# THE NEW BOOK OF KNOWLEDGE ANNUAL

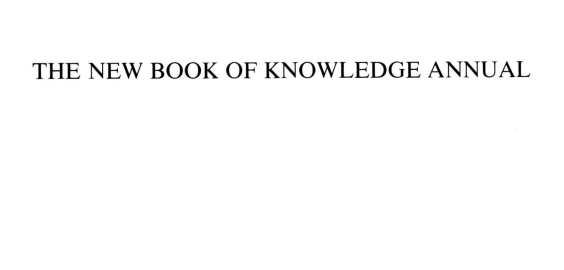

# THE NEW BOOK OF KNOWLEDGE ANNUAL

The Young People's Book of the Year

Grolier Incorporated, Danbury, Connecticut

1992
Highlighting Events of 1991

ISBN 0-7172-0623-8
ISSN 0196-0148
The Library of Congress Catalog Card Number: 79-26807

 COPYRIGHT © 1992 BY GROLIER INCORPORATED

# STAFF

| | |
|---|---|
| EDITORIAL DIRECTOR | LAWRENCE T. LORIMER |
| EXECUTIVE EDITOR | FERN L. MAMBERG |
| ASSOCIATE EDITOR | PATRICIA A. BEHAN |
| ART DIRECTOR | MICHÈLE A. McLEAN |
| DIRECTOR, ANNUALS | DORIS E. LECHNER |

## YOUNG PEOPLE'S PUBLICATIONS

| | |
|---|---|
| EDITOR IN CHIEF | GERRY A. GABIANELLI |
| ART DIRECTOR | NANCY HAMLEN |
| EDITORS | SARA A. BOAK |
| | ELAINE HENDERSON |
| | GEORGIANNE HEYMANN |
| | VIRGINIA QUINN McCARTHY |
| | JEROME NEIBRIEF |
| PHOTO EDITOR | LISA J. GRIZE |
| CHIEF, PHOTO RESEARCH | ANN ERIKSEN |
| MANAGER, PICTURE LIBRARY | JANE H. CARRUTH |
| PRODUCTION EDITOR | SHEILA ROURK |
| INDEXER | PAULINE M. SHOLTYS |
| FINANCIAL MANAGER | JEAN GIANAZZA |
| EDITORIAL LIBRARIAN | CHARLES CHANG |
| DIRECTOR, ELECTRONICS | CYNDIE L. COOPER |
| EDITORIAL ASSISTANTS | KAREN A. FAIRCHILD |
| | LINDA R. KUBINSKI |
| | MARY T. BERTOLAMI |
| | JOAN FLETCHER |

## MANUFACTURING

| | |
|---|---|
| DIRECTOR OF MANUFACTURING | JOSEPH J. CORLETT |
| PRODUCTION MANAGER | BARBARA A. PERSAN |
| PRODUCTION ASSISTANT | A. RHIANON MICHAUD |

# CONTENTS

# CONTRIBUTORS

**BORZA, Eugene N.**
Professor of Ancient History, The Pennsylvania State University; Author, *The Classical Tradition*; *Fire From Heaven: Alexander at Persepolis*; *Philip II, Alexander the Great and the Macedonian Heritage*; *In the Shadow of Olympus*: *The Emergence of Macedon*

ANCIENT GREECE

**BRAUNTHAL, Gerard**
Professor Emeritus, University of Massachusetts, Amherst Campus; Author, *The West German Legislative Process; Political Loyalty and Public Service in West Germany: The 1972 Decree Against Radicals and Its Consequences*

BERLIN

**DOHERTY, James G.**
Curator of Mammals, The Bronx Zoo; General Curator, New York Zoological Society

ANTELOPES

**DUBROFSKY, Melvyn**
Professor of History and Sociology, and Chairperson, Department of History, State University of New York at Binghamton; Author, *We Shall Be All: A History of the IWW; John L. Lewis: A Biography; "Big Bill" Haywood*

LABOR MOVEMENT

**HAHN, Charless**
Stamp editor, *Chicago Sun-Times*; Co-author, *British Pictorial Envelopes of the 19th Century*

STAMP COLLECTING

**HOLLANDER, Louis**
Former Vice President, Amalgamated Clothing Workers of America; Secretary-Treasurer, New York AFL-CIO

LABOR MOVEMENT

**KAPLAN, Elizabeth**
Series editor, *Ask Isaac Asimov*; Author, *Biology Bulletin Monthly*

BIOMES

**KURTZ, Henry I.**
Author, *The Art of the Toy Soldier; John and Sebastian Cabot*

PORTRAITS IN STONE
PEARL HARBOR: A DAY OF INFAMY

**LINGARD, C. Cecil**
Director, *Canada Yearbook*

NORTHWEST PASSAGE

**NELSON, Florencia Bazzano**
Professor, Rochester Institute of Technology; Visiting Professor, School of the Art Institute of Chicago

LATIN AMERICAN ART AND ARCHITECTURE

**PASCOE, Elaine**
Author, *South Africa: Troubled Land*; *Neighbors at Odds: U.S. Policy in Latin America*; *Racial Prejudice*; *The Horse Owner's Preventive Maintenance Handbook*
CHANGE IN SOUTH AFRICA

**RHINES, Karin L.**
Program Administrator, Westchester County Health Department; Co-author, *Discover Science*
BIOLOGICAL CLOCK

**SHAPIRO, William E.**
Executive Editor, *Worldmark Encyclopedia of the Nations*; Author, *Lebanon*; *Statue of Liberty*; *Pearl Harbor*
ANTARCTICA IN DANGER

**SHOEMAKER, Earl**
Contributor, *Numismatic News* and *Coins Magazine*; History Lecturer, University of Wisconsin
COIN COLLECTING

**SMITH, Allen**
Professor of Economics, Eastern Illinois University; Author, *Understanding Economics*; *Understanding Inflation and Unemployment*; Author, *Economic Alert*, a weekly syndicated newspaper column
ECONOMICS

**SMITH, Charles D.**
Professor of History, San Diego State University; Author, *Islam and the Search for Social Order in Modern Egypt*; *Palestine and the Arab-Israeli Conflict*
ARABS

**STEPHANI, Julie**
Editor, *Crafts 'n Things* magazine
POPULAR CRAFTS

**TERZI, Gail M.**
Forest Biologist, Regulatory Branch, U.S. Army Corps of Engineers; Contributor, *Insect Biochemistry Journal*
BEETLES

**TESAR, Jenny**
Author, *Global Warming*; *Scientific Crime Investigation*; *The Waste Crisis*; *Threatened Oceans*; *Shrinking Forests*; *Endangered Habitats*; *Food and Water: Threats, Shortages and Solutions*; *Introduction to Animals* (Wonders of Wildlife series); series consultant, *Wonders of Wildlife*; designer, computer programs
SPACE BRIEFS
A SUNSATIONAL EVENT

**WOOLF, Lynn Marcinkowski**
Science writer; former editor, *Raintree Illustrated Science Encyclopedia*
ANTELOPES

# IN THE PAGES OF THIS BOOK...

How closely did you follow the events of 1991? Do you remember the people who made news during the year? What about the trends—what was in and what was out? Who won in sports? What were the top songs, films, and television shows? What important anniversaries were celebrated? All these helped make up your world in 1991—a year that was like no other.

Here's a quiz that will tell you how much you know about your world—about what took place during the past year and about other things, as well. If you're stumped by a question, don't worry. You'll find all the answers in the pages of this book. (The page numbers after the questions will tell you where to look.)

In January, 1991, international forces led by U.S. General ''Stormin' Norman'' launched attacks on Iraq and Iraqi-occupied Kuwait at the start of Operation _____. (*17;40;64*)

In October, nations in both Europe and America began a year-long commemoration of the (300th/400th/500th) anniversary of Christopher Columbus's arrival in America. (*34;194*)

Two baseball teams that were at the bottom of their leagues in 1990 rose to face each other in the World Series in 1991. Which teams were they? (*166*)

Macaulay Culkin was a hot property during the year following the success of his hit film _____, which became one of the top money-making movies of all time. (*228*)

Mission to Planet Earth is (a fifteen-year satellite program/a Martian space expedition/a fund-raising album by rock musicians.) (*127*)

Mount Rushmore turned 50 years old in 1991. Name the four U.S. presidents whose faces are carved on the mountain. (*204*)

In June, U.S. Supreme Court Justice _____ resigned; in July, _____ was named to succeed him. (*26;28;66*)

American Mike Powell made a historic leap into the record books when he set a new world record in the (100-meter dash/long jump/pole vault). (*182*)

At age 4 he wrote the tune ''Twinkle Twinkle Little Star,'' and before he reached his teens he was a famous composer. Who was this ''whiz kid'' whose life was celebrated by music lovers around the world in 1991? (*222;242*)

In the Soviet Union, hard-line Communists tried to overthrow President _____ in August. But massive demonstrations spearheaded by Russian Republic President _____ led to the coup's failure three days later. (*30;56;65*)

Giant pandas are in danger today. Part of their problem is the dwindling supplies of their diet, which consists mostly of (rice/bamboo/chicken). (*70*)

What TV shows won Emmys as the best comedy and drama series in 1991? (*268*)

Led by the amazing Michael Jordan, the _____ won their first NBA title in 1991. (170)

In Eastern Europe, the collapse of Communism led to the re-emergence of old ethnic rivalries. In 1991, these rivalries erupted into a civil war in (Poland/Albania/Yugoslavia). (62)

In November, five U.S. presidents gathered together for the first time in history. Who were the five presidents and why did they meet? (37)

The 125th anniversary of the birth of Beatrix Potter was celebrated in 1991. She was the author of _____, one of the most popular children's books of all time. (270)

In 1991, the U.S. Congress voted to repeal a law that prohibited women in the military from (repairing tanks/flying warplanes in combat/driving ammunition trucks). (29)

These beautiful "underwater gardens" are found in tropical waters near the equator, and they are being bleached, polluted, and damaged in other ways. What are these fascinating habitats? (92)

When 17-year-old _____ reached the top of women's tennis in 1991, she was the youngest woman in the world ever to be ranked number one. (163;180)

The Environmental Protection Agency announced in April that the ozone layer over the United States was thinning at a faster rate than had been thought. This thinning is dangerous because the ozone layer absorbs harmful ultraviolet radiation from (Mars, Krypton, the sun). (23)

In July, ecliptophiles from around the world gathered in Hawaii to view the astronomical event of the year. What was it? (132)

A new TV comedy took audiences by storm in 1991. But its main characters—the Sinclairs—weren't just ordinary family members. The scaly crew were all _____! (227)

Through a new (shuttle/travel/computer) technology called virtual reality, you might one day be able to explore the moon without leaving your living room. (100)

In September, the Soviet Union's three Baltic republics became independent nations. Name the three republics. (32)

In 1991, scientists developed a new picture of the _____, a flightless bird that has been extinct about 300 years. (91)

In February, the governor of California announced emergency plans to deal with a massive (food/water/housing) shortage. (19)

What current heartthrob is being compared to Elvis Presley? (263)

In 1991, for the first time ever, Israel and all its _____ neighbors met officially face to face for peace talks. (36;50)

The 100th anniversary of the world's most popular indoor sport—(basketball/bowling/chess)—was celebrated in 1991. (184)

South Africa reached a turning point in 1991 when its government began to put an end to its system of rigid racial discrimination. What is this policy called? (54)

Kevin Costner won the 1991 Academy Award as best director for the film _____, which also won best-picture honors. (248;255)

By December, all the American hostages that had been held in captivity in (Iran/Iraq/Lebanon) had been released. (38;53)

# THE WORLD IN 1991

A U.S. soldier poses against a backdrop of burning oil wells in Kuwait during the Persian Gulf War in early 1991. The war broke out after Iraq ignored a United Nations deadline for removing its troops from Kuwait, which Iraq had invaded in August, 1990. The United States and its allies launched an air campaign on January 16, 1991, inflicting heavy damage on Iraq. Five weeks later, allied ground troops swept into Kuwait and southern Iraq, driving out the Iraqis in a decisive campaign that lasted less than 100 hours. Burning oil wells, set afire by retreating Iraqi troops, were only part of the destruction suffered by both Iraq and Kuwait in the conflict.

# THE YEAR IN REVIEW

Extraordinary events marked the year 1991. January saw the outbreak of the Persian Gulf War, which included the largest U.S. ground offensive since World War II and ended six weeks later in victory for the United States and its allies. In August, an attempted coup in the Soviet Union set off a chain of events that by year's end had led to nothing less than the breakup of the country. And throughout the year, there were new steps toward peace in several of the world's trouble spots.

The brief and decisive Persian Gulf War was triggered by Iraq's invasion of Kuwait, its small, oil-rich neighbor, in August, 1990. The Iraqis had remained in Kuwait despite condemnation by the United Nations and countries around the world. Finally, in January, 1991, the United States and its allies (which included Britain, France, Saudi Arabia, and others) launched Operation Desert Storm to drive them out, as well as to reduce the threat of Iraq's growing military power.

The military action achieved its goals. But Kuwait suffered heavy damage from the Iraqi occupation, including environmental damage from hundreds of oil wells set on fire by the Iraqis. Iraq, too, suffered in the war. Allied bombing destroyed transportation, communication, and power networks. And economic sanctions, which prevented Iraq from selling its oil or trading with other countries, also took a toll.

The sanctions stayed in effect through 1991 to ensure that Iraq met the terms of the U.N. agreement that ended the war. Among these terms, Iraq was required to demolish its stores of chemical and biological weapons and to dismantle its nuclear weapons program. U.N. inspectors found that Iraq was much closer to developing nuclear weapons than had been thought.

Iraqi leader Saddam Hussein remained in power after the war, and many people suspected that he would soon try to rebuild his military might. But meanwhile, there were new hopes for peace in the troubled Middle East. In the atmosphere of cooperation that developed after the war, Israel and its Arab neighbors agreed to hold talks. The Arab countries have been at odds with Israel since its creation as a Jewish homeland in 1948, and the first round of these talks, held in Madrid, Spain, in the fall, marked the first time they had all met officially to discuss the issues that divide them.

The fall also brought more good news—the release of Western hostages, including all the Americans, who had been captured by Iranian-backed terrorist groups in Lebanon. The last and longest-held American hostage, Terry Anderson, was released in early December. He had been held for almost seven years. And Lebanon itself, torn by civil war since the mid-1970's, seemed at last to be on the road to peace.

Meanwhile, dramatic events were taking place in the Soviet Union. Since the mid-1980's, under President Mikhail Gorbachev, the Soviets had gradually moved away from their repressive Communist system and toward reform. Then, in August, 1991, a group of Communist hard-liners attempted to take control of the government and turn back the clock. The attempt collapsed after thousands of Soviet citizens took to the streets to oppose it. But in the wake of the coup, the Soviet Union fell apart. One by one, its fifteen republics declared independence. And although Gorbachev was restored as president, Boris Yeltsin—the pro-reform president of the Russian republic and the leader of the opposition to the coup—emerged as the most powerful figure in the country. In December, he and the leaders of two other republics, Ukraine and Belorussia, announced that they would form a commonwealth outside the framework of the old Soviet Union. Eight other republics joined them. The Soviet Union, a major world power for most of the century, simply ceased to exist.

The growing Soviet turmoil was reflected in the countries of Eastern Europe, most of which have rejected Communism in recent years and are struggling to develop democratic systems. Along with this has come a rebirth of old ethnic rivalries. In 1991, ethnic rivalries erupted into civil war in Yugoslavia, where Croats and Slovenes attempted to secede from the Serbian-dominated union.

But the shifting politics of the Soviet Union and Eastern Europe did lead to important reductions in nuclear arms. Before the Soviet coup, Gorbachev and U.S. President George Bush signed a new Strategic Arms Reduction Treaty (START), reducing the U.S. and Soviet stockpiles of strategic (long-range) nuclear weapons. After the coup, both countries volunteered further reductions of nuclear weapons. But as the Soviet Union collapsed, there was concern about who would control its nuclear arsenal.

There were encouraging developments in other parts of the world, too. Western European countries who belong to the European Community (EC) moved toward closer economic and political ties. And in South Africa, the rigid system of racial discrimination known as apartheid fell in a series of sweeping reforms. Although the country was still troubled by violence, black and white leaders sat down late in the year to work out a new system that would allow all races a voice in the government.

While dramatic political events such as these took center stage for much of the year, economic problems caused growing worry in the United States. The country continued to suffer from an economic recession, and unemployment neared seven percent. The natural world grabbed newspaper headlines, too. Concern continued to mount over worldwide environmental threats caused by pollution. And 1991 seemed to have had more than its share of natural disasters, including volcanic eruptions in Japan and the Philippines, a devastating cyclone in Bangladesh, and severe flooding in China. And California continued to struggle with a five-year-long drought.

But the year ended on a hopeful note. On December 7, Americans marked the 50th anniversary of the Japanese attack on Pearl Harbor, which had brought the United States into World War II in 1941. They looked back over a troubled half century that had been dominated by the Cold War, the long period of tension between the United States and the Soviet Union. In 1991, with change sweeping through the former Communist world and signs of peace emerging in many trouble spots, that chapter of history was over. What lay ahead was unknown, but a new chapter was clearly beginning.

# JANUARY

**4**    In Poland, the parliament approved the nomination of Jan Krzysztof Bielecki as premier. Bielecki succeeded Tadeusz Mazowiecki, who had held the position since 1989.

**6**    In a runoff presidential election in Guatemala, conservative Jorge Serrano Elias was elected president. He succeeded Vinicio Cerezo Arévalo, who had been president since 1986.

**13**    Soviet Army troops killed fifteen people and injured more than 140 others in Vilnius, the capital of the republic of Lithuania. The slayings occurred as Soviet forces cracked down on the supporters of independence for the republic. Lithuania and the other Baltic republics, Latvia and Estonia, had been independent from 1918 to 1940, when they were taken over by the Soviet Union. All three republics have taken steps toward regaining their independence despite strong opposition from the Soviet government.

**14**    In the Soviet Union, Valentin Pavlov was named premier. He succeeded Nikolai I. Ryzhkov, who had held the position since 1985.

Newspaper headlines screamed "War!" as Operation Desert Storm began against Iraq.

Protesters surround Soviet Army troops in Vilnius, the capital of the Soviet republic of Lithuania. Soviet troops killed fifteen people in a crackdown on the Lithuanian independence movement.

**16**  International forces led by the United States launched air and missile attacks on Iraq and Iraqi-occupied Kuwait. The attacks—the start of Operation Desert Storm—began one day after the deadline set by the United Nations for Iraq's withdrawal from Kuwait. (Iraq had invaded its small neighbor on August 2, 1990, a move condemned by most of the world's nations.) As the month progressed, the allies claimed to have significantly destroyed strategic targets and military equipment in Iraq while suffering relatively few casualties. Iraq responded with missile attacks on Saudi Arabia and Israel, causing minimal damage. On January 23, Iraq began releasing huge quantities of oil from Kuwaiti facilities into the Persian Gulf. The massive spill caused much ecological damage and threatened water desalination plants in Saudi Arabia.

**17**  Crown Prince Harald became king of Norway. He succeeded to the throne on the death of his father, Olav V, who had reigned since 1957.

**25**  President George Bush nominated Edward Madigan as U.S. Secretary of Agriculture, to succeed Clayton K. Yeutter. Yeutter's resignation had been announced on January 7. (On March 7, the Senate confirmed the nomination.)

**26**  In Somalia, President Mohammed Siad Barre was ousted in a coup. Ali Mahdi Mohammed assumed the presidency. Barre was forced to flee the country after ruling as a dictator for 21 years.

# FEBRUARY

**1** A strong earthquake struck Pakistan and Afghanistan. More than 700 people were killed, and thousands of homes were destroyed or badly damaged.

**17** Cape Verde held its first free presidential elections since the nation gained its independence from Portugal in 1975. Antonio Monteiro Mascarenhas was elected president. He defeated Aristides Pereira, who had been president since the country's independence.

**23** In Thailand, Premier Chatichai Chunhawan was ousted in a military coup. Chunhawan had been premier since 1988. (On March 3, Anand Panyarachun was named premier.)

**25** Member nations of the Warsaw Pact agreed to dissolve the 36-year-old military alliance. The Warsaw Pact was established in 1955 between the Soviet Union and the Eastern European nations under its control: Albania, Bulgaria, Czechoslovakia, East Germany, Hungary, Poland, and Rumania. It was formed as a counterpart to the North Atlantic Treaty Organization (NATO), the defense organization of the United States and Western European nations. Albania resigned in 1968; East Germany ceased to exist in 1990; and, with the collapse of Communism in the area, the other Eastern European nations had declared their independence from the Soviet Union and demanded the withdrawal of Soviet troops stationed on their soil. (The Pact was officially disbanded on July 1.)

**27** In national elections in Bangladesh, the conservative Bangladesh National Party won the most seats in parliament. The party's leader, Khaleda Zia, became prime minister.

While a solid majority of Americans supported the Persian Gulf War, there was a strong minority who opposed it. But while debates over war and peace raged throughout the country, both sides felt great concern for the soldiers and their families. This cartoon comments on the wide chasm, or "gulf," that separated supporters and opponents of the war.

**California's drought led to a massive water shortage, and "drought busters" monitored illegal water use.**

## CALIFORNIA'S WATER CRISIS

Weather predictions of "clear, sunny skies" no longer delighted Californians as their state entered its fifth year of drought. Below-average precipitation since 1986 had caused a massive water shortage, particularly in southern California. The drought was so severe that on February 15, California Governor Pete Wilson announced emergency plans to combat it.

Three-quarters of California's 30 million residents live in southern California. But most of the state's precipitation falls in the north. Dams, reservoirs, and aqueducts funnel water from north to south, turning a natural desert into a lush area of irrigated farms and backyard swimming pools.

During the first years of the drought, few efforts were made to conserve water. But with reservoirs and streams drying up, California faced a serious crisis. Local, state, and federal agencies took various steps to deal with the problem. People were ordered to drastically cut back on their use of water. Public water fountains were cut off. Some communities made it a crime to water lawns, fill swimming pools, and wash cars at home.

California farmers were especially hard hit by the drought. Many of the crops grown in the state, such as alfalfa and cotton, require huge amounts of water. The farmers, who were almost totally dependent on irrigation, accounted for 85 percent of California's water use. Many people felt that farmers were wasting a great deal of water by growing crops that weren't suited to a dry climate. As the crisis worsened, water that the farmers received from the state's reservoirs was cut back.

No one knew how long the drought would last. But it seemed likely that the water shortage would result in major changes in California's economy and in the lifestyle of its people.

# MARCH

**3** Iraqi military leaders accepted a cease-fire in the Persian Gulf War, which began January 16. The first weeks of the war were marked by massive aerial bombing of Iraq and Iraqi-occupied Kuwait. On February 23, the allies launched a ground and air offensive. By February 27, Iraqi forces had been defeated, and U.S. President George Bush announced the liberation of Kuwait and the suspension of allied military operations. The cease-fire resolution, adopted by the United Nations Security Council, required Iraq to void its annexation of Kuwait, return Kuwaiti property, accept liability for damages resulting from its invasion and occupation of Kuwait, release all prisoners of war, and end all military action. (On April 6, the Iraqi government formally accepted the cease-fire terms, and the U.N. Security Council officially declared an end to the war on April 11.)

In the first free presidential elections in São Tomé and Príncipe, Miguel Trovoada was elected president. He succeeded Manuel Pinto da Costa, who had been president since the country gained independence from Portugal in 1975.

**12** It was reported that 200-million-year-old fossilized dinosaur bones had been found on Mount Kirkpatrick in Antarctica. Some of the bones were from a plant-eating dinosaur thought to have been about 25 feet (7.6 meters) long. Another fossil came from a meat-eating dinosaur, which may have been feeding on the plant-eater. This was only the second time that dinosaur fossils were found in Antarctica. Scientists said that the discovery definitely proved that dinosaurs once lived on every continent.

**24** In a runoff presidential election in Benin, Nicephore Soglo was elected president. He defeated Mathieu Kerekou, who had been president since seizing power in 1972. Soglo's victory marked the first time that a president of an African country was forced out of power because of an election defeat.

**26** In Mali, President Moussa Traoré was overthrown in a military coup. Traoré had ruled Mali since seizing power in 1968. (On April 2, Soumana Sacko was named to succeed him.)

**31** In Albania's first multiparty national elections since World War II, the ruling Communist Party retained power. Albania was the last Eastern European nation to hold multiparty electons since the collapse of Communism in the region. In May, Ramiz Alia resigned as Communist Party leader but remained as the country's president. (Despite the election results, widespread demonstrations and a general strike soon broke out to protest Communist rule. As a result, the Communist government resigned on June 4. Ylli Bufi was named premier, heading a nonpartisan cabinet—a cabinet not dominated by any political party. It was Albania's first non-Communist government in 47 years.)

U.S. Marines patrol the streets of Kuwait City. The United States and its allies liberated Kuwait on February 27, seven months after Iraq had invaded the Persian Gulf country. In March, Iraqi military leaders accepted a cease-fire—ending Operation Desert Storm.

# APRIL

**11**    The space shuttle *Atlantis* completed a six-day mission. The main objective of the mission was the launch of Gamma Ray Observatory, an astronomy satellite. The 17-ton satellite was the heaviest ever carried on a shuttle. The mission crew consisted of Kenneth D. Cameron, Jerome Apt, Linda M. Godwin, Steven R. Nagel, and Jerry L. Ross.

**20**    In national elections in Iceland, the conservative Independence Party won the most seats in parliament. David Oddsson, the party's leader, became prime minister. He succeeded Steingrimur Hermannsson, who had been prime minister since 1988.

**26**    Six weeks after national elections in which no party gained a majority in parliament, Esko Aho became premier of Finland. Aho, head of the Center Party, succeeded Harri Holkeri, who had been premier since 1987.

**30**    A devastating cyclone struck Bangladesh. More than 125,000 people were killed, and millions were left homeless. Many people were threatened by starvation due to food shortages, and by disease caused by unsanitary health conditions.

Justin Lekhanya, prime minister of Lesotho, was ousted in a military coup. He had ruled since seizing power in a coup in 1986. Elias P. Ramaema was named to succeed Lekhanya.

Millions of people were left homeless after a powerful cyclone struck coastal areas and offshore islands in Bangladesh. The storm was one of the worst to hit the country.

# IT'S IN THE AIR!

Every day, people dump tons of pollutants, or wastes, into the air. As the pollutants build up in the atmosphere, they are causing dramatic changes that threaten life on our planet. In April, two announcements caused new concern about these threats.

**Ozone.** The U.S. Environmental Protection agency (EPA) reported that the ozone layer over the United States was thinning more than twice as fast as had been thought. The ozone layer is 10 to 30 miles (16 to 48 kilometers) above Earth's surface. It absorbs harmful ultraviolet radiation from the sun. But the ozone layer is being destroyed by chemicals, mainly chlorofluorocarbons (CFC's) that are used in refrigeration and in other ways. As the ozone layer thins, more ultraviolet radiation reaches Earth. The radiation can cause skin cancer and harm plants and animals.

The nations of the world have agreed to stop producing most ozone-destroying chemicals by early in the next century. But the large amounts of chemicals already in the atmosphere will continue to harm the ozone layer for years. As a result, the EPA said, about 12 million Americans will develop skin cancer over the next 50 years.

**Global Warming.** Also in April, the U.S. National Academy of Sciences recommended that the United States act promptly to reduce the threat of global warming. This threat is caused by the buildup of carbon dioxide and other gases in the atmosphere. The gases act like the glass in a greenhouse: They allow warmth and light from the sun to reach Earth, but they prevent heat from escaping back into space. As more heat is trapped, the atmosphere becomes warmer. Scientists generally agree that in the next 50 years or so, the average temperature will rise enough to change weather patterns, harm agriculture, and perhaps melt polar ice caps and raise sea levels. The climate change could also cause many kinds of plants and animals to die out.

Most of the gases that cause global warming are released when fossil fuels such as coal and oil are burned in factories and motor vehicles. Americans, who make up 5 percent of the world's population, produce over 20 percent of these gases.

# MAY

**4** U.S. President George Bush was hospitalized after experiencing an irregular heartbeat. He was released after two days and resumed his normal work schedule. It was later announced that the condition resulted from Graves' disease, a form of hyperthyroidism (overactive thyroid gland). The disease is easily treated.

**6** The space shuttle *Discovery* completed an eight-day mission. The main purpose of the military mission was to conduct experiments for a planned antimissile defense system. The seven-member crew included Michael L. Coats, Guion S. Bluford, Jr., L. Blaine Hammond, Jr., Gregory J. Harbaugh, Richard J. Hieb, Donald R. McMonagle, and Charles Lacy Veech.

**12** In Nepal's first free elections in 32 years, the centrist Nepali Congress Party won a majority of seats in a new House of Representatives. Girija Prasad Koirala became prime minister. He succeeded Krishna Prasad Bhattarai, who had been prime minister since April, 1990.

**15** In France, Edith Cresson became the nation's first female premier. She succeeded Michel Rocard, who had resigned after three years in office.

**21** In India, former Prime Minister Rajiv Gandhi was assassinated while campaigning to regain power. It was widely suspected that the killing had been carried out by Tamil militants who wanted a separate state for their people in the neighboring country of Sri Lanka (Ceylon). In 1987, as prime minister, Gandhi had sent Indian troops to Sri Lanka to help enforce a peace accord between the government and the Tamil separatists. However, the troops often engaged in violent clashes with the militants. (Gandhi was part of a family dynasty that had dominated Indian politics since the country's independence in 1947; he was the son of Prime Minister Indira Gandhi and the grandson of Prime Minister Jawaharlal Nehru.)

President Mengistu Haile-Mariam, who ruled Ethiopia since 1977, resigned and fled the country. He had headed Africa's harshest Marxist government, and he left behind a nation in which various rebel groups had been fighting a civil war for more than ten years. (In July, the rebel groups set up a temporary government to rule the country until free elections were held.)

**24** In South Korea, Chung Won Shik was named premier. He succeeded Ro Jai Bong, who resigned after five months in office.

**31** In Angola, the government and rebel forces signed a peace agreement, ending the country's sixteen-year-old civil war. The agreement called for the nation's first free elections to be held in 1992.

The coelacanth has six fins. Four move as pairs, as if they were primitive legs. Scientists have been studying coelacanths to learn if they are our water-dwelling ancestors.

## YOUR FISHY FAMILY TREE

Human beings and all other four-legged land animals are believed to have descended from ocean creatures that lived millions of years ago. Some biologists believe that these ancestors are strange, primitive fish called coelacanths (pronounced SEE-luh-kanth). In May, German biologists presented new evidence to support this theory.

Coelacanths existed as long as 370 million years ago, and it was long believed that they were extinct. But in 1938 a fisherman netted one in the Indian Ocean. Over the years more of these rare fish were captured and studied. The German biologists analyzed blood proteins from live coelacanths. They found that these proteins are like the blood proteins of frogs—the earliest land animals. Scientists consider the structure of proteins to be an important clue to relationships among animals: the more alike the proteins, the closer the kinship. Despite the new evidence linking coelacanths and amphibians, many more studies must be done to determine if coelacanths really are our water-dwelling ancestors.

# JUNE

**12** In Russia, the largest of the Soviet Union's fifteen republics, Boris N. Yeltsin was elected president. This was the first time in Russian history that a leader was directly elected by the people.

**14** The space shuttle *Columbia* completed a nine-day mission. The mission's primary objective was to study how humans and other organisms (29 rats and 2,478 jellyfish) adapt to space flight and weightlessness. The crew of seven astronauts included Bryan D. O'Connor, James P. Bagian, Francis A. Gaffney, Sidney M. Gutierrez, Millie Hughes-Fulford, Tamara E. Jernigan, and Margaret Rhea Seddon.

**15** In national elections in India, no single party won a majority in parliament. The Congress Party, which received the most votes, chose P. V. Narasimha Rao to be prime minister. Rao succeeded Chandra Shekhar, who had been prime minister since late 1990.

**17** In Jordan, Taher Masri was named premier. He succeeded Mudar Badran, who had held the position since 1989. (In November, Masri was replaced by Sherif Zeid ibn Shaker.)

**27** U.S. Supreme Court Justice Thurgood Marshall announced his retirement. A leader in the civil rights movement, Marshall became the first black named to the Court when he was appointed in 1967.

In June, hundreds of thousands of people turned out to honor members of the U.S. armed forces who had served in the Persian Gulf War. The largest celebrations were parades held in New York City (*below*) and Washington, D.C.

A blizzard of ash in the Philippines: In a massive volcanic eruption, Mount Pinatubo spewed blankets of ash over thousands of square miles of land.

## ERUPTIONS IN THE RING OF FIRE

During June, two volcanoes—Mount Unzen in Japan and Mount Pinatubo in the Philippines—erupted. The volcanoes were part of the Ring of Fire, a circle of active volcanoes that edge the Pacific Ocean. The heavy volcanic activity in the ring is caused by the movements of sections of the earth's crust, called plates. As the plates collide, some are pushed downward and some are lifted upward. High temperatures deep inside the earth melt the sinking plates and produce gases. The melted rocks and gases rise within the volcano, until finally an explosive eruption occurs. When the hot, melted rock spews out of the volcano, it's called lava.

On June 3, Mount Unzen began to erupt after six months of lava flows. This volcano, which last erupted in 1792, is on the island of Kyushu, about 30 miles (50 kilometers) east of Nagasaki. The blasts killed 38 people and forced more than 7,000 people from their homes.

A few days later, Mount Pinatubo began to erupt, after lying dormant for more than 600 years. Located on Luzon Island, the volcano is about 55 miles (90 kilometers) northwest of Manila. The eruptions continued for more than a week, throwing huge columns of ash and smoke high into the air. Skies were darkened as far away as Manila. Thick blankets of ash settled over thousands of square miles of land, and the fallout caused about 200 deaths. More than 100,000 people fled from communities near Mount Pinatubo. In addition, about 16,000 Americans who lived and worked at Clark Air Base, a large U.S. military installation east of the volcano, were evacuated. (In July, it was announced that the United States wouldn't renew its lease on the heavily damaged base.)

# JULY

**1** President George Bush nominated Clarence Thomas to the U.S. Supreme Court. Thomas, a judge of the Court of Appeals for the District of Columbia, was named to succeed Thurgood Marshall, who retired in June. (The Senate confirmed the nomination on October 15.)

**15** Two months of heavy rains caused severe flooding in central China. More than 1,700 people were killed, and millions were left homeless.

**17** In London, the leaders of the seven major industrial nations ended their 17th annual summit meeting on world economic issues. The countries represented were Britain, Canada, France, Germany, Italy, Japan, and the United States. Mikhail S. Gorbachev, President of the Soviet Union, met with the participants to describe plans for changing his country's economic system and to request financial aid.

**22** A Japanese fish-processing ship and a Chinese freighter collided in the Pacific Ocean, 22 miles (35 kilometers) northwest of Washington State. The Japanese ship sank, creating an oil spill that polluted beaches and killed hundreds of seabirds in Olympic National Park.

**31** U.S. President George Bush and Soviet President Mikhail S. Gorbachev ended a two-day meeting in Moscow. The two leaders signed the Strategic Arms Reduction Treaty (START)—the first agreement in history to reduce the number of long-range nuclear warheads held by the two nations. Previous treaties had reduced only the rate at which the weapons could be produced. START must be ratified by the U.S. Senate and the Soviet parliament before taking effect.

Presidents George Bush and Mikhail Gorbachev share a moment of amusement during the signing of START —a historic agreement to reduce the number of long-range nuclear warheads held by the two nations.

## WOMEN IN COMBAT

By July 31, both houses of the U.S. Congress had voted to repeal a 43-year-old law that prohibited women from flying warplanes in combat. The action came in response to the highly capable and dedicated performance of the 35,000 American women who served in the Persian Gulf War. These women weren't in combat (fighting) positions. They weren't allowed to serve in infantry or artillery units. Nor were they allowed on fighting ships or combat planes. But women worked in supply units, crewed missile units, repaired tanks, drove ammunition trucks, and served aboard Navy tenders. Female pilots flew helicopters that transported troops, food, and fuel into combat zones. Two U.S. women were taken prisoner and eleven were killed (five in action) during the war.

Congress's action renewed the debate over whether women should be allowed to fight side by side with men. Those in favor say that women have a right to equal opportunity. They say that many women can meet the physical demands of serving on a gun crew or in an infantry unit. They also say that combat experience is usually needed to be eligible for higher ranks and top jobs in the Armed Services; thus, current law discriminates against women by limiting career advancement.

Opponents say that putting women in combat positions could harm national security because it would destroy the closeness of male soldiers and weaken their fighting power. They worry that women wouldn't be held to the same physical standards as men, and that weak members could endanger a combat unit. And, they say, many enlisted women who now make important contributions might leave the service if combat were required.

A U.S. Army advertisement calls on soldiers to "be all that they can be." In the coming years, it will be debated whether this includes the right for women to stand on the front lines in time of war.

# AUGUST

**9** U.S. Attorney General Dick Thornburgh resigned after three years in office. (On October 16, President Bush nominated William P. Barr for the position. On November 20, the Senate confirmed the nomination.)

**11** The space shuttle Atlantis completed a nine-day mission. A main objective was to study the human body's ability to adapt to space travel. The crew consisted of John E. Blaha, Michael A. Baker, James C. Adamson, G. David Low, and Shannon W. Lucid.

**19–21** In the Soviet Union, hard-line Communists tried to oust President Mikhail S. Gorbachev. But the attempt failed when hundreds of thousands of anticoup demonstrators, led by Russian Republic President Boris N. Yeltsin, resisted the takeover. After three days of overwhelming opposition—both in the Soviet Union and in countries around the world—the coup ended and Gorbachev was returned to power. (On August 24, Gorbachev resigned as leader of the Communist Party; on August 29, the Soviet parliament suspended all activities of the Communist Party and ordered an investigation into its role in the coup. These actions ended 74 years of Communist domination in the Soviet Union.)

**27** In Togo, Kokou Koffigoh was named prime minister by a national, pro-democracy conference. The appointment effectively ended the 24-year military rule by President Gnassingbe Eyadema.

Moscow's streets were lined with tanks as hard-line Communists tried to overthrow Soviet President Mikhail Gorbachev. Massive demonstrations led to the coup's failure.

**Mount Huxley, Kings Canyon National Park, California. This is one of the many magnificent parks maintained by the U.S. National Park Service—which celebrated its 75th anniversary in August.**

## CELEBRATING AMERICA'S NATIONAL PARK SERVICE

On August 25, the U.S. National Park Service celebrated its 75th anniversary. Since its beginnings in 1916, the agency's responsibilities have grown to include 357 parks, seashores, monuments, historic homes, and other sites, covering a total of more than 80 million acres. In addition to such natural treasures as Yellowstone, Yosemite, Grand Canyon, and Acadia national parks, the agency protects the Atlanta house where Martin Luther King, Jr., was born, battlefields of the Civil War, Independence Hall in Philadelphia, and memorials such as Mount Rushmore in South Dakota. It also maintains some 26 million artifacts, including ancient Indian pottery, the pistol used by John Wilkes Booth to assassinate President Abraham Lincoln, and the sewing machine used by the Wright Brothers to make wing covers for their flying machines.

Today, however, some of the most magnificent properties are threatened by overcrowding and pollution. About 265 million people visited the sites in 1991. Traffic jams were common in the most popular parks; in Yosemite, visitors produced some 25 tons of garbage a day. Water pollution in the Everglades has drastically reduced the numbers of wading birds. Air pollution hides beautiful views and kills trees in the Great Smoky Mountains. Logging activities next to Mount Rainier and Olympic national parks have filled streams with silt and killed fish. Marble is deteriorating at the Jefferson Memorial in Washington, D.C.

Reversing this damage and preventing additional harm is essential if the National Park Service is to meet its three basic objectives: to preserve the past, manage the present, and invest in the future.

# SEPTEMBER

**6** The Soviet Union recognized the independence of the Baltic republics of Estonia, Latvia, and Lithuania. The three republics had been independent nations before being annexed by the Soviet Union in 1940.

In Suriname, Ronald Venetiaan was chosen president. He succeeded Ramsewak Shankar, who had been overthrown in a military coup in December, 1990, after almost three years in power.

**15** In national elections in Sweden, a coalition of four parties received the most votes. The coalition's leader, Carl Bildt of the Moderate Party, became premier. He succeeded Ingvar Carlsson, who had been premier since 1986.

**17** The 46th annual session of the United Nations General Assembly opened at U.N. headquarters in New York City. Samir Shihabi of Saudi Arabia was elected to serve as assembly president for one year. U.N. membership increased to 166 nations with the admission of seven new members: North Korea, South Korea, Estonia, Latvia, Lithuania, the Marshall Islands, and Micronesia.

**18** The space shuttle *Discovery* completed a five-day mission. The main objective of the flight was to launch the Upper Atmosphere Research Satellite (UARS), which will study the ozone layer. The five-member crew included John O. Creighton, Kenneth S. Reightler, Jr., Charles D. Gemar, James F. Buchli, and Mark N. Brown.

**19** In Austria, mountain climbers discovered the mummified body of a man who lived 4,600 years ago. The body had been frozen in a glacier in the Tirolean Alps. The ice preserved the body, preventing decay. It was the oldest and most complete remains of a person from the Neolithic Age ever found in Europe. The man wore leather and fur clothing lined with hay, and he clutched a copper ax. Beside the body were a flintstone knife, flint for lighting fires, kindling wood in a small pouch, and a leather quiver filled with arrows.

**26** In Rumania, Petre Roman resigned as premier after two years in office. (On October 16, Theodor Stolojan was chosen to succeed him.)

**27** U.S. President George Bush announced that the United States would eliminate all U.S. tactical (short-range) nuclear weapons in Europe and Asia, and remove them from U.S. ships and submarines around the world. (On October 5, Soviet President Mikhail S. Gorbachev announced that the Soviet Union would also reduce its arsenal of land- and sea-based nuclear weapons.)

**30** In Haiti, President Jean-Bertrand Aristide was ousted in a military coup. Aristide had taken office in February as Haiti's first freely elected president. (On October 8, Joseph Nerette became president.)

# LIFE UNDER GLASS

On September 26, eight researchers sealed themselves in a giant greenhouse-like structure, called Biosphere II, in the Arizona desert. (A biosphere is a closed system of living things that is completely self-sufficient and cut off from any other system.) Biosphere II was named after the Earth, which the researchers call Biosphere I. The four men and four women plan to live in the airtight environment for two years, obtaining everything they need from their enclosed world. Only sunlight, electricity, and electronic communications will enter the structure.

Biosphere II covers almost 3 acres of land and is designed to imitate the Earth's environment—its different climate zones and habitats are desert, savanna, marshland, tropical rain forest, and ocean. Each habitat contains a variety of plants and animals. There's also a farm, living quarters, labs, and recreational facilities. The Biospherians will raise their entire food supply and recycle all wastes produced within the greenhouse. Computers will monitor the entire system.

The researchers hope to gain a better understanding of how various organisms interact with their environment. Some of what they learn may help in solving the planet's pollution problems. And some information may one day be useful in colonizing space.

**Eight researchers enter Biosphere II, where they will remain sealed off from the world for two years.**

# OCTOBER

**12** Parades and other special events in Europe and the Americas began a year-long commemoration of the 500th anniversary of Columbus's arrival in the New World. On October 12, 1492, Columbus stepped ashore on one of the Bahama Islands, probably present-day San Salvador. His discovery led to the settlement of European colonies in the Western Hemisphere.

**13** In national elections in Bulgaria, the Union of Democratic Forces won the most seats in parliament. The opposition group thus replaced the Communists as the country's major political force. Filip Dimitrov became premier. He succeeded Dimitar Popov, who had been premier for ten months.

**20** In California, fire roared through residential neighborhoods in Oakland and Berkeley, destroying more than 2,500 homes. At least 24 people were killed and 148 injured. The flames were fueled by gusty winds, high temperatures, low humidity, and the extremely dry conditions caused by more than five years of drought in the area.

**One of the worst fires in U.S. history roared through the Oakland–Berkeley area of California. At least 24 people were killed, and more than 2,500 homes were destroyed.**

## THE 1991 NOBEL PRIZES

**Chemistry:** Richard R. Ernst of Switzerland, for his work in nuclear magnetic resonance imaging, a technology widely used by doctors to examine the inside parts of the human body, and by scientists in doing chemical analyses of complex molecules.

**Economics:** Ronald H. Coase, a British-born American, for his explanations of basic economic issues—such as the role of government in a free market system, and how and why companies exist (why, for example, there's a McDonald's rather than many thousands of individual hamburger vendors).

**Literature:** Nadine Gordimer of South Africa, for her novels and short stories, which portray human relations under apartheid—her country's system of racial discrimination, segregation, and white minority rule.

**Peace:** Aung San Suu Kyi of Burma (Myanmar), "for her nonviolent struggle for democracy and human rights." Suu Kyi, who has been under house arrest since 1989, is a leader of the democratic opposition to Burma's military government.

**Physics:** Pierre-Gilles de Gennes of France, for his studies explaining the behavior of molecules in such materials as liquid crystals, superconductors, and "super" glues.

**Physiology or Medicine:** Erwin Neher and Bert Sakmann of Germany, for discovering how to record and observe ion channels, tunnel-like passageways from the inside to the outside of a cell. Their work has led to a better understanding of the causes of such diseases as diabetes and cystic fibrosis and the development of special drugs to treat them.

---

**20** In national elections in Turkey, the True Path Party won the most seats in parliament. The party's leader, Suleyman Demirel, became prime minister. He succeeded Mesut Yilmaz, who had held the office for four months, following the resignation of Yildirim Akbulut.

A major earthquake struck northern India. More than 1,000 people were killed, and thousands more were injured.

**23** Cambodia's four warring factions, together with representatives of eighteen other nations, signed a peace treaty designed to end 21 years of fighting. The treaty, to be supervised by the United Nations, included a plan for free elections and a transition to democratic rule.

**31** In national elections in Zambia, Frederick Chiluba was elected president. Chiluba defeated Kenneth D. Kaunda, who had been president since Zambia gained its independence from Britain in 1964.

# NOVEMBER

**4** Israel and Arab nations concluded six days of talks in Madrid, Spain. It was the first time that Israel and all its Arab neighbors met officially face to face for peace talks since Israel became an independent nation in 1948. The Arab countries represented were Syria, Egypt, Jordan, and Lebanon. The Palestinians were also represented, as were the United States and the Soviet Union, co-sponsors of the conference. The meeting was to be followed by individual negotiations between Israel and the Arab representatives.

**5** Severe floods and landslides caused by tropical storm Thelma struck the islands of Leyte and Negros in the Philippines. More than 5,000 people were killed and about 50,000 people were left homeless.

**6** Kiichi Miyazawa was chosen premier of Japan by the nation's parliament. He succeeded Toshiki Kaifu, who had been premier since 1989.

**21** Boutros Ghali, an Egyptian diplomat, was chosen to become Secretary General of the United Nations by the fifteen members of the organization's Security Council. He would serve a five-year term, beginning January 1, 1992. He succeeded Javier Pérez de Cuéllar of Peru, who had served two terms.

U.S. President George Bush speaks at the Israeli-Arab peace talks, held in Madrid, Spain, for six days. It was hoped that these talks would be just the first step toward settling some of the region's bitter disputes.

George Bush, Ronald Reagan, Jimmy Carter, Gerald Ford, and Richard Nixon: a historic gathering to dedicate the Ronald Reagan Presidential Library, in Simi Valley, California.

## A NEW PRESIDENTIAL LIBRARY

On November 4, for the first time in history, five U.S. presidents gathered together. The occasion was the dedication of the Ronald Reagan Presidential Library in Simi Valley, California. Joining Reagan for the event were President George H. Bush and former Presidents Richard M. Nixon, Gerald R. Ford, and Jimmy Carter. Also in attendance were the wives of the five presidents and Lady Bird Johnson, the widow of President Lyndon B. Johnson.

The $60-million Ronald Reagan Presidential Library contains more than 47 million documents of the Reagan administration. Said Reagan: "Certainly it is my hope that the Reagan library will become a dynamic intellectual forum where scholars interpret the past and policymakers debate the future."

The first presidential library, the Franklin D. Roosevelt Library in Hyde Park, New York, opened on July 4, 1940. There are also presidential libraries for Herbert Hoover, Harry S. Truman, Dwight D. Eisenhower, John F. Kennedy, Lyndon B. Johnson, Richard M. Nixon, Gerald R. Ford, and Jimmy Carter. Each of the libraries contains important papers and records from the president's days in office.

# DECEMBER

**1** The space shuttle *Atlantis* ended a seven-day military mission. The main objective of the mission was the launch of a Defense Support Program satellite, one of a network of satellites designed to give the U.S. military early warning of missile attacks. The mission crew consisted of Frederick D. Gregory, Thomas J. Hennen, Terence T. Henricks, F. Story Musgrave, Mario Runco, Jr., and James S. Voss.

**4** Terry A. Anderson, the last American hostage in Lebanon, was released by his kidnappers after nearly seven years in captivity. The release brought to an end the eight-year hostage crisis, during which pro-Iranian terrorist groups in Lebanon had held seventeen Americans, of whom three were killed. The terrorists had also held hostages from other nations, and two Germans still remained in captivity.

**5** U.S. President George Bush announced the resignations of two of his cabinet members: Secretary of Transportation Samuel K. Skinner would become Bush's chief of staff; and Secretary of Commerce Robert A. Mosbacher would run Bush's re-election campaign.

**6** In Poland, Jan Olszewski was named premier. He succeeded Jan Krzysztof Bielecki, who had held the post since January.

Joseph Cicippio, Terry Anderson, and Alann Steen enjoy their freedom after years in captivity in Lebanon. Anderson was the longest-held hostage and the last American hostage to be released.

# 1992

## . . . AND LOOKING AHEAD TO 1992

**THE OLYMPICS.** *The Winter Olympics will take place from February 8 through February 23 in Albertville, France. Among the new events will be Nordic skiing and freestyle skiing. The Summer Olympics will be held July 25 through August 9 in Barcelona, Spain. New events will include baseball and badminton.*

**EXPO 92.** *From April 20 through October 12, the largest world's fair in history will take place in Seville, Spain. The fair's theme, "The Age of Discovery," commemorates all the discoveries made since 1492, when Christopher Columbus reached the Americas.*

**PRESIDENTIAL ELECTIONS.** *On November 3, U.S. voters will go to the polls to choose a president and vice-president for the following four years. The election will mark the 203rd anniversary of the nation's first election in 1789, in which George Washington received every vote cast.*

**ANNIVERSARIES.**

• *The 500th anniversary of **Christopher Columbus**'s arrival in the New World, which led to the settlement of European colonies in the Western Hemisphere.*

• *The 300th anniversary of the **Salem Witchcraft Trials,** in Salem, Massachusetts. More than 200 people were accused of witchcraft, and 20 were put to death in the largest witchhunt in U.S. history.*

• *The 125th anniversary of the passage of the **British North American Act,** which founded the modern nation of Canada.*

• *The 125th anniversary of the U.S. **purchase of Alaska** from Russia for $7.2 million.*

**8** Three major republics of the Soviet Union—Russia, Ukraine, and Belorussia—created a new Commonwealth of Independent States outside the framework of the Soviet Union. The step followed months of growing turmoil in which central authority had broken down as republic after republic seceded from the union. In forming the commonwealth, the three republics declared that the Soviet Union "no longer exists" and invited other republics to join them. (Within two weeks, eleven of the twelve republics had joined the commonwealth. Soviet President Mikhail Gorbachev resigned on December 25, and the Soviet Union was dissolved.)

**19** Paul Keating became Prime Minister of Australia. He succeeded Bob Hawke, who had held the post since 1983.

# OPERATION DESERT STORM

Just before 7 P.M. (U.S. Eastern Standard Time) on January 16, 1991, a Tomahawk cruise missile streaked north toward Baghdad, Iraq, from the USS *Wisconsin,* off the coast of Kuwait in the Persian Gulf. The opening shot of the Persian Gulf War had been fired.

The war pitted forces of the United States and its allies against those of Iraq. They fought to drive Iraq out of the small, oil-rich Persian Gulf country of Kuwait, which Iraq had invaded in August, 1990, and also to halt Iraq's growing military power. Iraq had a huge army and stores of chemical weapons, and it was rumored to be developing nuclear weapons. This, coupled with the ambitions of its leader, Saddam Hussein, threatened stability in the Middle East.

The war lasted just six weeks and ended in victory for the allies. But while Iraq was driven out of Kuwait, the long-term prospects for peace in the region were unclear.

## THE OUTBREAK

When Iraq invaded its neighbor Kuwait on August 2, 1990, most of the world was taken by surprise. The United Nations quickly condemned the action and imposed economic sanctions. And, fearing that it would be the next to be invaded, Saudi Arabia asked the United States for help. The United States responded with Operation Desert Shield, a military build-up that eventually brought about 540,000 U.S. troops to the region, along with planes, missiles, and Navy ships. They were under the command of Army General H. Norman Schwarzkopf.

The U.S. forces were joined by some 265,000 troops from other countries, including Saudi Arabia, Britain, France, Egypt, Syria, and Kuwait itself. (About 40 countries supported the war effort in various ways, although only some of these sent forces.) Facing them were between 545,000 and 590,000 Iraqi soldiers, massed in and around Kuwait. Meanwhile, nearly half of Kuwait's population fled the country, and there were reports of atrocities committed by Iraqi troops.

Operation Desert Storm pitted the forces of the United States and its allies against those of Iraq. The six-week air and ground war resulted in victory for the allies.

The United Nations set a deadline—January 15, 1991—by which Iraq was supposed to withdraw from Kuwait. The weeks leading up to the war were filled with last-minute efforts to avoid a conflict. But these efforts failed; Iraqi leader Saddam Hussein claimed that Kuwait was now a province of Iraq and said that he would fight a ''holy war'' against the allies. January 15 arrived, and there was no change in the situation. The next day, Operation Desert Storm began when the allies launched the air attack that opened the war.

**THE AIR WAR**

In the early days of the war, allied planes jammed Iraqi radar and inflicted heavy damage on Iraqi targets, seeking to knock out the ''command and control'' systems that allowed Iraqi leaders to direct their forces. ''Smart'' bombs, which zeroed in on their targets electronically, and other high-tech weapons played an important part in this phase, although they accounted for only a portion of the total bombs dropped.

The air war lasted five weeks. Apart from a few clashes along the Saudi-Kuwait border, the only major ground action during this part of the war took place at the small Saudi town of Khafji. After Iraqi forces took over this town, which had been deserted, Saudi forces drove them out on January 31.

Otherwise, allied forces continued to pound away at Iraq from the air. Iraq claimed that the United States was intentionally killing civilians, including about 300 who died when an air raid shelter was bombed on February 13. But the allies said that they were targeting only military installations. Some allied planes were lost, and Iraq took 45 prisoners of war, 21 of them Americans. Some of the prisoners were shown on Iraqi television, and they appeared to have been tortured.

Meanwhile, the Iraqi air force stayed on the ground, its planes hidden in protected bunkers. (Iraq also moved some planes to Iran, where they were impounded.) Iraq's chief response to the allied bombing was to launch Scud missiles from mobile and fixed bases toward cities in Saudi Arabia and in Israel. Israel wasn't a party to the war. But Saddam hoped to draw Israel into the fight and thereby gain support from other Arab countries, most of whom have opposed Israel ever since that country was created as a Jewish homeland in 1948.

The plan failed—Israel refused to fight, and among Arabs only Jordan, Yemen, and the Palestine Liberation Organization (PLO) sided with Iraq. People in both Israel and Saudi Arabia responded to Scud attacks by rushing to shelters and donning gas masks that would protect them if one of the missiles carried a chemical warhead (none did). The United States also set up batteries of Patriot missiles in both countries. These missiles zeroed in on approaching Scuds and knocked most of them out of the sky. Still, some Scuds found their targets, inflicting damage and casualties. In the worst attack, 28 U.S. soldiers were killed when a Scud hit a military barracks in Dhahran, Saudi Arabia, on February 25.

By that time, the allies had achieved air superiority—they controlled the skies, and

Saddam Hussein, the brutal leader of Iraq, initiated the crisis when he invaded Kuwait in August, 1990. Despite the fact that he was defeated in the war, he was still firmly in control of his country by the end of 1991.

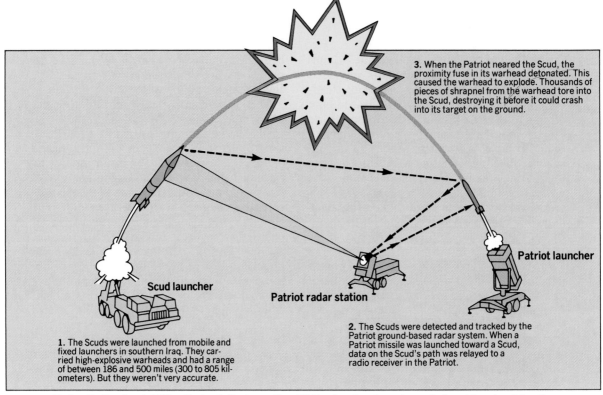

**3.** When the Patriot neared the Scud, the proximity fuse in its warhead detonated. This caused the warhead to explode. Thousands of pieces of shrapnel from the warhead tore into the Scud, destroying it before it could crash into its target on the ground.

**Patriot launcher**

**Scud launcher**

**Patriot radar station**

**2.** The Scuds were detected and tracked by the Patriot ground-based radar system. When a Patriot missile was launched toward a Scud, data on the Scud's path was relayed to a radio receiver in the Patriot.

**1.** The Scuds were launched from mobile and fixed launchers in southern Iraq. They carried high-explosive warheads and had a range of between 186 and 500 miles (300 to 805 kilometers). But they weren't very accurate.

During the Persian Gulf War, the Iraqis fired more than 70 Scud surface-to-surface missiles at Israel and Saudi Arabia. The United States countered by deploying the Patriot air-defense system in those two countries.

An Iraqi boy tries to sell produce amid the ruins of bombed out shops and homes in Baghdad, Iraq's capital. Both Iraq and Kuwait suffered heavy damage in the war.

Iraqi communications and supply lines were disrupted. It was time for the next phase of the war to begin.

### THE GROUND WAR

On February 23, the United States launched its biggest ground offensive since World War II, involving more than 200,000 allied troops. Surprise and deception were important parts of the strategy. At first, allied troops were concentrated just south of Kuwait, with a large force of U.S. Marines off the coast. This led the Iraqis to expect an attack at the Saudi-Kuwait border and an amphibious landing. But just before the attack, U.S., British, and French armored and air assault groups took up new positions farther west, on the Saudi-Iraq border. With its command systems disrupted by the air war, Iraq was unable to detect these movements.

When the offensive began, the allies attacked from several points. The units that had taken up new positions to the west headed north into Iraq and then turned east, outflanking and encircling Iraq's forces with lightning speed. Tens of thousands of Iraqi

Worshippers in Saudi Arabia and children in Israel all donned gas masks to protect them in case the Scud missiles carried chemical warheads. None did.

soldiers surrendered or deserted. The allies defeated a division of Iraq's elite Republican Guard—the best of the Iraqi units—in the largest tank battle since World War II.

At the same time, Saudi, Kuwaiti, Egyptian, and Syrian units, along with U.S. Marines, moved north from Saudi Arabia directly into Kuwait. On February 27, Kuwait City was liberated. The ground war, which had lasted less than 100 hours, was over.

### AFTER THE WAR

Under the terms of a U.N. cease-fire, Iraq agreed to give up its claim to Kuwait, return Kuwaiti property and pay for damages, release prisoners of war and other detainees, and permit the United Nations to supervise the destruction of its ''weapons of mass destruction''—chemical, biological, and nuclear weapons. Sanctions on imports of food and other essentials were lifted, but other economic sanctions were to remain in place until Iraq complied with these terms. In May, U.S. troops withdrew to Kuwait, and a U.N. peacekeeping force set up a demilitarized zone in southern Iraq.

Casualties on the allied side were considered remarkably low—223 soldiers were killed in combat, including 148 Americans. Another 120 American soldiers died in noncombat incidents. Iraqi casualty figures were difficult to determine because it wasn't clear how many Iraqi soldiers had deserted—or how many there had been to begin with. The United States estimated that perhaps 100,000 had been killed but acknowledged that the actual figure could be 50 percent lower or higher. Other estimates ranged from 25,000 to 50,000.

Civilian casualties were even more difficult to determine. Kuwaiti resistance leaders estimated that 7,000 Kuwaitis had been killed by Iraq during the occupation. Iraq didn't release official figures, but at the time of the cease-fire various Iraqi reports put the number of civilian casualties at about 1,400. Later estimates, also unofficial, ranged from 5,000 to 15,000. In addition, Kuwait and Iraq both suffered heavy damage in the war.

**Kuwait.** In Kuwait, the cost of rebuilding was estimated at $100 billion. Iraqi soldiers had blown up Kuwaiti oil wells, burned and looted buildings, and killed animals in the Kuwait City Zoo. Basic services such as water and power were restored to much of Kuwait City within a few months of the allied victory, with the help of the U.S. army. But large areas of the country remained laced with land mines planted by the Iraqis, and burning and leaking oil wells damaged the environment. Some people estimated that it would be years before these problems were solved. As a result, many of the Kuwaitis who had fled during the Iraqi invasion were slow to return to their country.

Iraq believed that the ground offensive would consist of an amphibious landing and an attack from the Saudi-Kuwait border. But the main attack came from allied air assault and armored groups positioned at the Saudi-Iraq border. Iraq's forces were encircled with lightning speed, and the ground war lasted 100 hours. On February 27, Kuwait City was liberated (*left*).

Kuwait faced other problems as well. Its conservative ruler, Emir Jabir al-Ahmad Al Sabah, had escaped when the Iraqis invaded. On his return, there were calls for greater democracy and a relaxation of his tight rule. The emir promised to hold elections for a new parliament in 1992. But the government's promises of reform seemed vague.

There were also reprisals against Palestinians living in Kuwait. Some Palestinians had sided with Iraq, but others hadn't. After the war, however, all Palestinians faced the anger of the Kuwaitis. Vigilantes attacked Palestinians, and a number of Palestinians (as well as Kuwaitis) were convicted on thin evidence of collaborating with the Iraqis. The attacks and the trials had largely ended by fall, but Palestinians continued to be forced out of the country. This left Kuwait short of workers, as many Kuwaitis refused to perform the manual labor that had been performed by the Palestinians.

**Iraq.** In Iraq, allied bombing had knocked out roads, electrical plants, and other facilities. A U.N. report said that the country had been "relegated to a pre-industrial age," and there were fears of widespread famine and disease.

Saddam Hussein remained in power. Right after the war, revolts broke out among Shi'ite Muslims in southern Iraq and among Kurds, who have long sought an independent state, in northern Iraq. Although the United States had called on Iraqis to rise up and overthrow Saddam, allied troops didn't aid in these revolts. The Shi'ite rebellion was put down quickly. As fighting intensified in the north, Iraq attacked Kurdish villages with helicopter gunships. (The terms of the cease-fire allowed Iraq to fly helicopters, but not other planes.)

Hundreds of thousands of Kurds fled to Iran and to refugee camps along the Turkish border. They feared that Saddam would attack civilians with chemical weapons, as he had during previous revolts. An international relief effort was mounted to bring food and medical supplies to the refugees. And allied troops moved in to establish a "safe zone," remaining in northern Iraq until mid-July.

Although the Kurdish situation remained unsettled, Saddam seemed to have firm control over most of Iraq by late summer. It also seemed that Iraq was failing to live up to the cease-fire. It gave the United Nations an incomplete list of its nuclear and chemical weapons facilities and tried to prevent U.N. teams from making a full inspection of the facilities. This brought a threat of new military action from the United States. Thus the

After the war, Kurds living in northern Iraq revolted to try to overthrow Saddam. But fearing that they would be attacked with chemical weapons, hundreds of thousands of Kurdish civilians fled the country.

# ENVIRONMENTAL TERRORISM

"Environmental terrorism" was the term U.S. President George Bush used to describe several Iraqi actions during the Persian Gulf War that caused great devastation.

Toward the end of the war, retreating Iraqi forces set fire to about 700 Kuwaiti oil wells. Smoke from the fires darkened the sky over Kuwait and as far south as Oman, on the Arabian Sea, and soot blanketed the desert. After the war, firms from the United States and other countries were brought in to put out the fires and cap the wells, but the work was difficult. By fall, most of the fires were out. But leaking oil from the wells poisoned the soil. Experts could only guess at the harm it would do. Meanwhile, there were fears that the heavy smoke and soot would cause illness as well as harm wildlife in the area.

Iraqi forces also opened the valves at Kuwaiti oil storage depots on the Persian Gulf, releasing the biggest oil spill on record—an estimated 450 million gallons, 40 times as big as the 1989 *Exxon Valdez* spill in Alaska. U.S. forces managed to stem the flood by bombing oil supply lines that led to the depots. But the huge spill had devastating effects on the gulf's delicate coral reefs and its wildlife (including the cormorant below). Animals such as the dugong (a relative of the manatee) and the green turtle, which were already in danger of dying out, were especially at risk. The gulf's fishing industry was also severely affected, and desalinization plants that supply the gulf countries with most of their water were threatened.

Americans strongly supported the war, and U.S. troops were welcomed home as heroes.

outlook for stability was unclear, and some people criticized the allies for not continuing the war and overthrowing Saddam.

### THE VIEW FROM THE UNITED STATES

For people in the United States, far from the fighting, the war had several striking aspects. One was the make-up of U.S. forces, which included many reserve units. Since the end of the military draft after the Vietnam War, the U.S. military had shifted many functions to these units, which serve part-time but are called to active duty when needed. The U.S. forces also included some 35,000 women. Although regulations barred them from combat roles, the Persian Gulf War put them closer to the fighting than any other war in U.S. history. Eleven women were among the casualties.

Another striking aspect of the war was media coverage. With satellite hookups, television networks were able to transmit on-the-spot reports from Saudi Arabia, Israel, and (for much of the war) from Iraq. This gave the events a sense of immediacy that kept many people glued to their television sets.

However, media coverage of the war was in fact highly restricted. The movements of the few reporters who were in Iraq were controlled by the government there, and their reports were censored. On the allied side, reporters' movements were limited, and reports were also censored. This brought protests from members of the press, who said they were being prevented from presenting an unbiased view of the war. But allied leaders said that the restrictions were needed so that secret information about military plans and troop movements wouldn't be given away.

The Persian Gulf War touched off some antiwar protests in the United States, as well as in other countries. But polls showed that Americans supported the war five to one. American flags and yellow ribbons—symbols of support for the troops overseas—were seen everywhere. Even people who opposed the war supported the troops, and returning soldiers were welcomed as heroes. Although it left many matters unsettled, the quick allied victory in the Persian Gulf War raised American confidence to levels that hadn't been seen for many years.

In 1992, the twelve European countries that make up the European Community (EC) are scheduled to eliminate the last barriers to free trade among them—forming the largest trade bloc in the world. Symbolizing this, a youngster totes the EC flag (*left*). Future plans have all the member countries using a common currency, called ECUs (*above*).

# A NEW EUROPE

By the end of 1992, twelve European countries plan to move one step closer to the goal of European unity: They are scheduled to eliminate the last barriers to free trade among them. These countries—which together make up the European Community (EC), or Common Market—will form the largest trade bloc in the world. And in the years that follow, they hope to strengthen their ties, moving toward political as well as economic union. There are many obstacles, but the result may one day be a United States of Europe.

The idea for creating the EC was born after World War II, which left much of Europe devastated. For centuries, Europe had been torn by conflicts between nations. Many believed that the best hope for the future lay in a union of European countries. In

this vision, economic union—eliminating barriers to trade between nations—would be the first step toward political union.

### ECONOMIC UNION

There are many barriers to buying goods from other countries. Countries may levy taxes, called tariffs, on imports. They may set quotas, which limit imported goods. They may set complex specifications for imported products. They may also subsidize (give money to) their own industries, through tax breaks or direct payments. And when goods move across borders, customs checks often require reams of paperwork and long delays. All this favors products that are made in the country by making it more difficult for foreign products to compete.

In Europe, the first steps toward removing these barriers were taken in the 1950's by six countries: Belgium, France, Italy, Luxembourg, the Netherlands, and West Germany. Under the Treaties of Rome—which were signed in 1957 and established the EC—these countries agreed to eliminate tariffs between them. They were joined in 1973 by Britain, Denmark, and Ireland; in 1981 by Greece; and in 1986 by Portugal and Spain. But while many tariffs were eliminated, other barriers remained. For example, West German "purity laws" barred imported beer, while Italian laws kept German pasta out of Italy.

In the 1980's, the EC members agreed to end such barriers. To do this, they had to take a major step: They had to give up some power. Until 1987, EC laws, or directives, had to be passed by *all* the member countries. But in that year, the members agreed to abide by directives that were passed by just a majority. That meant that in trade matters, the EC could overrule the individual governments of its member countries.

With this step taken, the EC moved to eliminate the last trade barriers by 1992. Under the plan, goods are to pass freely across borders, with a single customs document replacing the stacks of papers previously required. Common manufacturing standards will apply. Banking and financial services will be integrated—people in one member country will be free to bank or invest money in any member country.

---

## GERMANY AND THE EC

The unification of Germany in 1990 created economic problems that seemed likely to affect not only Germans but all the members of the European Community. After World War II, when Germany was divided, West Germany developed a very strong economy. It was a founder, and soon one of the most important members, of the EC. But in Communist East Germany, the government-controlled economy gradually deteriorated.

With the collapse of the East German government in 1989 and the reunification of Germany a year later, many hoped that life would quickly improve for East Germans. But this didn't happen. Without government subsidies, outmoded East German businesses couldn't compete with those of the west. They closed their doors, and unemployment soared. Western companies didn't rush to take their places, and it was clear that it would take time to solve the problems of the east.

East Germans, out of work and seeing little hope of improvement, began to complain that they were second-class citizens and that Germans in the prosperous west were ungenerous for not helping more. They staged demonstrations to protest the situation. West Germans, meanwhile, complained about stiff new taxes that were imposed to help pay the cost of reunification—a cost that could be as high as $600 billion. They also faulted Germans in the east for not working harder, saying that the easterners lacked drive and initiative after living for so many years under Communism.

All these problems hurt the German economy, and they seemed likely to affect other EC members as well. By late 1991 the German economy was improving. But still, Germany's problems made EC members less willing to expand the community to include Eastern European countries. Many of those countries faced similar problems as they tried to rebuild their economies after years of Communism.

---

The plan for 1992 also called for the end of border checks for travelers, so people could move, live, and work anywhere within the community. But as 1992 drew nearer, this was still being debated. Some people wanted border checks to remain in effect to control drug traffic and terrorism. And wealthier EC countries feared a flood of immigrants from less wealthy members.

### QUESTIONS FOR THE FUTURE

EC members also discussed future steps, including plans to form a central European bank and to create a common currency. Since the 1980's, European currencies have been linked by a theoretical unit called the ECU. Each country's currency has a value in ECUs, and this helps stabilize exchange rates among them. The ECU may become the common currency for all the member countries —although Britain seemed unwilling to give up its own currency, the pound sterling.

There are questions about expanding the EC, too. With the collapse of Communism, Eastern European countries are developing Western-style market economies. Many are eager to join the EC. So are Turkey and some Western European countries that have remained outside. But EC members are concerned about including new members whose economies lag behind their own.

The idea of political union raises still other questions. How much power should member governments give up? How should they be represented in the EC's governing structure? The members don't agree. Nor do they agree on military matters. Some members, including Britain, want the North Atlantic Treaty Organization (NATO) to continue as Europe's main defense organization, even though NATO includes the United States and Canada. Others, including France, want Europe to develop its own defenses.

Still, the EC members have been able to act together internationally. For example, the EC tried to arrange a cease-fire when civil war broke out in Yugoslavia in 1991.

A "United States of Europe" may be many years away. Even so, the EC will be a powerful force in world trade after 1992. Its gross national product—the value of goods and services produced in a year—will be the largest in the world. And with 340 million people, the EC will be an important market for companies in the United States and elsewhere that do business abroad.

Palestinians and an Israeli soldier confront each other in the Israeli-occupied West Bank. The area has long been a source of friction between Israel and its Arab neighbors. It was hoped that the 1991 Middle East peace conference might be a start in solving some of the problems in this troubled region of the world.

# THE MIDDLE EAST: STRIVING FOR PEACE

The Middle East has long been one of the most troubled regions of the world, the site of long-running conflicts both within and between nations. In 1991, however, the situation seemed to be changing, and there were new hopes for settling some of the region's most bitter disputes.

One of the most hopeful events of 1991 was the release of Western hostages who had been held by terrorist groups in Lebanon. Other important developments included a historic conference between Israel and neighboring Arab countries.

### ISRAEL AND THE ARABS

Israel and its Arab neighbors have been at odds with each other since Israel's creation as a Jewish homeland in 1948. At that time, under a United Nations plan, the British-controlled territory of Palestine was to be divided into a Jewish state and an Arab state. The Arab state was to include territory on the West Bank of the Jordan River and an area on the Mediterranean coast called the Gaza Strip.

But the Arab state was never created. Israel was immediately attacked by the Arab countries around it; in the fighting, Jordan ended up controlling most of the West Bank, while Egypt took the Gaza Strip. Palestinians who were driven from their land by the fighting fled to refugee camps in these territories and in neighboring countries. They bitterly denied Israel's right to exist, and Arab governments backed their position.

War broke out again in 1967, and this time Israel captured both territories. It also captured the Sinai Peninsula, which it later returned to Egypt, and the Golan Heights, taken from Syria. Many Israelis felt that these territories should rightfully be part of Israel, and they began to establish settlements there.

Egypt has been the only Arab country to officially recognize or make peace with Israel. The Palestine Liberation Organization (PLO) and other groups representing Palestinian Arabs have repeatedly called for the creation of a Palestinian state, and they have attacked Israel with terrorist and guerrilla tactics. In 1987, Palestinians in the West Bank and Gaza Strip territories revolted against Israeli occupation.

That revolt continued to smolder in 1991. Yet several developments brought new hope that a peaceful solution might be found. In the past, events in the Middle East were often complicated by Cold War tensions between the United States (which supported Israel) and the Soviet Union (which supported the Arabs). But in 1991, this rivalry seemed to be at an end. Israel and the Soviet Union resumed diplomatic relations, which the Soviets had broken off in 1967. Moreover, the Soviets were focusing on their own internal problems and weren't in a position to provide much support to the Arabs.

In addition, the United States allied itself with Saudi Arabia and other moderate Arab countries to defeat Iraq, one of the most hard-line Arab states, in the Persian Gulf War. Together, these two developments brought the Arab world closer to the United States and created what seemed to be a historic opportunity to bridge the gulf between Israel and the Arabs.

The result was a peace conference that convened in Madrid, Spain, on October 30. Sponsored by the United States and the Soviet Union, the conference brought Israeli and Palestinian representatives together in their first official meeting. Also attending were representatives of Syria, Egypt, Lebanon, and Jordan.

The conference didn't produce any solutions, but it gave both sides a chance to air their positions—which they did in terms that were often bitter. And Israel and the Palestinians at least agreed to discuss the issue of Palestinian self-rule. But there was no progress on other issues, such as the status of the West Bank and the other occupied territories. The six-day meeting was followed by individual negotiations between Israel and the Arab participants, which began in Washington, D.C., in December.

But not all Arabs and Israelis supported the peace process. One major Palestinian group staged terrorist attacks during the conference, and that prompted Israel to shell Palestinian bases in southern Lebanon. Israel also opened a new settlement in the Golan Heights during the conference. In recent years Israel has been flooded with immigrants, mostly from the Soviet Union, and it has established many settlements in the occupied territories. This issue has created strain between Israel and the United States, which opposes the creation of such settlements while the status of the territories is unresolved. The opening of the new Golan settlement during the Madrid conference seemed to be a sign that Israel wouldn't give up these territories easily.

In Lebanon, seaside resorts once again began to attract vacationers, as the war-torn country started to rebuild. Peace seemed to be returning to Lebanon after fifteen years of civil war.

## ISLAMIC FUNDAMENTALISM

Islamic fundamentalists, who reject Western culture and values and believe that traditional Islamic rules and values should govern society, have become an important factor in the Middle East. This trend began in 1979, after Iranian fundamentalists led by Ayatollah Ruhollah Khomeini overthrew the government and established a state governed by Islamic law. Under their government, religious doctrine ruled all aspects of life, and opponents of the regime were suppressed. Khomeini also urged Muslim fundamentalists in other countries to follow his path and take control of their countries.

Khomeini died in 1989, and since then Iran has become somewhat more moderate. The country has deep economic problems, and solving them will require better relations with other countries. However, Iran is still governed by religious rulers, and Islamic fundamentalism remains a strong force there.

Fundamentalism has also gained ground in other Muslim countries. Fundamentalists hold seats in Egypt's parliament. They are also challenging the PLO for leadership of the Palestinian Arabs. And armed fundamentalist groups are fighting the governments of Egypt, Lebanon, Morocco, and Tunisia.

Experts who have studied Middle Eastern politics say that Islamic fundamentalism, despite its rigid rules, appeals to many people because it gives them a sense of pride and cultural identity. It remains to be seen whether any of the fundamentalist groups will succeed, as Khomeini did, in controlling their countries. But fundamentalism seems certain to continue to play an important role in the Middle East.

### LEBANON

Peace finally seemed to be returning to Lebanon in 1991, after more than fifteen years of bloody civil war. The war broke out in 1975 as a conflict between Muslim and Christian groups; Muslims, who form the majority of the population, wanted a greater voice in government. But over the years Lebanon was torn by fighting between dozens of factions—independent Muslim and Christian militias, Palestinian guerrilla forces, Syrian and Israeli troops. In all, 150,000 people were killed.

After a period of intense fighting in 1989, Lebanon's legislature agreed on a peace plan that gave Muslims more power. But hard-line Christian forces under General Michel Aoun held out. Then, in the fall of 1990, Aoun's forces were finally crushed by the Syrian army, which had first entered Lebanon in 1976 and had controlled sections of the country ever since.

With the support of the Syrians, the Lebanese government established a peace zone in Beirut, the capital, which had long been divided between Muslim and Christian groups. Private militias in this zone surrendered their weapons, and the city was unified. In 1991, this peace zone was extended to include 1,000 square miles (1,609 square kilometers) around the capital.

Within this area, the Lebanese people were at last able to start rebuilding their war-torn country. Slowly, refugees and exiles began to return, and businesses began to reopen. Several foreign airlines resumed flights that had been canceled during the fighting. And investors began to discuss rebuilding Beirut's once-beautiful seaside hotels, which had been destroyed in the civil war.

But the peace was still fragile—after so many years of hatred and fighting, there were fears that war could break out at any time. And rival factions still operated outside the government-controlled zone. Palestinian guerrillas had bases in the south, and Israeli troops patrolled a strip of Lebanese territory along the southern border. Radical Muslim groups, such as the Iranian-backed Hezbollah (Party of God), continued to operate in some areas. Several splinter groups that were tied to Hezbollah had staged kidnappings and other terrorist actions in the past, and at the beginning of 1991 they held a number of Western hostages.

### THE WESTERN HOSTAGES

Most of the hostages were released in 1991, including all six of the Americans. The releases stemmed from negotiations led by the United Nations and Iran. Iran had long strongly opposed the West and, along with Syria, Iraq, and Libya, was believed to have been behind many terrorist actions in the 1980's. But in 1991, in the atmosphere that followed the Persian Gulf War, Iran seemed

Terry Waite, a British envoy of the Anglican Church, was one of the numerous hostages released in 1991. Waite was kidnapped in 1987 when he went to Beirut to try to free some of the hostages.

interested in improving relations with the West. Through Hezbollah, it was in a position to put pressure on the groups that held the hostages.

John McCarthy, a British journalist who had been kidnapped in Lebanon in 1986, and Edward A. Tracy, an American held since October of that year, were released in August. McCarthy carried a message from his captors to the United Nations. It suggested that all Western hostages might be released if Israel released some 300 imprisoned Palestinian and Lebanese guerrillas. Israel, in turn, said that it would release the prisoners in exchange for seven Israeli soldiers who had been captured in Lebanon in the 1980's or, if the soldiers had been killed, for confirmation of their deaths.

Negotiations began. In September, after Israel released 51 prisoners, a radical Muslim group released Jack Mann, a retired British airline pilot who had been kidnapped in 1989. In October, after Israel released fifteen more prisoners, Jesse Turner, an American professor who had been held for almost five years, was freed. In November, two more hostages were freed: Thomas Sutherland, a dean at the American University of Beirut held since June, 1985; and Terry Waite, a British envoy of the Anglican Church who was kidnapped in 1987 when he went to Beirut to negotiate hostage releases. And in December, the last Americans were freed. They were Joseph J. Cicippio, an American University official held since September, 1986; Alann Steen, a University journalism professor held since January, 1987; and Terry Anderson, a journalist kidnapped in March, 1985. Anderson, the longest-held American hostage, was the last to be released.

Only one Westerner, a French relief worker, was taken hostage in 1991, and he was released within a few days. But two Germans were still being held. Their kidnappers belonged to a different group than the other hostage takers, and at year's end negotiations were under way to gain their freedom. Meanwhile, the release of the other Westerners seemed a good sign for future stability in the Middle East.

Recent events in South Africa have led to the crumbling of its rigid system of racial discrimination. One sign of this was school desegregation. At about ten percent of the country's white public schools, parents voted to end segregation in 1991.

# CHANGE IN SOUTH AFRICA

The year 1991 saw a historic event in South Africa—the crumbling of the basic laws of apartheid, the rigid system of racial discrimination that had allowed a white minority to dominate every aspect of life in the country. But while the end of legal apartheid marked a great step forward for South Africa, the country faced a difficult future.

### A HISTORY OF REPRESSION

The system of apartheid was put in place after 1948, when the National Party came to power in South Africa. Whites had dominated the country since the 1700's, but apartheid turned that domination into law. Everyone was classified by race—white, black, colored (mixed race), Asian. Blacks were denied political power, and other non-white groups were allowed only a limited voice in government. Housing, education, employment, and social services were strictly segregated.

Protests against these policies were harshly suppressed. Black groups that opposed them, such as the African National Congress (ANC), were banned. Individials who spoke out against them were jailed.

With legal protests suppressed, some op-

ponents of apartheid turned to violence. The country seemed to be heading toward civil war. Meanwhile, outside South Africa, apartheid produced a growing outcry. Many nations imposed economic sanctions against South Africa, limiting or cutting off trade.

The white South African government was slow to respond to these pressures. But in 1989, a new government headed by F.W. de Klerk came to power and began to ease some of the restrictions of apartheid. In 1990, banned groups such as the ANC were legalized. And ANC leader Nelson Mandela, who had been imprisoned for 27 years and had become a symbol of the fight against apartheid, was freed.

### TOWARD CHANGE

Soon after Mandela's release, the government and black leaders began to meet to discuss ways in which a new constititution might be drawn up. But they remained far apart in their vision of South Africa's future.

The ANC held firmly to the principle of "one man, one vote," which would inevitably lead to black majority rule. The government continued to seek a system of "group rights," under which any minority group, white or other, would be able to veto measures passed by the majority—a proposal that the ANC saw as a way of preserving white privileges. The ANC also wanted power to be turned over to a transitional government while a new constitution was drawn up, a step de Klerk's government was unwilling to take.

While agreement on these issues seemed far away, the government continued to dismantle the structure of apartheid. The most important steps came in June, 1991, when the parliament repealed a group of laws that formed the foundations of apartheid. They included the Land Acts, which reserved 87 percent of South Africa's land for whites (who make up just 13 percent of the population); the Group Areas Act, which imposed residential segregation; and the Black Communities Act, which defined the separate status of black townships. Repeal of these laws meant that a black South African would be able to live, and buy land, anywhere in the country. Also repealed was the Population Registration Act—the basic law that classified all South Africans into racial groups.

These reforms were sweeping enough to convince many people that South Africa was on a course that couldn't be reversed. As a result, many countries lifted economic sanctions in April, 1991. Among them was the United States, which lifted sanctions in July. And the International Olympic Committee ended a 21-year-old ban on South African participation in the Olympic Games.

As far-reaching as the reforms were, however, black South Africans still had no vote and no voice in government. Worse, years of poverty and desperation were helping to feed violence in black areas.

## FACTIONAL VIOLENCE

Violence between black groups had been growing since the mid-1980's, and it had erupted on an appalling scale in 1990. By mid-1991, this factional fighting had taken thousands of lives. Much of the violence involved clashes between members of the ANC and the Inkatha Freedom Party, a rival group whose members include many Zulus (the country's largest ethnic group). But while political rivalry between black groups lay behind many of the clashes, in some cases armed bands attacked other blacks randomly, with no clear reason.

In January, 1991, ANC leader Nelson Mandela and Mangosuthu Gatsha Buthelezi, the Inkatha leader, met for the first time. They agreed to work together to end apartheid. But this only slowed the pace of the violence for a while. In September, the government, the ANC, and Inkatha signed a formal accord to end the violence—but even then the killing continued.

The ANC charged that the police and security forces were taking sides in the conflict —standing by while Inkatha forces attacked people, and even training some armed gangs. But it wasn't clear that ANC supporters were always blameless victims. And the ANC's image suffered a blow in 1991 when Winnie Mandela, the wife of ANC leader Nelson Mandela, was convicted on charges of kidnapping and acting as an accessory to assault. The charges stemmed from a 1988 incident in which her bodyguards allegedly abducted four black youths and tortured them at her home. One of the youths died.

While whites largely remained untouched by the factional fighting, it contributed to their fears about the future. Most whites supported reform, but many were uneasy about what lay ahead. Meanwhile, militant right-wing groups who opposed *any* reform became increasingly vocal in 1991. Some vowed to take up arms and plunge the country into civil war rather than give up their privileged position.

## APARTHEID'S LEGACY

In September, De Klerk outlined a plan for a new constitution that would give everyone the vote, regardless of race, but included a number of checks on majority power. The ANC rejected the plan, and progress toward a new constitution seemed to falter.

There seemed to be no easy solution to the problems created by the years of apartheid. Just as abolishing slavery and ending legal segregation didn't put blacks in the United States on an equal footing with whites, so the years of white supremacy in South Africa were likely to leave a bitter legacy of poverty, discrimination, and mistrust between the racial groups.

Yet South Africans, black and white, had brought their country to a turning point. And the events of 1991 raised hope that they would find ways to solve their problems and steer their country to a peaceful future.

ELAINE PASCOE
Author, *South Africa: Troubled Land*

# THE SOVIET UNION AND EASTERN EUROPE: NEW DIRECTIONS

On the morning of August 19, 1991, Soviet citizens woke up to some startling news: According to the government news agency, President Mikhail Gorbachev was ill and had been replaced by a group of officials called the Committee for the State of Emergency. As the news spread, people realized that Gorbachev, who had led the country cautiously toward reform for the last six years, wasn't really ill. Instead, Communist hard-liners had staged a coup, trying to oust Gorbachev and take control of the country.

Within just three days, however, the coup had collapsed. Hundreds of thousands of Soviet citizens had poured into the streets to protest it. Governments around the world had condemned it. Gorbachev returned as president, and the coup leaders were arrested.

Life didn't return to normal in the Soviet Union, however. The failed coup set in motion a chain of events that ended the long domination of the Soviet Communist Party and led to the breakup of the Soviet Union itself. Because the Soviet Union had long held a position as one of the world's nuclear superpowers, these dramatic changes were watched around the world.

## CAREFUL REFORM

Gorbachev had come to power in 1985, at a time when the Soviet Union faced a serious economic crisis. Under the Soviet economic system, the government controlled all aspects of the economy—it owned the land and factories, decided what would be produced, and set wages and prices. Years of this system had led to serious shortages of basic goods, even food and housing.

Gorbachev developed new policies to deal with the crisis. He lessened government control of the economy with a policy called *perestroika,* or "restructuring," which permitted some private enterprise. The Soviet government was restructured, too. The leading role of the Communist Party, previously guaranteed by the constitution, was ended. Voters were allowed to have a choice among candidates in elections. And under a policy called *glasnost,* or "openness," Soviet citizens were allowed to criticize the system for the first time in many years. Gorbachev also released the countries of Eastern Europe from Soviet domination, a step that brought him the 1990 Nobel Peace Prize.

But these reforms weren't enough to solve the country's problems. The Communist Party remained entrenched; many party officials enjoyed privileged lives that they were unwilling to give up. The government still controlled most aspects of the economy. Gorbachev wavered back and forth, pushing for reform at some times and drawing back at others. Late in 1990, he appointed several hard-liners to his government, seeking to appease this group. But others warned that the hard-liners wanted total control.

Meanwhile, a spirit of rebellion began to spread throughout the country. Independence movements formed in many of the Soviet Union's fifteen republics, and there were clashes between ethnic groups as well. In January, 1991, the government sent troops into seven republics, including the Baltic republics of Lithuania, Latvia, and Estonia, which had pressed hardest for independence. Fifteen protesters were killed by the troops in Lithuania.

Then in the spring and summer of 1991, Gorbachev and leaders of the republics negotiated a new union treaty that would have permitted the republics to have more freedom from central control. It was this treaty, which was to be signed on August 20, that prompted the hard-liners to attempt the coup. They had already lost control of Eastern Europe and had seen their privileged position threatened; now they saw the Soviet empire slipping away.

## THE COUP

The coup was led by Soviet Vice-President Gennadi I. Yanayev and seven other high government officials. They acted while Gorbachev was on vacation at his *dacha,* or country house, on the Black Sea, placing the Soviet president and his family under house arrest. After announcing the takeover, the coup leaders imposed curfews and press

Cheering crowds unfurled the Russian republic flag in Moscow, after Soviet hard-liners failed in their attempt to oust President Mikhail Gorbachev. The coup attempt marked the beginning of the end of the Soviet Union.

censorship and banned any activities that would oppose their move. On their orders, troops took up positions in Moscow, throughout the Baltics, and in other key regions.

Many Soviet citizens were slow to react to the coup. But in Moscow, opposition was led by Boris Yeltsin, president of the Russian republic. Yeltsin had long urged radical reforms and had quit the Communist Party in 1990. In June, 1991, he had won the election for the Russian presidency in a landslide. Now he spearheaded opposition to the coup, working from the Russian parliament building, which is known as the "White House."

Fearing that the coup leaders would

Boris Yeltsin (*above*), president of the Russian republic, led the resistance to the takeover. His opposition resulted in the coup's failure and led to the return of Gorbachev and his family (*left*).

storm the White House and arrest Yeltsin, crowds of Moscow citizens surrounded the building. By late morning on August 19, several tank crews defected to the Russian side, as well. Yeltsin, mounting one of the tanks, denounced the coup to the cheering crowd. Over the tense hours that followed, the crowd built a barricade around the White House, using abandoned cars and buses and construction debris. Meanwhile, Yeltsin and his supporters broadcast uncensored news over the radio, and they kept phone lines open to inform foreign journalists of events.

In other countries, the coup was almost universally condemned. U.S. President George Bush reacted tentatively at first, calling the takeover "disturbing" but suggesting that the United States could work with the new leaders. However, by August 20 he had joined other world leaders in opposing the coup and supporting Yeltsin. Leaders of several Soviet republics also backed the Russian president and called for Gorbachev's return. In Leningrad, the second largest Soviet city, a crowd of 200,000 rallied. Some 400,000 gathered in Kishinev, the capital of the republic of Moldavia. And in Lithuania, as in Moscow, crowds gathered to defend the parliament building from troops.

Several people were reported to have been shot by troops in Lithuania and Latvia. But elsewhere, the Soviet Army clearly seemed reluctant to move against the Soviet people. Faced with overwhelming opposition inside and outside the country, and without the support of the armed forces, the coup collapsed on August 21. One of its leaders, Interior Minister Boris K. Pugo, committed suicide; the others were arrested. Gorbachev resumed the presidency and returned to Moscow early on August 22.

### COMMUNISM FAILS

In the days and weeks after the failed coup, the Soviet government was in turmoil. Faced with clear evidence that Communist Party leaders and many members of his government had backed the coup, Gorbachev resigned as Communist Party leader. But he retained the presidency. He also dismissed his cabinet and the heads of the military and the KGB, the feared Soviet secret service.

Boris Yeltsin emerged from the coup with national and international support, and he and other liberals demanded greater reforms. They rejected many of Gorbachev's new government appointments, forcing him to name people they supported instead. And at their urging, on August 29, the Soviet legislature suspended all activities of the Communist Party. This ended the rule of the Communists, who had controlled almost all aspects of life in the country since 1917.

Soviet citizens were quick to approve. Around the country, statues of Vladimir Lenin, the founder of Soviet Communism, and other Communist leaders were toppled by crowds. The city of Leningrad, named for Lenin after the Russian Revolution, took back its original name: St. Petersburg, for the Russian czar Peter the Great.

Meanwhile, an interim parliament and a new State Council, led by Gorbachev and including representatives from several republics, was set up to run the central government. But the central government didn't seem to have much control over the country —the Soviet republics were rushing to declare independence.

Soviet citizens showed their anger at the Communist Party's role in the attempted coup by toppling statues of former Communist leaders.

## A TIME OF TURMOIL

During the coup, Lithuania had reaffirmed its declaration of independence issued in 1990, and Estonia and Latvia had announced their immediate independence. The three Baltic states were quickly recognized by other nations, and their independence was acknowledged by the Soviet government on September 6. These countries had been annexed by the Soviets during World War II and had long protested Soviet rule.

Right after the coup, a number of other republics followed the Baltics and also declared their independence: Armenia, Georgia, Moldavia, Belorussia, and Ukraine, one of the Soviet Union's most important agricultural and industrial regions. Their independence wasn't immediately recognized by other countries. However, the push for independence threatened the very existence of the Soviet Union. Five republics boycotted the new interim parliament. Several republics began to withhold funds from the central government and develop their own currencies and economic systems. In the Russian republic, Yeltsin operated with special emergency powers, and he announced a package of radical economic reforms that were designed to bring a Western-style market economy to the republic quickly. And a few republics, including Ukraine, even announced plans to establish their own armies.

Instead of a union, the country seemed likely to become a collection of independent states. This raised important questions for

Despite Soviet President Mikhail Gorbachev's attempts to bring reform to the Soviet Union, the country's fifteen republics declared their independence in 1991. By year's end, what was once the Soviet Union no longer existed.

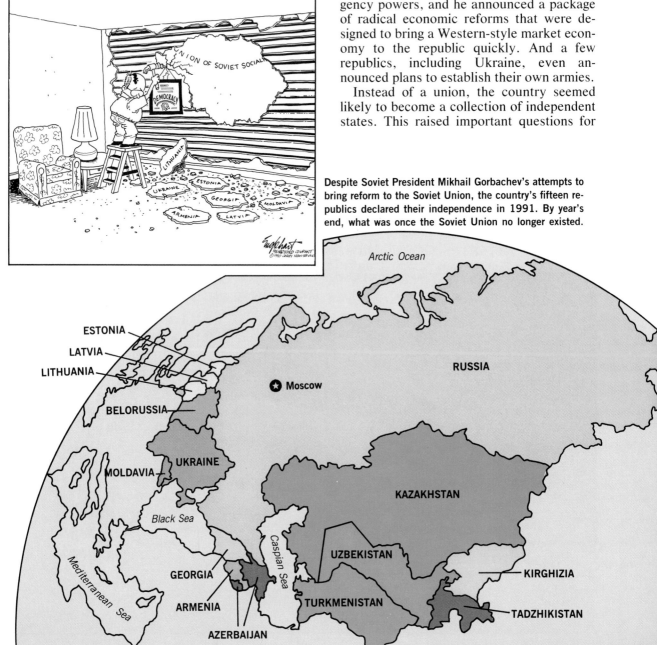

the rest of the world: If the Soviet Union broke up, who would be responsible for its debts? Would each former republic have a separate foreign policy? Who would control the vast Soviet arsenal of nuclear weapons? There were also fears that fighting might break out between former republics and between ethnic groups that were at odds with one another in several republics. Such groups had already clashed in Georgia, Azerbaijan, and other republics.

But some form of cooperation was needed if these states were to survive. For one thing, they were dependent on each other economically. Discussions continued on how some form of union might be maintained. But by late 1991, little progress had been made. In addition, the people of the crumbling Soviet Union seemed to be facing their worst winter ever. Poor harvests combined with a breakdown in the Soviet distribution system to create severe shortages of food and other essentials.

In the cities, people began to hoard food, expecting the worst. There were fears that food riots might break out. If conditions became bad enough, some people warned, hard-liners might again attempt a coup—and the people, tired of turmoil and shortages, might not resist it this time. Late in 1991, the United States and other Western countries said that they would provide food and loans to help the Soviets through the winter. And Russia began to finance the bankrupt central government and control its budget.

On December 1, Ukraine confirmed its independence in a referendum. Just a week later, Russia, Ukraine, and Belorussia announced the formation of a new Commonwealth of Independent States, outside the old Soviet system. Members were to be independent but would share economic and foreign policies. Other republics announced that they would join the commonwealth, too.

Russia next took control of the Soviet government's ministries. By the end of the year, Gorbachev's role in the government had ended, and the old Soviet Union no longer existed. But there were still many questions that remained. Could the commonwealth solve the massive economic problems? And who would control the military? One thing was clear: What was once the Soviet Union was entering a new chapter in history.

## MILITARY QUESTIONS

The Soviet Union's movement toward democracy ended the Cold War, the long stand-off between the West and the Communist countries. But important military questions remained to be solved.

**NATO and the Warsaw Pact.** One of these involved the North Atlantic Treaty Organization (NATO), the military alliance formed after World War II by the United States, Canada, and Western European countries to oppose the spread of Communism in Europe. The Soviets and their Eastern European allies had formed a similar organization, the Warsaw Pact. But in 1990, with Soviet domination of Eastern Europe at an end and all these countries moving toward democracy, the two alliances announced the end of their conflict. And in July, 1991, the Warsaw Pact officially disbanded.

That left the question of what role NATO would play in the future. Some Europeans suggested that they should handle their own security, outside the alliance. But others favored continuing to rely on NATO. And there was discussion of extending the alliance's protection to Eastern Europe. Some Eastern Europeans worried that hard-liners might return to power in the Soviet Union and try to regain control of their countries.

**Nuclear Weapons.** A second military question concerned the huge stockpiles of nuclear weapons built up by the United States and the Soviet Union during the Cold War. In July, at a summit meeting in Moscow, Gorbachev and U.S. President George Bush signed a new Strategic Arms Reduction Treaty (START), setting new limits on long-range nuclear weapons. But the August coup and the turmoil that followed it created new worries. As central authority collapsed in the Soviet Union, there were fears that individual republics or even terrorist groups might gain control of some of the vast stockpiles of Soviet nuclear weapons.

In September, Bush announced a unilateral (one-sided) reduction in U.S. nuclear weapons. He hoped this would encourage the Soviets to take similar steps. And Gorbachev responded by announcing cuts in Soviet nuclear forces. But both sides still had huge nuclear arsenals. And as the Soviet system collapsed late in the year, it wasn't clear who would control the Soviet nuclear weapons. Russia and other republics who had such weapons in their territories promised to abide by the arms-control agreements and even destroy some nuclear weapons. But the unclear status of these weapons remained a cause for concern for many people around the world.

For many of the countries of Eastern Europe, the end of Communism led to the resurfacing of old rivalries between ethnic groups. Nowhere was this more evident than in Yugoslavia, where a civil war erupted between the two largest groups, the Serbs and Croats.

## YUGOSLAVIA'S CIVIL WAR

Old ethnic rivalries erupted in a civil war in Yugoslavia in 1991. This country includes six republics that reflect its major ethnic groups. There is a long history of friction between many of these groups, especially between Serbs and Croats, the two largest. But for years the country was held together by Josip Broz Tito, who set up a Communist government after World War II and ruled until his death in 1980.

Since Tito's death, nationalist feelings have grown. In 1990, the Yugoslav Communist Party collapsed, and this ended the last unifying force in the country. Full-scale separatist movements emerged in the republics of Croatia and Slovenia.

In June, 1991, these republics declared independence, saying that they would no longer be dominated by Serbia, the largest Yugoslav republic. Fighting broke out almost immediately, as Croat and Slovene forces battled Serbian-led federal forces and Serbian militias. And the fighting continued despite efforts by the European Community (EC) to negotiate a peace.

In Croatia, the situation was complicated by the fact that many ethnic Serbs live within the republic's borders, and they strongly opposed independence. Some of the heaviest fighting took place in the eastern part of the republic. Several Croatian towns and cities were devastated—Vukovar, one of the largest towns, was practically destroyed, and Dubrovnik, a historic port city, was shelled by federal forces. Thousands of people, both Serbs and Croatians, were killed or injured or became refugees.

In November, a U.N.-sponsored cease-fire also failed to take hold, and the fighting prevented a U.N. peacekeeping force from taking up positions. Meanwhile, EC members and the United States imposed economic sanctions on Yugoslavia, hoping to stop the war. Late in the year, the EC said that it would recognize the independence of Croatia and Slovenia. But most countries held back, fearing that recognizing the republics would only fuel the conflict, which had already produced the heaviest fighting in Europe since World War II.

## EASTERN EUROPE

The economic and political troubles faced by the Soviet Union were echoed in many of the former Communist countries of Eastern Europe. Since 1989, when the Soviets had relaxed their control over this region, most of these countries had moved toward democracy, market economies, and closer ties with the West. But in 1991, many people in these countries were finding the change difficult.

Changing from a state-run to a market economy, in which businesses are owned and run by private individuals and prices and wages are set by the economic law of supply and demand, brought goods to store shelves. But it also brought hardships. When prices were no longer controlled by the government, the cost of living rose. Factories that were no longer run by the government couldn't make a profit and so closed their doors. That created unemployment. And many people who were used to government support, no matter how meager, resented the few who developed their own businesses and began to get ahead in the new economy.

Because their situation didn't improve quickly, many people in these countries became discouraged and cynical. In Poland, where voters had turned the Communists out of office in 1989, only 40 percent bothered to vote in parliamentary elections in 1991. More than 100 parties competed in the elections, and none won more than 12 percent of the vote. The elections seemed to show that voters were unhappy with the pace of economic change but uncertain what to do.

The end of Communism also allowed old ethnic rivalries to emerge once again. In Czechoslovakia, for example, strain increased between the country's two main ethnic groups, the Czechs and the Slovaks. Slovaks argued that the Czech republic, the larger of the two units that made up the country, dominated their region and was receiving most of the benefits of change. Some Slovaks wanted to separate from Czechoslovakia and form an independent country. Czechoslovak President Vaclav Havel proposed reforms that would give the two republics equality, and he urged voters to decide the unity question in a referendum.

In the few countries where Communism still held sway, however, people increasingly rejected it. In 1990, Bulgaria had been the

Hoping to escape political repression and economic hardship, thousands of Albanians fled across the Adriatic Sea to seek refuge in Italy. Most were turned back.

only Eastern European country in which Communists won a free election. In 1991, voters turned the Communists out of office, giving an opposition group a majority in parliament.

And in Albania, where a repressive Communist regime had isolated the country even from the Soviet Union, thousands of refugees fled across the Adriatic Sea to Italy, hoping to escape the repression and economic hardship of their homeland. Most were sent back. But anti-government demonstrations erupted after the Communist Party won parliamentary elections in the spring of 1991. In June, the new government was forced to resign. A nonpartisan government was appointed to lead the country until new elections could be held in 1992.

The turmoil and confusion in these countries showed the difficulty of dismantling Communism. Even so, the people of Eastern Europe, like those of the Soviet Union, seemed determined to continue on the road to change.

# NEWSMAKERS

When U.S. troops went into action in the Persian Gulf early in 1991, two military leaders were in the forefront of the news. **General H. Norman Schwarzkopf** (above), head of the U.S. Central Command, led the forces that drove Iraq from Kuwait. Nicknamed Stormin' Norman, the 56-year-old general captivated audiences with his blunt, direct manner in televised briefings during the war. When he returned to the United States in April and announced his retirement from the Army, there were rumors that he might seek political office. Similar rumors circulated about **General Colin L. Powell** (left), chairman of the Joint Chiefs of Staff and, as such, the highest U.S. military leader. Powell, 54, was the youngest person and the first black to hold that post. The son of Jamaican immigrants, he had risen through the ranks during his 33-year army career and had also served as national security adviser under President Ronald Reagan. During the Persian Gulf War his calm, easygoing manner won him widespread admiration.

With the collapse of the Soviet Union in 1991, **Boris N. Yeltsin**, president of the Russian republic, became a world figure. Yeltsin, a reformer who had quit the Communist Party in 1990, had often opposed Soviet president Mikhail Gorbachev. But in August, 1991, he successfully rallied opposition to a coup that tried to oust Gorbachev. After the coup attempt, the Soviet republics declared independence. Yeltsin then led a movement that replaced the Soviet system with a commonwealth made up of former republics. As head of the largest and most powerful of these states, he seemed likely to play a leading role.

**Edith Cresson** became prime minister of France in May, 1991—the first woman ever to hold the position. Named to the post by French president François Mitterrand, she had held other cabinet positions, including minister of foreign trade. She was known for her outspokenness and had earned the nickname *la battante* —"the fighter"—early in her career.

After 24 years on the U.S. Supreme Court, **Justice Thurgood Marshall** (left), 82, announced his retirement in June, 1991. As an attorney before he was named to the court in 1967, Marshall had argued and won landmark civil rights cases. Among them was *Brown* v. *Board of Education of Topeka, Kansas,* which ended school segregation. He was the first black Supreme Court justice, and he became known for strongly worded opinions that often championed individual rights. To succeed Marshall on the court, President George Bush named **Clarence Thomas** (below), 43. An attorney and former head of the federal Equal Employment Opportunity Commission, Thomas had criticized earlier civil rights policies and court decisions. After his nomination, Anita Hill, a law professor, accused him of having sexually harassed her ten years earlier, when she had worked for him. On October 15, after long and heated hearings, the Senate confirmed Thomas's appointment by one of the narrowest margins in history, 52—48. The new justice was expected to support the conservative positions the court has taken in recent years.

**Lynn Martin** was confirmed as U.S. Secretary of Labor in February, 1991. A former schoolteacher, she had been a Republican congresswoman from Illinois from 1981 to 1991. Martin, 51, succeeded Elizabeth Dole in the post.

Was **U.S. President Zachary Taylor,** who died in office in 1850, assassinated? Taylor (shown below on his deathbed) fell ill after eating huge quantities of iced cherries and milk at the dedication of the Washington Monument on July 4, 1850. He died five days later of what seemed to be natural causes. But in 1991 a historian pointed out that the president's symptoms were consistent with arsenic poisoning. Taylor had opposed slavery, the biggest issue of his day. Could supporters of slavery have done him in? To answer the question, Taylor's remains were removed from his crypt in Louisville, Kentucky, and tested. No trace of arsenic was found—showing that Taylor died a natural, if untimely, death.

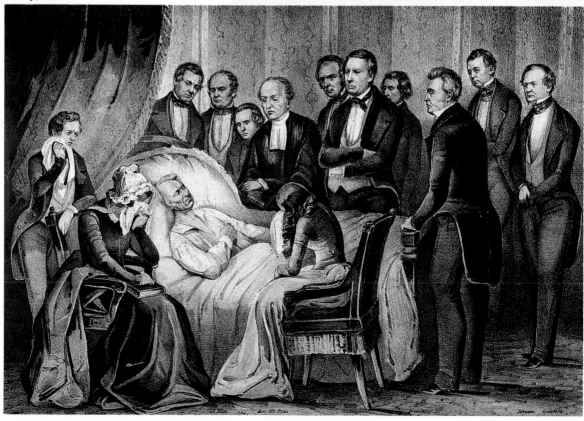

# ANIMALS

The tokay gecko is an amazing creature. It can perform gravity-defying stunts that would put a circus acrobat to shame. Tokay geckos, which live in Asia, are members of one of the most numerous and widespread animal families—the lizards. These reptiles have been around since prehistoric times, and the roughly 3,000 members of the family have developed some remarkable features.

Roly-poly, cuddly-looking giant pandas face extinction—and most of their problems are caused by people.

# GIANT PANDAS— PRECIOUS TREASURES IN TROUBLE

Giant pandas are among the most loved animals in the world. Their cuddly looks and good-natured antics draw thousands of visitors to those few zoos lucky enough to possess a pair. When the Chinese government lends a pair of pandas to a zoo in another country, visitors wait on lines for hours to catch a glimpse of them. In 1986, when a panda was born in a zoo in Tokyo, Japan, thousands of people phoned every day just to hear a recording of the baby's cry.

But today pandas are in danger. There are fewer than a thousand pandas in the wild, and about a hundred in zoos. How have these animals come to be endangered? Unfortunately, it's mostly people who are driving them toward extinction.

All the wild giant pandas live in dense bamboo forests in a small area in the mountains of central China. A little less than half live on reserves especially established for them in this area. But over the years, more and more of the bamboo forests have been cut up to make way for farms, villages, and roads—and bamboo is the panda's main source of food. To make matters worse,

poachers (illegal hunters) have been killing pandas in great numbers for their magnificent pelts.

With the extinction of the panda a very real threat, an alarm has been sounded. People everywhere—including the Chinese government, conservationists, the World Wildlife Fund, and zoos around the world—are finally taking steps to protect this much-loved animal.

## THE LIFE OF A GIANT PANDA

The giant panda is a chubby, roly-poly creature with a short tail. Its white body is accented by black legs and a wide black band across the back. Its large round white head is topped by small black ears. The panda is especially known for the large black patches around its eyes, which give the animal an endearing and lovable look.

Mature giant pandas are about 5 feet (1.5 meters) long and can weigh more than 200 pounds (90 kilograms). Their stiff, coarse fur, which is about 2 inches (5 centimeters) long, serves as a warm coat in their cold and snowy mountainous habitat.

Pandas love to frolic. They've been seen doing somersaults and belly-flops down snowy slopes. They sometimes swim and climb trees. And in zoos they play with rubber balls and other toys. Yet pandas are loners—they are unsociable and solitary animals who spend most of their day eating and sleeping. They have little or no contact with other pandas except during the once-a-year mating season, from March to May.

When a female panda is ready to give birth, she builds a nest of leaves, twigs, and other vegetation in a cave or a hollow tree. Pandas give birth to one or two cubs, but the mother nurses only one, leaving the other to die. She is devoted to the surviving cub and can be seen carrying the helpless and blind offspring around in her teeth, much as a cat carries a kitten. She will rear the cub for a year and a half, by which time it will weigh about 120 pounds (55 kilograms) and be able to fend for itself.

A typical female can breed for only seven or eight years, from the time she is 6 or 7 years of age to about 14. She will give birth a total of just four or five times, but only two cubs will make it to adulthood. The reproductive rate of pandas in zoos is even lower.

Given the chance, a panda will eat a wide variety of foods—including meat. If it happens upon a dead rodent or other small animal, it will happily devour it. But pandas are so slow moving—the best they can manage is a slow trot—that they can't easily catch other animals. As a result, they have had to find other foods to live on. Pandas will eat

## PANDA-MONIUM

- Pandas live for as long as 30 years.

- A giant panda weighs about 4 ounces when it is born, and around 200 pounds when fully grown. One *giant* giant panda weighed in at 400 pounds.

- The giant panda's closest relative is the bear, and the Chinese call the animal *daxiong mao,* which means "large cat bear."

- To obtain enough nutrition, a giant panda must spend sixteen hours a day eating bamboo. In one year it may eat as much as 5 tons of the plant.

- When it eats, a panda sits on its haunches—just like a human being.

- Pandas make a wide variety of sounds. They moo and moan, whine and snort, bleat and chirp, growl, squeal, bark, and roar.

grasses, flowers, roots, and other vegetation. And in zoos, some pandas have even eaten chicken, muffins, and honey.

But the panda's basic food is bamboo, a woody grass that grows as tall as trees. Bamboo, however, isn't a nutritious food, and it's also hard for pandas to digest. As a result, pandas must eat great amounts of bamboo every day—perhaps as much as 85 pounds (38 kilograms). They eat not only the bamboo shoots and leaves but the stalks as well, using their powerful jaws and teeth to crush and tear away the hard outer covering to get at the softer pith.

The pandas' dependence on bamboo for 99 percent of their diet, along with their low reproductive rate, are two factors that have contributed to their dwindling numbers. But the major cause of their decline is the intrusion of people into the pandas' steadily diminishing habitat.

### SAVING THE PANDA

For China's giant pandas to survive, they need only two things: to be left alone and to have enough bamboo to eat. These are simple needs, yet for those who want to save these animals from extinction, these needs have been difficult to meet.

Pandas once roamed across wide areas of China, finding ample supplies of bamboo on which to feast. But over time, as human population grew, pandas were pushed into ever smaller areas of bamboo forest. Starting in the early 1960's, the Chinese government began to establish protected reserves for them. Today, a little less than half of China's pandas live on thirteen small reserves, twelve of them in Sichuan province and one in Shaanxi province. But they aren't alone even on these reserves. Thousands of people also live there, and they've cleared some of the land for farms and cut down stands of bamboo to use as fuel for heating and cooking. The Chinese government has lured some of these people away from the reserves with promises of financial aid, but most refuse to leave their ancestral homeland.

The fact that the thirteen reserves are, for the most part, separate from one another has

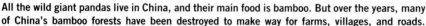

All the wild giant pandas live in China, and their main food is bamboo. But over the years, many of China's bamboo forests have been destroyed to make way for farms, villages, and roads.

Despite the bamboo problem, the illegal killing of pandas is the major reason for their decline. Here, a policemen's chalkboard informs Chinese citizens about the capture and sentencing of poachers.

created two other problems for the pandas. One has to do with the nature of the bamboo plant. There are many kinds of bamboo. But a peculiar characteristic of bamboo is that all the plants of each type flower, produce seeds, and then die at the same time. Many years—sometimes a hundred years—will go by before new bamboo sprouts and grows enough for it to be fit to eat. In the past, when the pandas could move on to an area that contained a different kind of bamboo, the temporary death of one kind of bamboo wasn't a problem. Today, however, the pandas have no place to go and face starvation if their area contains only one or two types of bamboo.

The second problem related to the separation of the reserves has to do with the mating and breeding habits of giant pandas. On each reserve there are only 10 to 50 animals. This has resulted in substantial inbreeding, which can weaken the pandas' genes and cause infertility and the death of newborns. And this adds to the problem of the pandas' already low reproductive rate.

To address these two problems, the Chinese government and the World Wildlife Fund have proposed that the existing panda reserves be linked together by planting corridors of bamboo between them. This would not only give the pandas more bamboo but would enable them to roam from reserve to reserve to find suitable mates. China has also announced plans to set aside an additional fourteen reserves, increasing the panda reserves by some 70 percent.

The Chinese government and various zoos around the world are also trying to find ways to improve the breeding of pandas in captivity. Thus far there has been little success, even with artificial insemination. Since 1963, 90 panda cubs have been born in Chinese zoos, but only 37 lived to reach the age of six months. And only three zoos outside of China—in Madrid, Spain; Tokyo, Japan; and Mexico City—have been able to breed pandas successfully.

However, despite all these problems, scientists say that poaching is the major reason for the decline of the giant panda. Panda pelts have sold for as much as $50,000 in Japan, Taiwan, and elsewhere. To try to stop this trade in panda pelts, the Chinese government has instituted life imprisonment and even the death penalty for anyone found poaching.

Are these efforts too few and too late? Let's hope not. Let's hope that China's magnificent giant pandas will not only survive but thrive.

# WHAT'S IN A FACE?

"Beauty is in the eye of the beholder" is an old saying. The faces on these pages may look very strange—or even ugly—to you. But you can bet that each of these animals is handsome to others of its kind.

An orange beak helps make the South American king vulture (*left*) a strikingly colorful bird. Unlike many other birds of prey, these vultures are thought to find their prey more by smell than sight.

"Weird" is the adjective that comes to mind for the axolotl (*above*)—a salamander whose name means "water toy" in the Aztec Indian language. The axolotl lives in water and breathes with the feathery gills that can be seen around its head.

The humpback wrasse (*right*) has a funny face, too. A bulging forehead and clownlike mouth give this colorful fish of the coral reefs a comical look.

The award for the strangest nose should clearly go to the star-nosed mole (*right*). But the 22 fleshy "rays" on the mole's nose aren't there just for decoration. They act as feelers, helping the little animal find food as it burrows beneath the ground.

The male mandrill (*below*) beats even the king vulture in the colorful face category. The mandrill, a kind of baboon, is an endangered species found in the rain forests of Africa. Only the males sport these vivid red and blue facial markings.

This male elephant seal (*left*) is still young. His nose is already big, but it will be even bigger when he's grown. A big nose is a status symbol for a male elephant seal. It helps the seal produce a loud roar. And because it can hold a lot of air, it helps the seal stay underwater for a long time. So, even though this bulging snout may look strange and funny to you, it's a beautiful thing for the elephant seal.

Get a grip gecko! A tokay gecko's bristly footpads and sharp claws allow it to travel almost anywhere.

# LEAPIN' LIZARDS!

What sort of creature can climb a glass window, walk upside-down across a ceiling, and bark like a dog? It sounds like the product of a cartoon creator's nightmare—a cross between Spiderman and Lassie. But this creature actually exists. It's a tokay gecko, a lizard that's found in parts of Asia.

The tokay gecko's feet are equipped with special pads that are covered with tiny bristles. The bristles are so fine that they can hook into the tiny pits and crevices that occur on all surfaces—even surfaces that, like glass, appear perfectly smooth to us. This allows the little lizard to perform some gravity-defying feats that seem impossible.

The tokay gecko is unusual in another way: When it is threatened, it opens its mouth in a menacing way—and barks. Few other lizards make sounds of any kind. The tokay gecko's bark is worse than its bite, however. The gecko will bite to defend itself; but, like most lizards, it would rather run than fight.

Geckos are just one group in the huge family of lizards. In all, there are some 3,000 different kinds of lizards, and they are among the most widespread of all animals. Some other well-known members of the lizard family are chameleons, anoles (often called false chameleons), iguanas, gila monsters, and skinks. (Salamanders aren't lizards; they are amphibians, while lizards are reptiles.)

Lizards vary enormously in size and appearance. The smallest lizards are certain geckos that are a mere three fourths of an inch (2 centimeters) long. The largest are the Komodo monitor lizards, or Komodo dragons, of Indonesia. They can range up to 10 feet (3 meters) long. But few other lizards approach this size—most are less than 2 feet (60 centimeters) long.

Some prehistoric lizards were even larger than the Komodo monitor. Lizards are an ancient group; scientists have found lizard fossils that date back 180 million years. The largest of the ancient lizards were the mosasaurs, which lived in the oceans and grew 20 feet (6 meters) long. But scientists think that most prehistoric lizards weren't too different from those that walk the earth today.

### GETTING AROUND

Lizards are closely related to snakes. Like snakes, most lizards have dry, scaly skin. In fact, there's even a lizard that looks just like a snake—the glass lizard, sometimes called the glass snake. This burrowing lizard has no limbs, and it gets around by wriggling. Certain skinks also have no legs, or their limbs are so small and weak that they are nearly useless.

Most lizards do have legs, however. And their legs and feet vary tremendously. Many desert-dwelling lizards have long legs that are useful for scrambling over rocks and dry ground. One desert dweller, the fringe-toed lizard, has fringes on its toes. The fringes act like snowshoes, allowing the lizard to move quickly across desert sands, or like little flippers, allowing it to dive into a dune and actually swim through the sand.

The racerunner, a striped, streamlined lizard that lives in the southeastern United States, probably holds the lizard land-speed record: 18 miles (29 kilometers) per hour. There are other ground-dwelling lizards that can run along on their hind legs, looking like tiny dinosaurs.

Many lizards can also swim. They move through the water by wriggling their bodies rather than using their limbs. And a few lizards have the amazing ability to walk on water. The basilisk lizard and certain other species that live along tropical rivers have fringed toes that allow them to scoot along the surface of the water on their hind legs.

Some lizards are adapted to life above ground—in trees. Most chameleons, for example, spend most of their lives moving slowly about in tree branches. They rarely

The fringe-toed lizard lives in the desert. The fringes on its toes act like little flippers, allowing it to dive into a dune and swim through the sand.

Most lizards are brownish-green; some are brightly colored. But the web-footed lizard of the Namib Desert in Africa has skin that is so colorless that its bones and blood vessels can be seen.

come down to the ground. These lizards have prehensile tails: tails that can grip branches. And their feet are specially adapted to work like pliers, grabbing tightly onto branches.

A group of Asian lizards called flying dragons are also tree dwellers. Despite their name, these lizards don't actually fly. But, like flying squirrels, they can glide from tree to tree by spreading out folds of skin along their sides.

The champions of lizard locomotion, however, must be the geckos. There are more than 700 kinds of these little lizards, few of them more than six inches (15 centimeters)

long. Besides their bristly footpads, most geckos have sharp claws that are useful for climbing trees. Some have tiny slits in their feet that act like suction cups, giving them an even stronger grip. With equipment like this, a gecko can travel anywhere.

### KEEPING WARM

Like other reptiles, lizards are cold-blooded—that is, they have no internal way of maintaining a constant body temperature. Instead, they rely on their surroundings to supply warmth. As you might expect, then, most lizards are found in areas where the climate is warm all year. Most are also active

Chameleons are the masters of color changing. They can display a range of hues—and even change the patterns on their skin. These lizards change color primarily as a physical reaction to temperature and light conditions and to reflect anger and fright.

during the day, when the sun warms the air. Geckos are among the exceptions—most geckos are nocturnal, sleeping during the day and coming out at night. They live only where nights are warm.

Lizards are adaptable creatures, however, and being cold-blooded hasn't stopped some kinds from making their homes in areas where the temperatures drop below freezing in winter. There are lizards that live in high mountain regions. Some even live as far north as the Arctic circle or as far south as the tip of South America. In cold-winter climates, lizards generally hibernate in deep crevices that are below the reach of frost. Before a lizard goes into hibernation, it puts away a store of fat, much of it in its tail.

Because they are cold-blooded, lizards put a lot of time and effort into regulating their body temperature, no matter where they live. A cold lizard moves slowly. This makes the lizard an easy mark for predators and also makes it more difficult for the lizard to get food. Thus, when the air is cold or when a lizard first wakes up in the morning, it will bask in the sun, perhaps on a warm rock.

Once the lizard has warmed up, however, it will move to a shady spot. If the lizard were to stay in the sun, its body temperature would continue to rise—and the lizard might die. A lizard may spend all day moving back and forth between sun and shade to keep its body temperature just right.

Some lizards have found other ways to regulate their temperature. Certain desert lizards, for example, burrow in the sand to escape the extremes of desert heat and cold. Some lizards can produce a bit of body heat by tightening their muscles and trembling all over. And some change color as the air temperature changes—growing darker to absorb more of the sun's heat in cold air, and growing lighter to reflect the sun when it's hot. But temperature regulation isn't the only reason why lizards change color.

### QUICK-CHANGE ARTISTS

Some lizards have bright, vivid colors and markings. On the other hand, one lizard, the web-footed gecko of the Namib Desert in Africa, has skin so colorless that its bones, blood vessels, and internal organs can be seen. But most lizards are mottled shades of brown and green—colors that help them blend in with their surroundings. And a number can grow lighter or darker to blend in even better. This camouflage helps the lizards escape the notice of predators—and thus survive.

There are lizards that can do more than grow light or dark, too. Some can actually change color. For example, American anoles, which are sometimes called false chameleons, can change from green to brown. But they can't match the abilities of the true chameleons of Africa. These lizards are the masters of color changing—they can display a range of hues and even change the patterns on their skin.

Chameleons can change color in about 90 seconds. And they do this primarily as a physical reaction to their environment (temperature and light conditions) or even to reflect moods (such as anger and fright). For example, during courtship, chameleons display a wide range of colors, from yellow and

The green iguana spends most of its time in trees near water in the tropical rain forests of South America. When threatened, it will dive into the water and hide.

The South African armadillo lizard is covered with hard, spiky scales. This form of protection makes it an unappealing meal for many of its enemies.

green to red and brown. Male chameleons may threaten each other with color, turning bright green or sporting yellow stripes. As a rule, the chameleon that displays the brightest colors will be the winner if the chameleons fight.

Chameleons don't just decide to change color; the change comes about automatically. A chameleon's skin has layers of cells that contain granules of various pigments, or colors. In response to some sensation, such as fear, the granules may bunch up or spread apart. This causes changes in pattern as well as color.

## ARTFUL DODGERS

Besides changing color, lizards have other ways of avoiding predators. When a lizard is threatened, it will often freeze, holding perfectly still until the danger has passed. This helps it avoid being seen. If freezing doesn't work, most ground-dwelling lizards will quickly dart to safety. Green iguanas, which live mostly in the tropical rain forests of South America, spend most of their time in trees near water. When the iguana is threatened, it will dive into the water and hide. Chuckwallas, which live in the deserts of the southwestern United States, make for the nearest rock crevice. Once inside, the chuckwalla puffs up its body so that it is wedged tightly in the crevice.

When threatened, the Australian frilled lizard hisses and unfolds a large collarlike frill around its neck.

Many lizards have another way of escaping predators. If a bird or some other predator catches the lizard by the tail, the tail simply breaks off. It lies wriggling on the ground while the lizard scampers safely away. (The glass snake's tail will break into several pieces, all of which wriggle.) The tail breaks at a special fracture line, and the lizard's blood vessels contract quickly so that little blood is lost. The lizard doesn't seem to miss its tail, and in time it grows a new one.

Horned lizards have another unusual defense. When a horned lizard is threatened, it can shoot a thin stream of blood from its eyes. The stream can travel as far as 3 feet (1 meter). It is thought that the blood confuses predators, although it may not be much help against large ones. But the horned lizard also has sharp spines along its head and neck, which make it a less appealing meal. In fact, snakes have been known to die while trying to swallow a spiny horned lizard.

The South African armadillo lizard is covered with hard, spiky scales that protect it in the same way. In addition, this lizard grabs its tail in its mouth when it is cornered. Most birds and snakes swallow their prey whole, head first—so this makes the armadillo lizard truly hard to swallow. The Australian moloch, or thorny devil, takes a similar tack. This strange-looking creature tucks its head between its forelegs, presenting predators with the thornlike spines on its back.

Other lizards rear or swell up or make some other threatening display when they are attacked. The Australian frilled lizard, for example, unfolds a large collarlike frill around its neck, opens its mouth, and hisses. The lizard looks frightening. But such displays are usually bluffs—most lizards aren't fighters.

A few lizards actually are dangerous. Large monitor lizards can deliver serious bites with their strong jaws and powerful blows with their long tails. But only two lizards are poisonous: the Gila monster and the beaded lizard. The Gila monster lives in the deserts of the southwestern United States and Mexico, and the beaded lizard lives in Mexico.

### HUNTERS

Insects are the ideal meal for most lizards. And lizards are very efficient insect catch-

Most lizards aren't dangerous. The Gila monster, however, is one of the few lizards that are poisonous.

ers, snapping up bugs and swallowing them whole. Molochs can gobble ants at a rate of 20 or 30 a minute, and one of these lizards was seen to eat 1,800 ants in one meal. Some city dwellers keep geckos in their apartments, to keep cockroaches and other insect pests in check.

Chameleons catch insects with their tongues. When the lizard spots a tasty-looking bug, its tongue—which can be 5.5 inches (14 centimeters) long—shoots out, unfolding like an accordion. The insect is caught on the tongue's sticky, forked tip and whipped back into the chameleon's mouth. Although chameleons move about very slowly, their tongues are incredibly fast. The complete operation takes less than half a second.

When a chameleon spots a tasty-looking bug, it shoots out its long, sticky tongue and whips the insect into its mouth. The whole operation takes less than half a second.

Insects aren't the only food of lizards. Some lizards eat small animals such as snails, crabs—or smaller lizards. Some eat eggs or newly hatched birds. Komodo dragons can eat small wild pigs, goats, and even deer. But most large lizards are plant eaters. For example, iguanas eat leaves, fruit, and even flowers. The marine iguana of the Galápagos Islands goes into the ocean at low tide to eat seaweed.

Many lizards can't lap up water directly. Some get the water they need from dew or rainwater that collects on the surfaces of leaves. The moloch drinks through its skin. When this lizard finds a puddle, it jumps in and begins to absorb water. A network of canals between its scales carries the water to the moloch's mouth, and the lizard swallows it.

### SHARP SENSES

Chameleons rely on their excellent vision to catch their prey. They are able to swivel their huge, bulging eyes in any direction—together or separately. When a chameleon takes aim at an insect, it turns both its eyes forward. This gives it binocular vision, which helps it judge the distance to its prey. At other times, the chameleon may look up or forward with one eye and down or back with the other, seeing two separate views at the same time. How the lizard's brain makes sense of this information is unknown.

Geckos that hunt at night have large eyes, designed to let in as much light as possible. The gecko's eyes are unusual because they have no retractable eyelids. Instead, they are protected by a hard, clear covering, somewhat like a windshield. The gecko keeps this covering clean by licking it with its tongue.

A gecko that hunts at night has large eyes that let in a lot of light, and they are protected by a hard, clear covering. The gecko cleans this covering by licking it with its tongue—just like a windshield wiper.

In contrast to the excellent vision of the chameleon and the gecko, the blind skink of South Africa can't see at all—as its name suggests. This lizard spends its entire life underground in darkness, where it has no need of vision.

Besides two eyes, most lizards have an organ that is sometimes called a third eye. This is a tiny spot in the lizard's forehead that is equipped with a lens and nerves similar to those of the animal's eyes. It is thought that the third eye acts as a kind of light meter, monitoring the level of light and perhaps even helping the lizard regulate its temperature.

Most lizards have good senses of taste and smell. And like snakes, many lizards use their tongues to find out about the world around them. A lizard will flick its tongue in and out of its mouth, picking up odors (actually chemicals) from the air or from objects that the tongue touches. The tongue carries the odors to the lizard's vomeronasal organs, two small pits on the roof of its mouth.

Lizards also have keen hearing, but few make any sounds. They communicate with each other through body language and, in some cases, color displays. The exceptions, once again, are the geckos. Different kinds of geckos may chirp, click, or, like the tokay gecko, bark. One type makes a loud call that sounds like "geck-o," giving rise to the name of these lizards.

## REPRODUCTION

Like snakes, most lizards hatch from eggs. After mating, females generally bury their eggs in the ground or in rotting logs. Child-raising ends right there for most female lizards—the mother leaves, and the baby lizards are on their own when they hatch. Certain female skinks, however, stay with their eggs to protect them. If the eggs are scattered, the mother skink will gather them up and put them back in the nest.

Some lizards, especially those that live in cold climates, keep their eggs inside their bodies and give birth to live young. Unlike mammals, however, lizards don't nurse their young or care for them after they are born.

Two kinds of lizards, the whiptails of the southwestern United States and Mexico and the lacertid lizards of Europe, have a very unusual method of reproduction. There are no males in these species—only females. The females lay eggs that hatch without being fertilized. All the offspring are female, and all are exactly like their mothers.

## LIZARDS IN DANGER

The predators that most lizards must watch out for are snakes, birds, larger lizards, and, in the desert, coyotes. But some lizards are also hunted by people. The chuckwalla was long an important food source for American Indians. The meat of the iguana is so prized in South America that the animal is known as the "chicken of the trees." Its skin is also valued, for leather goods.

Some lizards have been hunted so much that their numbers are now greatly reduced. By some estimates, as much as 95 percent of the iguana population has been killed by hunters. In addition, the natural homes of many lizards are destroyed as wild areas are taken over by people. Thus today there are efforts to protect some of these fascinating and varied creatures.

# THE BEAUTY OF BUTTERFLIES

Imagine a field of wildflowers, waving gently in a summer breeze. Suddenly, one of the flowers takes wing, soaring into the air. Of course, it's not a flower—it's a butterfly, one of summer's prettiest and most welcome sights.

Butterflies are found in every part of the world except the cold poles. There are about 20,000 different kinds, 700 in North America alone. They range in size from the giant birdwing of the New Guinea forests, which may have a wingspan of 10 inches (25 centimeters), to tiny blue butterflies of Afghanistan that measure just 1/4 inch (6.3 millimeters) across. And their beautiful wings display an astonishing variety of colors and patterns.

### FLYING FLOWERS

The colors and patterns on a butterfly's wings are created by rows and rows of tiny overlapping scales. (It's these scales that give butterflies and their close cousins, moths, their scientific name: Lepidoptera, Greek for "scaly winged.") Each type of butterfly carries a pattern of scales in colors unique to its species. And these patterns often serve a purpose.

Many butterflies display bright or iridescent colors and bold patterns. This helps them identify others of their kind and find mates. Some are drably mottled to blend in with their surroundings. This helps them hide from predators. And some have both features—their wings are dull on the undersides, so that the butterfly is hard to spot when it is resting with its wings upright. But when the butterfly takes flight, it flashes the boldly patterned upper sides of its wings.

Some butterflies have wings that also serve as clever disguises. The beautiful orange viceroy butterfly has wings that mimic the pattern and color of the monarch butterfly. Monarchs are usually shunned by hungry birds because they taste terrible. Since birds can't tell a viceroy from a monarch, they usually pass up the viceroy as well. Buckeye butterflies have wingspots that they flash when a bird or other predator comes too close. The spots, which look like big, staring eyes, startle the bird long enough for the butterfly to make a getaway.

Besides giving butterflies their unique colors and patterns, the scales on a butterfly's wings serve another purpose. If you've ever touched a butterfly's wing, you may know that the scales come off quite easily—you may have noticed them as dust or fine powder on your fingers. At first, this may not seem like an advantage. But it allows butterflies to escape easily from spider webs. The scales may stick to the web, but the butterfly can just fly away. Some scientists think that butterflies may have originally had feathers, and that scales evolved as a feature that helped them survive.

### NECTAR DRINKERS

The colors and patterns of butterfly wings are remarkable, but butterflies are surprising in other ways, too. Most butterflies feed on the sugary nectar of flowers, and they are especially adapted to do so. Many types of butterflies prefer to feed on just a few favorite kinds of flowers. How do they find their favorites? Partly by scent—butterflies smell with their antennae, and they can distinguish the scent of one flower from another.

Butterflies also find their flowers by sight. Their eyes are very sensitive to ultraviolet light, which means that they see the world quite differently than we do. To a butterfly, flowers stand out because they glow with reflected ultraviolet light.

When a butterfly lands on a flower, it knows instantly whether it's about to get a good tasting meal. That's because butterflies taste with their feet—through taste receptors located on the front legs. The receptors are especially sensitive to sugar. When a butterfly has found a good-tasting flower, it unrolls its coiled, tubelike proboscis, or tongue, and sucks up the nectar. In many butterflies, the proboscis and other mouth parts are specially adapted to feeding on certain types of flowers.

Compared to some other animals, butterflies may not rank high in brainpower. But scientists who have studied these insects say that butterflies seem able to develop mental "maps," using landmarks to find their way home to favorite roosting spots at night. And when a butterfly can't find one of its favorite flowers, it's able to learn to drink nectar from other kinds.

### LIFE CYCLE

An adult butterfly's life is short—many live just a few weeks, although some types live as long as eighteen months. The butterfly's most important job during this brief span is to reproduce, completing a life cycle that will produce more butterflies of its kind.

After mating, female butterflies lay their eggs—anywhere from 50 to 1,000 of them—on or near plants that will serve as food for the larvae, or young, when they hatch. Different kinds of butterflies choose different plants. Monarchs, for example, always lay their eggs on milkweed.

The eggs may stay dormant for many months until they hatch. Then caterpillars

---

## BUTTERFLY OR MOTH?

Butterflies and moths are closely related and have many features in common. In fact, it's often hard to tell a butterfly from a moth. Here are some guidelines.

• Butterflies are often more brightly colored than moths.

• A butterfly's body is slender, while most moths are stout.

• Butterflies are usually active during the day, while moths are active at night.

• The antennae of most butterflies are narrow, with clublike enlargements at the tips. A moth's antennae have no enlargements, and they may have feathery plumes.

• At rest, butterflies usually hold their wings erect, while most moths fold their wings flat.

These guidelines aren't foolproof. There are drab butterflies and brightly colored moths, for example. Some moths are active during the day, and some have clublike enlargements on their antennae. But in most cases, checking these features will tell you whether you're looking at a butterfly or a moth.

Some butterflies accomplish amazing feats for their small size. There are dozens of kinds of butterflies that migrate south when summer ends, traveling hundreds or even thousands of miles. Admiral butterflies head for Florida. In Europe, butterflies called

Many butterflies have bright or iridescent colors (*top* and *bottom*). The Buckeye butterfly (*above*) has wingspots that look like big, staring eyes. These colors and patterns on a butterfly's wings are created by rows and rows of overlapping scales. But some butterflies have so few scales that their wings are transparent (*left*).

emerge and go to work eating the food plant—and growing. As the caterpillar grows, it repeatedly sheds its skin and grows a new one. Caterpillars continue to eat and grow for anywhere from a few days to several months—and sometimes even longer. Some butterflies that live in the far north spend up to fourteen years as caterpillars, hibernating through the cold winters.

Finally, the caterpillar finds a place for pupation, the next step in its development. For this stage, the caterpillar spins a tiny silken pad on a leaf or twig. It sheds its skin and emerges as a pupa, and hangs upside down from the pad. Then a thin, hard shell forms around the pupa. During pupation, which lasts from days to months, the pupa (now called a chrysalis) is transformed into an adult butterfly. When the change is complete, the new butterfly cracks open the shell, wriggles out, and spreads its wings. The wings are limp at first, but as soon as they are dry and stiff the butterfly is ready to take to the air.

painted ladies cross the Mediterranean Sea. But the most famous migrating butterflies are the monarchs, which travel a distance of 2,000 miles (3,220 kilometers) from the eastern United States to Mexico. There they gather in groups of as many as 200 million.

How the butterflies manage to travel so far with their fragile wings was long a mystery. But scientists who have studied these butterflies now say that the insects take advantage of air currents, so that they actually float south, rather than fly, for much of the journey. Air currents may carry them high into the atmosphere—butterflies have been spotted by glider pilots at altitudes up to 7,000 feet (2,135 meters). Butterflies will even hitch rides on storm winds, if the winds will take them closer to their destination.

For monarchs, the return journey is made over several generations. In spring, the females lay their eggs. When the new butterflies emerge, they fly a distance north, mate, and repeat the cycle. The next generation travels farther north. This continues until late summer, by which time the butterflies have reached Canada. Then it's time to head south again.

## AN IMPORTANT ROLE

Butterflies have many natural enemies, including birds and some kinds of wasps that feed on caterpillars. And while butterflies are a welcome summer sight to most people, their caterpillars aren't. By gobbling up plants, caterpillars do a great deal of damage to crops and gardens. Thus farmers and gardeners often kill them with pesticides. By some estimates, only two out of every 100 butterfly eggs produce adult butterflies.

Butterflies lay so many eggs that, normally, such losses are no cause for alarm. But today there is concern that butterflies, especially the rarer kinds, are in danger. As people take over more land for agriculture and development, some of the plants that butterflies depend on—as sources of food and as places to lay eggs—are disappearing. This makes it difficult for the butterflies to survive.

Butterflies play an important role in nature. They serve as food for many creatures, and they help plants reproduce by carrying pollen from flower to flower as bees do. They are more than just a pretty sight—they are part of the web of life on Earth.

## BUTTERFLIES IN YOUR GARDEN

If you'd like to see butterflies, you can tramp through fields and meadows in search of them. But why not plant a garden that will bring them to you?

A small, sunny patch of earth—even a windowbox —is all you need. You can grow flowers in your butterfly garden from seed, or you can get plants from a nursery. Some common garden flowers that butterflies enjoy are clover, coreopsis, daisies, joe-pye weed, phlox, verbena, and zinnias.

Plant a mixture of flowers, so that your garden will attract a variety of butterflies. Then sit back and see who comes to dinner.

# ANIMALS IN THE NEWS

A new chapter in the story of the **California condor** began in 1991. These birds, vultures with wing spans up to 10 feet (3 meters), are nearly extinct. In 1987 the last wild birds were captured and taken to the San Diego Wild Animal Park and the Los Angeles Zoo to be bred in captivity. The breeding program was successful, and by 1991 there were 52 birds. In October, the first steps were taken to release two of the captive-born chicks into the wild. It's hoped that by January, 1992, the giant condor will once again soar over North America.

In 1991, the U.S. Fish and Wildlife Service proposed that five kinds of **Pacific salmon** be listed as endangered species. These fish are born in rivers and travel downstream to live in the sea; they return to the rivers to spawn. But many rivers, such as the Columbia River in the Pacific Northwest, have been dammed to provide hydroelectric power. The young fish can't cross the dams, so they can't complete their life cycle. In order to save the salmon, a costly plan is being considered— to create currents strong enough to push the fish along their way to the sea.

The **San Diego Zoo,** one of the leading zoos in the United States, celebrated its 75th anniversary in 1991. There were special events throughout the year, from the opening of a new gorilla habitat exhibit to a "save the rhino" walk that raised money for the zoo's wildlife conservation programs. An important part of the festivities was the zoo's fourth annual wildlife art contest. Students in four age groups, ranging from kindergarten through twelfth grade, were invited to enter artwork on the theme "Celebrate the Colors of the Wild." The picture above was painted by Jake Card, and it was the third-place winner in the category for grades four through six.

"Dive into a Texas-size undersea adventure" is the motto of one of the newest aquariums in the United States—the **Texas State Aquarium** in Corpus Christi, Texas, which opened in 1990. The aquarium is designed to give visitors the feeling that they are traveling deeper and deeper into the waters of the Gulf of Mexico. Exhibits focus on coastal marshes, tidal pools, barrier islands, animals of the waters near the shore, coral reefs, and deep-sea exploration. One exhibit shows how oil and gas platforms—common off the Texas coast—provide a habitat for such creatures as redfish, groupers, barracudas, and sharks. There are displays that focus on the plight of endangered species such as the sea turtles of the Gulf Coast, and others that demonstrate how tides and waves act on the shore and how the Gulf shoreline has changed over the years. Altogether there are more than 250 species of sea life— and 350,000 gallons of seawater—at this Texas-size aquarium.

**Champion Whisperwind on a Carousel,** a standard poodle known as Peter to his friends, was named best-in-show at the 1991 Westminster Kennel Club dog show in New York City in February. Peter was chosen over 2,500 other dogs to win the title, which effectively made him top dog in the United States. But success didn't come easily—Peter had spent six hours on the grooming table while his fabulous fur was fluffed and trimmed for the final competition.

The **dodo,** a flightless bird that has been extinct for about 300 years, is usually pictured as a fat, clumsy creature. But now scientists have developed a new picture of the bird. The model at left, which went on display at the Royal Museum of Scotland in Edinburgh in 1991, was based on bones and other remains of wild dodos that once lived on the island of Mauritius, in the Indian Ocean. It shows a bird that's smaller and sleeker than earlier versions. Those versions had been based on pictures of captive dodos that were kept as pets—and were probably pampered and overweight.

# THE FRAGILE CORAL REEFS

Strange formations tower above the ocean floor, pierced by narrow, sandy canyons and deep, dark grottoes. The delicate fronds of sea anemones and sea fans wave slowly in the water. Thousands of creatures—vivid tropical fish, eels, crabs, shrimp—swim and scuttle through the eerie underwater twilight, turning the scene into a shimmering world of color.

Welcome to a coral reef, one of the richest and most fascinating habitats on Earth. Coral reefs are found in warm waters throughout the world. Each is a complete community of living things that depend on each other to survive. And the life of a reef is incredibly varied—a single reef can support as many as 3,000 different kinds of ocean plants and animals. Altogether, the world's coral reefs are home to about a million different species—including 2,000 kinds of fish.

But coral reefs are delicate, and today they are in danger. All around the world, the reefs are dying—and with them, the rich communities of life that they support.

## AN UNDERWATER WONDERLAND

The huge and exotic formations that make up coral reefs are built up over hundreds and thousands of years by tiny sea animals called coral polyps. While corals are found in all the oceans of the world, reef-building corals live only in the warm, clear waters of the tropics. They can't live in waters that are colder than 65°F (18°C).

Corals belong to the same family as sea anemones and jellyfish. A coral polyp may be no bigger than the eraser on a pencil. Its body is tubular, and it has a mouth surrounded by tiny tentacles. The coral's skeleton, formed of limestone, grows outside its body. It forms a cup that protects the coral, just as shells protect crabs and many other ocean creatures. During the day, the coral's tentacles rest in the cup. At night, they reach out to search for small prey and push food into the coral's mouth.

Most corals live together in colonies. When the polyp dies, its limestone skeleton remains. And as more and more coral skeletons pile up, they may form the base of a

coral reef. The reef will continue to grow very slowly, only a few inches a year at most. But over centuries, a reef can grow to tremendous size. Still, the only living part of the reef is the top layer of coral polyps.

A reef may be made up of many thousands of coral colonies, created by billions of coral polyps. Each kind of coral takes a form that is different in size and shape. Some shapes resemble tree branches, flowers, or mushrooms. Many corals have been named for the fascinating shapes and patterns they form—brain coral, star coral, hat coral, staghorn coral. Besides hard corals, there are soft corals, such as sea fans. They are closely re-

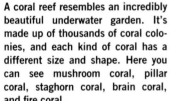

A coral reef resembles an incredibly beautiful underwater garden. It's made up of thousands of coral colonies, and each kind of coral has a different size and shape. Here you can see mushroom coral, pillar coral, staghorn coral, brain coral, and fire coral.

Looking like blossoms in a garden, the corals' tentacles reach out of their limestone shells to capture tiny animals that float by. Most corals feed at night.

lated to the hard corals, but their skeletons are flexible, so that the formations wave in the ocean currents.

The colors of the living coral polyps give color to the reef—red, green, orange, blue, yellow. In most cases these colors come not from the polyps themselves but from microscopic plants, called zooxanthellae. These one-celled plants actually live in the tissues of the coral polyps. They help provide the polyps with nutrients.

The fascinating structures formed by corals are only the beginning of the reef community. A coral reef creates a special kind of underwater world. Ocean waves carry tiny plants toward the reef. The plants take root and thrive there, forming a cover of vegetation. This plant life, along with the coral polyps themselves, provides food for fish and other creatures. These animals in turn attract predators. And the complex formations of the reef provide shelter for a wide range of living things.

The reef becomes a bustling community where plants and animals depend on one another. It resembles an incredibly beautiful underwater garden, filled with oddly shaped formations and blooming with the colors of the living corals and the strange creatures that dwell there.

## REEFS IN DANGER

Today, however, these fascinating underwater gardens are in trouble all over the world. Large areas of coral reefs are dying. There are several reasons for this, and scientists aren't sure of all the forces that are harming the reefs. But it's clear that in many cases people are responsible for the damage.

**Coral Bleaching.** One of the most mysterious problems is coral bleaching. In the Caribbean and in other regions, vast areas of coral reefs have lost their brilliant colors and turned a sickly white. The reason is that the polyps have suddenly expelled the tiny one-celled plants that live inside them. Without the plants, the polyps are transparent—you can see right through to the white limestone skeletons.

The coral polyps don't die right away without their plant partners. They can still use their tentacles to catch tiny bits of food from the water around them. But they obtain fewer nutrients, and so they have less energy. When a coral reef bleaches, it stops growing.

Scientists think that bleaching occurs when the coral polyps are stressed in some way. In the past, short episodes of bleaching, affecting small areas, have often been noted. Many of these episodes were related to increases in water temperature. Once the water temperature returned to normal, the partnership between the plants and the polyps resumed, and the reefs recovered.

But since the mid-1980's, coral bleaching has been widespread. Episodes of bleaching have been more frequent and have lasted longer. In the Caribbean, they have been so severe that large areas of coral reef haven't been able to recover. Instead, the polyps have died. When a coral reef dies, the living community that it supports dies with it.

Some scientists think that widespread coral bleaching is related to global warming, or the greenhouse effect. This is a worldwide warming trend caused by the buildup of carbon dioxide and other gases in the Earth's atmosphere. These gases, which are produced when fossil fuels like oil and coal are burned, act like the glass in a greenhouse. They allow sunlight to enter the atmosphere, warming the Earth's surface. But they prevent heat from escaping back into space.

As yet there is no firm evidence that the greenhouse effect is behind the increase in coral bleaching. Thus scientists are continuing to look for other causes. But bleaching is only one of the threats that coral reefs face.

**Pollution.** Some coral reefs are literally being smothered by growths of underwater plants, mainly various kinds of algae. This is happening to the only true coral reef in North America, off the Florida Keys. Algae now grows like grass all over this reef, killing the coral polyps and preventing new coral colonies from starting.

Some scientists think that pollution is behind the growth of these plants. Sewage is released into the ocean, and runoff from farmland carries fertilizers into the sea. This provides nutrients to feed a spurt of plant growth. But again, not all scientists are convinced—some think that the plant growth may be related to long-term climate changes or other factors.

Other forms of pollution are clearly threatening coral reefs, however. Runoff from farmland can carry pesticides as well as fertilizers. These chemicals, sprayed on crops to kill insect pests, are deadly to many ocean creatures as well. And they aren't the only danger. Industrial wastes can be carried into the ocean, too. Some harmful chemicals travel hundreds or thousands of miles to the reefs, carried first by rivers and then by ocean currents. Residue from paper-making plants in the midwestern United States has been found in the coral reefs off the Florida Keys, for example.

Microscopic plants called zooxanthellae live in the tissues of the coral polyps (right) and give the polyps their colors; without the plants, the polyps are transparent. In recent years, the polyps have been expelling these tiny plants, and vast areas of coral reefs are losing their brilliant colors and are turning a sickly white (below)—called coral bleaching.

Development of land along the coast poses another kind of threat. When towns and resort hotels are built along the coast, or when land is cleared for farming, trees and other soil-holding plants are stripped away. Then erosion begins—rain washes the soil into the ocean. In many areas, coral reefs are being smothered in a buildup of silt that has been carried into the ocean from the shore. Silt can also smother reefs when harbors are dredged, to make them deep enough for big ocean ships.

Oil spills—from tankers, offshore drilling rigs, and other facilities—are another threat to the reef communities. How much damage is done depends on the size of the spill. In 1991, during the Persian Gulf War, massive amounts of oil were released into the Persian Gulf, the site of some of the world's most beautiful reefs. Scientists expected the damage to be extensive, and they weren't sure that the reefs would be able to recover.

**Upsetting the Balance.** Most of the time, the reef community stays in a state of natural balance. Natural forces, such as predators and disease, keep any one species from overwhelming the others. This ensures that the incredible variety of plants and animals on the reef is maintained. But sometimes, something happens to tip the balance. Then the reef community can be harmed or even killed.

In recent years, scientists have been concerned about plagues of natural predators in some reefs. Off the eastern coast of Africa, swarms of sea urchins have devastated some reefs. Sea urchins are normally an important part of the reef community. But something has made their numbers grow out of control.

In much the same way, vast sections of coral have been killed by crown-of-thorns starfish in the Great Barrier Reef, off the coast of Australia. The starfish are natural predators of the coral, but as with the sea urchins something has caused their numbers to increase. One theory is that people have caused the outbreak by collecting too many giant tritons. These shellfish are one of the few natural predators of the starfish. But other scientists don't agree. And no one is sure if these reefs will recover.

People have also upset the balance of the coral reefs directly. Reefs have always provided rich fishing grounds for people. But the demand for fish and shellfish has increased as the world's population has grown. In addition, tropical fish are wanted for aquariums, and shellfish for souvenirs and collections. Some of the reefs' most marvelous animals, such as the fantastic giant clams of the Pacific, have been harvested to the point where they are in danger of dying out.

New fishing technology is part of the problem. Large numbers of fish are caught in traps. In some areas, fish are driven out of the reefs and stunned, so that they can be caught easily, by setting off charges of dynamite in the water—destroying a section of reef at the same time. Tropical fish for aquariums are often caught with sodium cyanide, a poison. A diver squirts poison into a coral formation, and stunned fish come spinning out of their hiding places. For every living

## THE WORLD'S CORAL REEFS

Altogether, there are more than 230,000 square miles (595,700 square kilometers) of coral reefs in the oceans of the world. Nearly all are found in tropical waters, within 30 degrees north and south of the Equator. The reefs are generally divided into three kinds—fringing reefs, barrier reefs, and atolls.

• A fringing reef forms in shallow water very near the shore, and it hugs the shoreline closely. The coral reefs of the Persian Gulf are of this type. Other major fringing reefs are found off the coasts of Central America, Sri Lanka, eastern Africa, and northwestern Australia.

• A barrier reef forms farther offshore. It protects the mainland from the ocean, and a quiet lagoon separates it from the shore. The most famous barrier reef is the Great Barrier Reef, off the northeastern coast of Australia. It stretches for about 1,250 miles (2,000 kilometers). Most of the reefs of the Caribbean are also barrier reefs.

• An atoll is a ring of coral reefs around an open lagoon. These reefs actually begin to form around an island, which then sinks or is submerged by rising sea levels. Only the reefs, and the quiet lagoon, remain. There are hundreds of atolls scattered across the open waters of the Pacific and Indian oceans.

fish that is collected in this way, as many as nine die—and so do the coral polyps in that section of reef.

Even tourists who come to visit the reefs and look at their beauty can harm the reef community. Boats churn up the water, divers kick up silt from the sea floor, and people drop litter and generally disturb the plants and animals of the reef.

People also damage the structure of the coral itself. Ship anchors scrape the coral and break it away. When a big ship runs aground on a reef, acres of coral can be destroyed. In some areas, coral reefs are being mined for limestone. And chunks of coral are harvested and sold as souvenirs or used to make jewelry and other items. A stalk of elkhorn coral, snapped off as a souvenir, may take 50 years to grow back. In the South China sea, coral harvesting has wiped out all but 20 of the more than 100 coral species that once flourished there.

When reefs are destroyed, the life they contain is lost. But there are other dangers, too. Many reefs protect islands or coastal land from the ocean. When they disappear, the land is exposed to the full force of ocean winds and currents. Thus the shore itself begins to erode.

### SAVING THE REEFS

Can anything be done to stop the destruction of the reefs? As grim as the situation seems, many scientists believe that it isn't hopeless. That's because a coral reef is a living thing. Given time and the right conditions, a reef—even one that has nearly died —can recover.

But if the reefs are to recover, scientists say, people must take action. Pollution must be stopped, so that reefs have the clean, clear water that they need. People who fish the reefs must learn that if they destroy the coral, they will destroy their own livelihood. And scientists need to find the causes of some of the mysterious events, such as coral bleaching and plagues of predators, that are harming the reefs.

This is a tall order. But already, progress is being made. Many reefs, including those off the Florida Keys and most of the Great Barrier Reef, are now protected by law. Fishing, pleasure boating, and freighter traffic

Crown-of-thorns starfish are natural predators of corals, but they contribute to the natural balance of the reef community. However, in Australia's Great Barrier Reef, something has made their numbers grow out of control, and they are devastating the corals.

are restricted in these areas. In the Philippines and in other areas where many reefs have been practically destroyed by overfishing, local communities are learning to fish without harming the reef community. People who fish with dynamite or cyanide can now be arrested.

The problems that face the coral reefs are complicated—they involve natural forces as well as the actions of people. Just as there is no single cause, there is no single solution. But as people become more aware of these problems and begin to act, there is hope that the fantastic underwater world of the coral reef can be saved.

# SCIENCE

A scientist examines a telescope mirror at a research station in Antarctica. Today this ice-covered continent, the last great wilderness, is endangered by pollution and other problems.

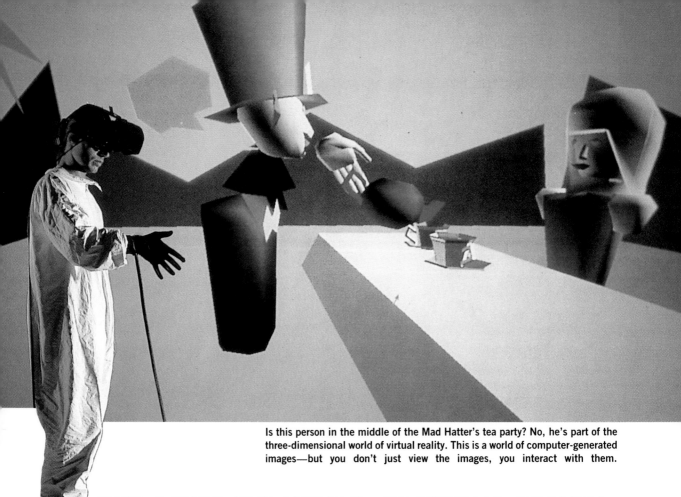

Is this person in the middle of the Mad Hatter's tea party? No, he's part of the three-dimensional world of virtual reality. This is a world of computer-generated images—but you don't just view the images, you interact with them.

# STEP INSIDE THE WORLD OF VIRTUAL REALITY

With a whack, you send the tennis ball speeding across the net. Your opponent returns it, and you race to meet her shot. Just in time, you connect with the ball and send it neatly back into the opposite corner of the court, scoring the final, winning point.

There's something odd about this tennis game, though: You're holding a racket, but you aren't really hitting a ball—you're just swinging at an image of a ball. And you aren't really on a tennis court. You're in a room by yourself, and your opponent is 300 miles (485 kilometers) away.

Welcome to the world of virtual reality, a brave new world of computer-generated images. Virtual reality begins with computer graphics—pictures created by computer. But what sets it apart from standard computer graphics is the fact that you don't just view the images. You actually become part of this computer world, interacting with it.

Virtual reality is still in its beginning stages. The field is also known as artificial reality (a name that seems to contradict itself) and cyberspace (a name taken from a popular science-fiction novel). And it's one of the hottest areas in computer research today. Researchers think that as virtual reality techniques are perfected, they will find dozens of uses—in scientific research, in medicine, in business and industry, and in personal recreation and entertainment.

## HOW IT WORKS

Virtual reality systems begin with a powerful computer that can generate complex computer graphics. In most systems, the viewer wears special headgear—goggles or a helmet. The computer-generated images are projected through this headgear, shutting out the real world so that you see only the "virtual" world. One system, for example, uses goggles that contain two tiny video display screens, one for each eye. The computer produces slightly different images for the right eye and the left eye. The two images create a three-dimensional, or stereoscopic, effect. Thus you don't just view the computer-generated scene; you actually seem to be *in* it.

You are able to interact with the scene through electronic sensors that report your movements to the computer. Sensors in the goggles or helmet track head movements; as you move your head, the computerized scene changes. In addition to the special headgear, many systems use a piece of equipment called a data glove—a glove that's packed with sensors and connected to the computer. As the glove reports your hand movements, the computer changes the images you see to reflect the actions you take.

Let's enter a "virtual" scene and see how it works. Put on the goggles, and you're suddenly in a strange room. Ahead of you are a desk and a chair. With the glove on your hand, you bend your index and middle fingers to "walk" over to the desk. There's a book on the desk. You reach out toward it, make a fist, and pick it up. When you open your fist, the book floats down to the floor. Now you point straight up—and begin to fly. Below you, the "virtual" room becomes smaller and smaller as it drops away and you soar into the air. Of course, you've never actually taken a step, much less left the ground.

Instead of a glove to report hand movements, some virtual reality systems use controls that are like the joysticks used in computer games. There's also a sensor-packed suit that can report *all* your body movements to the computer, allowing you to enter into the scene completely. Other variations include treadmills that allow you to "walk" through a computer-generated scene, and tennis rackets that are wired with sensors. Advanced systems let two people interact in the same scene at once—for a game of virtual tennis, for example.

As exciting as it sounds, however, virtual reality is still a long way from mimicking the real world accurately. The images produced by the computers are simplified and lack detail. There's often an unnatural pause between an action you take and the change in the scene that should follow. When you reach out to touch a "virtual" object, your hand will pass right through it, and you won't feel a thing.

Researchers expect to solve these problems with better graphics and more powerful computers. They are also developing systems that would add realistic sound and the senses of touch and smell to virtual worlds, making them seem truly real. But even without these improvements, people are beginning to find practical uses for virtual reality.

## VIRTUAL WORLDS

Although virtual reality isn't widely used yet, systems are being developed for many different fields. And researchers have even more ideas for the future.

The National Aeronautics and Space Administration (NASA) is developing a virtual reality system that allows scientists to "visit" distant planets without leaving Earth. The system begins with information that has been gathered by unmanned probes, such as the Viking orbiters that surveyed Mars. This information is translated into computer images of the planet's surface. With a set of 3-D goggles and a joystick-like device, scientists can then "fly" over Martian mountains, zoom into valleys for a close-up look, and even come in for a direct landing.

The system is called the Virtual Interface Environment Workstation (VIEW), and it gives scientists a way to visualize the detailed information that's obtained in unmanned space research. Such systems may be used on future manned missions, too. For example, astronauts in a safe base on Mars could use a virtual reality system to direct a remote-controlled rover hundreds of miles away. The rover would explore the planet's surface, feeding video images into the virtual reality system. When the images showed something especially interesting, the astronauts would stop the rover for a closer look. Wearing the special gloves, the astronauts could manipulate the rover's robot arm to pick up rock samples.

This concept—visiting dangerous places through virtual reality—is sometimes called "telepresence." (When a remote-controlled robot is added, the term is "telerobotics.") The same concept may be useful in areas other than space exploration. For example, similar systems could be used to explore the ocean floor or to handle dangerous materials such as nuclear fuel and toxic wastes.

Telepresence is only one way in which virtual reality can be used. There are already systems that allow architects to provide their clients with realistic previews of their designs. With a virtual reality preview, you can "walk" through a building before ground has even been broken for construction. Would you like that window to be placed a little to the left, to improve the view? Just reach out, grab the window, and put it where you want it. You can even "shrink" or "grow," to see how a room will look from the point of view of a child or an adult.

In the military, pilots may one day use virtual reality to practice bombing runs over enemy targets. In business, executives may hold virtual conferences even though they are hundreds of miles apart. Their computers

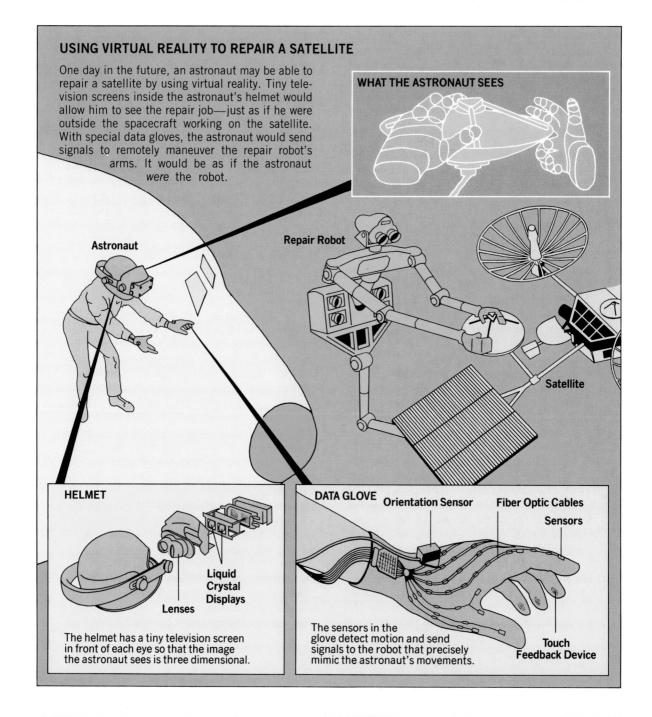

## USING VIRTUAL REALITY TO REPAIR A SATELLITE

One day in the future, an astronaut may be able to repair a satellite by using virtual reality. Tiny television screens inside the astronaut's helmet would allow him to see the repair job—just as if he were outside the spacecraft working on the satellite. With special data gloves, the astronaut would send signals to remotely maneuver the repair robot's arms. It would be as if the astronaut *were* the robot.

**WHAT THE ASTRONAUT SEES**

**Astronaut**

**Repair Robot**

**Satellite**

**HELMET**

**Liquid Crystal Displays**

**Lenses**

The helmet has a tiny television screen in front of each eye so that the image the astronaut sees is three dimensional.

**DATA GLOVE** **Orientation Sensor** **Fiber Optic Cables**

**Sensors**

The sensors in the glove detect motion and send signals to the robot that precisely mimic the astronaut's movements.

**Touch Feedback Device**

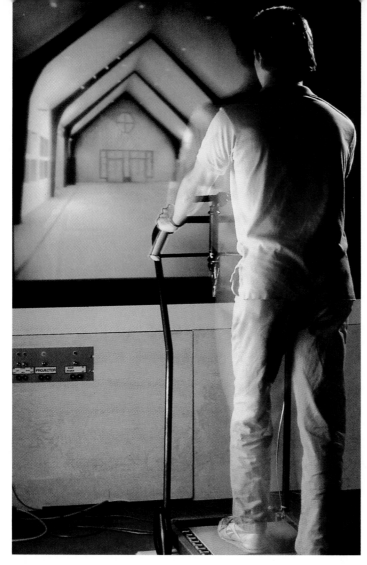

In this virtual reality system, a building design is put into a computer's memory. Sensors in a treadmill pick up foot motion, allowing a person to experience the feeling of walking around inside the building.

space. To establish radio contact, they would just "touch" a plane.

For many people, however, the most exciting potential of virtual reality is in the area of personal use. So far, the systems are much too expensive for most people to consider owning. But some video-game makers are already bringing elements of virtual reality systems to their products. And super-real video games are only the beginning. If virtual reality systems are developed to the point where they become common equipment in homes, the possibilities seem endless.

People could enter virtual worlds to learn new skills—anything from juggling to driving a car. Elderly and disabled people could use virtual reality systems to shop or play strenuous sports. Students could visit distant

would be linked by telephone lines, and they would share the same virtual setting.

Virtual reality can also be used in medicine. Doctors can preview surgery, actually practicing the operation on a virtual "patient." In one system that's being developed, X-ray images would be projected onto a set of see-through goggles. Doctors could then look at their patients and see the internal organs at the same time, as if they had X-ray vision.

City planners could use virtual reality to find out if a new skyscraper would block too much sunlight or to visualize the traffic flow through a new highway interchange. Some researchers are developing a virtual reality system for air traffic control. Instead of blips on a flat radar screen, controllers would see planes moving in a three-dimensional air-

places and far-off times, rather than just read about them. You might wander through the forest in the days of the dinosaurs, and even take the form of a dinosaur if you chose to.

With computers sending information back and forth over telephone lines, you could play virtual tennis or another game with a friend in a distant city. Or you could enter one of your favorite stories and become a character in it. One experimental system, for example, puts you in the middle of the Mad Hatter's tea party from *Alice's Adventures in Wonderland*. You can even pour the tea.

For now, virtual reality systems for the home are still far in the future. But one day, you may be able to sit down, slip on your sensor-filled glove and your 3-D goggles, and become an armchair astronaut—heading for the moon without leaving your living room.

# YOU ARE WHAT YOU EAT

• You eat three square meals every day. You've heard that this will give you all the energy and nourishment you need. Yet you feel tired all the time, and your doctor says you may be undernourished. How can that be?

• Your parents complain that you snack all the time and never seem to eat a decent meal. Yet you feel healthy, and you have plenty of energy. Should you cut out your snacks?

• Your diet is the same as the rest of your family's—but you're overweight, and they're not. Should you go on a diet? What foods should you cut out?

If you're like most people in North America, you get enough to eat. But that doesn't mean that you eat wisely—many people don't. Now, however, many people are changing their diets. They are learning that

what they eat affects their health—not only today but possibly many years from now.

## WHAT SHOULD YOU EAT?

Your body needs more than 50 different chemicals to be healthy. These chemicals are called nutrients. They are usually divided into six main groups: proteins, carbohydrates (starches and sugars), fats, vitamins, minerals, and water. Each nutrient has a specific job to do in your body; eating more of one won't make up for a shortage of another.

All the nutrients can be found in food. But different foods contain different types of nutrients. How can you be sure that you're getting the nutrients you need? One way is to eat a variety of foods each day. Your diet should include the following:

**Fruits and Vegetables.** These give you carbohydrates, which provide your body with its main source of energy. They also give you vitamins, especially vitamins A and C, and they contain fiber. Fiber is a part of plants, the part that gives plant cells their shape. It isn't completely broken down by your digestive system, and it provides few nutrients. But it helps move food and waste through the digestive system.

One guideline is to eat four servings of fruits and vegetables a day. You could have an orange at breakfast, a salad at lunch, an apple after school, and green beans with dinner. Vary the fruits and vegetables, so that you get all the vitamins you need.

**Bread and Cereal.** Foods like bread and cereal are made from grain, and they're rich in B vitamins and iron. They are also a good source of carbohydrates. But many breads and cereals are made from grain that has been processed, or refined, and has lost a lot of its nutritional value. Try to eat whole-grain breads and cereals. They contain fiber and many important minerals that aren't found in refined products. Try to have four servings of bread or cereal a day.

**Milk, Cheese, and Yogurt.** These dairy foods give you several important vitamins, and they are rich in calcium—a mineral that's especially important when you're growing. Many experts in nutrition recommend that children have three servings a day. They also suggest that you choose low-fat dairy foods, such as yogurt and low-fat milk, more often than fatty ones like cheese.

**Meat, Poultry, Fish, Eggs, and Dried Beans and Peas.** These foods are all good sources of protein, which is especially important for building new body tissues. Many of them also provide minerals, such as iron and zinc, and B vitamins. It's a good idea to have two helpings of foods from this group each day. This isn't a problem for most Americans—in fact, many people in North America eat more meat than they need.

You may have missed seeing some of your favorite foods on this list. What about candy, cookies, french fries, potato chips? They aren't here because they provide little nutritional value. That's why they're called junk food. Junk foods fill you up, so that you're not hungry for more nourishing foods. And eating too much of foods that are high in sugar, fat, and salt—like candy and fast-food burgers—can be harmful to your health.

How good a shopper are you? Today you almost have to be a detective to sort out all the information that leads to good nutrition. You would have to carefully study this label to find out that this can of pasta contains sugar and is high in fat and salt.

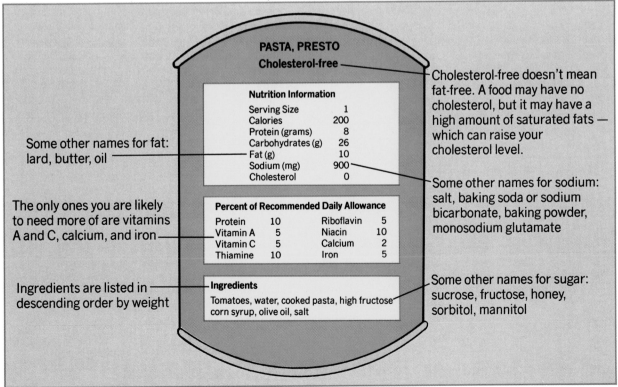

**PASTA, PRESTO**
**Cholesterol-free**

**Nutrition Information**

| | |
|---|---|
| Serving Size | 1 |
| Calories | 200 |
| Protein (grams) | 8 |
| Carbohydrates (g) | 26 |
| Fat (g) | 10 |
| Sodium (mg) | 900 |
| Cholesterol | 0 |

**Percent of Recommended Daily Allowance**

| | | | |
|---|---|---|---|
| Protein | 10 | Riboflavin | 5 |
| Vitamin A | 5 | Niacin | 10 |
| Vitamin C | 5 | Calcium | 2 |
| Thiamine | 10 | Iron | 5 |

**Ingredients**
Tomatoes, water, cooked pasta, high fructose corn syrup, olive oil, salt

Some other names for fat: lard, butter, oil

The only ones you are likely to need more of are vitamins A and C, calcium, and iron

Ingredients are listed in descending order by weight

Cholesterol-free doesn't mean fat-free. A food may have no cholesterol, but it may have a high amount of saturated fats — which can raise your cholesterol level.

Some other names for sodium: salt, baking soda or sodium bicarbonate, baking powder, monosodium glutamate

Some other names for sugar: sucrose, fructose, honey, sorbitol, mannitol

## STAYING SLIM AND HEALTHY

Why are junk foods less desirable? Well, first there's the problem of calories. A calorie is a unit of measure for the amount of energy that can be obtained from food. If you take in the proper number of calories, you will stay at a healthy weight. If you eat more calories than your body can use, you will store the excess as fat and gain weight.

How many calories you need depends on several factors, including age and how active you are. A fairly active 12-year-old needs between 2,200 and 2,800 calories a day. Some teenagers who participate in active sports can use 4,000 calories a day. But if you're a couch potato, this will be far too many.

It's easy to eat too many calories, especially if you like junk food. For example, a hamburger-with-everything-on-it from your favorite fast-food restaurant has about 600 calories. Add french fries, a soda, and an apple turnover, and you've eaten over 1,200 calories—in one meal. If you don't eat lightly for the rest of the day, you'll gain weight. But you still haven't provided your body with the nutrients it needs.

If you need to lose weight, you have to eat fewer calories than your body uses. One way to do this is to exercise more, so that you burn up more calories. In fact, exercise is one of the best ways to get rid of extra pounds—and it promotes good health in other ways, too.

You'll also need to watch the amount you eat. But even if you're dieting, your body needs the same amounts of vitamins and minerals. It's important for people who are trying to lose weight to choose foods that are low in calories but high in nutrients. Stay away from sugary foods that provide only empty calories (with little nutritional value). Stay away from high-fat foods, too—ounce for ounce, fats have twice as many calories as proteins and carbohydrates.

If you're fond of fried foods and snacks like potato chips, you have more to watch out for than extra pounds. Diets that are high in salt and fat have been shown to be a factor in heart disease, strokes, and other serious health problems. These problems usually affect older adults. But the conditions that cause them may begin early in life, and a good diet can help prevent them.

Fat is a necessary part of the diet—no one should try to eliminate it. But as a rule, no more than a third of your total daily calories should come from fat. This means watching out for more than french fries. Most red meats, such as beef, are very high in fat. So are dairy products made from whole milk.

You also need to be concerned about the *kind* of fat that's in your diet. Saturated fat—the kind found in fatty meats, butter, whole milk, and certain tropical oils—is thought to raise the level of a substance called cholesterol in the blood. Cholesterol can form deposits on blood-vessel walls and clog arteries. Although it takes years for this to happen, many researchers think that people should begin to watch their cholesterol levels while they are still growing up. (Cholesterol is also found in foods—in all meat and dairy products. And while it's most important to limit foods that are high in fat, you should also watch how much cholesterol you eat.)

Eat more foods like these, which provide the necessary nutrients.

## EATING WISELY

Is eating between meals really so bad? Not necessarily. In fact, many experts in nutrition say that snacking is important for children, especially younger and active children. Kids burn up calories faster than adults; but at the same time, children usually eat less than adults at mealtimes because their stomachs are smaller. So children actually need to have snacks between meals.

But whether snacking is good or bad really depends on what you snack on. If you reach for cookies, candy, and potato chips, you just fill up on empty calories. And because these junk foods are high in sugar and fat, they are more likely to spoil your appetite for your next meal. You'll eat less, and thus you may not get the nutrients you need.

Does all this mean that you should never eat another candy bar, swear off hamburgers forever, or never let a potato chip touch your lips? Not at all. It just means that you should keep a careful eye on what you eat—and avoid eating too much junk food. If you're getting the nutrients you need from healthy foods like fresh fruit, vegetables, and whole grain cereals, you'll have room in your diet for a candy bar or a few potato chips now and then. The important thing is not to overdo it.

Because so many people today are concerned with what they eat, food producers and even restaurants have begun to offer a wide variety of healthy foods. It's easy to find low-fat milk, whole-grain bread, cereals that are low in sugar and salt, and even fat-free ice cream in most supermarkets. You can even get a reduced-fat hamburger at a fast-food restaurant.

Remember to read the labels on food packages carefully, however. Many products on the market today are labeled ''low cholesterol'' or ''light,'' and these terms may be misleading. A food may contain no cholesterol at all, but it still may be very high in saturated fat. Thus it can still contribute to high cholesterol for the person who eats it. The term ''light'' on a label may just mean that the product *tastes* lighter. Even if the product has fewer calories or less fat than the standard version, it can still have plenty of both—and so it probably isn't a much healthier food.

You can also make a lot of healthful foods at home. For example, you can use whole-grain flour when you make pancakes for breakfast. You can make a shake with yogurt and fresh fruit. With many recipes for cookies and cakes, you can reduce the amount of sugar called for by as much as a third or a half—and still produce delicious treats. The same is true for the amount of salt you use in your food. You don't have to cut salt out; just use less of it.

If you're hungry between meals, pick up an orange or a carrot instead of a cookie. Try plain popcorn instead of chips, and yogurt instead of ice cream. Have a glass of juice instead of soda. And if it's close to dinner time, skip the snack altogether and save your appetite.

If you eat a well-balanced, nutritious diet, you'll look and feel healthy. It's the best thing you can do for yourself—for today and for the rest of your life.

**Eat fewer foods like these, because they provide little nutritional value.**

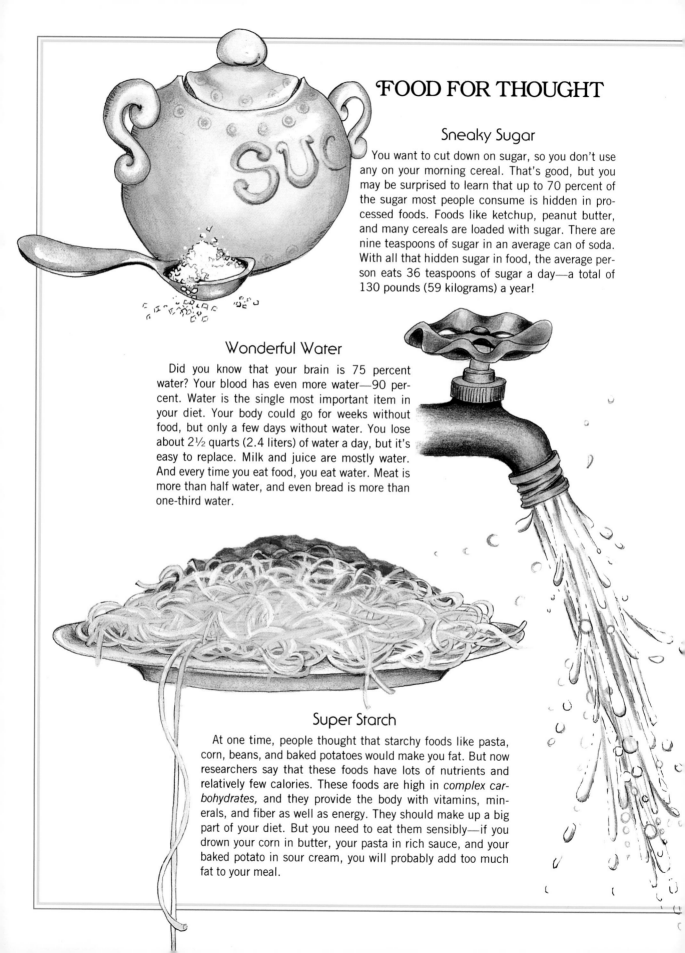

# FOOD FOR THOUGHT

## Sneaky Sugar

You want to cut down on sugar, so you don't use any on your morning cereal. That's good, but you may be surprised to learn that up to 70 percent of the sugar most people consume is hidden in processed foods. Foods like ketchup, peanut butter, and many cereals are loaded with sugar. There are nine teaspoons of sugar in an average can of soda. With all that hidden sugar in food, the average person eats 36 teaspoons of sugar a day—a total of 130 pounds (59 kilograms) a year!

## Wonderful Water

Did you know that your brain is 75 percent water? Your blood has even more water—90 percent. Water is the single most important item in your diet. Your body could go for weeks without food, but only a few days without water. You lose about 2½ quarts (2.4 liters) of water a day, but it's easy to replace. Milk and juice are mostly water. And every time you eat food, you eat water. Meat is more than half water, and even bread is more than one-third water.

## Super Starch

At one time, people thought that starchy foods like pasta, corn, beans, and baked potatoes would make you fat. But now researchers say that these foods have lots of nutrients and relatively few calories. These foods are high in *complex carbohydrates,* and they provide the body with vitamins, minerals, and fiber as well as energy. They should make up a big part of your diet. But you need to eat them sensibly—if you drown your corn in butter, your pasta in rich sauce, and your baked potato in sour cream, you will probably add too much fat to your meal.

## Tomato Tale

For years, people believed that tomatoes were poisonous. People grew the plants for decoration. But they thought that if you ate a tomato, you would die before morning. The fact that we eat and enjoy tomatoes today is due in part to a man named Robert G. Johnson. In 1820, Johnson stood on the courthouse steps in Salem, New Jersey, and ate a whole basket of tomatoes, in front of hundreds of people. They thought he had gone crazy—until they saw that he not only lived but didn't even get sick.

## Breakfast Benefit

Do your parents insist that you eat breakfast before you go to school—even though you're running late and would rather skip it? Well, they're right. Breakfast can help you feel better and perform better at school. In one study, children who ate breakfast did better at problem-solving than those who skipped the meal. That doesn't mean that you should sit down to a heavy meal of bacon and eggs every morning, though. A good breakfast might consist of fruit or juice, whole-grain cereal, and milk.

## Fast-Food Facts

On an average day, about a fifth of all Americans eat at a fast-food restaurant. More than 200 people order hamburgers *every second*! But they aren't getting much nutrition for their money. In most fast-food meals, almost half the calories come from fat. These meals are also high in salt and low in fiber and important nutrients. But you can enjoy nutritious fast food if you order wisely. Order a smaller burger, and top it with lettuce and tomato instead of cheese. Have low-fat frozen yogurt instead of ice cream, and top pizza with vegetables instead of meatballs and sausage.

# WELCOMING WILDFLOWERS

As European settlers came to North America and, over the years, pushed westward, they found a continent in bloom with wildflowers. In the East were golden marsh marigolds, handsome white trillium with its three distinctive petals, goldenrod, oxeye daisies, and milkweed. The Midwest bloomed with false indigo, evening primroses, ironweed, and black-eyed Susans. Farther west, the settlers found blazing stars, wild sunflowers and asters, swamp thistle, bluebonnet, Indian blanket, coneflowers, and California poppies.

On high mountain peaks, delicate wildflowers such as fringed gentian, dwarf columbine, old man of the mountain, and Alpine forget-me-not bloomed during the short summers. Wildflowers even bloomed in the scorching heat of the southwestern deserts—wild cotton, verbena, desert marigolds, and several kinds of flowering cactus.

Native Americans and early settlers found uses for many of these native plants. For example, yellow coreopsis, which grows wild in Texas, was used to produce dyes, and its seeds were put inside mattresses to repel bedbugs and fleas. Joe-pye weed, a wildflower of the East, was thought to ease fevers. It was just one of the many wild plants used for medicinal purposes by the Indians.

To many settlers, however, most of these wildflowers were nothing more than weeds. Native wildflowers began to disappear as forests were cleared and meadows were plowed into farmland for growing crops. More vanished as towns and cities spread. Around their homes, people preferred trimly mowed lawns to meadows of wildflowers. And when people planted flower gardens, they usually preferred plants from abroad—tulips, hybrid roses, peonies, and others. These plants had been cultivated for years to produce showy flowers. They soon filled the gardens of North America, just as in Europe. Wildflowers in the garden were gatecrashers, to be ripped up and weeded out.

Today, however, wildflowers are more appreciated. There are several reasons. Concern for the environment has made many people more aware of the value of native species of plants. Many wildflowers are much tougher and more resistant to drought, pests, and disease than are cultivated plants. They can thrive in conditions that are too poor to support traditional garden plants.

Native wildflowers are also part of the heritage of North America. Today there are very few areas on the continent that look as they did when settlers first arrived. Some people are concerned that, as the population continues to grow and towns and cities continue to spread, many

kinds of wildflowers will die out altogether. If that were to happen, it would affect the birds, insects, and other animals that depend on these plants. And a piece of North America's heritage would be lost forever.

Thus people are studying native flowering plants, working to preserve the areas where these plants are found, and even planting meadows and gardens that are filled with masses of beautiful and fragrant wildflowers.

### LEARNING ABOUT WILDFLOWERS

There are about 4,000 different kinds of wildflowers in North America, and learning about them can be both challenging and fun. Many nature centers have information about wildflowers and provide wildflower walks in spring and summer, so that people can see and learn about these plants. There are also field guides and other books that give information about the plants.

If you live or vacation in the country, take your own wildflower walks in the woods and fields, and see how many native flowers you can spot. If you live in the city, take a closer look at vacant lots—some of the "weeds" in these neglected areas may be tough little wildflowers, trying to make a comeback in the middle of the city. On your hikes, carry a wildflower guide and a pocket magnifying glass, to help you identify the plants, and a notebook in which to record your observations. If you like to draw, you might want to make sketches of the flowers.

Identifying wildflowers can be tricky. Examine the structure of the flower, the way the flowers and leaves are arranged, and where you find the plant growing. Then check your observations against the information in a wildflower guide to find the plant's name. The common, or folk, names

*Opposite page: Top—white trillium; Bottom—evening primrose. This page: Right—fishook barrel cactus; Below left—fringed gentian; Below right—coneflowers.*

*Joe-pye weed* was named for an Indian medicine man and was used to cure fevers. It was one of the many wild plants used by the Indians to treat illnesses.

*Indian pipes* are usually completely colorless. Because they lack chlorophyll, they can't produce their own food; they live off decaying matter in the forest's soil.

of many wildflowers are fascinating. Often there's a story behind the name. Joe-pye weed, for example, is supposed to have been named for an Indian medicine man.

To identify wildflowers accurately, however, you'll need to use their scientific names. That's because the same plant often has several common names. For instance, the great mullein is also called velvet dock, Aaron's rod, Adam's flannel, blanket leaf, bullock's lungwort, candlewick, feltwort, hare's-beard, and stamp-pad leaf. And those are just the English-language names—there are more names, in more languages, in Europe, where this plant also grows. But you can't go wrong with the scientific name, which is *Verbascum thapsus*.

One thing you *shouldn't* do on your walks is dig up wildflowers and take them home. In some cases, doing this may even be illegal— some wildflowers are so rare that they are protected by law. It's not even a good idea to pick the flowers of rare plants—if the flowers are picked, there will be no seeds to produce the next generation of plants.

Even some of the more common wildflowers are having a hard time surviving the spread of towns and cities. They should be left to grow in the wild, too. But usually you can pick the flowers of common plants without doing great harm. Just make sure that there are several plants of the same kind nearby—and don't pick *all* the flowers. That way, you can be sure that some of the plants will set seed and that wildflowers will bloom in the same place next year.

You may want to preserve the flowers that you pick by pressing or drying them. By doing this, you can build a collection of wildflower specimens. Keep notes on each of your specimens—the name of the flower and where and when you found it.

### A WILDFLOWER GARDEN

If you have an unused corner in your yard, why not plant a garden of wildflowers? A wildflower garden needs less watering than a traditional garden, and there is less need for pesticides, fertilizers, and other chemicals that can harm the environment. Growing

**Pink lady's slippers** *are common woodland wildflowers. They are members of the orchid family and get their name from their graceful pouchlike flowers.*

*The* **jack-in-the-pulpit,** *also called an Indian turnip, is known for its unusual hooded flower formation. This formation is actually a modified leaf called a spathe.*

wildflowers also helps preserve these native plants. And wildflower gardens have a natural beauty all their own.

Although a wildflower garden requires less work than a traditional garden once it's established, getting started takes some effort. The best way to obtain plants is to grow them from seed. Rather than collecting seeds from the wild, buy them—that will help protect wild plants. Many garden centers sell mixtures of wildflower seeds, and dozens of seed companies specialize in wildflowers.

By learning about the plants, you can make sure that you plant wildflowers that do well in your region. You can select plants that attract wildlife—hummingbirds love Indian paintbrush, and monarch butterflies are attracted by milkweed, for example. And you can plan to have flowers blooming all through the spring and summer. Choose the site for your wildflower garden carefully, too. Most wildflowers, including the ones that are usually included in seed mixtures, need lots of sun. For these plants, your garden should have six to eight hours of sun-

shine each day. If you want to plant your garden in a shady spot, be sure to choose plants that do well in shade.

To plant your garden, begin by tilling the soil to break up the ground and eliminate unwanted weeds. Then scatter the wildflower seeds over the ground and press them down. (If you're planting a large area, a good way to sow the seeds evenly is to first mix them with sand.) If the weather is dry, water the area regularly until the seeds sprout and the seedlings are beginning to grow.

Once your wildflower garden is established, it will almost take care of itself. You may want to pull out unwanted plants and add some new ones from time to time. If you've planted a large area, mow it once a year in early spring, to keep trees and bushes from taking hold. But if you let the wildflower plants set seed, your garden will bloom year after year with very little help from you. You'll have a natural garden that's good for the environment. And you'll have a beautiful piece of North America's heritage, too.

**113**

# THE MYSTERIES OF MEMORY

*Memory—that strange deceiver!*
*Who can trust her? How believe her—*
*While she hoards with equal care*
*The poor and trivial, rich and rare;*
*Yet flings away, as wantonly,*
*Grave fact and loveliest fantasy?*
Walter de la Mare (1873–1956)

Do you remember what you had for dinner last Monday? How many continents there are? Can you name the members of your favorite rock group? How about the Seven Dwarfs in *Snow White*?

Chances are that you knew all these things —at one time. But if you are like most people, you remember only some of them now. All day, every day, people are bombarded with information and experiences. Why is it that we remember some things perfectly, while others are forgotten?

How memory works is a question that has fascinated scientists for a long time. Researchers still don't have all the answers. But they know a great deal about memory, and they have come up with some fascinating theories about the way it works.

### HOW MEMORIES FORM

Psychologists (scientists who study how the mind works) divide the process of memory into three steps. First, you *receive and register* something—for example, you look in the phone book for the number of your favorite pizzeria, and you read the number on the page. An image, or memory trace, of the number is held very briefly in your mind. This step is sometimes called sensory memory.

To remember the telephone number for more than an instant, you must take the next step—*retention*. Memories may be retained in two ways. Short-term memories are held only as long as you actively think about them. To remember the pizzeria's phone number, you may repeat it to yourself until you dial it—and then promptly forget it. But long-term memories may be held for hours, weeks, and even years.

Long-term memories may be formed when you consciously try to memorize something or when you just think about it a lot. There are also "flashbulb" memories—memories of events that were so special (or so upsetting) that they are etched in your mind in perfect detail.

The third step in the memory process, *retrieval*, takes place when the information is remembered and used. If you want pizza again next week, you may be able to recall the phone number without looking it up. A specific cue, such as the name of the pizzeria, may help you recall it.

Even if you don't remember the number and have to look it up again, it will probably be familiar to you when you see it. This kind of retrieval, called recognition, is easier than recall. And that's why many students prefer taking tests that consist of true-or-false and multiple-choice questions (which ask them to recognize correct answers) rather than short-answer and essay questions (which ask them to recall information).

### INSIDE THE BRAIN

One of the greatest puzzles about memory is still the question of what, exactly, happens inside the brain when memories are formed. Scientists have identified an area of the brain, called the hippocampus, that is involved in transferring information from short-term to long-term memory. When the hippocampus is damaged, people can't form new long-term memories—they couldn't even remember this sentence. But scientists still don't know exactly how memories are formed in the brain or where they are stored.

They have theories, however. Most scientists believe that when a memory is formed, the connections between the brain's nerve cells are changed in some way. The brain is made up of billions of these nerve cells, called neurons. Neurons have long, treelike branches called dendrites and axons. Each dendrite can receive signals from thousands of other neurons, and each axon can pass the signals on to thousands more.

Scientists think that each time we learn something new, such as a new phone number, signals flash through a unique pattern or circuit of neurons. In some way, the connections between the neurons in this circuit are

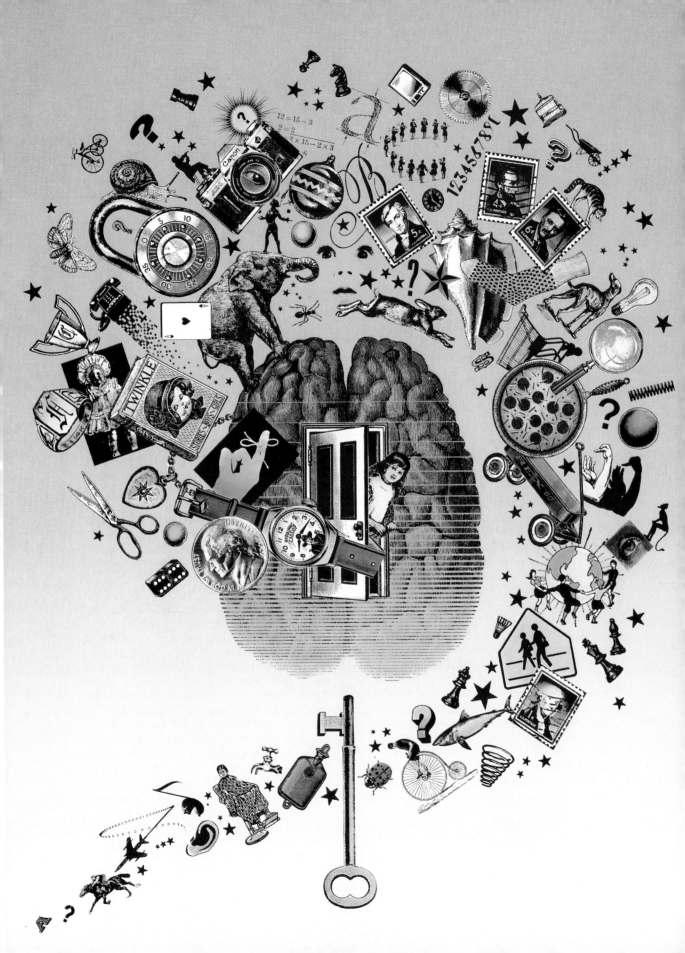

## PICTURE THIS PICTURE

A few people have the ability to recall everything they see or encounter, for a short time at least. This kind of memory is often called photographic memory. People with photographic memory can read a page in a book, close the book, and recite the words on the page perfectly. They are able to remember a complete image of the page and "read" it from memory.

Do you have a photographic memory? To find out, look at this picture for 30 seconds. Then close your eyes and see how many items you remember.

Don't worry if you can't remember many, or even most, of the items. You might envy people with photographic memories, especially at exam time—but it's not the advantage that it seems. To produce a single fact, a person with a photographic memory might have to mentally sift through pages of unnecessary information. Researchers estimate that one out of every ten children has a photographic memory. But this special ability fades over time as people learn to be more selective about what they remember.

strengthened by the signals. The more times the circuit is used—the more times you repeat the phone number, for example—the stronger the connections become. And once the connections are strong enough, the brain can reactivate the circuit and retrieve the memory.

### DON'T FORGET!

If every new experience or bit of information that you encounter forms a unique neuron circuit in your brain, why is it that you forget some things but remember others?

Memories often fade quickly. An hour after dinner you would find it easy to remember what was on your plate. The next day you might remember only the main course. And a week or a month later you most likely would have forgotten all about that meal. If it's true that memories are formed by connections between neurons, then, it seems likely that those connections grow weaker over time.

One of the most common types of forgetting is called retrieval failure. You search your mind for a name or some other bit of information but just can't come up with it—even though it's "on the tip of your tongue."

But a few hours later the information comes to you without difficulty. It's almost as if you got a busy signal when you first tried to recall the information; later, the line was clear.

A memory may also be blocked by other information. Suppose, for example, your friend has a cat named Lizzie. Then she gets a second cat and names it Clarence. When you try to recall the new cat's name, you may have trouble because the name "Lizzie" pops into your mind. Or you may remember "Clarence" but have difficulty recalling the first cat's name. This type of forgetting is called interference—new information interferes with information that is already stored in your memory.

Sometimes people forget because they want to. Consciously or unconsciously, people often push memories of painful experiences out of their minds. Pleasant memories seem to last much longer, and be easier to recall, than unpleasant ones.

Your memory can play tricks on you, too. Think back to a past experience—perhaps your first day at school. Chances are that you remember only a few events clearly. But as you search your memory, your mind will fill in details that may not be true. Incidents that took place on other days, or that never took place at all, may become mixed with accurate recollections. And the false memories seem just as real as the accurate ones. This process is sometimes called confabulation or refabrication.

Amnesia is a kind of memory illness in which people can remember almost nothing. In one type of amnesia, people forget a period or even all of the past. This type is rare, however, and usually lasts just a short time. In a more common type of amnesia, a person is unable to form new memories. This type usually results from a brain injury or disease. People who suffer from it remember the past, but they can't remember people they meet or learn anything new.

Older people are often more forgetful than young people. Researchers think, however, that there's nothing in the aging process itself that causes memory to weaken. Instead, younger people are better at remembering because they use their memory more—in studying for school, for example. The more you use your memory, the better it becomes.

## SHARPEN YOUR MEMORY

While no one can remember everything, you can try to improve your memory through a number of different techniques.

• One of the simplest methods is overlearning. If you are studying for a test, for example, keep studying long after you feel you know all the material that the test will cover. Repetition will strengthen your memory and improve your ability to recall the information.

• Another way to improve memory is through the use of mnemonic devices—mental images and word tricks that trigger memories. One of the oldest of these devices is called the method of Loci (locations). It was developed by orators in ancient Greece, to help them remember their speeches.

To use this method, you first memorize a series of familiar places, preferably places that are part of your daily routine. Try picturing the places you see when you get up in the morning—your bed, the bathroom sink, your closet, the breakfast table. Now suppose your mother asks you to stop at the store and buy eggs, milk, bread, and dog food. Picture eggs in your bed, milk filling the bathroom sink, loaves of bread hanging in your closet, and dog food served up on the breakfast table. Later, to recall the shopping list, just take an imaginary tour of the familiar places and note the unusual items that you "stored" there.

• You can use mental pictures in other ways, too. For example, when you meet someone new, try to form a mental picture using the person's name. It helps if you can link the name to something in the person's appearance. If Mrs. Bushnell has a full hairstyle, you'll remember her name when you think of her "bushy" hair. Mental pictures can also help you spell. You'll remember that *i* comes before *e* in "piece" if you think of a piece of p*ie*.

• Another mnemonic device is to store information as a rhyme: "In fourteen-hundred ninety-two/ Columbus sailed the ocean blue."

• You can also use an acronym, a word formed from the first letters of the words you want to remember. "HOMES" is an acronym for the individual names of the Great Lakes.

• In the same way, you can make up a short phrase to remember a list of facts. The phrase "when a just man makes a just vow" can help you remember the names of the first eight U.S. presidents because the first letters of the words are the same as those of the presidents' names.

The continent of Antarctica is the world's last great unspoiled wilderness. But its fragile environment is threatened.

# ANTARCTICA IN DANGER

The land is cloaked in darkness for much of the year. Bitterly cold winds of up to 200 miles per hour (320 kph) howl across the barren landscape. The temperature is a bone-chilling −80°F (−60°C). And except for a few patches along the coast, there is no visible land. There are no grassy plains; no lakes or rivers; no trees; no land mammals. Instead, ice—some of it nearly 3 miles (4.8 kilometers) deep—stretches as far as the eye can see.

This is the continent of Antarctica, land of the South Pole—the coldest, harshest, most desolate place on Earth. Antarctica is the world's last great unspoiled wilderness. And today this great wilderness is in danger—from people.

As forbidding as it is, Antarctica attracts more and more people to its icy shores each year. Scientists by the thousands, from many countries around the world, work at research stations there. Tourists, many of them naturalists and advocates of environmental protection, are also flocking to Antarctica.

The problem is that these people, tourists and scientists alike, are damaging Antarctica's fragile environment. And, until recently, there were also fears that oil- and mineral-hungry nations would try to exploit these valuable resources in Antarctica, doing even greater damage. Environmentalists and other concerned individuals had horrifying visions of offshore oil platforms in the waters around Antarctica, and of open-pit mines on the continent itself.

In 1991, mining and oil exploration in Antarctica was prohibited for fifty years, under

an international agreement. That greatly encouraged people who are concerned about the continent's environment. But that step was just a start in removing the dangers that still threaten Antarctica.

### SCIENTIFIC RESEARCH

Scientists are Antarctica's only permanent human inhabitants. More than twenty countries now have scientific research stations there, and during the summer months there may be as many as 4,000 scientists and support staff. These researchers have long traveled to Antarctica to take advantage of its relatively unpolluted environment, which makes the continent a natural laboratory.

Biologists study the millions of penguins and other birds that live along the shore and on the ice. They study fish that produce their own natural antifreeze, allowing them to survive in the frigid waters. Geologists study meteorites that have landed on the continent. Vulcanologists study the gases from

Mount Erebus, a volcano near the coast. Astronomers study cosmic rays in the atmosphere, and they have conducted experiments to detect the radiation left over from the "Big Bang" that created the universe.

Environmental scientists study pollutants that drift to Antarctica from other parts of the globe. And they are learning how the thinning of the atmosphere's ozone layer is affecting Antarctica's wildlife—and therefore how it may affect life in the rest of the world. This layer shields the Earth from much of the sun's harmful ultraviolet radiation, which can damage plants and animals. It is being destroyed by chemicals known as chlorofluorocarbons (CFC's), which are used in aerosol sprays and as refrigerants. The problem is most severe over Antarctica, where a so-called "ozone hole" has appeared. The nations of the world are now working on an agreement to end the production of CFC's by the year 2000.

All these scientific studies are important.

Scientists are the only people who live and work permanently on Antarctica, and more than twenty countries have research stations there. Here, scientists are conducting experiments on an ice floe.

But surprisingly, many of the scientists stationed in Antarctica are responsible for much of the pollution that already exists. In some areas, their garbage litters the landscape, or it's burned, sending poisonous fumes into the air. Some stations have been abandoned, and rusted metal drums and old equipment are scattered about. Raw sewage has been allowed to flow into the surrounding seas. And the scientists have sometimes unintentionally harmed the continent's wildlife. For example, a penguin rookery was partially destroyed during the building of an air base at one scientific station.

Supply ships that serve the scientific stations also create problems. Early in 1989 an Argentinian supply ship, the *Bahía Paraíso,* hit a reef and spilled thousands of gallons of oil in the sea. Soon after, a research and supply ship from Peru also ran aground, causing additional oil pollution. These spills caused the death of krill (tiny shrimplike animals that are vital to the Antarctic food chain) and possibly of thousands of skua chicks, penguins, and cormorants.

## TOURISM

Another major problem that has developed in recent years is the influx of tourists. Tourism began in the mid-1950's, but as recently as the early 1980's, only a few hundred tourists made their way to Antarctica. In 1989, however, seven tour companies brought some 3,000 visitors to the continent. Tourists continue to flock there—and their tour ships are increasingly fouling the waters around Antarctica.

In addition, the tourists themselves disrupt the continent's natural environment. For example, many tourists want to visit penguin rookeries. But their mere presence can interfere with the breeding of the penguins and the raising of the penguin chicks. Tourists also disrupt the scientific research. Many tour groups visit research stations, where they may accidentally damage fragile equipment.

Still, the damage that's done by scientists and tourists is small compared to the damage that might be done if people began to exploit Antarctica's rich natural resources.

## RESOURCES OF ANTARCTICA

Long before Antarctica was discovered in 1820, some scientists had predicted that a continent existed at the bottom of the world. They also speculated about the kinds of resources that would be found there. One French explorer, Yves-Joseph de Kerguélen-Trémarac, predicted in 1772 that "wood, minerals, diamonds, rubies and precious stones, and marble will be found [in Antarctica]."

The first resource to draw people to the southern seas, however, was its rich marine life, especially the seals and whales. Today there are more than 30 million seals in Antarctic waters, including crabeater (the most numerous), southern elephant, Weddell, Ross, Antarctic fur, and leopard seals. But during the late 1800's and early 1900's, millions were killed, especially fur seals. Whales, such as the sperm, blue, humpback, fin, and minke, were also hunted and greatly reduced in number. In this century, fin fish and krill have been harvested in the waters around Antarctica. Because krill is eaten by penguins, whales, fish, and many other marine animals, it's very important to the ecology of the area.

There are no important land animals or plants in Antarctica. A few insects live there, mostly in warmer areas near the sea. The plant life consists mainly of mosses and lichens; there are only two flowering plants.

There are, however, mineral resources in Antarctica. According to the United States Geological Survey, there may be deposits of coal and iron ore, as well as gold, nickel, platinum, chromium, uranium, copper, and others. Traces of natural gas have been found in core samples taken from the bed of the Weddell Sea, so there may also be commercial quantities of oil and natural gas in the seas surrounding the continent.

Would it be possible to conduct profitable mining operations in Antarctica? Many peo-

Some of the scientists stationed in Antarctica are responsible for polluting the continent. They may, for example, abandon a research station and leave rusted metal drums and old equipment littering the landscape.

ple don't think so. For one thing, the climate is so harsh that mining crews would find life very difficult. Also, it would be hard to get at many of the minerals, because only a few of the known mineral deposits are in ice-free areas. And even if the minerals could be mined, it would be expensive to mine them and transport them to world markets.

These major problems would seem to indicate that large-scale mining in Antarctica wouldn't be profitable. Still, many countries and environmental groups fear that mining operations of *any* kind could severely damage the continent's environment, and they have been trying hard to prevent that from happening.

## PROTECTING THE CONTINENT

What can be done to protect Antarctica? The concerned nations of the world have tried to protect Earth's last unspoiled environment since June, 1961, when the Antarctic Treaty went into effect. This treaty states that "Antarctica shall be used for peaceful purposes only." Military bases and weapons testing were prohibited, as was the disposal of radioactive waste. This was the first concerted attempt by the nations of the world to protect Antarctica.

A later agreement prohibited the killing of fur, Ross, and southern elephant seals and set limits on the catch of Weddell, crabeater, and leopard seals. A third agreement pro-

tected many different species of fish from over-fishing; and it prohibited fishing in certain areas, so that the stocks of some species could be replenished.

The most recent and most important attempt to preserve Antarctica in its natural state occurred in October, 1991, when 24 countries signed a treaty banning all mining and oil exploration on the continent for 50 years. The agreement also set new rules for wildlife protection, waste disposal, and marine pollution. Among the countries that signed the treaty were the United States, Canada, the Soviet Union, and China.

Discussions were also under way to limit the number of tourists visiting Antarctica

More than 35 species of penguins—including the gentoo penguins above—make their home in Antarctica. Tourists flock to get a glimpse of the flightless birds and watch them waddle along the land. But the presence of so many people may confuse the penguins and interfere with their breeding habits and the raising of their chicks.

every year, and the environmental group Greenpeace International is inspecting scientific research stations to ensure that pollution there is brought to a halt. Greenpeace is one of several organizations that are working to protect Antarctica. Others include the Environmental Defense Fund and the Antarctic and Southern Ocean Coalition, which is made up of more than two hundred environmental groups.

These groups oppose not only mineral and oil exploration but any activity that would ruin the unspoiled environment of the continent. Their efforts, along with those of concerned governments and people around the world, can help ensure that endangered Antarctica remains as it is today—the Earth's last great wilderness.

# CROP CIRCLES: FACT OR FICTION

Stonehenge is an ancient monument in southern England. When it was built some four thousand years ago, it formed a circle of giant stones almost 100 feet (30 meters) in diameter. Who built Stonehenge? No one knows. It remains one of history's greatest mysteries.

Today, not far from Stonehenge, other mysterious circles have been appearing. These, however, aren't circles of stone— they are circles of flattened stalks of wheat and other crops. One circle was 300 feet (90 meters) in diameter. Most often, the circles appear alone. But there have also been circles within circles and linked circles, as well as other forms shaped like rectangles, triangles, arcs, bars, keys, and crosses. The patterns (such as those shown on these pages) are intriguing, beautiful, and puzzling.

The shapes appear during the growing season in June and July, and they usually appear at night. The stalks of wheat—and other crops such as corn and sugar beet—are rarely broken; they are just flattened, and they continue to grow. If the crops are flattened when they are still green, they will eventually stand upright again and the pattern will fade away.

Crop circles have been found in more than 30 countries, including the United States, Canada, Australia, and Japan. But most have been found in England. Some crop circles were seen there as long ago as the 1600's. In those days, many people believed that the circles were formed by dancing fairies—or by "mowing devils" who cut the patterns in the crops with giant scythes.

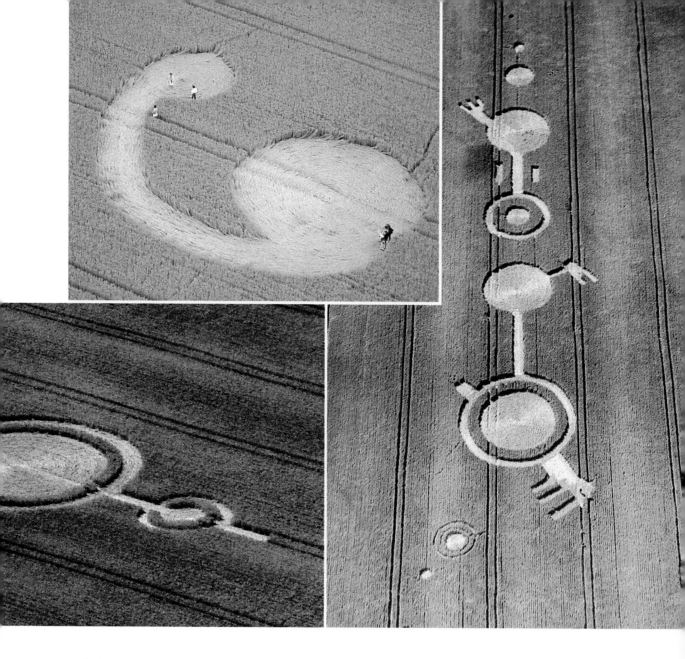

Today, as more and more circles are being found—there were some 600 sightings in 1990 and 1991 alone—scientists are searching for answers. Who or what is making these patterns? Are they formed by fungi in the soil? Do hordes of hedgehogs cause them as they run crazily in circles during their mating season? Are they made by UFO's or by some "unknown" intelligence? Are they caused by the downdrafts of hovering helicopters? Or are they all nothing more than a hoax? These are some of the early theories that were advanced.

By 1991, the leading theory was that the circles were formed by swirling currents of electrically charged air. But in September, two men claimed that *they* had created the crop circles in southern England—as a joke. They did it, they said, by trampling out the circles with wooden boards tied to their feet. Many people thought the mystery was solved. But others weren't so sure. They said that even if the men had created some of the circles, they couldn't have created the ones that appeared in different parts of England on the same night, and the ones that have appeared in other countries.

Only time and a thorough investigation will reveal who or what has made the circles. For now, they remain as mysterious as ever.

In April, astronauts aboard the *Atlantis* space shuttle took two spacewalks—a planned one and an unplanned one. They were the first spacewalks by U.S. astronauts since 1985.

# SPACE BRIEFS

The launch of sophisticated satellites, a ride on a monorail in space, spectacular new views of Venus, and a close encounter with an asteroid were among the highlights of the 1991 space year.

### 1991 SHUTTLE MISSIONS

The first space shuttle mission of 1991 took place in early April, when *Atlantis* roared into space. The main objective of this mission was the launch of Gamma Ray Observatory, an astronomy satellite designed to detect and measure high-energy gamma radiation. This radiation, which doesn't penetrate the Earth's atmosphere, is created during violent events in the universe, such as the birth and death of stars. But before the satellite could be launched, it was discovered that its long antenna boom had become jammed. As a result, astronauts Jerry Ross and Jerome Apt had to take an unplanned spacewalk outside *Atlantis* to loosen the boom. It was the first spacewalk by U.S. astronauts since 1985.

The following day, Ross and Apt went for a second spacewalk, this time a scheduled one. The two men spent six hours testing equipment and techniques that might someday be used for moving about while building an orbiting space station. "This is the way to travel," exclaimed Ross after riding an electric cart back and forth on a monorail that he and Apt had constructed along one side of *Atlantis*.

In late April, *Discovery* was launched on a military mission. The astronauts released and later retrieved a satellite that studied *Discovery*'s exhaust plumes and other chemicals purposely released into space. The experiments were intended to help the U.S. military design an antimissile defense system. In addition, a series of instruments aboard the shuttle gathered data to help distinguish speeding warheads and missiles from natural phenomena such as the Northern Lights.

In June, *Columbia* spent nine days in space as its crew performed detailed medical studies. The astronauts gave blood and urine samples and underwent various tests to learn what changes occurred in their bodies during liftoff and during their time in space. Scientists hope to use this information to develop ways to solve medical problems that develop in zero gravity, particularly during long flights. Also aboard *Columbia* were 29 rats and 2,478 jellyfish. Once back on Earth, the animals were studied to see how they had adapted to space flight and weightlessness.

*Atlantis* returned to space in August. Its crew deployed a giant Tracking and Data Relay Satellite almost identical to three satellites already in orbit. The purpose of these four communications satellites was to rapidly transmit large volumes of data between orbiting spacecraft and ground stations. The astronauts also conducted experiments on the human body's ability to adapt to the weightlessness of space.

In September, *Discovery* went aloft to launch the Upper Atmosphere Research Satellite (UARS)—the first satellite in a fifteen-year program called Mission to Planet Earth. The purpose of this mission is to gather extensive information on Earth's environment, climate, and natural resources. UARS will be used to study the effects of pollution on the ozone layer in the upper atmosphere; scientists hope to gain a better understanding of what causes the periodic thinning of the layer, especially over Antarctica.

The year's final shuttle flight took place in late November, with the launch of *Atlantis*. The main accomplishment of the mission was the launch of an Air Force satellite that can give early warning of a missile attack. Originally planned as a ten-day mission, the flight was cut short after seven days because one of the three navigational devices aboard the *Atlantis* had failed.

### VISITS TO OTHER PLANETS

Hundreds of years ago, two famous people —Ferdinand Magellan and Galileo—greatly increased people's knowledge of Earth and space. Magellan was a Portuguese navigator who, in 1519, led an expedition that would be the first to sail around the world (although

## NAME A CRATER!

Imagine a crater named after a beautiful movie star, or a mountain named after your favorite author. As Magellan orbited Venus, it found thousands of previously unknown craters, valleys, mountains, and other features. All these features will be given names. If the National Aeronautics and Space Administration (NASA), which is responsible for Magellan, has its way, all the features will be named after famous women.

NASA has asked the public to suggest women for this honor. The women must have died at least three years ago. No religious or political figures of the 19th or 20th centuries are eligible. NASA will select the names and forward them to the International Astronomical Union, which is responsible for assigning names to features on other planets. All chosen names will become official in 1994.

If you would like to suggest someone, send her name, her birth and death years, and a brief explanation of why she deserves the honor to: Venus Names, Magellan Project Office, 4800 Oak Grove Drive, Pasadena, CA 91109

Magellan himself was killed during the voyage). Galileo was an Italian astronomer. In 1610, using a telescope he had built himself, he discovered many wondrous objects in the universe, including moons revolving around Jupiter. In 1991, spacecraft named after these two men provided new data on the solar system.

The spacecraft Magellan was launched by the United States in 1989 on a mission to Venus. In September, 1990, soon after Magellan went into orbit around Venus, it began taking radar images of the planet. Radar was used because the surface of Venus is hidden beneath a dense blanket of clouds—it cannot be seen with instruments that depend on light. Radar images consist of a combination of bright and dark areas, depending on the texture of the planet's surface: bright areas are rough, and dark areas are smooth.

By piecing together the radar images, scientists have created the most detailed maps ever of the Venusian surface. The maps revealed that the surface is very rugged, with long channels and valleys, huge craters, and gigantic lava flows. The surface of the planet also appears to be comparatively young. This has led scientists to believe that Venus has active volcanoes, and that the lava may completely "repave" the planet every few hundred million years.

Magellan also obtained, in August, 1991, the first before-and-after pictures of a huge landslide on Venus. The face of a steep cliff near the Venusian equator had collapsed, covering a smooth valley with rocky debris. The landslide was believed to have been caused by a "venusquake."

The spacecraft Galileo was launched by the United States in 1989 to travel to Jupiter, reaching the planet in 1995. Galileo's booster rockets weren't powerful enough to launch the craft on a direct path to Jupiter. Instead, Galileo was sent on an indirect route that would include a bypass of Venus and two orbits of Earth. Gravitational interactions with the planets would give Galileo the boost needed for the long voyage to Jupiter.

In October, 1991, during its second orbit of Earth, Galileo reached the asteroid belt beyond Mars. It flew within 1,000 miles (1,600 kilometers) of the asteroid Gaspra—the first time ever that a spacecraft encountered an asteroid. The information gathered by Galileo is expected to greatly increase scientists' understanding of asteroids, their composition, and how they formed.

There was, however, one serious problem with the spacecraft. Galileo has three antennas to handle communications with Earth-based stations: two small antennas and one large antenna. Only the large antenna can transmit a heavy volume of pictures and data. The problem began in April, when the large antenna didn't open completely. The Gaspra information had to be recorded on board Galileo, to be transmitted back to Earth when the large antenna is fully deployed. If that doesn't happen, the data can be transmitted by the small antennas when Galileo returns near Earth in late 1992 for its final boost toward Jupiter. But this option doesn't exist once Galileo reaches Jupiter: If the large antenna can't be fully deployed, another means of transmitting the data has to be found.

## THE SOVIET SPACE PROGRAM

The Soviet Union's manned space program centers around Mir, its giant space station. Mir was launched in 1986, and it has been occupied by teams of cosmonauts for extended periods of time. From December, 1990, until May, 1991, its residents were Viktor Afansev and Musa Manarov. Their activities included a variety of experiments and four spacewalks.

About a week before Afansev and Manarov ended their mission, they were joined by

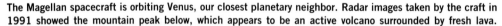
The Magellan spacecraft is orbiting Venus, our closest planetary neighbor. Radar images taken by the craft in 1991 showed the mountain peak below, which appears to be an active volcano surrounded by fresh lava.

## A MEMORIAL FOR ASTRONAUTS

On May 9, 1991, the Astronauts Memorial, a monument honoring American astronauts killed in the line of duty, was dedicated at Kennedy Space Center in Florida.

The memorial is a highly polished black granite wall consisting of 93 panels. It's 42.5 feet (13 meters) high and 50 feet (15 meters) wide, and it's mounted on a computer-controlled platform that turns to track the sun. As the Earth rotates, the wall does too, so that its back is always to the sun. The names of the astronauts are carved through the granite; thus sunlight shines through the letters, making them glow against the black granite. The face of the wall reflects the sky, creating the impression that the names are shining in the heav-ens—an impression that has led to the memorial's popular name: Space Mirror.

The names of fifteen astronauts are carved into the granite. Three of these astronauts died in a launchpad fire while preparing for the Apollo 1 mission in 1967; seven died when the space shut-tle *Challenger* exploded in 1986; and five died in plane crashes.

A plaque on the memorial reads: "Whenever mankind has sought to conquer new frontiers there have been those who have given their lives to the cause. This Astronauts Memorial . . . is a tribute to the American men and women who have made the ultimate sacrifice, believing the conquest of space is worth the risk of life."

two other cosmonauts, Anatoly Artsebarsky and Sergei Krikalyov, plus a British chemist, Helen Sharman. Sharman was chosen from 13,000 applicants to become the first Briton in space. In order to join the flight, she had to spend fourteen months training and learn-ing Russian. Sharman remained on Mir for eight days, during which time she performed several experiments, spoke by radio to So-viet President Mikhail Gorbachev, and placed the first flower delivery order from outer space. On May 26, Sharman, Afansev, and Manarov returned to Earth. Artsebarsky and Krikalyov remained aboard Mir.

JENNY TESAR
Author, *Global Warming*

# EYES IN THE SKY

Satellites orbiting high above the Earth are like giant eyes. Their cameras, radar, and other instruments can be aimed at every part of the Earth's surface, from crowded cities to isolated ocean areas. They operate day and night, in clear weather and in storms. They map wetlands, locate oil deposits, and monitor volcanoes. They also collect information that helps scientists to unlock the secrets of climate patterns, ocean and air interactions, changes in polar ice packs, and other natural processes. The words spoken many years ago by the famous rocket engineer Wernher von Braun have come true: "The more we go into space, the more we'll find that the most interesting planet to study from space is Earth."

Scientific satellites study the Earth and space, greatly increasing our knowledge of natural processes. Instruments aboard the Upper Atmosphere Research Satellite, or UARS (*above*), create temperature profiles, measure concentrations of ozone and other substances, map wind fields, and determine the amount of energy coming from the sun. Scientists hope to use this data to better understand changes in the upper atmosphere's ozone layer.

Communications satellites use receivers, amplifiers, and transmitters to pick up and relay various kinds of communication signals around the Earth. Intelsat 6 (*above*) can simultaneously handle 120,000 telephone calls and three television channels. Communications satellites are also used to transmit computer data, carry educational and health information to remote villages, and listen for distress signals from ships and aircraft (and then relay the vessel's location to rescue teams).

**Earth resources satellites** survey the Earth, gathering data on natural resources, land formations, animal migrations, and other phenomena. Data from Landsat satellites (*above*) have been used in numerous ways—to map transportation networks, observe crop harvests, assess forest fire damage, determine soil conditions, map water pollution, trace beach erosion, estimate runoff from melting snow, and monitor urban growth.

**Weather satellites** collect meteorological data over large areas of the Earth's surface. They then relay the data to ground stations, which provide people with timely weather information, including advance warnings of developing storms. Geostationary Operational Environmental Satellites, or GOES (*above*), let meteorologists measure the movement of certain clouds at different altitudes to obtain their wind direction and speed, and to better understand atmospheric circulation patterns.

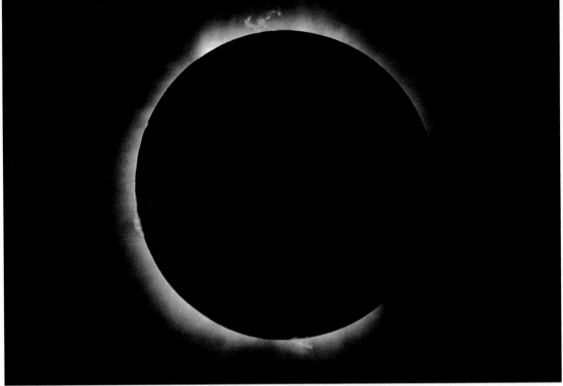

A total solar eclipse on July 11, 1991 lasted up to seven minutes. It was the astronomical event of the year.

# A SUNSATIONAL EVENT

On the island of Hawaii, people stood on roofs, airport runways, and lava flows. In Mexico, people climbed ancient Olmec pyramids. In California, people crowded beaches and mountaintops. They all had specially equipped cameras or pinhole viewers aimed at the skies. And they all had the same goal: they wanted to watch the sun disappear. But this wasn't just some spectacular sunset they were waiting for—it was the astronomical event of the year.

On July 11, 1991, the moon passed directly between the sun and Earth, covering the sun and casting a shadow. For parts of the Earth that were in the direct path of the moon's shadow, the sun appeared to have completely disappeared. It was a total solar eclipse, plunging those parts of the Earth into total darkness. In some places, the eclipse lasted for almost seven minutes. No one now living will get to see a longer eclipse —not until the year 2132 will the Earth again experience an eclipse of this significance.

The total eclipse cut a path that began over the western Pacific Ocean. Because of the Earth's rotation, it appeared to move eastward, across the island of Hawaii to south-

ern Mexico and parts of South America. Around the area darkened by the total eclipse was a much larger area that experienced a partial eclipse; only part of the sun was covered by the moon, producing a slight darkening of the sky. In southern California, 80 percent of the sun was covered, whereas in New York less than 20 percent of the sun was covered.

## DIAMOND RINGS AND SHIMMERING HALOS

What's so magnificent about a total eclipse? What exactly did the viewers see?

As the moon began to pass in front of the sun, it appeared to take a round bite out of the edge of the sun. Moving at 6,000 miles (10,000 kilometers) per hour, the moon covered more and more of the sun. Just before totality, viewers saw one last glimpse of the sun peeking out—a burst of white light that made the black moon look as if it were encircled by a diamond ring. Then, when the sun was completely covered, another wondrous sight appeared: the brilliant outer atmosphere of the sun, called the solar corona. (Normally, the sun's glare conceals the corona from viewers. The corona can be seen only during a total eclipse.) It appeared to form a wide, white halo around the dark moon. Also visible were enormous flames of burning gases called prominences, which shot outward from the sun's inner atmosphere, called the chromosphere.

Because the sky was dark, people within the path of the total eclipse saw stars and planets, which normally are visible only at night. Some also noticed strange behavior in birds and other animals, which became confused by the suddenly cool temperatures and dark skies. Songbirds stopped singing, and mammals moved to their nests to sleep.

As the Earth and the moon continued in their orbits, the moon's shadow moved out into space. For viewers on Earth, the end of the eclipse was heralded by the appearance of another diamond ring. The corona became obscured, and the sun once again began to shine its light onto the viewers.

### RARE OPPORTUNITIES

Total solar eclipses provide rare opportunities for astronomers to study the sun's atmosphere. Generally, total eclipses take place far from astronomical observatories. Scientists must make costly expeditions to set up temporary viewing sites. But the 1991 eclipse passed directly over a major observatory on the summit of Mauna Kea, a high volcanic mountain on the island of Hawaii. This observatory has the world's biggest collection of high-powered telescopes.

Unfortunately, the view at Mauna Kea was somewhat obscured. The major problem was dust in the Earth's atmosphere. This dust had come from the June explosion of Mount Pinatubo, a volcano in the Philippines. The dust, in addition to thin clouds that had formed over Mauna Kea, made it difficult to study the sun's infrared emissions.

Nonetheless, the astronomers immediately added to our knowledge of the sun. They found that the chromosphere extended some 3,700 miles (6,000 kilometers) beyond the sun's surface, making the sun larger than scientists had thought. Studies also indicated that the chromosphere was hotter and denser than had been thought.

As astronomers analyze all the data they gathered, they hope to solve certain mysteries. Why, for example, is the corona some one million degrees hotter than the sun's surface? What happens to interplanetary dust— particles left over from the creation of the

## LOOKING AT THE SUN

Never look directly at the sun during an eclipse! This is extremely dangerous, even when there isn't an eclipse. The sun's rays can cause permanent eye damage and may even cause blindness.

The safest way to look at an eclipse is through a pinhole viewer. Poke a pinhole in one side of a cardboard box. Opposite the pinhole, on the inside of the box, tape a sheet of white paper. Put the box over your head with the pinhole behind you. As you face away from the sun, the sun's rays will pass through the pinhole and project an image of the eclipse onto the white paper in front of your eyes.

People who want to look directly at the sun during an eclipse must look through extra-dark welding goggles or blackened X-ray negatives.

Whatever method you choose, be sure to talk with your parents or a teacher before viewing an eclipse.

solar system—as gravity pulls the dust toward the sun? Does it form a ring around the sun, as some scientists believe? And what is the relationship between the sun's magnetic field and the solar wind?

To discover the answers, more eclipses must be studied. Although the next total solar eclipse, which will occur over the southern Atlantic Ocean in 1992, won't last as long as the 1991 eclipse, astronomers are already preparing to view it. Like many of the people who gathered to watch the eclipse in July, these astronomers are clearly "ecliptophiles"—people who love eclipses.

JENNY TESAR
Author, *Global Warming*

133

MAKE
&
DO

You've made or bought the perfect gift. Now present it in the perfect wrapping: a colorful bag decorated with cutouts, stickers, ribbons, lace, and other materials. You can even match the design of the bag to its contents —felt animal cutouts for a cuddly teddy bear, glitter-paint strawberries for a homemade jam, or construction-paper flowers for a pretty potted plant.

If you become an orienteer, you'll never get lost in the woods! And you'll experience the excitement of a sport that combines the skills of navigation and cross-country running.

# INTO THE WOODS!

Pat was lost. A thick clump of trees loomed darkly a short way ahead, beyond a pile of small boulders. To the right, the ground rose steadily up a rooted and rocky slope. Which way to go? Pat looked at the compass, then studied the map. A "topographic" map, it showed every detail of the forest, the complete lay of the land. "Okay —I've got it," thought Pat. "Here's the pile of boulders, and here's the slope, which rises to the south. I've got to go north, down the slope. The map says there's a stream at the bottom . . . I see it." And Pat was off at a fast trot, hopping over fallen logs, toward the stream, no longer lost. "Control point number five should be just west of that willow."

Pat isn't just a hiker in the woods; Pat is a participant in orienteering, a sport that combines the skills of navigation and cross-country running. In orienteering races, the idea is to travel through unfamiliar woodland areas as quickly as possible. But unlike other races, the competitors—who are called "orienteers"—don't have to follow the same route. Each must, however, reach a series of landmarks, or control points, in a particular order. The winner is the person who reaches the control points, and the finish line, in the shortest time. But how the participants get to each control depends on their ability to read a topographic orienteering map and use a compass.

## THINKING ALL THE TIME

To "orient" yourself means to find your bearings, to understand where you are in relation to your surroundings. That's why in orienteering, a map and a compass are indispensable. While orienteering is a physically demanding sport, it's just as demanding mentally. A good orienteer is thinking all the time, consulting the map, checking the compass, looking for landmarks—often while moving at top speed in the direction of the next control.

The topographic maps used in orienteering are called "O-maps." They are very detailed, much more than the average road map. Lakes, streams, rivers, ponds, swamps, wooded areas, and clearings are all represented, as are hills and valleys, trails and roads, and vegetation. Contour lines indicate the lay of the land—close together, they signify steep ground; farther apart, they mean the slope is more gradual. O-maps will frequently identify such tiny details as boulders and small caves and ditches. In addition to roads, O-maps will point out human-made objects such as fences, cabins, and power lines. Of course, the control points are marked too.

In the woods, the control points are usually designated by orange and white markers. But even with the map, the controls aren't easy to find. They aren't supposed to be; otherwise, it would be too easy for you to accidentally happen upon one. In addition to map and compass, every orienteer carries a scorecard. To prove that you have reached a control, you must use the special hole punch that is kept at each checkpoint and punch the card—in much the same way that a train conductor punches a ticket. Then it's back to the map and compass and the search for the next control.

Here's where the heavy brainwork starts. Examining the map, you realize that control point number six is just beneath a low ridge about a half mile to the east. The route straight to the ridge looks like flat ground, through the woods, of course, although otherwise easy to cover.

But wait: The map says that some wetlands lie in there, perhaps even a mosquito-infested swamp. Would it be better to take the direct route, which might mean sloshing through a lot of muck? Or would it be faster to take the roundabout route that goes through higher and drier ground?

A quick decision is needed—you're losing time! "It hasn't rained much lately. Maybe the wetlands have dried out a bit . . . " And off you go toward the swamp. Thinking, always thinking, you approach the wet ground

Every orienteer must use a special map and compass to reach a series of landmarks, or control points. The control points are designated by white and orange markers. When you reach one, you must use a special hole punch to punch your scorecard.

and look for vines hanging from trees that may help you swing across. And as you dash onward, you're watching for your landmark, the low ridge.

Some other orienteer, in the meantime, has chosen the high ground, reaching the ridge by circling in from the north. It's a longer run, but there's little chance of getting bogged down with a bunch of frogs!

Which route would you have chosen?

### YOU CAN COMPETE, AND YOU CAN HAVE FUN

Orienteering developed in Sweden in the early 1900's, and to this day, many of the world's best competitors are from Scandinavian countries. The sport remains so popular in Sweden that an event lasting several days can attract thousands of participants.

Orienteering reached North America in the 1940's, but it didn't receive much attention for two decades. People in the military, however, saw the value of orienteering in the training of soldiers—it was a means of learning survival skills and the ways of the wilderness. In 1970, the first United States orienteering championships were held, and five years later, the first North American championships took place.

Orienteering has grown enormously in popularity. People of all ages are drawn to the sport, and there are clubs for both young people and adults. And not all orienteers are racers. Today orienteering is a recreational pastime as well as an intensely contested sport. Many participants enjoy just navigating and walking through orienteering courses. A hike in the woods is an invigorating exercise, and the mental stimulation of deciphering an O-map adds considerably to the fun. (Other types of orienteering involve travel by horseback, bicycle, cross-country skis, canoe, and even wheelchair.)

What about bad weather? In this sport, there's no such thing. Orienteering events are rarely canceled; they have been held in furious rainstorms and even blizzards. If you're going into the wilderness to confront nature, you've got to be ready to face all it has to offer, whether mild or unforgiving.

What's the best way to practice for orienteering competition? If you're going to become a serious contender, you must be in good shape, since the physical side of the sport requires stamina and speed. Cross-country running is a recommended exercise. The mental side of orienteering is just as important: A good runner who can't read an O-map will spend a lot of time running around in circles. So of equal value to physical conditioning is technical training, learning to read and interpret O-maps.

You can sharpen your ability by running over orienteering courses while reading your map. You can also sit at home studying a map and trying to picture in your mind exactly what the locality looks like. One top competitor received a lot of technical training when he was an O-map maker. His job was to take a "base map," a general map of a proposed orienteering area, and walk through the woods and fill in all the details. In this way, he learned how to pick out significant landmarks, how to read the rises and falls of a region, how to gauge the density of brush and forest.

Because more and more people of different ages and abilities have taken up orienteering, six different types of orienteering courses have been laid out.

The beginners' course enables participants to become used to reading maps, by finding and following easily located streams and trails. Advanced beginners must be able to leave the streams and trails now and then to find a control point, and then return to the original course they were following. On these courses, the controls are usually located at boulders, trees, or other large landmarks. On the third type of course, orienteers must move successfully cross-country while searching out large landscape features, such as a vast rock formation.

The top three courses are all equally difficult, but they vary in length, ranging up to 10 miles (16 kilometers). The world's best orienteers often compete on courses with few major terrain features, so very advanced skills are necessary, including the ability to identify subtle changes in landforms. The control points are usually located farther away from each other and in spots that are harder to find. At this level, you've got to be good—and even the top orienteers get lost occasionally.

When it comes right down to it, orienteering is a simple sport, requiring only that you get from "here" to "there." You're usually on your own, too, unless you're orienteering

## BE PREPARED!

When you go into the woods, it's wise to pay heed to the Boy Scout motto: "Be prepared." You've got to bring suitable gear. But "being prepared" can mean different things: A hiker on the Appalachian Trail probably requires a large backpack, including tent, sleeping bag, clothing, an extra pair of shoes, cooking stove, and plenty of food. An orienteer, on the other hand, needs just an O-map, a compass, and proper clothing.

• **O-map.** All orienteers carry O-maps of the area in which they are competing. Intricately detailed, these maps are extremely accurate representations of the territory.

• **Compass.** All orienteers use special compasses. The baseplate type of compass, in which the needle rests in a clear plastic baseplate, allows you to set a course from your current location to where you want to go. Another type of orienteering compass hooks onto your thumb; it's easy to use because you can hold it on the map as you are moving through the woods. But you can't set your course with it.

• **Clothing.** Competitive orienteers frequently prefer nylon running suits, gaiters (lightweight shin guards, which provide extra protection for the lower legs), and a sturdy pair of running shoes. If you aren't racing, but are just in the woods for an orienteering hike, then choose any loose, comfortable clothing and a pair of hiking boots. Shorts usually aren't recommended—they aren't protective enough. It's also a good idea to carry a whistle, to signal for help in case of injury.

in a team. In an orienteering race, you may not even see any of the other competitors: Everyone starts at a different time, to eliminate the possibility of contestants following each other. And if you're particularly pleased with yourself when you reach the finish line, you have a right to be. You've accomplished something. Plus, you've had the pleasure of experiencing nature in the most basic way—finding your way through a wilderness on foot. As one orienteer said, "I love the outdoors. Orienteering gives me one more way to go to the woods and enjoy myself."

# LET'S FACE IT

One of the best-known tourist attractions in the United States turned 50 years old in 1991. It's a huge sculpture, carved in solid granite, and on a clear day it can be seen from as far as 60 miles (100 kilometers) away.

This famous monument was chiefly the work of American sculptor Gutzon Borglum, who began carving it in 1927. After Borglum's death in early 1941, the work was completed under the direction of his son Lincoln.

To learn the name of the monument, you need a pencil and a sheet of lined paper. Carefully follow the directions given below. Hint: It will be easier if you rewrite the complete words at each step. The solution is on page 413.

1. Print the words GUTZON BORGLUM. Leave the words separated as you continue to work.

2. Remove the fourth letter from the left.

3. Find the second vowel from the left. Move it in front of the first vowel from the left.

4. Insert an E between the R-G combination.

5. Find the second consonant from the right. Replace it with an S.

6. Put an M after the first letter from the left.

7. Place an R after the fifth vowel from the left.

8. Remove the letter that comes after A in the alphabet.

9. Reverse the order of the last two letters of the first word.

10. Insert an H between the E-G combination.

11. Move the first three letters of the second word to the end of that word.

12. Reverse the order of the first five letters of the second word.

13. Remove all G's.

Borglum's spectacular sculpture in South Dakota honors four U.S. presidents: George Washington, Thomas Jefferson, Theodore Roosevelt, and Abraham Lincoln.

# TIP
# TOP
# TIES

It's a hot new fad: Take Dad's old neckties and decorate them in exciting new ways. Glue on bangles and beads. Add pieces of lace that you have colored with felt-tip markers. If the tie has a design, highlight the curves and curlicues with glitter paint or sequins. Try using puff paints to write a serious or a silly message on a solid-color tie: "Save the Whales!" "It's my birthday!" "Hi, there!" "I'm soooooo cool!" Paste on felt cutouts of animals, pink birthday candles, or yellow smile faces. Cover the entire front of the tie with bright red feathers—or with feathers dyed to match your school colors. Ask your best friends to autograph a solid-color tie. There are dozens of ways to change an ordinary necktie into a work of art. Your creations will be fun to wear. And they will make terrific presents for family and friends—even dear old Dad.

# STAMP COLLECTING

The year 1991 saw hundreds of new stamps issued by countries around the world. Favorite subjects, such as animals and famous people, were joined by new ones, including the Persian Gulf War.

In that war, allied military forces led by the United States drove Iraqi troops from Kuwait early in 1991. Kuwait marked the event with a set of special liberation stamps, showing doves in the colors of allied flags. Other countries also issued stamps on this theme. Among them were Saudi Arabia, Micronesia, and Palau and the Marshall Islands in the Pacific, both of which had soldiers serving in the operation. The United States issued a stamp that showed the medal given to all U.S. soldiers who served in the operation, which was named Desert Shield/Desert Storm.

### U.S. STAMPS

The United States issued an unusually large number of stamps in 1991, and the main reason was an increase in postal rates early in the year. Because the new first-class rate of 29 cents wasn't set until the last minute, the Postal Service released several stamps that carried the letter F instead of the rate. Fittingly, a flower and a flag were shown on two of these stamps.

American history was an important theme in 1991. A sheet of ten 29-cent stamps marked the entry of the United States into World War II in 1941. The stamps, each different, showed important events and people of the war. On the sheet, they were arranged above and below a world map that showed the locations of major events.

A far older historic event was shown on a 50-cent airmail stamp: the arrival of the first Americans, who crossed from Asia to what is now Alaska thousands of years ago. Asia and Alaska are now separated by the Bering Strait, but it's thought that during the Ice Age a bridge of land linked the regions. This stamp was part of the America series, issued in cooperation with Spain, Portugal, and the twenty-five member countries of the Postal Union of the Americas.

As always, important people from the past were honored on stamps. Among them was the composer Cole Porter. A group of fa-mous comedians, including Abbott and Costello and Laurel and Hardy, were shown in caricatures by the well-known artist Al Hirschfeld. Jan Matzeliger, inventor of a shoe-lasting machine (which shaped the upper parts of shoes) in the 1880's, was shown on a new stamp in the Black Heritage series. And stamps also honored Dennis Chavez, who was the first Hispanic U.S. senator, and former Supreme Court Chief Justice Earl Warren. These two stamps were controversial because they were printed in Canada—the first U.S. stamps ever printed outside the United States.

A new airmail stamp showed Harriet Quimby, who in 1911 became the first U.S. woman to fly solo across the English Channel. A colorful hot-air balloon was featured on a 19-cent stamp. And ten attractive 29-cent stamps focused on space exploration.

Two new "love stamps" were also released. A 29-cent stamp showed the world in the form of a heart, and a 52-cent stamp showed a pair of lovebirds. Love stamps have been among the most popular U.S. issues in recent years.

Sports were featured on a stamp that marked the 100th anniversary of basketball and in five stamps honoring Olympic track and field events. These looked ahead to 1996, when the Summer Olympics will be held in Atlanta, Georgia. Several other stamps, including a 29-cent stamp and a $9.95 express mail stamp, featured the five linked rings that are the Olympic symbol.

### STAMPS AROUND THE WORLD

Canada's 1991 stamps covered everything from modern art to prehistoric life. A new stamp in the Masterpieces of Canadian Art series showed Emily Carr's painting *Forest, British Columbia*. Painted in the late 1920's, this work evokes the strength and splendor of the northern forests.

Four Canadian folktales—from Nova Scotia, Alberta, Quebec, and Labrador—were shown on a group of 40-cent stamps. Canada also honored its heritage with four stamps showing Ukrainian settlers of the 1800's. Ukrainians today make up one of Canada's largest ethnic groups.

# 1991 STAMPS FROM AROUND THE WORLD

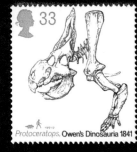

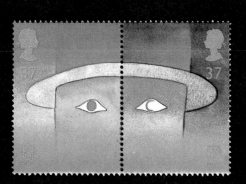

EASTER 1984

MINNIE MOUSE

**...ANDS 45¢**

Turks & Caicos Islands

WORLD CUP "ESPAÑA 82"

DONALD DUCK and DAISY DUCK

Commonwealth of **DOMINICA** 60¢

...NIA

**LESOTHO** 15S

Chip 'n' Dale with a Christmas cracker

**Turks & Caicos Islands**

SCROOGE McDUCK

**80¢**

EASTER 1981

HUEY

© MCMLXXXI Walt Disney Productions

**BHUTAN 4CH**

THE LIGHTHOUSE OF ALEXANDRIA, EGYPT

**Sierra Leone**

1¢

MICKEY MOUSE

Space Ark Fantasy

Le 2 **Sierra Leone**

MICKEY MOUSE

Space Ark Fantasy

Le 3 **Sierra Leone**

DONALD DUCK

Space Ark Fantasy

3¢ **Sierra Leone**

GOOFY

Space Ark Fantasy

FROM "BEDKNOBS AND BROOMSTICKS"

...Productions

**LA 7¢**

DIAMONDS OF SIERRA LEONE

Le 250 **SIERRA LEONE**

Commonwealth of **DOMINICA**

TOM SAWYER

MARK TWAIN

1985 CHRISTMAS

**$1.00**

Aunt Polly's Pain Killer

Dramatic designs depicted dangerous public-service occupations—police and fire departments, search and rescue groups, and ski patrols—in another group of four Canadian stamps. Canada also honored four famous doctors: neurosurgeon Wilder Graves Penfield; Jennie K. Trout, Canada's first woman physician; Harold R. Griffith, who pioneered in anesthesia, and Frederick G. Banting, who discovered insulin.

In June, Canada marked Environment Week with five colorful stamps showing different public gardens. Each featured a flowering plant in the foreground, with a view of the garden behind. Canada also completed its series on small craft with stamps showing a kayak, a rowboat, a dinghy, and a canoe. And it began a new five-stamp series on Canadian rivers. Canada also added four stamps to a series depicting fossils of ancient plants and animals.

Britain also showed ancient life on stamps—in this case, dinosaurs. Each of the five stamps in this set showed a detail of a dinosaur skeleton and a silhouette of the prehistoric creature. Stamps from British Antarctic Territory and New Zealand were among others showing dinosaurs in 1991.

Space was the theme of the 1991 Europa stamps, issued by members of the Conference of European Posts and Telecommunications Administrations. Several countries showed satellites, but Britain took an unusual approach and showed abstract designs. They were issued in se-tenant pairs, in which two stamps together made up each of two designs.

Yet another unusual British set was a se-tenant booklet of ten stamps that made up a fanciful scene with a rainbow, charms, black cats, four-leaf clovers, and other items relating to superstitions about luck. Britain's more traditional issues included five commemoratives depicting roses and five dog stamps that reproduced paintings by the 18th-century artist George Stubbs.

Animals were featured on stamps from many countries. Two Swiss stamps showed a rabbit and a pair of barn owls, while Germany depicted endangered dragonflies. Suriname showed colorful jungle birds, Australia featured insects, and Gambia showed butterflies. Zambia depicted some of the animals in *Aesop's Fables*.

Animals also appeared on twelve stamps from the United Nations Postal Administration. In se-tenant blocks of four, these stamps showed the wildlife of different regions of Europe. They saluted the environmental work of the U.N. Economic Commission for Europe.

The United Nations also issued a special group of six stamps with colorful designs by children. These stamps publicized the Convention on the Rights of the Child, a document that has been adopted by many countries as a way of ensuring the protection and well-being of children.

Several Irish stamps—including one showing a child's horse tricycle of 1875 and a "love" stamp that showed a boy and a girl kissing—were among the many other interesting releases of the year. Israel issued a group of stamps with special messages: "Greetings," "Keep in Touch," and "Happy Birthday." A German stamp honored the famous composer Wolfgang Amadeus Mozart, while a Soviet stamp showed the human rights activist and Nobel Prize winner Andrei Sakharov. And several countries showed cartoon characters on their stamps. These included the Flintstones and the Jetsons (on stamps from Mongolia and St. Vincent), Archie (on stamps from Antigua and Barbuda), and a growing number of Walt Disney characters.

### A TOPICAL COLLECTION

Stamps featuring Disney characters have been issued by many countries since 1970, when the first such stamp appeared. These stamps make a good subject for a topical collection—a collection built around a single theme.

In 1991 alone, there were new Disney stamps from such countries as Bhutan, Gambia, Lesotho, Uganda, Antigua and Barbuda, Dominica, and Grenada. They included some unusual ones—Bhutan, for example, showed Disney characters exploring the wonders of the world, while Antigua and Barbuda showed Mickey Mouse as a Japanese sumo wrestler. In fact, there are so many Disney stamps that some collectors focus on certain characters, such as Mickey or Donald Duck.

CHARLESS HAHN
Stamp Editor, *Chicago Sun-Times*

# 50¢

# LET'S HAVE A TAG SALE

Do you have toys that you no longer play with? Clothing that no longer fits? Comic books you've read and don't want to keep? Do you have other unused items that are gathering dust or cluttering drawers and closets? If so, why not hold a tag sale! You can sell these items to people who want them, and make some money along the way.

First, gather everything you want to sell. Clean all the items so that they look as good as possible. Then organize them—all the books in one box, all clothes in another box, all your toys in still another.

Ask your parents if they have anything they would like to donate to your tag sale. Invite friends to set up tables with their tag sale items. Generally, the larger the sale—that is, the more items there are for sale—the more buyers it will attract. If some of your friends would like to participate but have no tag sale items, suggest that they make lemonade or cookies to sell.

Mark the price of each item on a tag or easily removable sticker. Then people can browse through everything for sale without having to find you and ask what the price is. People like to feel they're getting a bargain, so don't price things too high. But don't ask too little, either. You might want your parents to help you with the pricing.

Many tag sale customers are at school or work during the week, so hold your sale on a Saturday or Sunday. Make signs announcing the sale, and ask local stores to display them. Also put advertising flyers in your neighbors' mailboxes.

It's finally tag sale day! Arrange all your tagged items, put a smile on your face, and get ready to say good-bye to old items as they leave for new homes.

# GOING PLACES

School's out for the summer, and all your classmates are traveling. Each student is visiting a place that contains his or her name. Abe is in the Scottish city of ABErdeen. Van is in PennsylVANia. Can you figure out where the other students are vacationing? (You may want to use maps in your encyclopedia to help you.)

Al is flying to an island country in the Mediterranean.

_ A L _ _

Ann is in the largest city in South Africa.

_ _ _ A N N _ _ _ _ _ _

Ben is swimming in a bay between India and Burma.

B E N _ _ _

Carl is exploring these caves in New Mexico.

C A R L _ _ _ _

Dan is seeing the desert in a country south of Egypt.

_ _ D A N

Ed is touring the capital of Alberta.

E D _ _ _ _ _ _

Eve is in a city on Lake Erie.

_ _ E V E _ _ _ _

Jack is photographing the capital of Mississippi.

J A C K _ _ _

Pat is on a cold, windy plateau in Argentina.

P A T _ _ _ _ _ _

Peg is visiting friends in the capital of Manitoba.

_ _ _ _ _ P E G

Peter is enjoying a sunny day in this city in Florida.

_ _ _ _ _

P E T E R _ _ _ _ _

Rita is riding a camel in this country in western Africa.

_ _ _ R I T A _ _ _

Ron is hiking through mountains in New York State.

_ _ _ R O N _ _ _ _ _

Stan is seeing the largest city in Turkey.

_ S T A N _ _ _

Tim is in Maryland's largest city.

_ _ _ T I M _ _ _

Tina is traveling through this South American country.

_ _ _ _ _ T I N A

**ANSWERS:** Malta; Johannesburg; Bengal; Carlsbad; Sudan; Edmonton; Cleveland; Jackson; Patagonia; Winnipeg; Saint Petersburg; Mauritania; Adirondacks; Istanbul; Baltimore; Argentina.

# HUNG UP ON HATS

Whatever the season, whatever the occasion, there's a perfect hat
for it. Perhaps it's an ordinary hat that you buy in a store. Much better,
though, is a one-of-a-kind hat that you yourself create.

Going to a funky party? Wear a beret decorated with glittering jewels . . . or a baseball cap covered with your collection of happy-face
buttons . . . or a glitzy sequined top hat. Spending the afternoon at the
beach? Keep the sun out of your eyes with a sombrero covered with
colorful pompoms and rickrack . . . or a visor with a dragonfly hovering on the brim . . . or a straw hat filled with dried flowers.

One of the simplest ways to decorate a hat is to tie a scarf around
the crown (the part of the hat that covers the head). Knot the scarf at
the back of the crown, letting the ends dangle over the brim (the part

that projects from the base of the crown). If the scarf is long enough, make a big bow. Wide ribbons can be substituted for scarves. This type of hat-decorating technique is a really terrific way to match hats to specific outfits—just replace one scarf or piece of ribbon with another.

Another way to match hats and outfits is to use leftover pieces of fabric from clothes that you or your mom have made or even altered. Cut a long, wide strip of the fabric on the bias (diagonal to the weave). Tie the strip around the crown of a straw hat. Or use the fabric to cover the edge of the brim.

Almost any small object can be glued onto a hat. In general, use a hot glue gun, which can be purchased at a craft store, to attach the objects. Begin by making a simple hat. Decorate a plastic visor with puffy satin hearts . . . or attach a red silk rose to a sailor's cap . . . or glue pastel teddy bears onto a baseball cap. Always try positioning the objects in different ways *before* you do any gluing. When you're completely satisfied with the arrangement, glue the pieces in place.

Some of the most beautifully decorated hats are those covered with lots of flowers and leaves. Use dried flowers or silk flowers—or use both together. If you're working with dried flowers, you must handle them gently. Most dried flowers are quite fragile. Begin by making a bow with long streamers. Use ribbon that complements the flowers and the hat. A blue-flowered ribbon would work well on a blue hat covered with red, white, and blue flowers. A peach ribbon would blend nicely with a cream-colored hat filled with peach-colored roses and dark green leaves. Center the bow on the back of the hat and glue it in place. Decide how you want to arrange the flowers and leaves. You

can circle the entire crown or put flowers only at the back. You can make a symmetrical (balanced) arrangement or one that's asymmetrical, with most of the flowers on one side of the hat.

To decorate a broad-brimmed hat for a boy or man, try using feathers, braid, or beads. For example, edge the base of the crown with silk braid that matches the shade of the hat. Join the ends of the braid on one side of the crown; then cover the ends with different kinds of feathers.

Macramé—decorative knotting—can be used to make braids to wrap around the crown of a hat. Cord, yarn, string, and even leather can be knotted and braided. A braid made of leather strips joined in square knots would look great on a cowboy hat. A more intricate braid of orange cotton string, with small beads threaded on the vertical strands, would work well on a white or cream boater.

Old jewelry, such as necklaces and bracelets, can also can be used as hat decorations. Loop a beaded Indian necklace around the base of the crown, and carefully glue it down. Cut the necklace at the back of the hat, gluing together the ends so that the beads or links join in a smooth line.

Beads can also be used individually, to create interesting patterns on a hat. Arrange the beads in a big bow on a visor . . . or combine beads with feathers to form a bird on the side of a felt hat . . . or create a bright yellow sunburst of beads on a beach hat. Sequins, buttons, glitter, and fake jewels can also be glued onto hats. And don't forget tiny mirrors—the Chinese used to decorate baby caps with mirrors to ward off evil spirits. Perhaps this ancient practice will work well for you, too!

If you collected shells on your last visit to the seashore, you can use them to decorate a hat. Place a strip of white or beige grosgrain ribbon around the crown of a hat. Cover the ribbon ends with a small grouping of scallop, clam, and whelk shells. Glue a few glittery pearls among the shells and your hat will be a true treasure!

Going on a picnic? Cover a visor or baseball cap with candy corn or popcorn. Be sure to first use several coats of acrylic spray to cover and preserve the food.

Paints also offer many possibilities. Use a brush and acrylic paints to create a design on a straw hat. Make an abstract design of squiggles or lightning bolts . . . or tint a spring garden on the hat . . . or create colorful masses of tropical fish. Before painting the design, you might think about spray painting the entire top surface of the hat. Spray paint it black, and then use neon paints for a bubble design . . . or spray paint it pale green, add a matching ribbon and bow, and then paint on lots of pink roses. Once a hat is painted, glue on glitter, fake jewels, or sequins. For example, place rhinestones on rose petals or add glitter waves among schools of circling fish.

Puff paints are also fun to use to create hat designs. Puff paints come in small squeeze bottles. Apply the paint, let it dry, and then turn over the fabric and iron the reverse side of the design. In seconds, the paint puffs up and becomes three-dimensional. Use puff paints to create a geometric design around the crown of a painter's cap . . . use them to write your name on a beret . . . highlight the pattern on a scarf with puff paints, and attach the scarf to a hat. Work carefully: puff paints are permanent, so you want to avoid mistakes.

Some hats are permanent creations. Many others can be redesigned if you get tired of them. It's easy to remove a scarf wrapped around a hat—and replace it with a different scarf, a ribbon, or a huge jeweled pin. Decorations attached with a hot glue gun can often be removed, too. Pull the objects off gently, to avoid tearing the hat or breaking the decorations.

As you become more experienced at decorating hats, consider making them not only for yourself but also for family and friends. You may even want to make enough to sell. Hats are great gifts, especially when they allow the wearer to express his or her personality and to stand out in a crowd.

If you make hats for other people, consider their interests and lifestyle. Felt ducks would look cute on an infant's hat . . . plastic baseballs and other sports charms are great for a boy's cap . . . fishing lures stuck in a grosgrain ribbon are perfect on a straw hat for Father's Day. If you give people hats they like, they, too, will soon be "hung up on hats."

# A LEAP OF LEOPARDS

You've probably seen a herd of cattle. But have you ever seen a leap of leopards?

A herd of cattle is a group of cattle. Similarly, a leap of leopards is a group of leopards. Many other groups of animals have also been given certain names. Some of these names are wonderfully descriptive: a shrewdness of apes, an unkindness of ravens, a labor of moles.

The names of 25 animals are listed below (in the left column). Match each to its group (in the right column).

| | | | |
|---|---|---|---|
| **1.** ant | | **a.** business |
| **2.** bee | | **b.** charm |
| **3.** crow | | **c.** colony |
| **4.** duck | | **d.** convocation |
| **5.** eagle | | **e.** crash |
| **6.** elephant | | **f.** descent |
| **7.** ferret | | **g.** exaltation |
| **8.** finch | | **h.** flock |
| **9.** fish | | **i.** gaggle |
| **10.** frog | | **j.** herd |
| **11.** goose | | **k.** host |
| **12.** kangaroo | | **l.** knot |
| **13.** lark | | **m.** murder |
| **14.** lion | | **n.** nest |
| **15.** locust | | **o.** ostentation |
| **16.** nightingale | | **p.** paddling |
| **17.** owl | | **q.** parliament |
| **18.** peacock | | **r.** plague |
| **19.** pony | | **s.** pride |
| **20.** rabbit | | **t.** rafter |
| **21.** rhinoceros | | **u.** school |
| **22.** sheep | | **v.** swarm |
| **23.** sparrow | | **w.** string |
| **24.** turkey | | **x.** troop |
| **25.** woodpecker | | **y.** watch |

**ANSWERS:** 1,c; 2,v; 3,m; 4,p; 5,d; 6,j; 7,a; 8,b; 9,u; 10,l; 11,i; 12,x; 13,g; 14,s; 15,r; 16,y; 17,q; 18,o; 19,w; 20,n; 21,e; 22,h; 23,k; 24,t; 25,f.

152

Next, go on a hunt. The names of all 25 animals are hidden in this search-a-word puzzle. Try to find them. Cover the puzzle with a sheet of tracing paper. Read forward, backward, up, down, and diagonally. Then draw a neat line through each name as you find it. One name has been shaded in for you.

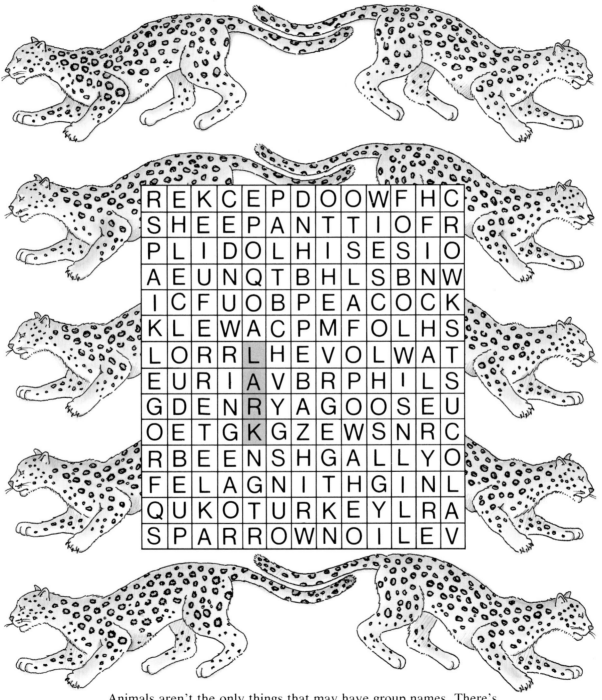

| R | E | K | C | E | P | D | O | O | W | F | H | C |
|---|---|---|---|---|---|---|---|---|---|---|---|---|
| S | H | E | E | P | A | N | T | T | I | O | F | R |
| P | L | I | D | O | L | H | I | S | E | S | I | O |
| A | E | U | N | Q | T | B | H | L | S | B | N | W |
| I | C | F | U | O | B | P | E | A | C | O | C | K |
| K | L | E | W | A | C | P | M | F | O | L | H | S |
| L | O | R | R | L | H | E | V | O | L | W | A | T |
| E | U | R | I | A | V | B | R | P | H | I | L | S |
| G | D | E | N | R | Y | A | G | O | O | S | E | U |
| O | E | T | G | K | G | Z | E | W | S | N | R | C |
| R | B | E | E | N | S | H | G | A | L | L | Y | O |
| F | E | L | A | G | N | I | T | H | G | I | N | L |
| Q | U | K | O | T | U | R | K | E | Y | L | R | A |
| S | P | A | R | R | O | W | N | O | I | L | E | V |

Animals aren't the only things that may have group names. There's a cluster of grapes, a slate of candidates, and a host of angels. You can even make up your own names for groups of things—for example, a learning of teachers, a cuddle of dolls, a babble of children.

An autumn garden will sprout right in your kitchen or dining room when you make this colorful harvest arch.

# POPULAR CRAFTS

Crafts enrich our lives in important ways. When we make something with our hands, using our own skills, we get a deep feeling of satisfaction. Sometimes we create an object using only our imagination as a guide. But even if we follow step-by-step instructions, we still put something of ourselves, something unique, into everything we make.

And when the project is completed, we aren't really finished! Now we can share what we've made—either by displaying our craft for others to see or by giving it to someone special. Often it isn't just the completed project that's given to others. Once a person discovers a good design, it can be passed along like a favorite recipe. Each person may change the design a bit, but these changes make the shared design more special.

There are so many different kinds of craft projects, using an almost endless variety of materials. Here are four popular projects for you to try.

### A HARVEST ARCH

Brighten your kitchen or dining room wall with a vegetable garden—one that will always looks fresh and pretty.

To make this harvest arch, you need a sheet of plastic foam, foam shapes, paper twist in various colors, natural-colored raffia, Spanish moss, dried or silk eucalyptus leaves, some dried flowers and wheat heads, heavy wire, a sharp knife, and a glue gun.

Begin by cutting out an arch shape from the plastic foam sheet—this will serve as the base. Attach a wire hanger to the back. Glue Spanish moss over the front and sides of the arch. Then glue short pieces of eucalyptus leaves to the front, letting some of the moss show from underneath.

Create several different kinds of fruits and vegetables by covering the foam shapes with the paper twist. For each item, cut two lengths of twist; overlap and glue them together along the edges, to form a tube. Place the tube over a foam shape, and twist and indent the paper until it has the form that you want. Add stems, tendrils, and leaves of green twist.

Glue the fruits and vegetables to the front of the arch. Place dried flowers and wheat among the leaves. Finish by making a flowing raffia bow and gluing it to the bottom center of the arch.

Your vegetable garden has sprouted, and it's ready to be displayed.

## STAR OF HEARTS

No weaving is necessary to create this charming hanging, which is based on an ancient Scandinavian craft.

You will need 24 wheat straws without heads, pre-woven straw ribbon, 9 straw roses, natural-colored raffia, ivory satin ribbon, a beige button, scissors, needle and thread, and a glue gun.

Cut the wheat straws to 10-inch (2.5-centimeter) lengths. Clean the straws and soak them in a mixture of vinegar and water for about fifteen minutes; this will make them flexible. Soak the straw ribbon for about five minutes before using it.

The center base will be an eight-pointed star made from the wheat straws. Place the 24 damp straws in a bundle and use thread to tie them together around the middle. Take two adjacent straws and tie them together 2 inches (5 centimeters) from the center tie. Skip one straw. Tie the next two straws together, also 2 inches from the center tie. Repeat until you have a circle of alternating single and paired straws.

Now you're going to create eight diamond shapes, which will form the star. Each diamond is made from a single straw and the pairs on its left and right, with the single straw coming down the center of the diamond. Start with a single straw. Take one straw from the pair at the left and, at the

Straw hearts and flowers are fashioned into this charming hanging, which is based on an old Scandinavian craft.

point where it's tied, bend it in toward the single straw. Then take one straw from the pair at the right and bend it in toward the single straw. Tie the three straws together at the point where they meet. Repeat until eight diamonds are formed. While the star is still wet, pin it on a board so it will dry flat.

This dainty ribbon doll will look just perfect tucked into that special little nook in your home.

After the star has dried, remove it from the board. Tie raffia over the thread ties, and add a drop of glue over the raffia knots. Cut off any straw that projects beyond the ends of the star.

Form the eight hearts from the strips of straw ribbon. Each heart consists of three strips, with the ends meeting at the top center point. Tie the ends tightly with thread.

Stitch the hearts onto the base. Tie satin bows onto the heart points, and top each bow with a straw rose.

Try hanging this lovely creation on a wall or window. It's sure to be a "star" attraction in any room.

## A RIBBON SWEETHEART

Add a touch of romance to a quiet corner in your home with this dainty ribbon doll.

You'll need about 5 yards (4.5 meters) of wide ribbon; 2 yards (1.8 meters) of narrow picot ribbon, in a coordinating color; and 1 yard (.09 meter) of narrow double-faced satin ribbon. You'll also need some white pre-gathered lace, four small ribbon roses, a beige knee-high stocking, a small amount of fiberfill, curly doll's hair, a small basket, and some dried flowers. Equipment includes needle and thread, scissors, a glue gun, and white craft glue.

Set aside about a foot of wide ribbon for the hat. Then cut ten 18-inch (4.6 centimeter) lengths of wide ribbon. Using a pencil and ruler, carefully divide each length into eight narrow strips, each 1/4-inch (0.6 centimeters) wide. Cut along the pencil lines, thus creating a total of 80 ribbon strips. Line up the strips and tie them together around the center with a piece of the satin ribbon. Put a dot of glue over the knot.

Fold the strips in half, at the point where they are tied —the satin tie is at the top, forming the "neck" of the dress. Take 24 strips from one side of the dress to form a sleeve. Cut off a couple of inches of ribbon from the ends of these strips and discard. Using a piece of the satin ribbon, tie the strips together at the hand end. Repeat this process for the other sleeve.

Form a waist a few inches down from the top of the dress. Use a length of satin ribbon for a belt, ending with long streamers in front.

Gently twist one of the sleeves backward six times. This will cause the ribbons of the sleeve to curve forward. Use the waist ties to tie the hand end of the sleeve to the front of the waist. Also tie the basket handle to the waist area. Then twist and form the second sleeve, slip its end through the basket handle, and tie it to the waist area.

The head is made from a circle cut from the knee-high stocking. Sew around the edge of the circle, pull the threads slightly, then stuff with fiberfill to form a ball. Pull the threads tight and knot. Glue the head to the top of the dress, with the threaded side to the back. Glue lace around the neck, and glue doll's hair to the head.

Make an oval hat from the remaining piece of wide ribbon, and glue lace around the edge. Using the picot ribbon, make a strap and multi-looped bow. Place the hat on the doll's head, securing it with glue. Now glue dried flowers and ribbon roses in the basket.

Set your ribbon doll on a little bench, and wait for everyone to notice her.

### WINDOWSILL DAISIES

One of the most popular quilt patterns is the "log cabin." It consists of strips of fabric sewn together in much the same way that logs are joined to build a house. In this wall hanging, that technique is used to create a window full of daisies. Beige calico fabric is used to form the window frame; four shades of blue fabric create the window panes.

After you've sewn the window quilt, you're ready to make the daisy-filled vase. Cut the vase from quilted fabric, and stitch

It will feel like springtime all year long whenever you catch a glimpse of this colorful quilted window filled with daisies.

it to the bottom of the window frame—with the top of the vase open. Cut stems, leaves, and flowers from pieces of colored fabric. Place the stems in the vase, and sew them to the window. Add the leaves and daisies. Put a small amount of fiberfill underneath the center of each flower, to create a puffy look.

Sew a rod casing onto the top back of the quilt, and slip a wooden dowel through it. Attach two curtain rings near the ends of the casing and your windowsill daisies are ready to hang—and to bring you a touch of springtime all year long.

JULIE STEPHANI
Editor, *Crafts 'n Things* magazine

# COIN COLLECTING

U.S. silver dollar marking the 50th anniversary of the United Service Organization (USO).

Coin collectors enjoyed quite a field day in 1991, with a great mix of issues from the United States, Canada, and other nations. In addition, the American Numismatic Association (ANA)—the national U.S. organization for coin collectors—celebrated its 100th year in 1991. More than 21,000 collectors flocked to the ANA's convention in Chicago, which was the site of the organization's first gathering back in 1891. Besides buying and selling coins, they were able to learn which coins are more valuable than others and why. And they had a chance to listen as experts described the proper techniques for preserving rare coins.

### U.S. COINS

The U.S. Mint offered several choices to collectors in 1991, among them three commemorative issues. Commemorative coins, like commemorative stamps, observe important events and anniversaries.

Three coins were produced by the Mint to mark the 50th anniversary of the Mount Rushmore Memorial in South Dakota. The four huge faces of presidents George Washington, Thomas Jefferson, Abraham Lincoln, and Theodore Roosevelt that appear on Mount Rushmore were begun by sculptor Gutzon Borglum in 1927 and were completed in 1941, after Borglum's death.

As part of the celebration of the anniversary, the Mint issued a silver dollar and a copper-nickel half dollar, each of which showed the sculptures. The Mint also produced a gold half eagle that showed an eagle swooping down on the mountain with sculptors' tools in its claws. Some of the proceeds from sales of the coins went toward preservation of the memorial.

Another 50th anniversary marked with a 1991 coin was that of the United Service Organization (USO). This organization serves members of the armed forces and their families all over the world, providing a range of services. In its best-known program, which began in World War II, the USO has sponsored overseas tours by hundreds of entertainers, who have performed for U.S. troops to boost morale. The silver dollar issued by the Mint to mark the anniversary not only paid tribute to the organization but also helped raise funds for USO programs.

A third commemorative silver dollar offered in 1991 saluted the U.S. men and women who served in the Korean War of 1950–53. The coin marked the 38th anniversary of the end of fighting in Korea. Part of the proceeds from sales of the coin were to go toward the cost of building a memorial to veterans of the war.

Canada's coins commemorating anniversaries of ship launchings: a silver dollar showing the *Frontenac* and a $100 gold-and-silver coin showing the *Empress of India.*

### COINS AROUND THE WORLD

Canada traditionally issues many coins each year, and 1991 was no exception. Ships and airplanes appeared on several new Canadian issues. One of these, a 1991 silver dollar, showed the *Frontenac,* the first

U.S. silver dollar commemorating the 50th anniversary of the Mount Rushmore Memorial in South Dakota.

Many nations issued coins honoring the Save the Children Fund, including these from Nepal and Mexico.

steamship to operate on the Great Lakes. The ship was launched in 1816, so the commemorative dollar marked its 175th anniversary. A $100 coin made of a gold and silver alloy depicted a second steamship, the *Empress of India*. This ship, launched in 1891, became famous for its speedy trans-Pacific voyages.

Continuing a program begun in 1990, Canada issued two coins depicting aircraft. Made of silver embossed with gold, the $20 coins featured a de Haviland Beaver, which was a popular float plane of Canadian design, and the Silver Dart, which in 1909 made the first heavier-than-air flight in Canada.

Hockey—the "national passion" in Canada—was depicted on another Canadian coin. A $200 gold piece showed children playing the game, with one of the children leaping with joy over scoring a goal.

Canada's $200 gold piece celebrating the country's "national passion"—hockey.

Seeking coins with a common theme—such as sports, aircraft, or ships—is a great way to organize a collection. One theme shared by many nations in 1991 was children. Gold and silver coins from such countries as Nepal, Cyprus, Mexico, Mongolia, Indonesia, and the Philippines honored the Save the Children Fund, an organization that aids children around the world.

With the Olympic Games slated for 1992, many nations issued coins that honored the athletes and events of the games. France, which will host the 1992 Winter Olympics, continued a series begun in 1989 with gold and silver coins depicting freestyle, slalom, and cross-country skiing; hockey; and ski jumping. Another coin in the series showed Pierre de Coubertin, who founded the modern Olympic Games in the 1890's.

The 500th anniversary of Columbus's first voyage to America was marked by coins from fourteen countries—Spain, Portugal, Mexico, and eleven nations of South and Central America. Austria issued gold and silver commemoratives honoring the famous composer Wolfgang Amadeus Mozart on the 200th anniversary of his death. Among other issues that proved popular with collectors were the first coins from the newly independent African nation of Namibia; gold, silver, and platinum coins from Australia, showing the country's unique wildlife; and Chinese coins, including a special issue that marked the tenth anniversary of China's popular Panda gold and silver coins.

### A RARE FIND

Most people who collect coins buy them from government mints or from coin dealers. And coin collecting can be an expensive hobby, especially when rare or precious-metal coins are involved. But late in 1990, a couple from Long Island, New York, acquired a rare coin in another way—with a metal detector. When their detector beeped, they dug in the earth and found a round silvery piece with a barely visible design. It turned out to be the eighth known specimen of a rare American colonial coin, the 1652 New England sixpence. The coin was a real buried treasure—it was worth about $30,000.

EARL A. SHOEMAKER
*Numismatic News*

# MANY FRIENDS COOKING

## GRAHAM CRACKER CAKE, from the United States

Thanks to Dr. Sylvester Graham, you can bake this crunchy cake from crackers named after him. Dr. Graham, who lived in the early 1800's, insisted that whole wheat flour was more healthy than white flour. And in *those* days, it was. Whole wheat flour was made by grinding the whole grain of wheat. For white flour, only the soft inside of the grain was used. The outer layers, rich with vitamins and minerals, were left out.

Today, white flour is "enriched" with the needed vitamins and minerals. But whole wheat flour is still naturally healthy. So are graham crackers, made from this flour. Use them for this one-bowl cake.

### EQUIPMENT

measuring cups
mixing bowl
measuring spoons
mixing spoon
chopper
8-inch-square cake pan

### INGREDIENTS

2 cups graham cracker crumbs
⅓ cup unsifted flour
2 teaspoons baking powder
1 cup sugar
½ cup shelled almonds
½ cup shelled walnuts
½ cup soft butter
2 eggs
1 cup milk
1 teaspoon vanilla
1 teaspoon butter
1 tablespoon flour

### HOW TO MAKE

1. Preheat the oven to 375°F.
2. Crush the crackers with your hands until you have 2 cups of coarse crumbs.
3. Put the crumbs into the mixing bowl with the flour, baking powder, and sugar. Stir.
4. Chop the almonds and walnuts into small pieces.
5. Add the soft butter, eggs, milk, vanilla, and chopped nuts to the mixing bowl.
6. Stir until the batter is well blended.
7. Grease the cake pan with the butter.
8. Sprinkle it with the flour and shake the pan until the bottom is evenly coated.
9. Pour the batter into the cake pan.
10. Bake the cake for about 45 minutes.
11. Remove the cake from the oven and let it cool. Cut into squares and serve warm.

This recipe serves 6 to 8 people.

## CHICKEN—LONG RICE SOUP, from Vietnam

Rice is the main food in the Vietnamese diet. Served boiled, fried, or made into noodles, rice appears at almost every meal. This dish consists of shredded chicken, bits of scallion, and a special cellophane noodle called "long rice," all served in a flavorful broth. You can buy "long rice" noodles in Oriental food stores. Or you can use Italian vermicelli.

### EQUIPMENT

large serving bowl
knife
medium saucepan
measuring cups
measuring spoons
mixing spoon

### INGREDIENTS

½ pound "long rice"
2 scallions
5 cups chicken broth
1 tablespoon soy sauce
   salt and pepper to taste
1 large chicken breast

### HOW TO MAKE

**1.** Place the chicken breast in the saucepan and add enough water to cover it. Bring the water to a boil and cook for three minutes. Lower the heat, cover, and simmer for 20 to 30 minutes. Remove the chicken breast and let it cool. Then skin and slice into thin strips.

**2.** If using "long rice," soak in warm water for 10 minutes. Break into pieces. If using other noodles, cook until tender following package directions.

**3.** Pile the noodles in the serving bowl.

**4.** Cut the scallions, both green and white parts, into small pieces.

**5.** Bring the chicken broth to a boil in the saucepan. Stir in the soy sauce. Season with salt and pepper. Add the cooked chicken strips and chopped scallions and cook for 1 minute over medium heat.

**6.** Pour the soup over the noodles. Serve hot.

This recipe serves 4 to 6 people.

# SPORTS

One of the most exciting sports events of 1991 was the women's final at the U.S. Open tennis championships. It was a battle of the "ages," and youth emerged the winner. Monica Seles (*left*), 17, who was ranked number one in the world, defeated legendary star Martina Navratilova (*right*), 34. Seles also won the Australian and French Opens during the year.

Cuban athletes got off to a running start at the gold medals in the 1991 Pan American Games when Alberto Cuba (number 264) finished first in the marathon.

# THE 1991
# PAN AMERICAN GAMES

One hot morning in August, 1991, a lean Cuban runner led a pack of marathoners through the streets of Havana, his nation's capital. After 26 sweltering miles, he entered Pan American Stadium, and, with his nearest challenger barely a heartbeat behind, Alberto Cuba strode across the finish line to win the first gold medal of the 11th Pan American Games. It was a coincidence that this champion's last name was the same as that of his country, and that his country was the host of the Games. But Alberto Cuba's

victory set the tone for what would follow: When the last medals were awarded more than two weeks later, Cuba—the country—had won 140 gold medals, ten more than the United States. For the first time since the Pan Am Games began in 1951, the United States finished second in golds.

The Pan Am Games, an Olympics-type competition for Western Hemisphere nations, are held every four years, each time in a different country. In 1991, some 6,000 athletes from 39 countries journeyed to Havana and Santiago, Cuba, to display their skills in track and field, swimming, basketball, baseball, softball, soccer, boxing, wrestling—in all, 29 sports.

Traditionally, competition in the Pan Am Games has been dominated by the United States, Cuba, and Canada. That didn't change in 1991. Despite Cuba's winning the most golds, the United States once again led in overall medals, with 352 (130 gold, 125 silver, and 97 bronze). Cuba was second with 265 (140 gold, 62 silver, and 63 bronze), and Canada finished third with 127 (22 gold, 46 silver, and 59 bronze).

But the glory didn't go only to the three athletic superpowers. Of the 39 countries participating in the Games, 26 won medals. Suriname, for example, garnered one gold, two silver, and one bronze. Haiti earned one bronze.

There were upsets, too. The United States women's basketball team, which hadn't lost in international competition since 1982, was nipped by Brazil, 87–84, in the qualifying round. Brazil wound up with the gold medal, defeating silver medalist Cuba, 97–76, in the final. The United States bested Canada for the bronze.

Another upset of a United States basketball team—this time, the men—came at the hands of Puerto Rico in the semifinals. With their top scorer sidelined because of an injury, the Americans fell, 73–68. Puerto Rico advanced to take the gold and Mexico the silver. The United States won the bronze with a hard-fought, foul-filled victory over Cuba.

In fact, the competition between the United States and Cuba, always heated, seemed particularly intense in 1991. The two nations have been at odds politically for more than 30 years, ever since Fidel Castro came to power and Cuba embraced communism. And athletic rivalries often reflect political ones.

Thus it was no surprise that the United States-Cuba baseball game attracted so much attention, especially since the sport is the national pastime of both countries. In the best-played game of the tournament, Cuba beat the United States, 3–2. Cuba eventually won the gold medal, defeating silver medalist Puerto Rico 18–3 in the final. The United States settled for the bronze. In the ten games it played, the Cuban team batted an astounding .399 and outscored its opponents by 145–27.

The gold medal in men's softball went to Canada, which topped the United States 3–1 in the final behind ace pitcher Terry Bell. In women's softball, the situation was reversed—the United States took the gold and Canada the silver. In the final, pitcher Lisa Fernandez won her fifth game of the tournament; the score was 14–1. U.S. pitcher Debbie Doom contributed three victories, two of which were perfect games (in which no opposing batter reaches base).

If the United States was upset in a few sports in which it usually excels, it also managed to turn the tables: It won a gold medal in soccer, outdueling silver medalist Mexico, 2–1, in overtime in the final. (Long-time powers Brazil and Argentina didn't send soccer teams to the Pan Am Games.)

U.S. swimmers also gathered the lion's share of medals, capturing 24 of 32 golds; American Amy Shaw splashed her way to three first-place finishes in three events. In freestyle wrestling, American Brad Penrith won a gold medal at the expense of Cuban world champion Alejandro Puerto; in all, U.S. freestylers amassed seven golds.

As always, Cuban boxers were in firm command, winning 11 of 12 gold medals; Steve Johnston of the United States was the only non-Cuban to punch his way to a championship. In weight lifting, the results were similar—Cubans snatched all but one of the gold medals awarded.

Ultimately, the nation of Cuba accomplished what it had set out to do: shine, both as host country and competitor.

The 1995 Pan American Games will be held in Argentina.

The Cuban baseball team routed most of its opponents, but could manage only a 3–2 victory over a strong U.S. squad. Cuba eventually won the gold medal, Puerto Rico the silver, and the United States the bronze.

# BASEBALL

Twins right-hander Jack Morris won eighteen games during the regular season, two in the playoffs, and two more in the World Series. He was named the Series MVP.

Never in baseball history had a team gone from last place in one year to a World Series championship the next. But in 1991, *both* Series contestants had been cellar dwellers the season before. And, in one of the most exciting Fall Classics in recent memory, the Minnesota Twins outlasted the Atlanta Braves, four games to three.

Manager Tom Kelly's Twins finished the regular season with an eight-game margin in the American League Western Division. It took only five games for them to dispatch the Eastern Division-leading Toronto Blue Jays in the American League Championship Series (ALCS). Minnesota center fielder Kirby Puckett won the ALCS Most Valuable Player award (MVP); he hit two homers and batted .429.

Atlanta topped the National League (NL) Western Division by only one game. They then required the full seven games to oust the Eastern Division champion Pittsburgh Pirates in the NLCS. For his victories in Games 2 and 6, 21-year-old Atlanta pitcher Steve Avery was named MVP of the NLCS. It was the Braves' first pennant since 1958, when their home was in Milwaukee.

The World Series was spectacular—three games went to extra innings, and interestingly, each of the seven contests was won by the home team. In Game 1, Twins starter Jack Morris held the Braves to two runs through the eighth inning; relievers Mark Guthrie and Rick Aguilera finished up. Meanwhile, Twins batters contributed five runs, including homers by first baseman Kent Hrbek and shortstop Greg Gagne. The final score: 5–2, Minnesota.

Game 2 saw two more Minnesota round-trippers, by designated hitter Chili Davis and third baseman Scott Leius. Kevin Tapani outpitched Atlanta's Tom Glavine for a 3–2 Twins victory.

Down two games, Atlanta wouldn't quit, going twelve innings to win Game 3 by the score of 5–4. The winning hit was a two-out single by second baseman Mark Lemke.

Lemke did it again in Game 4. With one out and the score tied in the last of the ninth, he tripled to left center; two batters later, he tagged up on Jerry Willard's fly to left, scoring the winning run on a close play at the plate. The 3–2 Atlanta decision tied the Series at two games apiece.

Game 5 was a rout: The Braves exploded to win 14–5, taking a three-games-to-two lead. Atlanta pounded out 17 hits, including two more triples by Lemke and Lonnie Smith's third homer of the Series.

Back in Minnesota for Game 6, the Twins needed to win or the Series was over. They won—in the second extra-inning game of the Series. Kirby Puckett led off the last of the eleventh with a homer to break a 3–3 tie.

The deciding game was a fitting end to a dramatic and well-played Series. Jack Morris pitched brilliantly, throwing ten scoreless innings. Meanwhile, Atlanta hurlers were shutting out the Twins through nine. But in the last of the tenth, Minnesota loaded the bases with one out, and Dan Gladden scampered home on Gene Larkin's pinch-hit single. The Twins were the champs—but both teams had played so well that neither deserved to lose. Morris, one of baseball's top pitchers for more than a decade, earned Series MVP honors.

During the regular 1991 season, Nolan Ryan of the Texas Rangers tossed the seventh no-hitter of his quarter-century career—a remarkable record. And Rickey Henderson of the Oakland Athletics surpassed Lou Brock to become baseball's all-time leading base stealer; he finished the season with 994.

Julio Franco batted .341 and became the first Ranger to win a hitting title. Atlanta's Terry Pendleton took the NL batting championship with a .319 average; that, along with his 22 homers and 86 runs batted in (RBIs), earned him the NL MVP award. The AL MVP, Cal Ripken, Jr., of the Baltimore Orioles, batted .323 and had 34 homers and 114 RBIs.

The NL Cy Young Award also went to an Atlanta player; Tom Glavine had a 20-11 record with a 2.55 earned run average (ERA). Roger Clemens of the Boston Red Sox received the AL Cy Young Award for his 18-10 record, 2.62 ERA, and 241 strikeouts.

Honored as rookies of the year were Twins second baseman Chuck Knoblauch, who hit .281 and had 25 steals, and first baseman Jeff Bagwell of the Houston Astros, who hit .294 and had 82 RBIs.

Atlanta third baseman Terry Pendleton led the National League in hitting and won the NL MVP award.

### 1991 WORLD SERIES RESULTS

|   |   | R | H | E | Winning/Losing Pitcher |
|---|---|---|---|---|---|
| 1 | Atlanta | 2 | 6 | 1 | Charlie Leibrandt |
|   | Minnesota | 5 | 9 | 1 | Jack Morris |
| 2 | Atlanta | 2 | 8 | 1 | Tom Glavine |
|   | Minnesota | 3 | 4 | 1 | Kevin Tapani |
| 3 | Minnesota | 4 | 10 | 1 | Rick Aguilera |
|   | Atlanta | 5 | 8 | 2 | Jim Clancy |
| 4 | Minnesota | 2 | 7 | 0 | Mark Guthrie |
|   | Atlanta | 3 | 8 | 0 | Mike Stanton |
| 5 | Minnesota | 5 | 7 | 1 | Kevin Tapani |
|   | Atlanta | 14 | 17 | 1 | Tom Glavine |
| 6 | Atlanta | 3 | 9 | 1 | Charlie Leibrandt |
|   | Minnesota | 4 | 9 | 0 | Rick Aguilera |
| 7 | Atlanta | 0 | 7 | 0 | Alejandro Pena |
|   | Minnesota | 1 | 10 | 0 | Jack Morris |

Visiting team listed first, home team second

# MAJOR LEAGUE BASEBALL FINAL STANDINGS

## AMERICAN LEAGUE

### Eastern Division

|  | W | L | Pct. | GB |
|---|---|---|---|---|
| Toronto | 91 | 71 | .562 | — |
| Boston | 84 | 78 | .519 | 7 |
| Detroit | 84 | 78 | .519 | 7 |
| Milwaukee | 83 | 79 | .512 | 8 |
| New York | 71 | 91 | .438 | 20 |
| Baltimore | 67 | 95 | .414 | 24 |
| Cleveland | 57 | 105 | .352 | 34 |

### Western Division

|  | W | L | Pct. | GB |
|---|---|---|---|---|
| *Minnesota | 95 | 67 | .586 | — |
| Chicago | 87 | 75 | .537 | 8 |
| Texas | 85 | 77 | .525 | 10 |
| Oakland | 84 | 78 | .519 | 11 |
| Seattle | 83 | 79 | .512 | 12 |
| Kansas City | 82 | 80 | .506 | 13 |
| California | 81 | 81 | .500 | 14 |

## NATIONAL LEAGUE

### Eastern Division

|  | W | L | Pct. | GB |
|---|---|---|---|---|
| Pittsburgh | 98 | 64 | .605 | — |
| St. Louis | 84 | 78 | .519 | 14 |
| Philadelphia | 78 | 84 | .481 | 20 |
| Chicago | 77 | 83 | .481 | 20 |
| New York | 77 | 84 | .478 | 20½ |
| Montreal | 71 | 90 | .441 | 26½ |

### Western Division

|  | W | L | Pct. | GB |
|---|---|---|---|---|
| *Atlanta | 94 | 68 | .580 | — |
| Los Angeles | 93 | 69 | .574 | 1 |
| San Diego | 84 | 78 | .519 | 10 |
| San Francisco | 75 | 87 | .463 | 19 |
| Cincinnati | 74 | 88 | .457 | 20 |
| Houston | 65 | 97 | .401 | 29 |

*League Championship Series winners

# MAJOR LEAGUE LEADERS

## AMERICAN LEAGUE

### Batting
(top 10 qualifiers)

|  | AB | H | Avg. |
|---|---|---|---|
| Franco, Texas | 589 | 201 | .341 |
| Boggs, Boston | 546 | 181 | .332 |
| Randolph, Milwaukee | 431 | 141 | .327 |
| Griffey, Jr., Seattle | 548 | 179 | .327 |
| Molitor, Milwaukee | 665 | 216 | .325 |
| C. Ripken, Baltimore | 650 | 210 | .323 |
| Palmeiro, Texas | 631 | 203 | .322 |
| Puckett, Minnesota | 611 | 195 | .319 |
| Thomas, Chicago | 559 | 178 | .318 |
| Tartabull, Kansas City | 484 | 153 | .316 |

### Home Runs

|  | HR |
|---|---|
| Fielder, Detroit | 44 |
| Canseco, Oakland | 44 |
| C. Ripken, Baltimore | 34 |
| Carter, Toronto | 33 |
| Thomas, Chicago | 32 |

### Pitching
(top qualifiers, based on number of wins)

|  | W | L | ERA |
|---|---|---|---|
| Erickson, Minnesota | 20 | 8 | 3.18 |
| Gullickson, Detroit | 20 | 9 | 3.90 |
| Langston, California | 19 | 8 | 3.00 |
| Finley, California | 18 | 9 | 3.80 |
| Clemens, Boston | 18 | 10 | 2.62 |
| Abbott, California | 18 | 11 | 2.89 |
| Morris, Minnesota | 18 | 12 | 3.43 |

## NATIONAL LEAGUE

### Batting
(top 10 qualifiers)

|  | AB | H | Avg. |
|---|---|---|---|
| Pendleton, Atlanta | 586 | 187 | .319 |
| Morris, Cincinnati | 478 | 152 | .318 |
| Gwynn, San Diego | 530 | 168 | .317 |
| McGee, San Francisco | 497 | 155 | .312 |
| Jose, St. Louis | 568 | 173 | .305 |
| Larkin, Cincinnati | 464 | 140 | .302 |
| Bonilla, Pittsburgh | 577 | 174 | .302 |
| Clark, San Francisco | 565 | 170 | .301 |
| Sabo, Cincinnati | 582 | 175 | .301 |
| Calderon, Montreal | 470 | 141 | .300 |

### Home Runs

|  | HR |
|---|---|
| Johnson, New York | 38 |
| Williams, San Francisco | 34 |
| Gant, Atlanta | 32 |
| McGriff, San Diego | 31 |
| Dawson, Chicago | 31 |

### Pitching
(top qualifiers, based on number of wins)

|  | W | L | ERA |
|---|---|---|---|
| Smiley, Pittsburgh | 20 | 8 | 3.08 |
| Glavine, Atlanta | 20 | 11 | 2.55 |
| Avery, Atlanta | 18 | 8 | 3.38 |
| Martinez, Los Angeles | 17 | 13 | 3.27 |
| Smith, Pittsburgh | 16 | 10 | 3.20 |
| Mulholland, Philadelphia | 16 | 13 | 3.61 |

Little Leaguers from Tai Chung, Taiwan, won the 1991 World Series, their fifth title in six years.

# LITTLE LEAGUE BASEBALL

Williamsport, Pennsylvania, the site of the Little League World Series, is nearly halfway around the world from Taiwan. Distance from home, however, hasn't lessened the talents of the young Taiwanese baseball players who have competed in Williamsport's Lamade Stadium each August. During the 22 years from 1969 to 1990, teams from their country have won fourteen championships. And in 1991, another group of hard-throwing, hard-hitting players extended the record, winning Taiwan's second consecutive title and its fifth in six years.

Every summer, eight regional champions play in the Little League World Series, which takes the form of a three-round tournament. The United States is represented by four of the teams; Canada, Europe, the Far East, and Latin America each send one. The 1991 champions hailed from Tai Chung, a city in western Taiwan. In the three games they played, they scored 31 runs while holding their rivals to a combined total of 3.

Under Little League rules, games are six innings long. In the final contest, Taiwan outclassed the U.S. champions, from San Ramon Valley, California, by the score of 11–0. Pitcher Pan Chih-Chiang struck out 14 of the 23 batters he faced. The game was scoreless through the first two innings, as San Ramon Valley's starting pitcher, Kevin Graham, kept Taiwan at bay with his 78-mile-per-hour fastball. But in the third inning, Fang Sheng clobbered a home run; and two innings later, Taiwan erupted for eight runs, four of which crossed the plate on Lin Wei-Chu's grand slam. A total of 36,000 fans, many watching from the hills surrounding Lamade Stadium, witnessed the game.

Taiwan had reached the final with a 3–2 defeat of the team from San Cristobal, Dominican Republic, in the first round, and a 17–1 rout of Glace Bay, Nova Scotia, in the semifinal. San Ramon Valley's victories came at the expense of Dunedin, Florida, 5–4, in the first round, and Staten Island, New York, 13–4, in the semis. Also taking part in the Little League World Series tournament were teams from Dhahran, Saudi Arabia (representing Europe), and Hamilton, Ohio. Since their first championship in 1969, teams from Taiwan·have won 47 contests while losing only 3. They have suffered just 2 losses in final games, against 15 wins.

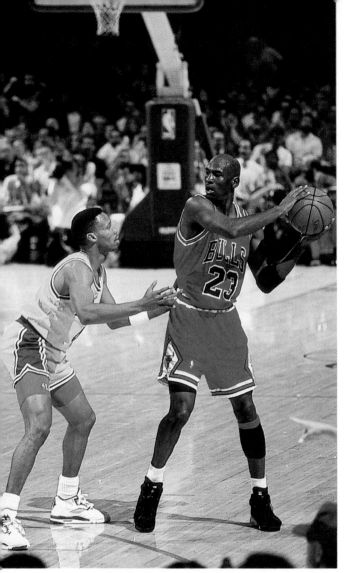

Michael Jordan led the Chicago Bulls to their first NBA championship. He was named MVP of both the regular season and the final playoffs.

# BASKETBALL

In every major sport, there have been great performers who have never played on championship teams. And after seven outstanding seasons in the National Basketball Association (NBA), Michael Jordan of the Chicago Bulls may have feared that he would suffer the same fate. But in 1991, Jordan's individual excellence combined with the superlative efforts of his teammates to bring the NBA title to the Windy City, as Chicago defeated the Los Angeles Lakers in the playoff finals, 4 games to 1.

Entering the playoffs, Chicago Coach Phil Jackson had reason to be confident. During the regular season, his Bulls forged a record of 61–21, best in the Eastern Division and second only to the Portland Trail Blazers' 63–19.

Chicago ripped the New York Knicks, 3 games to 0, in the first round of the playoffs, and then eliminated the Philadelphia 76ers in five. In the Eastern Conference finals, they met the Detroit Pistons—NBA champions for the two previous seasons. Led by Jordan, Chicago swept Detroit in four games; the last was a 115–94 rout.

In the Western Conference playoffs, Los Angeles dispatched the Houston Rockets in a three-game sweep and the Golden State Warriors in five. Then, facing Portland in the conference finals, the Lakers knocked off the Trail Blazers in six contests.

The NBA finals were touted as a showdown between Michael and Magic—the Bulls' Jordan and the Lakers' Earvin Johnson—both guards, and considered the sport's two best players. But teams, not individuals, win or lose.

Closely fought Game 1, played in Chicago, had 28 lead changes. With fourteen seconds left in the contest, and the Bulls leading by two points, Lakers forward Sam Perkins took a pass from Magic Johnson and sent a three-point shot deftly through the hoop. The final score was 93–91, Los Angeles.

The second game was close until halftime; Jordan was sluggish in the first two quarters. But he and his teammates erupted in the third period and ultimately ran away with the game by a score of 107–86. Jordan poured in 33 points, forwards Horace Grant and Scottie Pippen added 20 each, and guard John Paxson totaled 16 on eight for eight shooting.

Game 3, played in California, was close all the way; Jordan had to cash in a jump shot with less than four seconds left to tie the game as the fourth quarter ended. Then Chicago's top-rated defense took over, holding the Lakers to only four points in overtime. The Bulls won, 104–96.

In Game 4, Chicago dominated. Led by Jordan's 28 points, five Bulls scored in double figures. The final count was 97–82.

Chicago now looked unbeatable. And they were. They took Game 5 by 108–101, thereby sweeping all three contests on the Lakers' home court. Scottie Pippen tallied 32 points, and Jordan netted 30.

## NBA FINAL STANDINGS

### EASTERN CONFERENCE

#### Atlantic Division

|  | W | L | Pct. |
|---|---|---|---|
| Boston | 56 | 26 | .683 |
| Philadelphia | 44 | 38 | .537 |
| New York | 39 | 43 | .476 |
| Washington | 30 | 52 | .366 |
| New Jersey | 26 | 56 | .317 |
| Miami | 24 | 58 | .293 |

#### Central Division

|  | W | L | Pct. |
|---|---|---|---|
| Chicago | 61 | 21 | .744 |
| Detroit | 50 | 32 | .610 |
| Milwaukee | 48 | 34 | .585 |
| Atlanta | 43 | 39 | .524 |
| Indiana | 41 | 41 | .500 |
| Cleveland | 33 | 49 | .402 |
| Charlotte | 26 | 56 | .317 |

### WESTERN CONFERENCE

#### Midwest Division

|  | W | L | Pct. |
|---|---|---|---|
| San Antonio | 55 | 27 | .671 |
| Utah | 54 | 28 | .659 |
| Houston | 52 | 30 | .634 |
| Orlando | 31 | 51 | .378 |
| Minnesota | 29 | 53 | .354 |
| Dallas | 28 | 54 | .341 |
| Denver | 20 | 62 | .244 |

#### Pacific Division

|  | W | L | Pct. |
|---|---|---|---|
| Portland | 63 | 19 | .768 |
| L.A. Lakers | 58 | 24 | .707 |
| Phoenix | 55 | 27 | .671 |
| Golden State | 44 | 38 | .537 |
| Seattle | 41 | 41 | .500 |
| L.A. Clippers | 31 | 51 | .378 |
| Sacramento | 25 | 57 | .305 |

**NBA Championship:** Chicago Bulls

## COLLEGE BASKETBALL

| Conference | Winner |
|---|---|
| Atlantic Coast | Duke (regular season) North Carolina (tournament) |
| Big East | Syracuse (regular season) Seton Hall (tournament) |
| Big Eight | Oklahoma State, Kansas (tied, regular season) Missouri (tournament) |
| Big Ten | Ohio State, Indiana (tied) |
| Big West | Nevada-Las Vegas (regular season and tournament) |
| Ivy League | Princeton |
| Metro | Southern Mississippi (regular season) Florida State (tournament) |
| Missouri Valley | Creighton (regular season and tournament) |
| Pacific-10 | Arizona |
| Southeastern | Mississippi State, Louisiana State (tied, regular season) Alabama (tournament) |
| Southwest | Arkansas (regular season and tournament) |
| Western Athletic | Utah (regular season) Brigham Young (tournament) |

**NCAA, men:** Duke
      **women:** Tennessee

**NIT:** Stanford

For Jordan, the Bulls' first championship was a perfect ending to another superb individual season. He was named the Most Valuable Player (MVP) of the final playoff series; he averaged 31.2 points and 11.4 assists.

Jordan was also the regular-season MVP; he led the NBA in scoring for the fifth consecutive year, averaging 31.5 per game. San Antonio center David Robinson grabbed the rebounding crown, averaging 13.0; and Utah guard John Stockton took the assists title for the fourth year in a row, averaging 14.2. Also during the regular season, Magic Johnson surpassed the record of Oscar Robertson for career assists, finishing the year with 9,921. Late in 1991, the sports world was saddened when Earvin Magic Johnson announced that he had tested positive for the AIDS virus and was retiring from basketball.

**College Play.** The Blue Devils of Duke won the National Collegiate Athletic Association (NCAA) men's championship, besting Kansas in the final, 72–65. Duke's junior center Christian Laettner was the game's MVP, scoring 18 points and adding ten rebounds. It was Duke's first NCAA title.

Coach Mike Krzyzewski's Blue Devils, who finished the year with a 32–7 record, reached the finals by stopping the University of Nevada at Las Vegas (UNLV) by 79–77 in the semifinals. In the other semifinal, Kansas ousted North Carolina, 79–73.

The NCAA women's champion was Tennessee. Sparked by guard Dena Head's 28 points, they defeated Virginia 70–67 in overtime. The Lady Vols also won the NCAA title in 1987 and 1989.

# FOOTBALL

The unusual grabbed the limelight on the gridiron in 1991. In the National Football League (NFL), a substitute quarterback took the New York Giants to a triumph in Super Bowl XXV. In the Canadian Football League (CFL) Grey Cup game, the Toronto Argonauts were rocketed to victory by their kickoff returner. And in college football, for only the second time in history, the Heisman Trophy was snared by a wide receiver.

## THE NFL PLAYOFFS AND SUPER BOWL XXV

In 1990, the Giants topped the National Conference Eastern Division with a 13–3

Running back Barry Sanders helped the Detroit Lions earn their first playoff berth since 1983.

regular-season record. The other playoff teams from the National Conference were the Central Division champion Chicago Bears, the Western Division champion San Francisco 49ers, and the wild-card teams, the Washington Redskins, the Philadelphia Eagles, and the New Orleans Saints.

Washington upset Philadelphia in the first round of the playoffs by the score of 20–6; also in the first round, Chicago triumphed by 16–6 over New Orleans. A week later, however, the Giant defense stifled the Bears as New York rolled, 31–3. And Washington suffered a 28–10 drubbing at the hands of San Francisco.

Thus New York faced San Francisco, which had won the two previous Super Bowls, in the National Conference title game. The contest wasn't decided until the last second. With the 49ers leading by one point, and no time left on the clock, Giants placekicker Matt Bahr split the uprights with a 42-yard field goal, his fifth three-pointer of the game, giving the Giants a 15–13 win.

In the American Conference, the Buffalo Bills led the Eastern Division, the Cincinnati Bengals were first in the Central Division, and the Los Angeles Raiders took the prize in the Western Division. Wild-card spots went to the Miami Dolphins, the Houston Oilers, and the Kansas City Chiefs.

The first round of the playoffs saw Miami come back from a 16–3 fourth-quarter deficit to beat the Chiefs, 17–16. Cincinnati, meanwhile, pasted Houston, 41–14. The following week, Buffalo dropped Miami in a shootout, 44–34. In Los Angeles, the Raiders eliminated the Bengals, 20–10.

The American Conference title game was a rout; Buffalo overpowered Los Angeles, 51–3, as the Bills intercepted five Raider passes.

A number of recent Super Bowls had been "yawners," heavily lopsided affairs essentially over by halftime. But Super Bowl XXV was a thriller, the game coming down to its final four seconds.

As usual, New York was powered by its defense. But just as important to the Giants' success was a second-string quarterback—Jeff Hostetler—and a 33-year-old running

Jim Kelly of the Buffalo Bills was once again among the top-rated passers in the NFL.

back—Ottis Anderson. Giant coach Bill Parcells had turned the signal-calling duties over to Hostetler after Phil Simms was hurt during the regular season. Anderson, acquired by New York late in his career, was considered to be well past his prime as a running back.

The Super Bowl was played in Tampa, Florida, on January 27. Hostetler completed 20 passes for 222 yards, and Anderson rushed for another 102. But even so, the game was close. Buffalo led 12–10 at the half, and the Giants led 17–12 after three quarters. The Bills pulled ahead again, but halfway through the last quarter, Matt

Bahr's 21-yard field goal gave New York a 20–19 lead.

The Giants held that lead to the very end, but just barely. With four seconds remaining in the game, Buffalo placekicker Scott Norwood attempted a 47-yard field goal, which missed, just wide to the right. New York had won its second Super Bowl in five years. Ottis Anderson was named the game's most valuable player (MVP).

### THE 1991 REGULAR SEASON

During the 1991 regular season, the Washington Redskins won fourteen games. The other National Conference titlists were New Orleans and the Detroit Lions; wild-card berths went to Chicago, the Atlanta Falcons, and the Dallas Cowboys.

Buffalo, Houston, and the Denver Broncos were division champs in the American Conference; the wild-card teams were Kansas City, the New York Jets, and the L.A. Raiders.

### THE CANADIAN FOOTBALL LEAGUE

On November 24, 1991, the temperature dipped below zero in Winnipeg, Manitoba, site of the Grey Cup game. But despite the cold, a ''rocket'' blazed brightly across the Winnipeg stadium turf; Raghib ''Rocket'' Ismail led the Eastern Division champion Toronto Argonauts to a 36–21 victory over the Western Division's Calgary Stampeders. Ismail gained a record 183 yards on kickoff returns, including an 87-yard touchdown, for which he was named the game's MVP.

### COLLEGE FOOTBALL

The University of Miami, 11-0 during the regular season, was ranked number one in college football; Miami trounced Nebraska (9-1-1) in the Orange Bowl. Washington (11-0) ripped Michigan (10-1) in the Rose Bowl; Notre Dame (9-3) defeated Florida (10-1) in the Sugar Bowl; Florida State (10-2) dropped Texas A&M (10-1) in the Cotton Bowl; and California (9-2) bested Clemson (9-1-1) in the Citrus Bowl.

Desmond Howard, a junior wide receiver from the University of Michigan, won the Heisman Trophy. He caught 61 passes for 950 yards and scored 23 touchdowns. The Heisman has now gone to juniors for four straight years.

Michigan wide receiver Desmond Howard won the 1991 Heisman Trophy as the best college player.

## COLLEGE FOOTBALL

| Conference | Winner |
|---|---|
| Atlantic Coast | Clemson |
| Big Eight | Colorado, Nebraska (tied) |
| Big Ten | Michigan |
| Big West | San Jose State, Fresno State (tied) |
| Pacific-10 | Washington |
| Southeastern | Florida |
| Southwest | Texas A&M |
| Western Athletic | Brigham Young |

**Citrus Bowl:** California 37, Clemson 13
**Cotton Bowl:** Florida State 10, Texas A&M 2
**Orange Bowl:** Miami 22, Nebraska 0
**Rose Bowl:** Washington 34, Michigan 14
**Sugar Bowl:** Notre Dame 39, Florida 28

**Heisman Trophy:** Desmond Howard, Michigan

## 1991 NFL FINAL STANDINGS

### AMERICAN CONFERENCE

#### Eastern Division

| | W | L | T | Pct. | PF | PA |
|---|---|---|---|---|---|---|
| Buffalo | 13 | 3 | 0 | .813 | 458 | 318 |
| N.Y. Jets | 8 | 8 | 0 | .500 | 314 | 293 |
| Miami | 8 | 8 | 0 | .500 | 343 | 349 |
| New England | 6 | 10 | 0 | .375 | 211 | 305 |
| Indianapolis | 1 | 15 | 0 | .063 | 143 | 381 |

#### Central Division

| | W | L | T | Pts. | PF | PA |
|---|---|---|---|---|---|---|
| Houston | 11 | 5 | 0 | .688 | 386 | 251 |
| Pittsburgh | 7 | 9 | 0 | .438 | 292 | 344 |
| Cleveland | 6 | 10 | 0 | .375 | 293 | 298 |
| Cincinnati | 3 | 13 | 0 | .188 | 263 | 435 |

#### Western Division

| | W | L | T | Pct. | PF | PA |
|---|---|---|---|---|---|---|
| Denver | 12 | 4 | 0 | .750 | 304 | 235 |
| Kansas City | 10 | 6 | 0 | .625 | 322 | 252 |
| L.A. Raiders | 9 | 7 | 0 | .563 | 298 | 297 |
| Seattle | 7 | 9 | 0 | .438 | 276 | 261 |
| San Diego | 4 | 12 | 0 | .250 | 274 | 342 |

### NATIONAL CONFERENCE

#### Eastern Division

| | W | L | T | Pct. | PF | PA |
|---|---|---|---|---|---|---|
| Washington | 14 | 2 | 0 | .875 | 485 | 224 |
| Dallas | 11 | 5 | 0 | .688 | 342 | 310 |
| Philadelphia | 10 | 6 | 0 | .625 | 285 | 244 |
| N.Y. Giants | 8 | 8 | 0 | .500 | 281 | 297 |
| Phoenix | 4 | 12 | 0 | .250 | 196 | 344 |

#### Central Division

| | W | L | T | Pct. | PF | PA |
|---|---|---|---|---|---|---|
| Detroit | 12 | 4 | 0 | .750 | 339 | 295 |
| Chicago | 11 | 5 | 0 | .688 | 299 | 269 |
| Minnesota | 8 | 8 | 0 | .500 | 301 | 306 |
| Green Bay | 4 | 12 | 0 | .250 | 273 | 313 |
| Tampa Bay | 3 | 13 | 0 | .188 | 199 | 365 |

#### Western Division

| | W | L | T | Pct. | PF | PA |
|---|---|---|---|---|---|---|
| New Orleans | 11 | 5 | 0 | .688 | 341 | 211 |
| Atlanta | 10 | 6 | 0 | .625 | 361 | 338 |
| San Francisco | 10 | 6 | 0 | .625 | 393 | 239 |
| L.A. Rams | 3 | 13 | 0 | .188 | 234 | 390 |

In 1991, Payne Stewart (*left*) won the U.S. Open. And Meg Mallon (*above*) won both the U.S. Women's Open and the Ladies PGA.

# GOLF

| PROFESSIONAL | | AMATEUR | |
|---|---|---|---|
| | **Individual** | | **Individual** |
| Masters | Ian Woosnam | U.S. Amateur | Mitch Voges |
| U.S. Open | Payne Stewart | U.S. Women's Amateur | Amy Fruhwirtch |
| Canadian Open | Nick Price | British Amateur | Gary Wolstenholme |
| British Open | Ian Baker-Finch | British Ladies Amateur | Valerie Michaud |
| PGA | John Daly | Canadian Amateur | Jeff Kraemer |
| World Series of Golf | Tom Purtzer | Canadian Ladies Amateur | Adele Moore |
| U.S. Women's Open | Meg Mallon | | |
| Ladies PGA | Meg Mallon | | **Team** |
| | | Walker Cup | United States |
| | **Team** | | |
| Ryder Cup | United States | | |

Mario Lemieux's scoring and leadership propelled the Pittsburgh Penguins to their first NHL championship.

# HOCKEY

If Wayne "the Great" Gretzky is the Number 1 player in the National Hockey League (NHL), Mario Lemieux proved in 1991 what his fans have always suspected: that he is Number l-A. Despite missing 50 regular-season games with a back injury, high-scoring Mario "the Magnificent" led the Pittsburgh Penguins to their first NHL championship. They defeated the surprising Minnesota North Stars, 4 games to 2, in the Stanley Cup finals.

Since joining the Penguins as an 18-year-old in 1984, Lemieux had established himself, alongside Gretzky, as one of the foremost players in the NHL. The Pittsburgh center had won several scoring titles and numerous individual awards, but the grand prize—the Stanley Cup—had always eluded him and his Penguin teammates. Until 1991.

The Penguins' championship was no fluke. They ended the regular season at the top of the Patrick Division with 88 points on a record of 41 victories, 33 losses, and 6 ties. It was Pittsburgh's first regular-season title. The other titlists were the Boston Bruins in the Adams Division, with 100 points; the Chicago Black Hawks in the Norris Division, with 106 points; and the Los Angeles Kings in the Smythe Division, with 102 points.

On the other hand, the Minnesota North Stars, who ultimately would face Pittsburgh in the Stanley Cup finals, barely qualified for the playoffs: The team's regular-season record was clearly below par—only 27 victories against 39 defeats, plus 14 ties, for 68 points.

In the opening round of the playoffs, the Penguins needed all seven games to oust the New Jersey Devils. Then, playing for the Patrick Division championship in the second round, Pittsburgh took the measure of the Washington Capitals, 4 games to 1. Opposed by the Boston Bruins for the Wales Conference championship in round three, the Penguins prevailed, 4 games to 2.

Over in the Campbell Conference, meanwhile, the North Stars were becoming the Cinderella team of the playoffs. In round one, they bumped Chicago, owners of the NHL's best regular-season record, in six games; Minnesota outscored Chicago 12 goals to 2 in the last three contests. The North Stars also needed six games to win round two, taking the Norris Division championship by defeating the St. Louis Blues. And in the Campbell Conference finals, Minnesota blew out the Edmonton Oilers, the defending Stanley Cup champions, in a quick five games.

Minnesota was on a roll. It took Game 1

## NHL FINAL STANDINGS

### WALES CONFERENCE

#### Adams Division

|  | W | L | T | Pts. |
|---|---|---|---|---|
| Boston | 44 | 24 | 12 | 100 |
| Montreal | 39 | 30 | 11 | 89 |
| Buffalo | 31 | 30 | 19 | 81 |
| Hartford | 31 | 38 | 11 | 73 |
| Quebec | 16 | 50 | 14 | 46 |

#### Patrick Division

|  | W | L | T | Pts. |
|---|---|---|---|---|
| Pittsburgh | 41 | 33 | 6 | 88 |
| N.Y. Rangers | 36 | 31 | 13 | 85 |
| Washington | 37 | 36 | 7 | 81 |
| New Jersey | 32 | 33 | 15 | 79 |
| Philadelphia | 33 | 37 | 10 | 76 |
| N.Y. Islanders | 25 | 45 | 10 | 60 |

### CAMPBELL CONFERENCE

#### Norris Division

|  | W | L | T | Pts. |
|---|---|---|---|---|
| Chicago | 49 | 23 | 8 | 106 |
| St. Louis | 47 | 22 | 11 | 105 |
| Detroit | 34 | 38 | 8 | 76 |
| Minnesota | 27 | 39 | 14 | 68 |
| Toronto | 23 | 46 | 11 | 57 |

#### Smythe Division

|  | W | L | T | Pts. |
|---|---|---|---|---|
| Los Angeles | 46 | 24 | 10 | 102 |
| Calgary | 46 | 26 | 8 | 100 |
| Edmonton | 37 | 37 | 6 | 80 |
| Vancouver | 28 | 43 | 9 | 65 |
| Winnipeg | 26 | 43 | 11 | 63 |

**Stanley Cup:** Pittsburgh Penguins

### OUTSTANDING PLAYERS

| | |
|---|---|
| **Hart Trophy** (most valuable player) | Brett Hull, St. Louis |
| **Ross Trophy** (scorer) | Wayne Gretzky, Los Angeles |
| **Vezina Trophy** (goalie) | Ed Belfour, Chicago |
| **Norris Trophy** (defenseman) | Ray Bourque, Boston |
| **Selke Trophy** (defensive forward) | Dirk Graham, Chicago |
| **Calder Trophy** (rookie) | Ed Belfour, Chicago |
| **Lady Byng Trophy** (sportsmanship) | Wayne Gretzky, Los Angeles |
| **Conn Smythe Trophy** (Stanley Cup play) | Mario Lemieux, Pittsburgh |

of the Stanley Cup finals, played in Pittsburgh, by the score of 5–4. Neil Broten scored two goals. His second tally, at the end of the second period, broke a 3–3 tie and put the North Stars ahead for good.

Game 2 belonged to the Penguins, who won 4–1. Wing Kevin Stevens netted two goals, the first assisted by Lemieux and Larry Murphy. Lemieux later added a goal of his own; Pittsburgh goalie Tom Barrasso contributed 39 saves.

For Game 3, the series moved to Bloomington, Minnesota, where the North Stars thrilled the home fans with a 3–1 victory. Dave Gagner and Bobby Smith snapped a scoreless tie in the second period with goals only 33 seconds apart. Mario Lemieux, suffering from back spasms, sat out the game.

Lemieux returned for Game 4, and he and his teammates almost put the contest on ice within three minutes. Kevin Stevens, Ron Francis, and Lemieux all notched goals in the opening 2:58 of the first period. The North Stars fought back, but goalie Barrasso again shined in the nets for Pittsburgh, ultimately stopping 35 shots. The Penguins won, 5–3, and the series was tied at 2 games apiece.

Home again for Game 5, Pittsburgh took a 4–0 lead but had to hold on to win, 6–4. Lemieux had a goal and two assists, and wing Mark Recchi scored twice. Now up 3 games to 2, the Penguins headed back to Minnesota for what would be the finest moment in their 24-year history.

Game 6 wasn't even close. Coach Bob Johnson's Penguins grabbed another early lead—on first-period goals by Ulf Samuelsson, Lemieux, and Joe Mullen—and never let up. Barrasso shut out Minnesota with 39 saves, and the final score was 8–0. Although their namesake is a flightless bird, this group of Penguins soared.

Mario the Magnificent had 44 playoff points—second only in NHL history to Wayne Gretzky's 47—and was awarded the Conn Smythe trophy as the playoffs' most valuable player (MVP).

For the regular season, Brett Hull of St. Louis won the Hart trophy as the league's MVP; he scored 86 goals, the third highest ever. The overall scoring leader was Gretzky—the Kings' center had 163 points on 41 goals and 122 assists.

U.S. women figure skaters soared in 1991. In February, Tonya Harding (*right*) won the U.S. championship and became the first American woman to land a triple Axel. In March, Kristi Yamaguchi (*above*) won the world championship; Harding was second and Nancy Kerrigan third— making the United States the first country ever to sweep the women's medals.

# ICE SKATING

### FIGURE SKATING

#### World Championships

| | |
|---|---|
| Men | Kurt Browning, Canada |
| Women | Kristi Yamaguchi, U.S. |
| Pairs | Natalya Mishkuteniok/Artur Dmitriev, U.S.S.R. |
| Dance | Isabelle and Paul Duchesnay, France |

#### United States Championships

| | |
|---|---|
| Men | Todd Eldredge |
| Women | Tonya Harding |
| Pairs | Natasha Kuchiki/Todd Sand |
| Dance | Elizabeth Punsalan/Jerod Swallow |

### SPEED SKATING

#### World Championships

| | |
|---|---|
| Men | Johann Olav Koss, Norway |
| Women | Gunda Kleeman, Germany |

# SKIING

### WORLD CUP CHAMPIONSHIPS

| | |
|---|---|
| Men | Marc Girardelli, Luxembourg |
| Women | Petra Kronberger, Austria |

### WORLD ALPINE CHAMPIONSHIPS

#### Men

| | |
|---|---|
| Downhill | Franz Heinzer, Switzerland |
| Slalom | Marc Girardelli, Luxembourg |
| Giant Slalom | Rudolf Nierlich, Austria |
| Super Giant Slalom | Stefan Eberharter, Austria |
| Combined | Stefan Eberharter, Austria |

#### Women

| | |
|---|---|
| Downhill | Petra Kronberger, Austria |
| Slalom | Vreni Schneider, Switzerland |
| Giant Slalom | Pernilla Wiberg, Sweden |
| Super Giant Slalom | Ulrike Maier, Austria |
| Combined | Chantal Bournissen, Switzerland |

# SWIMMING

Several world records in swimming were broken in 1991. Two athletes, in particular, set notable marks. In January, at the World Championships in Australia, Joerg Hoffmann of Germany (*below*) broke the men's record in the 1,500-meter freestyle by more than four seconds, finishing in 14:50.36. The previous record, held by the legendary Vladimir Salnikov of the Soviet Union, had stood since 1983. In August, at the European Championships in Greece, Krisztina Egerszegi (*right*), a 17-year-old from Hungary, knocked nearly two seconds off the mark for the women's 200-meter backstroke. Her time was 2:06.62. At the same meet, she also notched a new record for the 100-meter backstroke, 1:00.31.

# TENNIS

In a sport in which teenage stars are commonplace, Jimmy Connors continued to play well at age 39. His high-spirited competitiveness thrilled the fans at the U.S. Open, where he reached the semifinals.

Monica Seles reached the top of women's tennis in 1991, winning three of the four Grand Slam events. She didn't compete in the other, Wimbledon, for which she was criticized. But the 17-year-old from Yugoslavia redeemed herself with a convincing victory at the U.S. Open. Seles was the youngest woman in the world ever to be ranked number one.

Heading the men's list was Stefan Edberg. The 25-year-old Swede won one Grand Slam event in 1991, the U.S. Open.

Edberg had started the year as the top-ranked man, but he was bumped to number two when Ivan Lendl bested him in the Australian Open semifinals. Lendl, in turn, was beaten in the finals by Boris Becker, 23, of Germany. Troubled by a stiff back early in the match, Becker lost the first set, 1–6. But he loosened up and won the next three sets by identical 6–4 scores. The Australian Open was Becker's fifth Grand Slam title, and it elevated him to the men's number-one ranking.

Seles, meanwhile, took the Australian final by outdueling Jana Novotna of Czechoslovakia, 5–7, 6–3, 6–1. She became the youngest woman ever to win the event.

On a roll, Seles went on to take the French Open, defending the title she had won in 1990. Her finals opponent was Arantxa Sanchez Vicario of Spain; the scores were 6–3, 6–4.

The men's competition saw the first all-American final since 1954. On a rainy, windy day in Paris, Jim Courier, 20, outlasted

---

## TOURNAMENT TENNIS

|  | Australian Open | French Open | Wimbledon | U.S. Open |
|---|---|---|---|---|
| **Men's Singles** | Boris Becker, Germany | Jim Courier, U.S. | Michael Stich, Germany | Stefan Edberg, Sweden |
| **Women's Singles** | Monica Seles, Yugoslavia | Monica Seles, Yugoslavia | Steffi Graf, Germany | Monica Seles, Yugoslavia |
| **Men's Doubles** | Scott Davis, U.S./ David Pate, U.S. | John Fitzgerald, Australia/ Anders Jarryd, Sweden | John Fitzgerald, Australia/ Anders Jarryd, Sweden | John Fitzgerald, Australia/ Anders Jarryd, Sweden |
| **Women's Doubles** | Patty Fendick, U.S./ Mary Joe Fernandez, U.S. | Gigi Fernandez, U.S./ Jana Novotna, Czechoslovakia | Larisa Savchenko, U.S.S.R./ Natalya Zvereva, U.S.S.R. | Pam Shriver, U.S./ Natalya Zvereva, U.S.S.R. |

**Davis Cup Winner:** France

## SELES IS NUMBER 1!

Her game is characterized by power. On the court, Monica Seles is a ferocious player with an unusual style: She uses a two-handed backhand, like some other players, *and* a two-handed forehand, unlike anyone else. Both are explosive, and Seles delivers the strokes with shrieklike sounds that have been compared to the shouts of a karate fighter. A natural left-hander, she has also perfected a one-handed forehand, which extends her reach. And Seles hits the ball early—"on the rise" —leaving her opponents no chance to breathe.

Born in Yugoslavia, Monica Seles was introduced to tennis by her father. She was European junior champ by age 10. In 1986, she and her family moved to Florida to further her tennis career.

In 1990, Seles won the French Open, becoming the youngest woman to win a Grand Slam title in over a century. A year later, at 17, the 5-foot 9-inch athlete achieved the top ranking in women's tennis, another first for one so young, while taking the Australian, French, and U.S. opens.

But controversy, too, beset Monica Seles in 1991. She withdrew from Wimbledon, claiming injuries. And she chose not to play in the Federation Cup, which led to her being banned from competing in the 1992 Olympics.

Andre Agassi, 21, by 3–6, 6–4, 2–6, 6–1, 6–4. Courier's triumph was his first in a Grand Slam event.

Seles caused an uproar at Wimbledon. Although top-seeded, she withdrew from the competition before play began. Seles said she had suffered injuries in a minor accident; she had also been treated for shin splints. Steffi Graf then became the number-one seed, and she didn't disappoint. The 22-year-old German, who had dominated women's tennis in 1988 and 1989, captured her third Wimbledon victory and her tenth Grand Slam title. In the final, Graf defeated Gabriela Sabatini of Argentina, 6–4, 3–6, 8–6.

On a historical note, defending champion Martina Navratilova, 34, was ousted in the quarterfinals by 15-year-old Jennifer Capriati. Thus for the first time since 1977, Navratilova didn't reach the Wimbledon semifinals; and Capriati became the youngest semifinalist ever to play at Wimbledon.

The men's competition featured the first all-German final in Wimbledon's 114 years. Underdog Michael Stich toppled Becker in straight sets, 5–4, 7–6, 6–4.

Edberg's victory in the U.S. Open finals was a rout of Courier—6–2, 6–4, 6–0. His fifth Grand Slam title, it strengthened the number-one ranking he had recently regained. The win was especially sweet for Edberg: In the previous year's U.S. Open, he had been eliminated in the first round.

Until Edberg's triumph, much of the excitement at the U.S. Open swirled about Jimmy Connors. The 39-year-old American thrilled the crowds by defeating much younger men round after round. He reached the semifinals, where he was ultimately undone by Courier.

In her U.S. Open final, Seles, too, faced an aging legend. She outplayed Navratilova by scores of 7–6, 6–1, placing herself at the very top of the sport.

# TRACK AND FIELD

As a rule, world records in track and field have short life spans. But one or two have lasted long periods of time. One such record, the men's long-jump mark, stood for 23 years. That record was set at the 1968 Olympics in Mexico City, when American Bob Beamon remained airborne for 29 feet, 2½ inches. He shattered the previous record by almost two feet.

Since then, little by little, long jumpers have gotten closer to Beamon's record, but no one surpassed it. However, in August, 1991, at the World Track and Field Championships in Tokyo, Japan, another American made a historic leap into the record books: Mike Powell soared 29 feet, 4½ inches, exceeding Beamon's mark by 2 inches.

Interestingly, Powell wasn't the man who was expected to break Beamon's record. That man was Carl Lewis of the United States, two-time Olympic long-jump champion. Lewis had won 65 consecutive long-jump events; his winning streak ended when Powell beat him with the record leap. But Lewis set an important world record of his own in 1991. More accurately, he lost the record for the 100-meter dash and then regained it. Lewis's old mark of 9.92 seconds was broken by Leroy Burrell, who ran a 9.90 in June. Two months later, at the World Championships, Lewis reclaimed the record with a 9.86 mark. Burrell was second in that event.

Lewis and Burrell took part in still another world record in 1991: They formed half the U.S. 400-meter relay team that set a new mark of 37.50 seconds in September. The other members of the quartet were Dennis Mitchell and Andre Cason.

Another significant track and field record fell in August, when Sergei Bubka set a new mark in the pole vault. Bubka, from the Ukraine in the Soviet Union, broke his own world record by vaulting 20 feet, ¼ inches. He became the first person ever to reach—and surpass—20 feet. Earlier in the year, Bubka had vaulted more than 20 feet in an indoor meet, but only outdoor marks are considered world records.

Mike Powell leaped into history when he broke Bob Beamon's record in the long jump, which had stood since 1968.

Carl Lewis's long-jump streak was ended, but he took the title of world's fastest human by setting the record in the 100-meter dash.

Clearing the crossbar, pole vaulter Sergei Bubka had reason to be triumphant. In recent years, he had upped the world record several times by ¼ or ½ inch; he finally went over 20 feet in 1991.

The triathlon—a race consisting of a swim, a bike ride, and a run—is growing in popularity among young people.

# SPORTS BRIEFS

The year 1991 saw important anniversaries in basketball and baseball, expanding interest in some lesser-known sports, and young people competing in the grueling triathlon.

### THINK YOU'RE IN GOOD SHAPE?

Do you think you're in good shape? Then try this: the triathlon, an endurance race made up of three parts—a swim, a bike ride, and a run. The triathlon has become extremely popular for adult competitors, and now triathlon competition is finding many enthusiasts among younger people. For juniors (aged 7 through 10), a race consists of a 100-meter (109-yard) swim, a 5-kilometer (3.1-mile) bike ride, and a 1-kilometer (.6-mile) run. For seniors (ages 11 through 14), each leg of the race is twice as long as it is for the juniors.

The triathlon program for young people is called IronKids, and the goal is to promote physical fitness among youth. In 1991, seventeen different IronKids competitions were held all across the United States, culminating in the national championships in San Antonio, Texas, in September. The national champions for 1991 were Jennifer Capelli, 10 years old, of Longwood, Florida (junior girls); Matthew Rother, also 10, of St. Peters, Missouri (junior boys); Katy Radkewich, 12, of Hudson, Ohio (senior girls); and Neal Herman, 14 of Lake St. Louis, Missouri (senior boys). But even though champions are crowned, the basic idea of the IronKids triathlon program is that "every finisher is a winner."

### A CENTURY OF HOOPS

Basketball is the world's most popular indoor sport. It's played in lavish arenas, shiny college fieldhouses, and noisy high school gyms. It's also played outdoors, by city kids rattling metal backboards in schoolyards, and by country kids tossing a ball up at a hoop hanging from the side of a barn. "Hoops," as the game is affectionately known, celebrated the 100th anniversary of its birth in 1991.

The beginnings of basketball were humble. In 1891, Dr. James Naismith, an instructor at the Training School of the Young Men's Christian Association (YMCA) in Springfield, Massachusetts, was looking for a game his students could play indoors during the harsh New England winter. So he nailed a couple of peach baskets to the gymnasium balcony and handed his young athletes a soccer ball. Dr. Naismith established a few basic rules, and the rest, as the saying goes, is history.

And what a history it is, full of exciting stories about great teams and great players: the original Celtics of the 1920's, led by "Dutch" Dehnert and Joe Lapchick; the Harlem Globetrotters, a team formed in 1927 and still popular today, which has boasted such stars as "Goose" Tatum and "Meadowlark" Lemon; and of course, the professional teams of the National Basketball Association, which originated in the 1940's.

When he nailed up those peach baskets, could Dr. James Naismith have imagined the popularity that his game would achieve in 100 years? Could he have imagined the stunning skills of players such as Michael Jordan, Earvin "Magic" Johnson, and Larry Bird? Could he have imagined high arching jump shots and resounding dunks? Could he have foreseen fine men's and women's teams from all over the world competing in the Olympics? Could he ever have guessed that the Basketball Hall of Fame would one day stand in Springfield, Massachusetts, where he invented the game a century earlier? Today, whenever a youngster laces up a pair of sneakers or dribbles a ball in staccato rhythm or stands on a foul line practicing

Basketball, B-ball, roundball, hoops: Whatever you call it, the game had a century of history behind it in 1991.

In 1991, baseball Hall of Famer Joe DiMaggio, shown here at the peak of his career, celebrated the 50th anniversary of his 56-game hitting streak.

free throws, the message is the same: "Thank you, Dr. Naismith, for inventing such a great game!"

## SHINING MOMENTS

Baseball, perhaps more than any other sport, has taken on the quality of myth, probably because the game is loved by so many millions of people. The year 1991 marked three special anniversaries—a 50th, a 40th, and a 30th—of events in major league baseball that have, in the passing years, achieved the status of legends.

*"Joltin' Joe and the Splendid Splinter."* In 1941, two remarkable baseball players had remarkable seasons. "Joltin' Joe" DiMaggio, the graceful center fielder of the New York Yankees, got at least one hit in each of 56 consecutive games, a record that

has never been broken. And Boston Red Sox left fielder Ted Williams, called the "Splendid Splinter" because of his hitting prowess, finished the 1941 season with a .406 batting average; no one since has batted .400 for a season, which represents two hits in every five at-bats.

DiMaggio and Williams were honored by major league baseball during the 50th anniversary year of their historic season. Both in their 70's, they are Hall of Famers. Many consider Joe DiMaggio the greatest all-round baseball player in history. And Ted Williams is considered to have been the greatest hitter in history.

*"The Giants win the pennant!"* One of the most dramatic moments in sports history occurred in 1951—when the Giants were still the New York Giants and the Dodgers were still the Brooklyn Dodgers. (Both teams later moved to California.) Since both had their homes in New York City, and since both

Dodger pitcher Ralph Branca's second pitch, Thomson unloaded a high line drive to left field. It soared into the stands. And radio announcer Russ Hodges shrieked the now-famous call: "The Giants win the pennant!"

*"Sixty-one home runs."* Babe Ruth's record of 60 home runs in one season, set in 1927, was considered unbreakable. But in 1961, New York Yankee right fielder Roger Maris hit 61. Maris was chased all season long by his teammate, center fielder Mickey Mantle, who finished with 54. Maris was named the American League's Most Valuable Player, and the mighty Yankees went on to win the World Series that season.

## NOW FOR SOMETHING DIFFERENT

Sure, nearly everyone loves basketball and baseball. And they're so familiar, like hot dogs with mustard, or the smell of wet grass on a summer morning. But how about trying something unfamiliar—a couple of

Zooming full-speed while lying flat on your back—that's what dry-land luge is all about.

were in the National League, their rivalry was especially heated. When the regular 1951 season ended, the two teams had identical records; so the pennant winner would be determined by a three-game playoff. The Giants won the first and the Dodgers won the second. Game three was played in the Polo Grounds, the Giants' home stadium. In the last of the ninth inning, the Giants were losing 4–2; with one out, two runners were on base, and Bobby Thomson came to bat. On

sports that are unusual to begin with, and are contested in unusual ways:

• Luge is normally a cold-weather sport, part of the program in the Winter Olympics. The competitor lies flat on his or her back on a sled and goes zooming down a snow-covered hill. But what would you have if you attached wheels to the bottom of the sled and went zipping along on dry land? "Dry-land luge," of course, which has been around for about fifteen years and is still trying to gain

Bicycle polo doesn't look very complicated, but hitting a ball with a mallet while cycling requires athletic skill and good eye-hand coordination.

in popularity. Basically, it's skateboarding on one's back, and, like skateboarding, the pastime has its critics. "Too dangerous," they say. Luge sleds have no brakes, and they are difficult to steer. In addition, dry-land lugers frequently practice on mountain roads—hoping that a truck won't round the next curve while they're descending a fast slope. For these reasons, highway police officers don't look too kindly upon the sport. But some dry-land lugers are hoping that if the sport grows in popularity, they may be able to get the backing necessary to set up competition on closed-off tracks—away from truck traffic.

• Then there's bicycle polo, the "every-day" person's answer to the traditional version of polo, which was originally played by aristocrats on horseback. And why not bicycle polo? Nearly everyone can buy, or borrow, a bicycle, but how many people have access to a horse? Each team has four players, and each player has a mallet and a bicycle. You ride up to the ball, and you try to knock it with your mallet into the goal. And, unlike traditional polo, women and girls, as well as men and boys, are invited to play. The game seems like a lot of fun, and interestingly, it was first played as long ago as the 1890's. Today, most bicycle polo competition takes place in the American West—that's right, the West, where not everyone rides horses!

## AN OLYMPICS EVERY TWO YEARS

The Olympic Games are held once every four years. Albertville, France, is the site of the 1992 Winter Olympic Games, and Barcelona, Spain, is the host city of the 1992 Summer Games. But thereafter, the Winter and Summer Games will no longer be held in the same year. Instead, they will be staggered: The 1994 Winter Games will take place in Lillehammer, Norway; the 1996 Summer Games, in Atlanta, Georgia; and the 1998 Winter Games, in Nagano, Japan.

# LIVING HISTORY

The year 1992 marks the 500th anniversary of an event that changed the course of history —the landing of Christopher Columbus in the New World. Here, he is shown kneeling as he claims the land for Spain. Columbus thought he had found a new trade route to Asia. In fact, he had reached one of the Bahama Islands, in the Caribbean. His 1492 voyage marked the discovery by Europeans of the Western Hemisphere, and it opened the way for European exploration and colonization.

189

# COME TO
# THE FAIR

Aromas of barbecued chicken and steaming corn-on-the-cob fill the warm September air. Sheep bleat and geese cackle. From the midway come shrieks of delight and the clang and clatter of carnival games and rides. Thousands of visitors jostle their way through a maze of canvas tents, viewing homemade pies and canned goods and stopping off at food stalls for cotton candy and fresh-squeezed lemonade.

This is a country fair, an American tradition. The best-known fairs are the big state fairs, which celebrated their 150th anniversary in 1991. But in late summer and early fall, there are thousands of country fairs, large and small, throughout North America.

## AN OLD TRADITION

A true country fair is a blend—it is part carnival, part farm display, part flea market, part outdoor junk-food feast. Attractions range from the ordinary (popcorn and pizza) to the beautiful (carriage parades and delicate needlework) to the downright strange (potato-peeling contests).

The blend of events is part of the tradition of the country fair. Fairs began in medieval Europe as sidelights to religious festivals. When pilgrims and worshippers gathered at a church or monastery for a festival, smart merchants and craftsmen saw an opportunity. They brought in their goods, pitched tents outside the monastery walls, and

Farm animals on display . . . prize-winning produce . . . amusement-park rides . . . a junk-food feast. Welcome to the country fair!

started trading. London's Bartholomew Fair, which started in the 1100's, was the first to add acrobats and other amusements. Gradually fun and trade rather than religion drew people to these fairs.

But North American fairs have an element that sets them apart from fairs that are held in other parts of the world. That element is agriculture, and it has been important ever since the first American fairs were held in the early 1800's.

The father of American country fairs was Elkanah Watson, a Massachusetts farmer and merchant who was a friend of Benjamin Franklin's. In the early 1800's, Watson retired from his business career and adopted a new mission: as he put it, "showing America how to farm"—and how to show off what it produced. He began by displaying his prize Merino sheep (a breed that had recently been imported from Spain) in a public square in Pittsfield, Massachusetts. The townspeople were fascinated, and Watson knew that he was headed in the right direction.

In 1812, Watson founded the Berkshire County Fair, an event that would become the model for all the country fairs that would follow. The fair offered prizes for the best produce and livestock. It featured a band and other entertainment as well. Members of the agricultural society paraded through the grounds, wearing badges of wheat on their hats. Farm animals were paraded, too, drawn along on floats. The star attraction was a plow pulled by 69 oxen and guided by the county's oldest citizen.

The fair was a wild success, and Watson's "Berkshire system" of country fairs quickly spread throughout the East Coast. Most fairs were started by farmers who banded together and formed fair associations, knowing that they would benefit from the publicity surrounding the event. The fairs grew larger each year until, in 1841, the first state-wide fair was held in Syracuse, New York.

In the years that followed, as Americans moved west across the continent, they took the idea of the country fair with them. In many farming areas, the annual fair became one of the biggest events of the year. It offered farm families a chance to show off their animals, produce, and handicrafts. They could see new farm tools and machines, swap information with other farmers, and buy products that weren't available in local stores. Horse races, political debates, and

Skills that were once essential to farm life, such as spinning yarn, are often demonstrated at country fairs.

other special events offered a welcome break from the hard work that was part and parcel of farm life for most of the year. So did the rides and games along the midway, which gradually became more and more important to the fairs.

## SOMETHING FOR EVERYONE

From their beginnings in New York, annual state fairs have grown into major events in about three-fourths of the states. Some of the biggest fairs, such as the State Fair of Texas and the Ohio State Fair, draw millions of visitors. There are big regional fairs, too, such as the Eastern States Exposition (The Big E) in Massachusetts. But the largest fair of all is in Canada—the Canadian National Exhibition in Toronto.

Many of today's fairs are a far cry from the agricultural fairs of the early 1800's. Large fairs are held on sprawling grounds with paved roads and permanent exhibition halls. Some have their own racetracks and even re-creations of historic buildings. The Ohio State Fair features some 69,000 exhibits spread throughout 40 buildings on 360 acres. The midway at the State Fair of Oklahoma features 100 rides and shows.

Elkanah Watson would feel lost amid the crowds, the noise of loudspeakers, the flashing lights of midway rides, and the general hustle and bustle of these fairs. There's something for everyone—circus acts, daredevil stunts, stock car races, concerts by famous country-and-western performers, international pavilions, exhibits on energy conservation and other timely subjects, demonstrations of archery and calf roping. The music in the air is more likely to be electronically amplified rock than a melody from an old-fashioned calliope.

But even the most commercial fairs give at least a nod to Watson's original goal of promoting agriculture. Cattle, sheep, pigs, and poultry are still shown and judged at most fairs, as are handicrafts, home-grown vegetables, and home-made baked goods and preserves. Farming equipment is still displayed and sold. Skills that were once essential to farm life, such as spinning and weaving, horse shoeing, and sheep shearing, are often demonstrated.

Small fairs especially emphasize farming, and many try to re-create the atmosphere of

Competitions are an important part of country fairs. One of the most popular pits teams of oxen against each other to see which can pull the heaviest weight.

old-time country fairs. But each fair has a flavor of its own. One Maine fair, for example, has an organic theme—all the produce on display is grown without chemical fertilizers or pesticides. The California State Fair, held in Sacramento since 1853, features a wine competition.

For many young people, competitions are an important part of country fairs. Members of local 4-H clubs and similar youth groups work on projects throughout the year—raising pigs or sheep, training a dog, growing or canning vegetables, baking bread, making a quilt, tracing their family history. They enter their projects in competitions at local and county fairs, where they gain experience in showmanship. Winners of these local contests advance to state or regional fairs, where they face stiff competition.

Children aren't the only competitors—there are contests for adults, too. But most of the millions of people who visit fairs each year do so just to have fun. You can wander through a tent full of bleating, freshly laundered sheep, all waiting their turn to be judged in the show ring. You can watch lumberjacks display their skills or observe teams of horses or oxen compete to see which can pull the heaviest weight. On the midway, you can ride the ferris wheel and the scram-

bler or test your pitching skill—and perhaps win a stuffed toy—at one of the game booths. At night, concerts and fireworks often provide the excitement.

Food is another big attraction. Hungry? Try barbecued beef or chicken, clam fritters, egg rolls, onion rings, pizza, rib-eye steak, french fries, sausage grinders, turkey sandwiches, hamburgers, hot dogs, or corn on the cob. Wash it down with soda, lemonade made right before your eyes, fresh cider, or a milkshake from the dairy barn. Later, sample watermelon, fresh-made fudge, funnel cakes, fried dough, apple fritters, candy apples, Belgian waffles, ice cream, or cotton candy. The list of choices is long enough to satisfy the pickiest eater.

Country fairs are no longer the only way for isolated farm families to meet, show off their work, and exchange information. And in some areas, fairs have disappeared as farmland has been taken over for houses, office buildings, and shopping malls. But the fairs that are still held are no less important, and no less popular, than they were in the 1800's. Even in areas where farming is no longer a way of life, thousands of people flock to country fairs. A fair offers great entertainment—and a chance for a first-hand glimpse of America's agricultural past.

# CHRISTOPHER COLUMBUS
## A Celebration of His Voyage of Discovery

In 1492, an Italian navigator sailing under the flag of Spain crossed the Atlantic Ocean and landed in the New World. The navigator was, of course, Christopher Columbus, or Cristóbal Colón as he was called in Spanish. And in 1992, there were plans to mark the 500th anniversary of his trip with dozens of special events.

Columbus is credited with the discovery of America. He wasn't the first to reach the continent—Indians had lived there for thousands of years. But to the Europe of his time, America was unknown. His voyage was made at a time when nations such as Spain were building empires that stretched around the world. Thus Columbus's discovery led to the founding of European colonies in the New World and, eventually, to the America we know today. (Much has been written about Columbus. But, oddly, no one knows what he really looked like. The portrait above, done in the 1800's, is one of many versions.)

In Columbus's day, demand for silk and spices had led traders to explore routes to the East Indies, as Asia was then called. Thus Europeans were familiar with parts of Africa and Asia. (Above, a map of the world as Europeans then knew it.) In the 15th century, improvements in ships and navigation techniques allowed longer voyages. (Right: an astrolabe, used by sailors to navigate by the stars.) Columbus, who was born about 1451 in the Italian port of Genoa, would have heard sailors' stories of far-off lands. He was a weaver's son and learned his father's trade. But he went to sea while still a boy, at first on short coastal voyages. By the time he was in his twenties, he was making longer trips. In 1476 he sailed on a ship bound for England—but the ship was attacked and sunk by a French privateer. Columbus, stranded, made his way to Lisbon, Portugal, then a center of trade and exploration.

In Portugal, Columbus made voyages for several traders. He also married, and he studied the latest theories of navigation. By this time, educated people knew that the Earth was round, not flat as had been thought for centuries. But they believed that the world was very small, and Columbus was convinced he could find a shorter route to Asia—by sailing *west* around the globe. This was a revolutionary idea. In 1484 he asked the ruler of Portugal to fund a voyage to find this western route. (Left: Columbus studying in Lisbon.)

Portugal turned down Columbus's proposal, so in 1485 he left for Spain. There, too, he had little luck at first. Spain was involved in a war with the Moors, who then controlled part of the Iberian Peninsula. The government had little time for wild schemes of discovery. But Queen Isabella, who ruled Spain with her husband, King Ferdinand, was interested. In 1486 she appointed a council to hear Columbus's plan and make a recommendation on it. The council debated the proposal for four years—and then decided against it. (Below: Columbus explains his theory to the Council of Salamanca, appointed by the queen.)

In 1492, the war ended, and Spain was victorious. Ferdinand and Isabella now decided to back Columbus's voyage, providing ships, crews, and rich rewards if the trip was successful. They even gave him letters of introduction to Asian rulers they were sure he would meet. On August 3, 1492, the expedition set sail. Two of the three ships, the *Niña* and the *Pinta,* were caravels, small ships used for coastal trading. The flagship, the *Santa María,* was only slightly larger. Columbus was brave to set out in these small ships. But in fact, he thought the trip would be short. He had underestimated the distance to Asia, and he had no idea that America lay in between. (Above: Ferdinand and Isabella say good-bye to Columbus. Below: The *Niña,* the *Pinta,* and, center, the *Santa María.)*

After stopping at the Canary Islands to pick up water and wood, the ships sailed west for more than a month. Finally, in the early hours of October 12, they sighted land and dropped anchor off one of the Bahama Islands (probably present-day San Salvador, formerly Watling Island). Soon after dawn, Columbus and some of his crew went ashore and claimed the land for Spain, naming it San Salvador. He believed he had reached the East Indies, and so he called the island people Indians. (Left: On shore, Columbus was greeted by a group of Indians—the first meeting between the Indian and European cultures. The surprise must have been great on both sides.)

Columbus sailed south, hoping to find Cathay (China). But after his flagship was wrecked off the island of Hispaniola, he returned to Spain, bringing gold bracelets, strange plants, and even several Indians. He was greeted as a hero. Ferdinand and Isabella may have doubted that he had reached Asia, but they were encouraged by the gold. They sent him back the next year to found a settlement. (Below: Columbus's return to the Spanish court.)

At the settlement on Hispaniola, Columbus proved to be a poor governor. He dealt harshly with the local Indians. The settlers, who were mostly interested in hunting for gold and had expected to live off the land, were disappointed by conditions on the island. They began to complain about their governor. In 1498, when Columbus returned to the settlement from a voyage to Spain, he found the settlers in rebellion. He restored peace by giving them

land grants and by assigning the Indians to them, to work as laborers. But they continued to complain. In 1500, Columbus was replaced as governor, stripped of all his titles, and sent back to Spain to answer charges. His titles were later restored, but he was never again allowed to govern in the New World. (Above: Columbus, in chains, returning to Spain in 1500. Left: the coat of arms of the Admiral of the Ocean Sea, one of the titles that Columbus held.)

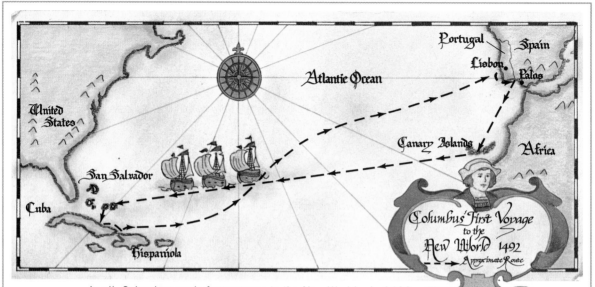

In all, Columbus made four voyages to the New World—in 1492, 1493, 1498, and 1502. On his last trip, which he hoped would restore his fame and fortune, he explored the coast of Central America and came in contact with the highly developed Indian civilizations there. But he never found the passage to the East Indies that he had believed was just over the horizon. He returned to Spain for the last time in 1504. (Left: a map showing Columbus's first voyage.)

Although Columbus brought back gold from his last trip, he didn't receive the recognition or reward he expected from the Spanish court. He spent his last years living in obscurity, bitter and unhappy. He died on May 20, 1506, in Valladolid, Spain. (Below: In this romanticized deathbed scene, Columbus holds the chains in which he was taken to Spain in 1500.)

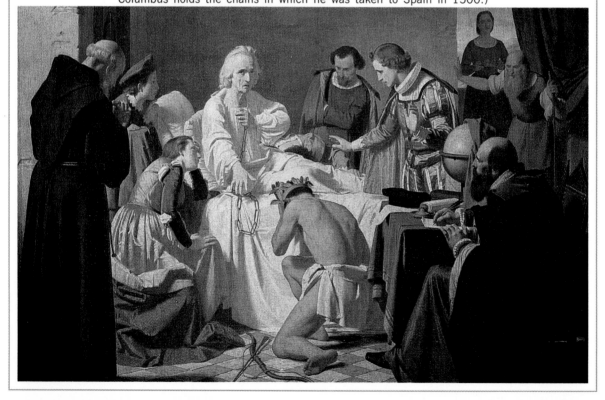

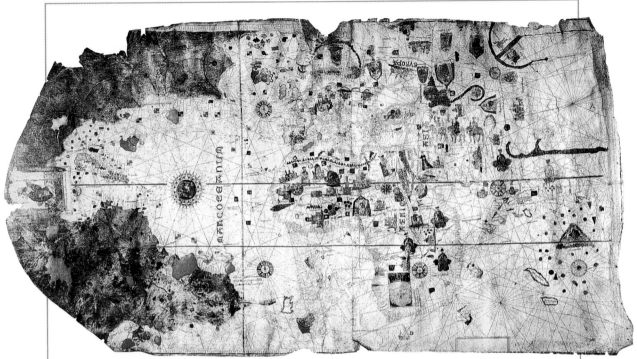

Many historians believe that other Europeans reached the Western Hemisphere before Columbus. There are theories that Phoenician, Roman, and Irish sailors made the trip. And there is evidence that Norse voyagers reached America around the year 1000. But Columbus, in a sense, was in the right place at the right time. His first voyage was made at a time when Europeans were ready to explore and colonize distant lands, and when new technology made it possible for them to do so. Columbus also discovered routes that took advantage of the trade winds, making the Atlantic crossing simple. Other explorers followed his lead, and within a few years Europeans had begun to realize the vast size of the continent to the west. (Above: a map showing the world, drawn in 1500, depicts the Old World and the New World. It shows how much the European view of the world had changed just a few years after Columbus's first voyage.)

Europeans also realized the potential of the New World. Spain and Portugal, followed by the Netherlands, France, and England, began to conquer and colonize the Americas. There were dark chapters in this story—the destruction of Indian civilizations, the establishment of slavery in the colonies. Nevertheless, the outcome was the growth of the societies that exist today in the Western Hemisphere.

For the 500th anniversary of Columbus's discovery, some thirty nations on both sides of the Atlantic planned events—parades, exhibitions, fairs, and much more. The Dominican Republic erected a $10 million lighthouse, the largest monument ever built to Columbus. Replicas of the explorer's ships were to sail to American ports. And in books, articles, and conferences, people examined once again the importance of that historic moment on October 12, 1492, when Christopher Columbus first sighted the New World.

Is this a giant eel? A partially submerged tree branch? Or is it the Loch Ness Monster?

# MYSTERY CREATURES

One-eyed giants known as cyclops... fire-breathing dragons... unicorns with magical horns... half-fish, half-human mermaids and mermen. These and other legendary creatures never existed. But long ago, many people believed that they were real—despite the fact that no one had ever found one.

There are mysterious creatures today, too. Thousands of people have reported seeing them in remote wilderness areas around the world. Among the most sought after mystery creatures today are the Loch Ness monster of Scotland, the Wildman of China, Mokele-Mbembe of Africa, and Bigfoot of the Pacific Northwest Coast of the United States.

### THE LOCH NESS MONSTER

Reports of a monster living in the deep, dark waters of Loch Ness, a lake in northern Scotland, have persisted for more than a thousand years. The Loch Ness Monster—affectionately known as Nessie—supposedly looks like a giant reptile. Like some dinosaurs that lived millions of years ago, it has a long neck and a small head. People

Scientists placed signs in areas of central China, asking villagers if they had seen the Wildman.

Mokele-Mbembe, the swamp creature of the Congo, supposedly resembles a long-extinct dinosaur.

### BIGFOOT

Similar to Wildman is Bigfoot, a huge hairy ape-man that has reportedly been seen in the forests of the Pacific Northwest since the early 1800's. According to some reports, he is 8 feet (2.4 meters) tall and weighs at least 500 pounds (227 kilograms). The Sasquatch in Canada, the Yeti (or Abominable Snowman) in the Himalayas of Asia, the Yowie in Australia, and the Almas in the Soviet Union are other apemen that people have reportedly seen.

have taken photographs of what they say is Nessie. But many expeditions, some using sonar and underwater cameras, have failed to find proof that Nessie exists. Many experts believe that if there is a Nessie, it will turn out to be a giant eel or a large seal.

### WILDMAN

Wildman is a tall, humanlike creature that people have reported seeing in the forests of central China. Researchers have found what is supposed to be some of Wildman's hair. Scientists analyzed the hairs and found that they were indeed from primates. Some experts are now considering the possibility that Wildman may be some unknown primate.

### MOKELE-MBEMBE

Somewhat similar to Nessie is Mokele-Mbembe, a black, lizardlike creature that people say they have seen in swamplands in the Congo, in Central Africa. Because of its small head, some people have likened it to a *sauropod*, a plant-eating dinosaur that lived millions of years ago. In 1981, two expeditions to the Congo failed to bring back proof that Mokele-Mbembe existed. But two years later, a mysterious creature "with a wide back, a long neck, and a small head" was seen by a Congolese zoologist.

Are these mystery creatures real or imaginary? Could Wildman or Bigfoot be some unknown species of primate? Could the Loch Ness Monster or Mokele-Mbembe be a type of dinosaur? These creatures probably aren't real—but no one knows for sure. In the meantime, people, including well-known scientists, continue to search for them.

A photographer claims that this apelike creature in California is Bigfoot. The search continues.

# PORTRAITS IN STONE

Not too long ago, a geologist stared straight into the eyes of Abraham Lincoln and pronounced the 16th president of the United States to be fit as a fiddle. The only noticeable problem to be seen on "Honest Abe's" weathered face, he said, was "a crack across the bridge of his nose."

No, the geologist wasn't hallucinating. He was inspecting a lifelike sculpture of Lincoln's face—60 feet (18 meters) high and carved out of the solid granite of Mount Rushmore in South Dakota. Lincoln's familiar bearded features and brooding eyes jut out of the side of the nearly 6,000-foot-high (1,830 meters) mountain, along with the carefully chiseled faces of three other U.S. presidents—George Washington, Thomas Jefferson, and Theodore Roosevelt.

The sculpted likenesses of these four great Americans make up the Mount Rushmore National Memorial—one of the largest sculptures in the world. The year 1991 marked the 50th anniversary of this world-famous monument, which is sometimes called "The Shrine of Democracy." And the geologist's inspection of the four massive faces was part of a $40-million preservation project.

Mount Rushmore celebrated its 50th anniversary in 1991. It took fourteen years to create the famous monument out of a mountain in South Dakota. Carvers were lowered in cagelike platforms and harness-seats, and they used jackhammers, drills, and other tools to sculpt the faces.

## A WORK OF ART

Mount Rushmore's grand golden anniversary celebration honored more than just a monument to American democracy and four great political leaders. It celebrated an epic work of art that is one of the true wonders of the world. Every year more than 2 million visitors from all corners of the world come to marvel at this incredible monument of stone.

How did the Mount Rushmore National Memorial come about? It began in 1923 as the brainchild of a South Dakota historian named Doane Robinson. Originally, Robinson proposed that giant statues of several popular Western heroes—such as Kit Carson and Jim Bridger—should be carved out of granite formations known as the "needles" in the Black Hills. To make this idea a reality, Robinson called in a Danish-American sculptor named Gutzon Borglum. Born in Idaho in 1867, Borglum had studied art in France, where he had become friendly with the great sculptor Auguste Rodin. By the early 1900's, Borglum had achieved a national reputation as a sculptor. His works included a large bronze statue of Civil War General Phil Sheridan and a monument honoring Pickett's Charge at the Battle of Gettysburg.

The statue that set him on the road to Mount Rushmore, however, was a massive bust of President Abraham Lincoln. Originally exhibited in New York City, it was seen by Robert Lincoln, the president's son. Robert was so moved by its realism that he remarked, "I never expected to see father again." (The Lincoln bust is now promi-

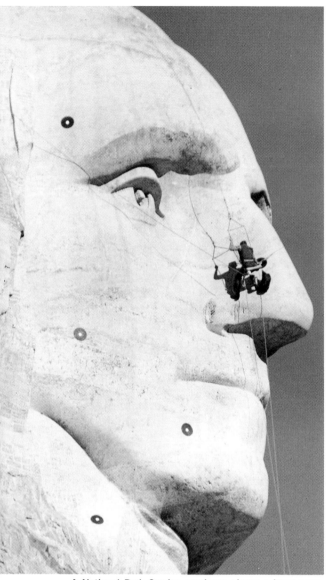

A National Park Service employee places a large paper dot over a crack on George Washington's nose. The dots target the areas where repair work is needed.

nently displayed in the Rotunda of the Capitol in Washington, D.C.)

After viewing the Lincoln bust, a group of people in Georgia asked Borglum to carve a monument on the side of Stone Mountain, honoring the soldiers and leaders of the Confederacy. He was fired from the project in 1924, after disagreements with the sponsoring group. But his work on the Stone Mountain sculpture attracted the attention of Doane Robinson.

Borglum went to South Dakota, first in 1924 and then again in 1925. After much discussion, it was decided that the memorial would honor great American presidents instead of Western heroes.

The four American presidents who were finally selected were chosen for their special contributions to the development of the United States. George Washington was picked because he led the fight for independence and then became the country's first president. Thomas Jefferson wrote the Declaration of Independence. Abraham Lincoln was the great leader who preserved the nation during the Civil War, while Theodore Roosevelt was chosen for his efforts to conserve our national resources.

Because of the scope of the project, Borglum searched for just the right locale. Mount Rushmore was chosen because of the fine texture and smoothness of the granite found on the mountain's peak. Also, the southeastern face of the mountain, where the four heads are positioned, is favored by direct sunlight most of the day.

The mountain was designated a national memorial site in 1925, but it wasn't until August of 1927 that work actually began. Creating a monument out of a mountain was no easy task.

### BLASTING AND ETCHING

First, dynamite was used to blast away the surface layers of rock and get at the hard granite underneath. During the years of blasting and chiseling, nearly 450,000 tons of rock were torn from the mountain.

Borglum established a studio at the base of the mountain. There he fashioned huge models of the four portraits; these would be used to guide the workers. After the drillers and powdermen finished their blasting, other workers began etching out the rough features of the presidents.

Using harness-seats and cagelike platforms suspended from winches, workmen were lowered and raised on the mountainside as they performed their various tasks. Drills and jackhammers were used to broadly shape the features. Next, hand-held hammers and wedging tools were employed

## LASTING WORDS

The four presidents honored at Mount Rushmore are famous for their words as well as for their important roles in American history. Here are quotations from each of them.

GEORGE WASHINGTON,
1st President, 1789–1797

*"The preservation of the sacred fire of liberty, and the destiny of the Republican model of government, are justly considered as deeply, perhaps as finally staked, on the experiment entrusted to the hands of the American people."*
Inaugural Address
April 30, 1789

THOMAS JEFFERSON,
3rd President, 1801-1809

*"We hold these truths to be self-evident, that all men are created equal, that they are endowed by their creator with certain unalienable rights, that among these are Life, Liberty, and the Pursuit of Happiness."*
Declaration of Independence
July 4, 1776

ABRAHAM LINCOLN,
16th President, 1861-1865

*"With malice toward none, with charity for all, with firmness in the right, as God gives us to see the right, let us strive on to finish the work we are in."*
Second Inaugural Address
March 4, 1865

THEODORE ROOSEVELT,
26th President, 1901–1909

*"Far better it is to dare mighty things, to win glorious triumphs, even though checkered by failure, than to take rank with those poor spirits who neither enjoy much nor suffer much, because they live in the gray twilight that knows not victory nor defeat."*
Speech Before the Hamilton Club (Chicago)
April 10, 1899

to further refine the facial features. Finally, the sculptured faces were polished smooth by means of small air hammers—a process called "bumping."

Teams of about 35 workers scrambled over the mountainside on any given day. Many of these people were recruited from the ranks of hard-rock miners. Over the years, a total of some 400 workmen took part in the project. They worked under the watchful eyes of Borglum, who closely supervised each stage of the "carving" process. Amazingly, not one worker was killed or seriously hurt while involved in the often-dangerous work.

It took fourteen years to complete the monument—although less than half that many were actually spent on construction. There were numerous delays due to changes in design, poor weather conditions, and insufficient funds. The first head, which was that of George Washington, was officially dedicated on July 4, 1930. The entire monument was completed in October, 1941, seven months after Borglum's death at age 74. The final details were supervised by his son Lincoln.

The total cost of the mammoth monument was just under $1,000,000. About 80 percent of the money came from the Federal government. The rest came from private donations. These included a $5,000 contribution from Charles E. Rushmore, the New York lawyer for whom the mountain was named.

Viewing the mountain today, one should keep in mind that each of the heads measures 60 feet from hair to chin—or about the size of a five-story building. Put in perspective, if you placed such an enormous head on a properly scaled body, you would end up with a man 465 feet (142 meters) tall.

Indeed, the Mount Rushmore National Memorial lives up to Gutzon Borglum's idea that a monument's size should reflect the importance of the men and events being commemorated. As he told the audience at the Mount Rushmore dedication ceremonies in 1927, "Let us place there, carved high, as close to heaven as we can, our leaders, their faces, to show posterity what manner of men they were."

HENRY I. KURTZ
Author, *The Art of the Toy Soldier*

# WHAT DO YOU MEAN BY THAT?

"*Breaking the ice* with a new classmate can be *a hair-raising experience*. I told Sally that *two heads are better than one* when it comes to figuring out how to do it. But she was so *green with envy* that everything I said to her went *in one ear and out the other*. The only thing I could do then was to *lead her by the nose*. But I let her think that I was upset about her problem by shedding a few *crocodile tears*."

These expressions might not make sense to someone who isn't very familiar with the English language. That's because they are idioms —commonly used phrases with special meanings that can't be figured out from the individual words in them. To understand the meaning of an idiom, you often have to know the story behind it.

## A HAIR-RAISING EXPERIENCE

This idiom is based on an actual scientific phenomenon. Thanks to something called the pilomotor reaction, people really do have hair-raising experiences. The pilomotor reaction is one of the body's responses to fear: Nerve endings under the skin cause hair on the head and body to stand up. A hair-raising experience, then, is a frightening one. The pilomotor reaction produces a tingling feeling that has given rise to some other expressions, too— "it made my skin crawl," for example.

## BREAK THE ICE

Have you ever found yourself with a group of people that you didn't know very well? You were probably quiet and a bit uncomfortable until someone came up to talk to you or crack a joke. That person "broke the ice," and soon you felt comfortable talking with everyone.

This idiom began with boatmen who worked on the Thames River in London, England. In winter, ice forms on this river. Today it can be easily broken up with power equipment; but years ago, boatmen had to chop their boats free of the ice before they could begin the day's work. Today "breaking the ice" means clearing the way to start a conversation or get a party going.

## TWO HEADS ARE BETTER THAN ONE

This expression doesn't mean that two-headed monsters have an intellectual edge over the rest of us. It means that two people, working together, can often solve problems that stump one person working alone. One person may see a solution that the other doesn't. By pooling their thoughts and talking the problem over, they come up with the answer. This is sound and very old advice—the expression appears in the Bible.

## IN ONE EAR AND OUT THE OTHER

Perhaps this has happened to you: You're in class, and the teacher is talking. Suddenly he asks a question—and calls on you for the answer. But you're not sure what the question is; in fact, you can't remember anything the teacher said in the last ten minutes!

"In one ear and out the other" means to hear something without really listening or paying attention to it. It's as if the teacher's words entered your head through one ear and passed right through, without being captured by your mind.

## CROCODILE TEARS

Do crocodiles cry? In Europe during the Middle Ages, people knew very little about animals of far-off places such as Africa, and they made up tall tales about them. One story was that a hungry crocodile would lure people by making sobbing noises, and then shed tears as it devoured its unlucky prey. Over the years, the expression "shed crocodile tears" came to be used for anyone who made a false show of grief.

So far as is known, crocodiles don't shed tears of any kind. But marine turtles secrete salty water from glands near their eyes, and that may be how the story got started.

## LEAD BY THE NOSE

A bull is a big, powerful animal. No amount of pushing and shoving could make a bull go someplace it didn't want to go. But many centuries ago, people found an easy way to lead bulls and other large farm animals. They put a ring in the animal's nose and tied a rope to the ring. The nose is very sensitive, so the animals learned quickly that it was best to obey even a gentle tug on the ring.

Today, when people are persuaded to do something without really thinking about it or using their own judgment, we say that they are being led by the nose.

## GREEN WITH ENVY

This expression comes to us by way of ancient Greece. The Greeks believed that emotions originated in specific parts of the body. Envy and jealousy were thought to come from the liver.

The liver secretes a substance called bile, which helps digestion. If a person's liver secretes too much bile, the extra bile gives a greenish-yellow cast to the skin and the whites of the eyes. This greenish-yellow tint is called jaundice, and it's a symptom of certain illnesses. But the Greeks thought that jealousy was the cause—the person had literally turned green with envy.

Ever since then, people have linked the color green with envy and jealousy. One of the most famous references is in William Shakespeare's play *Othello*, in which jealousy is called ''the green-ey'd monster.''

211

Scarecrows don't seem to be frightening many birds these days—but they make the landscape more interesting.

# WHO'S AFRAID OF SCARECROWS?

For as long as people have grown their own food, they have found it necessary to protect their crops from birds and other wild animals. Wherever there is farmland, crows —which are perhaps the most destructive birds—can be seen scratching at the ground to get at seeds and pulling up seedlings with their beaks. Today, in North America alone, birds cause more than $100 million worth of damage to crops every year.

In England during the Middle Ages, farmers would send their sons into the fields to shoo the birds away. Known as bird scarers, these young boys would patrol the fields, watching for crows and other birds that wanted to make a meal out of the seeds and young plants. The bird scarers would shout, use noisemakers, wave their arms about, and throw stones at the birds to frighten them off.

When the bubonic plague, or Black Death, struck Europe, almost half the people on that continent died. Every son of every peasant was now needed to work in the fields. The young boys could no longer be spared to work as bird scarers. With everyone working the crops, the birds had a field day feasting on the seeds and shoots.

As a result, medieval peasants had to find another way to frighten away the birds. And so they built scarecrows—figures that they hoped would look like real people to the hungry birds.

But these weren't the first scarecrows. Bird scarers and scarecrows were actually used long before the Middle Ages, even in ancient times. And, in just about every country of the world, humanlike figures—in one form or another—have been used to scare away pests.

### ONCE UPON A SCARECROW

Ancient Egypt was one of the world's first great civilizations. The Egyptians farmed the land along the mighty Nile River more than 3,000 years ago. In the early 1900's, archeologists discovered and explored the tombs of the pharaohs, or emperors, of ancient Egypt. They found great treasures in the tombs. They also found wall paintings, and some of them depicted bird scarers. This is the earliest known record of farmers' attempts to protect their crops from birds.

The ancient Greeks were probably also the first to use scarecrows that looked like people. They placed wooden statues of Priapus, the god of fertility and the protector of gardens, in their wheat fields and vineyards. This idea later spread to Rome and then throughout the rest of Europe.

When European colonists first settled in the New World in the early 1600's, they found that the American Indians were using scarecrows, as well as bird scarers, to protect their corn crops. The Zuni Indians, who lived in the Southwest, had many different and unusual kinds of scarecrows, which they called "the watchers of the corn sprouts."

The colonists, however, created scarecrows that were similar to those that had been built in Europe for centuries. They stuffed old clothing with hay, leaves, grass, or straw, used a large gourd for the head, and stuck on a straw hat. The figure was then mounted on a long pole and placed in the field. Sometimes a farmer would find that the scarecrow's clothes had

## BUILD YOUR OWN SCARECROW

It's easy to build your own scarecrow. All it takes is imagination and some old clothes, some rags or other material for stuffing, a bucket or other object to serve as the head, and a couple of sturdy sticks or pieces of wood. Here's how to build a scarecrow that's 5 feet (1.5 meters) tall.

1. Nail or tie the two sticks together to form a cross. One stick should be about 7 feet (2 meters) long, the other about 2 feet (0.6 meters). The shorter piece should be fastened about 12 inches (30 centimeters) from the top of the longer one.
2. Slip the longer stick through one leg of a pair of pants; let the other leg hang free.
3. Put a shirt or jacket on the shorter stick.
4. Stuff the pants and the jacket or shirt with rags, straw, or leaves.
5. Make a head out of a stuffed pillowcase, an old bucket, or a plastic pumpkin left over from last Halloween and mount it on top of the longer stick.
6. Use your imagination! Add finishing touches such as a belt or jewelry. Paint on a face. Put a cowboy hat or baseball cap on your scarecrow.
7. Dig a narrow hole in the ground about two feet deep. Place the bottom end of the stick in the hole and pack tightly with dirt and stones.

tinue to enjoy building them. Some of today's scarecrows resemble those used by the colonists, although generally they are found only on small farms or in vegetable gardens. But other scarecrows—far more stylish and whimsical in appearance—have begun to dot the countryside, especially in the fall.

### THE WELL-DRESSED SCARECROW

Many of the early scarecrows were probably just wooden stakes driven into the ground and draped with pieces of cloth that would flap in the breeze. The farmers hoped that the birds would mistake the scarecrows for people and be frightened off. This seemed to work—for a while, at least. In time, the birds became aware that these figures amid the crops couldn't hurt them.

disappeared during the night—a poor tramp may have liked the scarecrow's garments better than his own.

Some scarecrows made today are similar to those made by the colonists. But how effective are they? Do they really frighten birds away? Many farmers doubt it. And ornithologists—experts on birds—say that loud noises and movement, not humanlike figures, are what really frighten the birds. This is why many farmers now use loudspeakers, firecrackers, and devices that sound like cannons to scare away birds. Farmers also treat seed with chemicals that are distasteful to birds.

Despite the fact that scarecrows probably don't work, people con-

awarded for the most original and artistic designs. The contests usually take place in September or October, and people gather from all over to participate. Some of the recent favorites have been scarecrows that looked like Cabbage Patch dolls, gremlins, dragons, robots, celebrities such as Michael Jackson, and cartoon characters such as Bart Simpson. One of the most popular was a scarecrow that looked like a giant crow—called a *scareperson*.

Whatever form they may take—from a bundle of straw to a witch on a broomstick—almost everyone agrees that scarecrows make the landscape more interesting. Their presence also adds a touch of nostalgia for those who love to remember the good old days. It seems that as long as people continue to work the soil and try to prevent their ancient enemies, the crows, from robbing the fields, scarecrows are here to stay.

Farmers then tried to make the scarecrows more humanlike. Instead of just draping pieces of cloth on a stick, they dressed the scarecrows with old clothing. They crafted heads and faces from old pots, wooden buckets, large turnips, or other items and topped them with hats. Many farmers began to fancy themselves as artists—or ''scarecrow sculptors.'' They built frightening figures, lifelike figures, humorous figures, silly figures—whatever struck their fancy. This artistic tradition has continued to this day. In fact, scarecrow contests are now being held in many towns across North America, with prizes

# JUST FOR YOU

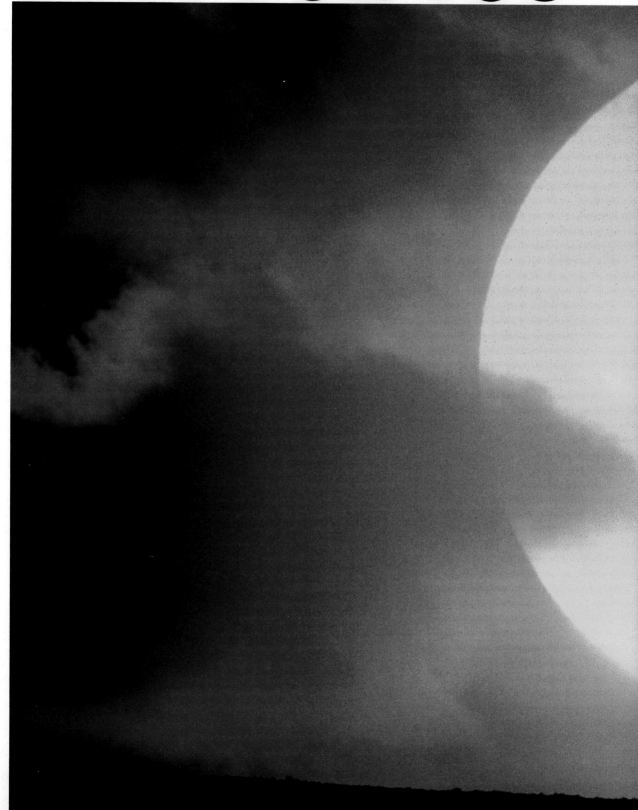

*Silhouetted against the setting sun, a young runner cuts a striking figure. Sports and fitness are as popular as ever with young people. And for fans and participants alike, sports offer exciting opportunities for careers as well as for enjoyment.*

The geodesic dome that towers above Science World contains a theater with the world's largest domed screen.

# A VISIT TO VANCOUVER'S SCIENCE WORLD MUSEUM

How would you like to blow square bubbles or bend light? Walk through a giant camera and crawl through a beaver lodge? Lose your shadow or stretch an echo? You can do all these things—and much more—at Science World in Vancouver, the largest city in the Canadian province of British Columbia.

Science World is a museum where visitors can see the wonders of the past and the technology of the future. But more than that, it's a hands-on learning center. Its displays en-

courage visitors to explore, to touch, to experiment—to enjoy the worlds of nature, science, and technology. There are also live shows, exhibitions, demonstrations, and films. The museum is designed to increase people's awareness and understanding of science as it plays a part in their everyday lives.

Science World was the idea of Barbara Brink, a resident of Vancouver. In 1977, she and her family were traveling across North

America. In cities such as Boston, Toronto, and Ottawa, she saw that science centers were drawing more and more visitors. Her children—and thousands of others—enjoyed the hands-on approach of these science centers so much that she suggested that one be built in Vancouver.

Her idea was accepted, and in 1980 some 80 science exhibits were displayed at the city's planetarium. It was an immediate success. This was quickly followed by a series of equally successful traveling exhibits. In 1982 a temporary center was opened in a donated storefront in Vancouver, and it attracted more than 100,000 visitors a year. Five years later, in 1987, Science World got a permanent home—at Expo Centre, the site of Vancouver's 1986 world's fair.

### A MULTI-LEVEL SCIENCE SHOWCASE

Science World has three levels. On the first level is Gravitram, where visitors can learn about potential energy and the force of gravity. On this level, too, are exhibitions and demonstrations of the latest in computer technology, as well as dazzling and puzzling displays of optical effects and illusions. A theater on this level is where visitors can watch experts explain a wide range of scientific phenomena.

Perhaps the most popular attractions on the first level are the laboratories where, every weekend, children between the ages of 5 and 14 can participate in fascinating experiments. How can heavy objects, such as

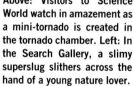
Above: Visitors to Science World watch in amazement as a mini-tornado is created in the tornado chamber. Left: In the Search Gallery, a slimy superslug slithers across the hand of a young nature lover.

people, float on water? Sign up for the workshop on Floaters and Sinkers. Are snakes cold and slimy? Find out at For Goodness Snakes! Do you want to learn about fingerprints, secret codes, and invisible ink? Just join the workshop called Science Detectives. How do a refrigerator and other household appliances work? Anyone can find out by taking part in the workshop called Appliantology. At Rocky 1, you will learn how to identify rocks and minerals and set up a rock collection. And at other workshops, young science enthusiasts can learn about animal camouflage, astronomy, electronics, and magnetism.

The second level contains Science World's Main Gallery, where a collection of exhibitions presents the basic principles of physics. There are also displays on the life sciences and technology. Many of these are interactive—you can, for example, actually touch a mini-tornado and stretch an echo.

Next to the Main Gallery is the Search Gallery, where a giant tree root hangs down from the ceiling. This gallery also features a whale skeleton, fossils, an ant farm, and a bee hive. Visitors to the Search Gallery are encouraged to get involved—they can even take things apart and put them back together again.

Also on the second level is the People and Science Gallery. This gallery is now the permanent home of one of Science World's most popular exhibits—Music Machines. Would you like to play the piano with your feet, make your own music in "jamming rooms," or alter your voice electronically? This is the place to do it.

The third level of Science World is the Omnimax Theatre. Located in the geodesic dome that was created for Expo '86, it has the largest domed screen in the world. Its diameter is more than 88 feet (27 meters), and its 28 speakers envelop the audience in its "wraparound sound."

One of the most popular films shown in the theater was *Blue Planet*—which showed the Earth as it appears from space. The audience viewed volcanoes, earthquakes, and typhoons, as well as the oceans and conti-

It takes the combined lung power of two small bubble-blowers to create this giant bubble at Science World's sheet-bubble exhibit.

How does a camera work? Visitors to the museum's "150 Years of Photography" exhibit found out by walking through this giant camera.

nents. They could see the snow-capped peaks of the Himalaya Mountains in Asia and the sand dunes of the Namib Desert in southwestern Africa.

### SPECIAL EXHIBITS

It isn't always necessary to visit Vancouver to see the wonders of Science World. While exhibitions are first shown at the museum, many are then sent to other parts of the province.

Some of the traveling exhibitions address the problems of today's world. One of the most interesting was "Hope: Seeing Our World Through New Eyes." It gave viewers a look at the exciting breakthroughs being made in Mexico, Kenya, India, and other developing countries in such areas as health, education, and environmental protection.

"Medicines From Around the World" presented a fascinating look at the history of medicines, including herbal medicines and natural drugs produced by the body.

A special light show included displays on candle making, silhouettes, a shadow zoo, ice carving, colored laser effects, light tricks with smoke, giant rainbows, and chemicals that glow in the dark.

"Special Effects: The Science of Movie and Television Magic" took visitors behind the scenes of the special-effects industry. There they saw how special effects artists are able to create worlds where anything can happen. Visitors saw reproductions of the movie studios that brought to the screen such popular films as *Star Wars*, *Ghostbusters*, and *Frankenstein*. It also showed how the dancing California raisins of TV advertisements and the werewolf for *An American Werewolf in London* were created.

A recent exhibition, "About Faces," explained how our facial features reveal so much about who we are. It also told how certain facial expressions have given rise to popular sayings—such as "keep a stiff upper lip," "she has her nose in the air," and "I'm all ears." And after a visit to Science World, you'll know the meaning of "What an eye-opener!"—a saying that's also an appropriate description of this magical museum.

# WHIZ KIDS

In 1991 music lovers marked the 200th anniversary of the death of Wolfgang Amadeus Mozart. Mozart wrote the tune we know as "Twinkle Twinkle Little Star" at age 4 and was a celebrated composer before he reached his teens. He is probably the best-known example of a prodigy—a person who masters a difficult field at an early age. But there have been many other "whiz kids" before and since Mozart, in math and other fields as well as music.

People have always been fascinated and awed by prodigies. And musical prodigies seem to capture peoples' hearts the most, perhaps because they perform in public.

Here are the stories of four of the best-known musical prodigies of recent times.

### YEHUDI MENUHIN

Violinist Yehudi Menuhin is considered by many people to be the greatest prodigy of the 20th century. The son of Russian immigrants, Menuhin grew up in San Francisco. While he was still a toddler, his parents began to take him to symphony concerts. He was fascinated by the violins at the concerts, and he pestered his parents to be allowed to play. In 1921, when he was 4 years old, he began to take lessons.

Just three years later, at 7, he made his concert debut. The next year he gave a recital at the Manhattan Opera House in New York City, and at 10 he played Beethoven's violin concerto with the New York Philharmonic. But his greatest triumph came when he made his European debut in Berlin, Germany, at age 11. The audience greeted his playing with enthusiasm that bordered on hysteria. The physicist Albert Einstein, who was in the concert hall, is said to have rushed backstage, embraced the boy, and exclaimed, "Now I know there is a God!" The next day, newspapers ran page-one stories proclaiming Menuhin as a wonder.

Thus began a string of world tours and performances that met with international acclaim. But for a child, there were drawbacks to this phenomenal success. Menuhin's father left his job so that the entire family could travel and stay together. That meant that the family depended on Yehudi's earnings from concerts and recordings for support—a big responsibility for a young boy. And because he toured so much, Menuhin missed the school experiences that are part of most people's childhood. He and his two younger sisters were educated by their parents and by tutors.

However, in later years Menuhin often credited the support given by his family for his early success. He didn't feel that he had missed anything as a child because he pursued music with a single-minded passion. "My main motive was just to play as well as I could," he told one interviewer.

**Yehudi Menuhin (shown here at age 9) is considered by many people to be the greatest prodigy of the 20th century.**

the son of a violinist. His father began to teach him to play at the age of 3 and quickly realized that his son had a great talent. He enrolled the boy in a music academy and, in a few years, moved the entire family to St. Petersburg to be near a famous violin teacher, Leopold Auer. The Heifetz family was very poor, and Auer at first refused to take Jascha on as a student. But after he heard the boy play, he pronounced him a genius and quickly accepted him.

Heifetz made his international debut in Berlin, Germany, at the age of 10, and he was an immediate success. For the next six years, he toured Europe. In 1917 he made his United States debut at Carnegie Hall. Critics highly praised the 16-year-old musician for his "surpassing talent" and "complete mastery." Tickets for all of his later concerts there sold out quickly, and at one performance the police had to be called in to clear the hall of gatecrashers.

Menuhin's success continued as an adult. Many critics have said that his career peaked in his teens, and that his later performances lacked the emotional power that had brought audiences to their feet in his childhood. But he remained a leading violinist and conductor, and even in his 70's, Menuhin was keeping a full concert schedule. He also founded two music schools and devoted time to working with young musicians.

## JASCHA HEIFETZ

Until his death in 1987, Jascha Heifetz was known as one of the world's greatest violinists. Born in Vilna, Russia, in 1901, he was Heifetz later moved to the United States, and as he grew older his career never faltered. His playing continued to be acclaimed, and his concerts set attendance records. One reason may have been that he never stopped trying to improve his playing. "There is no top," he once said. "There are always farther heights to reach. If one thought himself at the pinnacle, he would slide back toward mediocrity by that very belief in his success." Until he gave his last concert in 1972, he practiced daily and held himself to high standards. He believed that audiences should applaud only good performances—and hiss poor ones.

## LORIN MAAZEL

The conductor of a symphony orchestra acts as a guide for the musicians. Thus most people usually think of a conductor as an older person—a seasoned musician who draws on experience to lead the group. But Lorin Maazel began his career as a conductor at the startling age of 9.

Maazel grew up in Los Angeles in the 1930's. His was a musical family—his father was a professional singer, and his mother was an amateur pianist. While Lorin was still quite young, his parents noticed that he could read musical scores and had an exceptional ear and memory for music. They found a teacher who agreed to train the boy as a conductor, and by the time he was 8 he was leading his school orchestra.

In 1939, Maazel attended a music camp in Michigan. A music critic saw him conducting the camp orchestra from memory and was impressed. Later that year, the camp orchestra appeared at the 1939 World's Fair in New York City—and its 9-year-old conductor received nationwide publicity. Soon, he was being invited to conduct well-known professional orchestras.

Unlike many prodigies, however, Maazel had a normal childhood. He conducted just a few concerts a year, mostly in the summer. The rest of the time he went to school and did the other things that kids his age were doing. In college, he drifted away from music, studying literature, philosophy, and languages. But in 1953, while in Italy on a scholarship, he was drawn back to conducting by chance. The conductor of an Italian orchestra fell ill, and Maazel was asked to fill in. His musical career then blossomed. He led some of the world's best-known orchestras, including the Cleveland Orchestra, the Vienna State Opera, and the Pittsburgh Symphony.

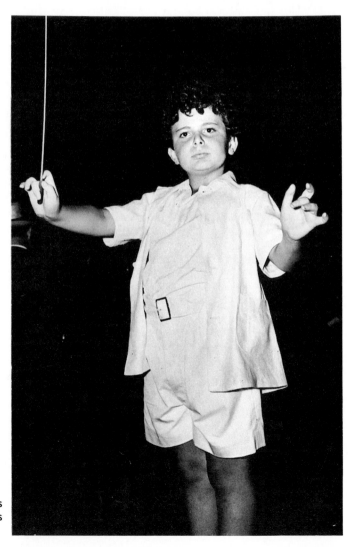

Lorin Maazel (shown here at age 9) has been the conductor of some of the world's best-known orchestras.

## MIDORI

There have been many other musical prodigies in recent years, but few have received as much attention as the violinist Midori Goto, who performs under the single name Midori. Born in 1971 in Osaka, Japan, Midori, too, grew up in a musical family. Her mother was a violin teacher as well as a concert performer, and by the time Midori was 2 she was humming tunes from her mother's concert pieces. For her third birthday, she was given a child-size violin. She practiced diligently and quickly mastered the basics.

When Midori was 8, a tape of her playing was given to a leading U.S. violin teacher, Dorothy DeLay. DeLay invited the youngster to play at a music festival in Aspen, Colorado, in 1981. Midori soloed with the New York Philharmonic at age 10, and soon she and her mother moved to New York City,

Midori (shown here at age 18) is currently receiving a great deal of attention. She began to play the violin at 3; as a teenager, she was praised for her flawless playing.

where Midori studied with DeLay at the Juillard School of Music. Before she reached her teens, she was juggling violin lessons, practice sessions, school, and a growing concert schedule.

Midori's career received a boost in 1986, when she was invited to play at Tanglewood, in Massachusetts, with the conductor and composer Leonard Bernstein. In the middle of her piece, a violin string broke. She

## WHAT MAKES A PRODIGY?

Why does a prodigy achieve so much at such a young age? Why do some prodigies go on to brilliant adult careers, while others slide into obscurity? Reseachers who have studied prodigies have only some of the answers. But it seems that these exceptional children develop from a special set of circumstances.

Prodigies usually appear in just a few fields—including math, chess, computer science, and music. These fields are demanding, but they have clear standards and excelling at them doesn't require years of general life experience. Also, the prodigy's talent is usually in one area only. A child who is exceptional in math, for example, may do only average work in other subjects.

Exceptional ability alone isn't enough. Children who become prodigies often pursue their interests intently, even single-mindedly. And they need support from their families and from society. Prodigies generally come from families who encourage their talents and who value hard work and discipline. And the fields in which prodigies appear are also fields in which advanced training is available to children, and in which success is rewarded with money or fame.

Many child prodigies begin with promise but fade in their teens or early 20's. This may happen because they are pushed too far too fast—they are asked to take on the responsibilities of an adult career while they are still children, and they miss too many childhood activities. The teens and 20's are a time when many people question authority and ask deep questions about their personal goals. For a prodigy, these years can be doubly hard.

calmly switched violins with a member of the orchestra and continued. Then a string on that violin broke—and she calmly switched instruments again. She finished the piece flawlessly, and critics raved about her playing and her coolness under pressure.

At 15, Midori was performing 30 concerts a year, and she recorded her first album. In 1989, she celebrated her 18th birthday with a recital at Carnegie Hall. It was her first recital there, and it marked the beginning of her career as an adult performer.

It is too soon to know if Midori will have a long and successful career, as prodigies such as Menuhin, Heifetz, and Maazel did. But she has made a brilliant beginning.

# SPOTLIGHT ON YOUTH

Sarah Williamson, 16, became the first girl to be elected mayor of Boys Town in May, 1991. Boys Town, near Omaha, Nebraska, was founded in 1917 by the Rev. Edward J. Flanagan as a place for troubled youths. Today it serves about 15,000 young people nationwide. Girls were first accepted in 1979 and today make up about 40 percent of the community. As mayor, Sarah would serve a one-year term—acting as student council president, representing Boys Town at public events, greeting visitors, and serving as a role model for the other young people. But her plans extended well beyond that year: She hopes to attend medical school.

At the age of 14, **Amani A. W. Murray** cut his first solo album in 1991. An accomplished jazz saxophonist, Amani had been playing for five years and had performed alongside jazz greats such as Dizzy Gillespie, Lionel Hampton, and Wynton Marsalis. His album featured some pieces that he had written himself. Amani's talent clearly made him a musical prodigy—but his success hadn't made him different from other kids his age. A ninth-grader at Bronx High School of Science in New York City, he enjoyed playing Nintendo when he wasn't playing his sax.

The Sinclairs are just another suburban family—mom, dad, and three kids—with one exception: They happen to be dinosaurs. This scaly crew took television audiences, especially young people, by storm in 1991 in the situation comedy *Dinosaurs.* Set in 60,000,003 B.C., the show imagines a time when dinosaurs were beginning to develop family life. And the characters, including Earl, the father, and Baby (below), don't seem very different from characters in other television situation comedies. What *is* different is the technology used to produce the show. The dinosaurs are giant puppets, with actors inside and the latest in electronic controls. The show was developed jointly by the Walt Disney Company and Jim Henson Produc-                    tions, creators of the Muppets.

*Home Alone* was the top money-making film of 1990—and one of the top moneymaking films of all time. And the success of its star, 10-year-old **Macaulay Culkin**, was equally dramatic. In the movie, Macaulay played Kevin McAllister, an 8-year-old who is accidentally left behind when his family goes on vacation and who manages to outsmart a pair of dim-witted burglars. Macaulay's role made him a hot property during 1991. He hosted the television show *Saturday Night Live* and was a guest on late-night talk shows. And late in the year he appeared in another feature film, *My Girl*—for a fee of $1 million.

**Ashley Reiter**, 17, was the 1991 winner of the Westinghouse Science Talent Search, the most prestigious science contest in the United States. A senior at North Carolina School of Science and Mathematics in Durham, North Carolina, Ashley won a $40,000 college scholarship for her winning entry, a project in fractal geometry. She thus joined a select group—over the contest's fifty years, five winners have gone on to win Nobel Prizes in their fields.

Are they works of art, or are they toys? The objects shown here are both—they're toys created by artists. "A Toy Tower for a Tall Tot" by Peter R. Thibeault (right) and "The Creators" by Eva Goetz-Adlerstein (below) were among a group of toys displayed at a special 1991 exhibit called **Playing Around: Toys by Artists**. Fifty artists, designers, and craftspeople contributed to the show, which was held at the DeCordova Museum and Sculpture Park in Lincoln, Massachusetts. Their handcrafted pull toys, puppets, scooters, and mechanical toys were mostly displayed on the floor, where young museum-goers could view them easily. The exhibit also featured an area called the Playpen where visitors could actually play with some of the toys.

If you love sports, you might consider a career in this field. There are many opportunities—from "star" football players to reporters who write about the games to designers of sports equipment.

# CAREERS IN SPORTS

Sports are an important part of life today. Millions of fans watch professional team sports such as football, basketball, and baseball. Recreational sports, from badminton to windsurfing, are more popular than ever. And a new emphasis on physical fitness has caused many people to begin exercise and other personal training programs.

For most people, sports are just one part of life. But for some, sports are a passion. If you are among those who truly love sports, perhaps you should consider a career in this field. Sports careers cover everything from "star" professional athletes to reporters who write about the games. For many of these careers, it's not even necessary to be an outstanding athlete. And many sports careers that were once considered "for men only" are now open to women as well.

### PROFESSIONAL ATHLETES

**Professional athletes** are the stars of the sports world. Top players in the most popular team sports sign million-dollar contracts. Incomes are also high for the top athletes in certain individual sports, such as golf, tennis, and boxing. And the leading athletes in many sports are celebrities—their names and faces are known everywhere. In many cases they can earn even more money in related ways—such as endorsing products in advertisements—than they earn directly from sports.

As glamorous as it sounds, however, a career in professional athletics has many drawbacks. First, not every sport offers opportunities for a professional career. In track and field, for example, most of the competition is amateur (unpaid). And in the sports where a pro career is possible, the competition is keen. For example, there are fewer than 300 players in the National Basketball Association. That means that most of the young people who aspire to careers as professional basketball players don't make it. In most sports, for every star player there are hundreds of lesser-known players who struggle to make a living.

Professional athletes also lead difficult lives. When they aren't playing, they are training. They're on the road a lot, traveling to competitions. And depending on the sport, games and competitions are often scheduled on nights and weekends. That makes it difficult to have a normal home and family life. Moreover, for players in demanding sports, pro careers don't last a lifetime. A player's career may be cut short by injury. And because youth gives players an edge in many sports, many athletes "retire" at an early age and go on to other careers even if they aren't injured.

Still, if you think you have the talent and determination that it takes, a pro sports career can be rewarding. Even if you don't make it to the top, you'll have the satisfaction of doing something you love—and getting paid for it.

Most pro athletes begin as amateur players in school sports. Outstanding high school athletes often win college scholarships; in team sports, outstanding college players are often spotted by scouts for major professional teams. So if professional athletics are your goal, you should begin working toward that goal while you are still in school.

Practice your sport as much as you can. Pay attention to nutrition and physical fitness, too, because athletic performance depends on your physical condition. And work on developing a positive mental outlook. The road to success as a pro athlete is long and hard. You will need to be able to accept setbacks and keep trying.

## COACHES

Coaching is a complicated job that requires many talents. Whether they work in amateur or professional sports, **coaches** must know everything about the game and about the players on their team. Then, using that information, they find ways to bring out the team's best possible performance.

A head coach oversees every aspect of a team, from scouting new players to developing fitness and nutrition programs to analyzing the weaknesses of opposing teams and developing game strategies. Many professional teams employ assistant coaches who concentrate on certain areas, such as the batting coach of a baseball team or the defensive line coach of a football team. Large teams also employ scouts, who comb the country for talented new players. The head coach oversees the work of all the assistants.

A coach's life is as demanding as an athlete's. The coach goes on the road with the team. And especially in professional jobs, the coach is under a lot of pressure. If the team doesn't do well, blame is often assigned to the coach. The coach may even be fired after a losing season. Coaches aren't paid as highly as top athletes, but those in professional sports make a very good living.

Coaches don't have to be outstanding athletes themselves, but they should have played enough to understand the fine points of the game from the athletes' point of view. Thus most coaches begin as players.

Coaches need other skills as well. They must be good communicators, so that they can get their ideas across to the players. They must be good judges of the skills and the personalities of the athletes they coach.

Coaching is a complicated job. A Little League coach, like a coach in a professional sport, must be able to bring out the team's best possible performance.

They should enjoy working with people. And they should be good leaders, able to inspire the players. Thus high school and college courses in English, speech, and psychology are valuable for a coaching career.

Many coaches get their first on-the-job experience while they are still in school, through volunteer and summer coaching jobs at city recreation leagues and camps. Most get their first full-time jobs as assistants in high school sports; later, they move on to college and finally professional sports.

After coaching for a number of years, some people move into team management or, in school sports, administration. For example, an **athletic director** develops and directs sports programs at a college or university. This is a big job—it involves managing budgets, raising funds, planning schedules for a wide range of events, and hiring and supervising coaches. At small schools, the athletic director may also provide information to the press and the public. While coaching itself doesn't require a college degree, athletic directors usually have a bachelor's degree in physical education, sports management, or business.

### INSTRUCTORS

**Instructors** teach sports to individuals and groups of amateurs. The increasing popularity of recreational sports has led to a growth in this career field in recent years.

There are two main kinds of instructors. Physical education instructors work in schools, developing programs and leading classes in a wide range of sports. Most "phys ed" instructors hold college or advanced degrees in the field. They need a wide knowledge of team and individual sports and of physical fitness.

Instructors of specific sports work wherever their sports are played—ski instructors at ski areas, aerobics instructors at fitness centers, and so on. Generally no college or advanced degree is required for this work. But instructors do need athletic skill, as well as a thorough knowledge of their sport and of physical training principles. Professional associations in some sports also offer certification programs for instructors. Such certification isn't always required; but, even if it isn't, it can help you in getting a job.

Like coaches, instructors of all kinds must be good communicators who enjoy working with people. Income in this field varies widely. Salaries for physical education instructors are about the same as those for other schoolteachers. Most other sports instructors are not highly paid. And those in seasonal sports, such as skiing, must often work at second jobs during the off-season. But instructors may earn more by advancing into a management job or going into business for themselves.

### SPORTS MEDICINE

Everyone knows that, to turn in the best performance, an athlete must be in top physical condition. And everyone knows that injuries can be disastrous in sports, ruining a team's season or a player's career. Maintaining peak condition and preventing injuries are the two chief concerns of sports medicine, a field that has grown rapidly in recent years.

Sports medicine offers two main careers. Most professional and many college teams employ **athletic trainers**. Athletic trainers are physical fitness specialists. They assess the athletes' condition and develop fitness training programs to strengthen any weaknesses. They give advice on nutrition and on protective equipment. At games they provide first

Suppose you love sports, but you're a clod on the playing field. You can still have a rewarding career in sports—by providing information to the public.

Colleges and universities with major athletic programs employ **sports information directors**, and professional teams employ **public relations specialists**. Their work is much the same. They prepare press kits that give information on the team and players, arrange and conduct press conferences and photo sessions, send out news releases, maintain files and scrapbooks on the team, arrange for press coverage of games, and make themselves available to answer questions and requests for specific information.

The goal in all this work is to present the team in the most favorable light possible. In many cases, assistants help the director. Some of the assistants may have specific responsibilities, such as writing news releases or keeping team and player statistics.

aid for injuries. And later they may supervise therapy and rehabilitation programs for injured athletes.

This career requires a four-year college degree; some athletic trainers hold master's degrees. In college, people who are interested in this career concentrate on medical, life science, and physical education courses. After college, they work as assistant athletic trainers for a period of time before being certified by a professional group, the National Athletic Trainers Association.

**Sports physicians** are the other main group of professionals in the sports medicine field. A sports physician is a doctor who specializes in physical fitness and sports-related injuries. The requirements for this career are similar to those for other medical specialties —college, four years of medical school, and a residency program that includes training in the specialty. Sports physicians must know about the demands of various sports and the injuries those sports are likely to produce.

Sports physicians may work for teams or clinics, have their own private practice, or conduct research into physical conditioning.

Besides these two main careers, sports medicine offers a number of related careers —in physical therapy and massage, for example. There are even dentists who specialize in sports dentistry.

**L.A. Laker Magic Johnson receives aid from the team doctor. Sports physicians must know about various sports and the injuries they are likely to produce.**

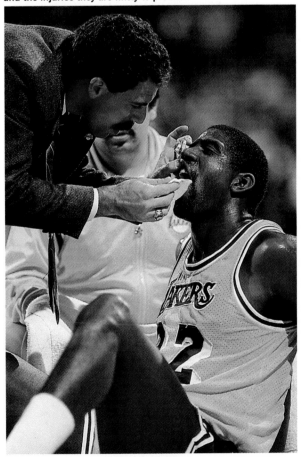

If you think a career in sports might be right for you, you should get involved in the sports that interest you. Play as much as possible, and learn the rules and regulations. Cover sports for your school newspaper. Find out if you can help coach teams in local recreation leagues.

There are professional organizations for nearly every sport and for nearly every sport-related career. Some are listed below. If you don't find a listing for an organization you might be interested in, check with your local library.

**American College of Sports Medicine**—P.O. Box 1440, Indianapolis, IN 46206

**Athletic and Educational Opportunities**—P.O. Box 31113, Chicago, IL 60631

**Athletic Equipment Managers Association**—723 Keil, Bowling Green, OH 43402

**College Sports Information Directors of America**—P.O. Box 114, Texas A & I University, Kingsville, TX 78363

**National Association of Sports Officials**—2071 Lathrop Avenue, Racine, WI 43405

**National Athletic Trainers Association**—1001 East 4th Street, Greenville, NC 27834

**National Fitness Foundation**—2250 E. Imperial Highway, El Segundo, CA 90245

**National High School Athletic Coaches Association**—3423 East Silver Springs Boulevard, Ocala, FL 32670

**U.S. Athletes Association**—3735 Lakeland Avenue, N., Minneapolis, MN 55422

**Women's Sports Foundation**—342 Madison Avenue, Suite 728, New York, NY 10017

Sports reporting is another information-related career. **Sportswriters** work for newspapers and magazines. They cover the games and prepare stories that give background information on the teams and players. **Sportscasters** work for radio stations and television networks. They may summarize the day's events in sports, provide "play-by-play" coverage of games, or prepare background and "color" reports that are filled with interesting information. **Photographers** and **camera operators** are also part of the sports-reporting team.

Besides a thorough knowledge of the sport, good communications skills are essential in this field. People who are interested in a career in sports information or reporting usually start by covering sports for their school newspaper, and they study journalism, communications, or public relations in college.

Hours are long, and the work often requires travel. But many sports information specialists make a good living—and they get first-rate seats for every game.

**OFFICIALS**

Every sport has rules and regulations. And in every competition, someone must supervise the play, settle disputes, and decide when points have been scored or rules have been broken. This is the job of officials—**umpires**, **referees**, **scorers**, **timekeepers**, **judges**, and others. Officials must know their sport and its rules inside and out, so that they can make decisions quickly and confidently. They must be sharp observers, even-tempered, and able to work under pressure.

The role of officials at a competition varies with the sport. So do the requirements for the career and the potential income. Sports officials generally have at least a high school degree. In most sports, in order to be certified, they must attend special training schools that are offered by professional sports associations.

Officials in major-league professional sports must also have years of experience officiating at minor-league and amateur games. Competition for these top jobs is keen. In the National Football League, for example, only a few officials are certified each year. All NFL officials are rated on their performance every year, and those who do poorly aren't hired the next year.

As in many sports careers, officials must often travel and work on nights or weekends. The work may also be seasonal. And while major-league officials can make a good living, those at lower levels are often not highly paid. Thus many sports officials hold second jobs.

## SPORTS AND BUSINESS

It's also possible to combine a love of sports with a traditional business career. For example, as professional sports have become big business, the role of the **agent**, or player's representative, has increased. Agents represent players in negotiations with team management, trying to get the best salary and working arrangement possible. They comb the players' contracts carefully, examining the wording, and keep the players up-to-date on legal matters that may affect their careers.

Agents are generally lawyers or accountants. Besides understanding contract law and financial matters thoroughly, they must be skilled negotiators and understand the regulations of the sport they are involved in. For their work, most agents earn a percentage (usually 10 percent) of the player's income. Thus an agent whose clients include several star players can count on a high income. But like many other sports careers, this one is competitive—there are even fewer top agents than there are top professional athletes.

There are many other careers that mix sports and business. Professional teams employ **marketing specialists** to promote ticket sales. They also hire **accountants** to watch the bottom line. There are **insurance agents** who specialize in providing "special risk" insurance for both athletes and teams. Or you might find a job in the **sporting goods industry**—designing sports equipment, marketing it to professional teams, or selling it in retail stores.

In all these fields, a knowledge and love of sports will give you an edge. So if sports are your passion, you may be able to make them your career—even if you aren't a star on the playing field.

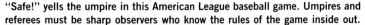

"Safe!" yells the umpire in this American League baseball game. Umpires and referees must be sharp observers who know the rules of the game inside out.

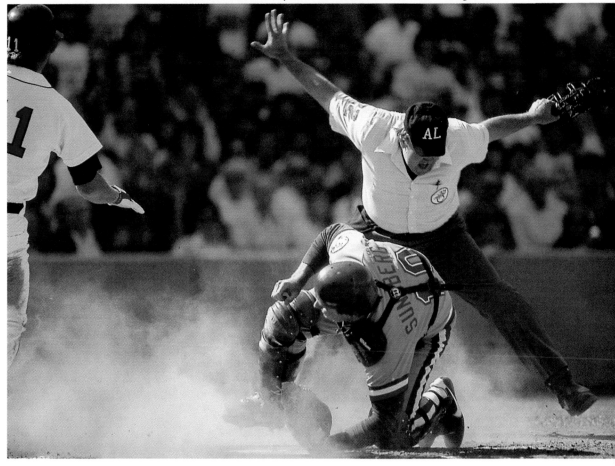

*Landscape,*
by Patricia Stone, 16,
Pittsburgh, Pennsylvania

# YOUNG PHOTOGRAPHERS

Photography can transform the world around us. Trees become pale ghosts. A door opens to reveal a world of enchantment. Even a simple carnation becomes something more when it is viewed through the camera's eye.

The young people who took the pictures on these pages clearly know about photography's magic powers. They were winners in the 1991 Scholastic/Ricoh Art Awards competition, which includes divisions in drawing and many other forms of art as well as photography. The contest is open to U.S. and Canadian students in grades 7 through 12.

Like many photographers today, these young people used a wide rage of techniques in their pictures—double exposures, hand tinting, computers. But all that's really needed to create magical pictures is a camera and an imaginative eye.

*Carnation,* by Emily Allison, 17, Glen Ellyn, Illinois

236

*Aspens in the Mist,* by Lynette Rencher, 16, Salt Lake City, Utah

Untitled,
by Mike McClure, 12,
Wichita, Kansas

*Fer Alisa,*
by Jeffrey Patterson, 17,
Newhall, California

*Portrait,* by Chanthou Ly, 17, Rochester, New York

*Wattie in Wonderland,* by Jonathan Nuner, 18, South Bend, Indiana

# CREATIVITY

Pierre Auguste Renoir was one of the best-known of the French Impressionist painters, and 1991—the 150th anniversary of his birth—brought renewed appreciation of his work. This painting, Madame Charpentier and Her Children, was acclaimed when it was first exhibited in 1879. It shows a celebrated Parisian hostess at home with her family, and it demonstrates Renoir's ability to blend the popular taste of his time with his own graceful style and creativity.

# MOZART— THAT MARVELOUS BOY

He composed his first piece of music by the time he was 5 years old. At the age of 8 he wrote his first symphony, and at the age of 12 his first opera. He grew up to become one of the greatest—some people would say *the* greatest—of the world's composers. When he died in 1791, at the young age of 35, he left behind hundreds of works, many of which are still widely performed and loved today.

The name of this musical genius was Wolfgang Amadeus Mozart, and 1991 marked the

Top: Mozart, age 11, at the clavichord. Above: a view of Salzburg, Austria, Mozart's birthplace, about the time the composer lived. Opposite page: Lincoln Center's banner proclaiming the Mozart bicentennial. The music is from an autographed copy of Mozart's motet "God Is Our Refuge."

200th anniversary of his death. In honor of the anniversary, festivals and special performances of Mozart's works were held all around the world.

### CHILD PRODIGY

Mozart was born in Salzburg, Austria, on January 27, 1756. He was christened Joannes Chrysostomus Wolfgangus Theophilus Mozart. But he was always called Wolfgang by his family, and he usually signed his music Wolfgang Amadeus (the Latin form of Theophilus, which means "beloved of God" in Greek). That is how he is known today.

Mozart's father, Leopold, was a violinist, a composer, and an assistant kapellmeister, or conductor, of the court orchestra of the archbishop of Salzburg. He and his wife, Anna Maria, had seven children. But only two—Wolfgang and his older sister, Maria Anna (nicknamed Nannerl)—survived.

When Nannerl was 8 her father began to give her music lessons on the harpsichord, a keyboard instrument resembling the piano. Wolfgang was 3 at the time, and he listened intently to his sister's lessons. Afterward, he would pick out chords on the keyboard. Leopold noticed his son's interest and decided to give him music lessons, too.

The boy learned quickly, throwing himself into the music with great seriousness. His father gave him increasingly difficult pieces to learn, and by the time he was 5 years old he was writing minuets (music based on dance rhythms that were popular at the time). Meanwhile, Nannerl had developed into an excellent musician.

Leopold Mozart decided that he had two exceptional children. In the 1700's, child prodigies—children with extraordinary talent—attracted a great deal of attention. Leopold knew that if Wolfgang and Nannerl performed before royalty and nobility, they could expect to receive money and gifts. Thus he decided that it was time to show his children's brilliance to the world. He didn't see this as exploiting their talents. In fact, he felt it was his duty to further their careers and help make the family financially secure.

In 1762, when Wolfgang was 6 and Nan-

Mozart came from a musical family with extraordinary talent. At this "jam session," Leopold plays the violin, Wolfgang is at the keyboard, and Nannerl is singing.

nerl was 11, their father took them to Munich, the capital of Bavaria. There they performed before the Elector, or ruler, of Bavaria, who called Wolfgang a "marvelous boy." From Munich the Mozarts traveled to Vienna, the capital of Austria, where they performed for the Empress Maria Theresa at the Schönbrunn Palace. She was so delighted with the performance that she gave each of the children a set of fancy court clothes.

Apart from his genius in music, Mozart at this time was more or less a typical boy. He was healthy, intelligent, and high-spirited, and he had a mischievous sense of fun— characteristics that would stay with him for the rest of his life. When he was introduced to the Austrian empress in Vienna, for example, he jumped into her lap, threw his arms around her, and kissed her. He also proposed marriage to the empress's 6-year-old daughter, Marie Antoinette, who would one day be the queen of France. Both incidents caused much amusement at the court.

The short tour was so successful that, the following year, Leopold Mozart decided to take the whole family on a much longer one —through Germany, France, England, and the Netherlands. The tour lasted three years and made the young Mozart the talk of Europe. He was called a "little magician" and a "wonderwork of nature." In his performances, he was constantly put to the test. He had to play with the keyboard covered with a cloth, and to play music at sight without having seen it before. These were things an experienced musician might have trouble doing, but the boy played perfectly.

Besides performing on the harpsichord and the piano, he also performed on the clavichord, the organ, and the violin. And he continued to compose. One day in London, when Leopold was ill and Mozart couldn't practice for fear of disturbing his father, he sat down and composed his first symphony. The year was 1764, and he was 8 years old. He would write two more symphonies within the next year.

The Mozarts returned home in 1766. The tour hadn't brought as much money as they

The Houston Grand Opera's production of *The Magic Flute*, Mozart's popular comic opera, was especially appealing—the sets were designed by children's book illustrator Maurice Sendak.

had hoped, and Leopold's salary from the archbishop was small. Thus they soon set out again for Vienna. Leopold hoped that the Austrian emperor would commission his son to write an opera, which was then considered the highest form of musical art. (At about this time, Wolfgang contracted smallpox. He survived this often-fatal disease, but it left his face pockmarked for life.) But the emperor didn't commission the opera—because, Leopold was convinced, his court musicians were jealous of Wolfgang's talent.

Wolfgang wrote the opera anyway, in 1768, and called it *La Finta Semplice* ("The Make-believe Simpleton"). A year later, the family had returned to Salzburg again, and the opera was performed at the archbishop's palace. As a reward, the archbishop gave Mozart the honorary title of concertmaster. But this position carried no salary, so Leopold and Wolfgang set out on a tour of Italy. Nannerl stayed home; she was now 18 and could no longer be considered a child prodigy. And at that time, it wasn't expected that a woman would have a career as a musician.

The trip to Italy was one of several that they would make in the next few years. Italy was then the musical center of Europe. Leopold felt that if his son was successful there, his future would be assured. The trip also provided a chance for Wolfgang to polish his skill at writing opera—Italy was the birth-

place of opera, and at that time nearly all operas were sung in Italian.

Italy received the boy well. He was applauded and honored. The pope awarded him the Order of the Golden Spur. The philharmonic society of the city of Bologna made him a member—even though he was just 14 and the minimum age for membership was supposed to be 20. In Rome, Wolfgang amazed everyone by writing down from memory the score of a difficult choral piece after hearing it performed just once, in the Sistine Chapel. And he was given commissions for two operas and several other works.

Leopold and Wolfgang returned to Salzburg in 1771. Wolfgang was 15, and his life as a mature composer and performer was beginning. Other musicians looked on him not as a child prodigy but as a potential rival.

### IN SEARCH OF SUCCESS

Wolfgang Mozart now drew a small salary in his position as concertmaster at the archbishop's court in Salzburg. He continued to compose new musical pieces, including his first piano concerto. But after so many tours and court performances, he hoped for a better position.

In 1777, he left the archbishop's service and set out on another tour, this time accompanied by his mother. They visited Mannheim, then one of the most important musical centers of Europe, and Paris. Mozart found his reception in Paris colder on this trip. Although he composed several new works that were well received, he didn't find the position he had hoped for. Then, in 1778, his mother fell ill and died suddenly in Paris.

Mozart returned to Salzburg, where he once again worked for the archbishop. His skills as a composer continued to grow. In 1781 he wrote the opera *Idomeneo,* considered by some to be his first truly great opera. But he was increasingly unhappy. The archbishop considered him a servant and treated him like one, and he often refused to let Mozart earn extra money by giving concerts for others. In 1781, Mozart left the archbishop's service once again.

Mozart planned to make his living independently in Vienna by performing, selling his compositions, and teaching. This was highly unusual; at that time, musicians were generally employed by a court or by some wealthy patron. Still, Mozart was confident that he would succeed. And despite his unclear future, in 1782 he married. His bride was 19-year-old Constanze Weber, the daughter of a musical family with whom Mozart boarded in Vienna. (They would have six children; only two sons would survive.)

Gradually, students began to come to Mozart. He sold several new compositions, and people flocked to his concerts. He wrote a new comic opera, *The Abduction from the Seraglio,* with spoken dialogue in German. It was a great success—even though the Austrian emperor remarked that it had "too many notes." (Mozart replied, "Just as many as it needs, Your Majesty.")

The Mozarts lived well in Vienna. They had a spacious apartment, dressed expensively, often entertained their friends, and kept their own carriage. Mozart also enjoyed gambling at billiards and cards. All this cost money, and he was often short of it. To earn more, Mozart kept up a busy schedule, giving concerts, teaching, and producing new compositions.

These years saw some of his greatest works, including the operas *The Marriage of Figaro* and *Don Giovanni* and the serenade *Eine kleine Nachtmusik* ("A Little Night Music"). Some of these works were better received in other cities than in Vienna. But in 1787, Mozart finally received an appointment at the Viennese court, as a composer of chamber music. The salary was small, but it was steady.

All the same, the Mozarts were deeply in debt and had trouble making ends meet. To make matters worse, both Wolfgang and Constanze fell ill. But Mozart continued to turn out new works at a furious pace. Among them was the comic opera *Così fan tutte* ("Women Are Like That"), which was a great hit in Vienna. Unfortunately, the emperor died soon after the opera's first performance, and the theaters were closed in mourning.

In 1791, Mozart produced what would be one of his last works and also one of his most famous, the comic opera *The Magic Flute*. It was written for a suburban theater run by a friend, and it contained some of the composer's most tuneful music. At the same time, he was working on several other projects. One of them was a mysterious commission for a Requiem Mass (church music that would be performed as a memorial to someone who had died).

According to the story, a stranger came to Mozart and offered him a large sum of money to write this work anonymously, on the condition that he wouldn't ask the name of the patron who wanted it. The patron was actually a Viennese nobleman who liked to commission works from composers and pass them off as his own. He wanted the mass to honor his wife, who had recently died. But Mozart, overworked and in declining health, became convinced that the mass would mark his own death. "One cannot change one's own destiny," he wrote in a letter. "Here is my death song."

By the late fall of 1791, Mozart was experiencing high fevers and severe stomach pains. Researchers today believe that he was suffering from kidney disease, but doctors at the time didn't know what was wrong.

Mozart himself was convinced that his rivals were poisoning him. In his last days, he worked frantically to complete the Requiem Mass. But it was still unfinished when he died, in Constanze's arms, at 1 A.M. on December 5, 1791. He was just 35 years old.

After a simple funeral, the composer was buried in an unmarked pauper's grave outside Vienna. Although it has long been thought that he was buried this way because he had little money, some researchers believe differently. They say the real reason was that elaborate religious funerals had been banned by the Austrian emperor. Whatever the reason, however, to this very day no one knows the exact site of Mozart's grave.

### MOZART'S LEGACY

The story of Mozart's life has captured the imagination of many people. For example, Mozart's belief that he was poisoned gave rise to rumors after his death that he had in fact been murdered by a rival, possibly the Viennese court composer Antonio Salieri. These rumors were the basis for the Broadway play *Amadeus* and the award-winning 1984 film of the same title. But historians agree that Mozart died a natural death.

Although Mozart died poor, he left a great legacy to the world—his music. His works include serious pieces that are among the greatest examples of classical music. They also include light, cheerful pieces that reflect his own sense of humor and fun—he even wrote songs with racy lyrics to entertain his friends. The first catalog of Mozart's works, the Kochel catalog, listed more than 600 works.

Mozart lived only 35 years. But he left behind hundreds of works, many still loved today.

If all the minor pieces that are known today are counted, however, there are more than 800 works by this prolific composer. Many of Mozart's works are as popular today as when they were first written, if not more so. And in 1991, the anniversary of his death, they were presented in special performances all over the world. In Salzburg, where the composer was born and where he is honored each year with a music festival, more than 600 concerts and special events were planned. Vienna hosted a Mozart festival in the spring and staged several Mozart operas and concerts throughout the year. Nine European countries collaborated in a festival called "Mozart's European Journey," staging concerts in cities where the composer had performed.

Mozart festivals were also held in Japan, Canada, and the United States. One of the most ambitious programs was that of New York City's Lincoln Center; the Center planned to perform, over a period of nineteen months, every note that Mozart had ever written. There were also dozens of new recordings of Mozart's works, books about him, TV specials, and even Mozart T-shirts, dolls, and coffee mugs.

Some people wondered if all this attention would be too much —if people would grow tired of Mozart and his works. But others dismissed that idea. As one music historian put it, "Mozart has stood up for 200 years. He's not going to wear out." Although the composer died young, his music seems likely to live on as long as there are people to play it and people to listen to it.

Kevin Costner (best director) in *Dances With Wolves* (best motion picture).

# 1991 ACADEMY AWARDS

| CATEGORY | WINNER |
| --- | --- |
| Motion Picture | *Dances With Wolves* |
| Actor | Jeremy Irons (*Reversal of Fortune*) |
| Actress | Kathy Bates (*Misery*) |
| Supporting Actor | Joe Pesci (*GoodFellas*) |
| Supporting Actress | Whoopi Goldberg (*Ghost*) |
| Director | Kevin Costner (*Dances With Wolves*) |
| Cinematography | Dean Semler (*Dances With Wolves*) |
| Song | "Sooner or Later (I Always Get My Man)" (*Dick Tracy*) |
| Foreign-Language Film | *Journey of Hope* (Switzerland) |
| Documentary Feature | *American Dream* |
| Documentary Short | *Days of Waiting* |

Patrick Swayze and Whoopi Goldberg (best supporting actress) in *Ghost*.

Glenn Close and Jeremy Irons (best actor) in *Reversal of Fortune*.

*Pierre Auguste Renoir was a master Impressionist artist. In one of his most famous paintings,* The Ball at Moulin de la Galette *(1876), he captured a happy but fleeting moment of Parisian life.*

# RENOIR—A GREAT IMPRESSIONIST

In the second half of the 19th century, a group of French painters brought a breath of fresh air to the world of art. Called the Impressionists, these artists sought to capture on canvas the momentary and magical effects of light in the natural world. Their ideas and their style were revolutionary in their day. But today the Impressionists are recognized as masters.

Among the greatest of the Impressionists was Pierre Auguste Renoir. Renoir's paintings have a warm, soft quality that has long made them popular favorites as well as great works of art. And in 1991, Renoir received

special attention on the 150th anniversary of his birth.

### EARLY YEARS

Renoir was born on February 25, 1841, in Limoges, a French city famous for ceramics. In 1845 the family moved to Paris, where his father, a tailor, hoped to find better opportunities. As a young boy, Renoir showed a natural talent for drawing. His father felt that he should use this talent in a trade, and so he was apprenticed at age 13 to a painter of china and porcelain.

Renoir learned to decorate china with tiny

roses, classical portraits, and other designs. He enjoyed the work. But it didn't offer a good future—machine methods of decorating china were being developed. By the time he was 17, he was looking for a new career. For a while, he decorated fans with scenes from classical paintings. This early training as a decorative artist would influence his later style, especially in his use of soft, glowing colors. But Renoir soon found his interests moving more toward fine art.

In 1862, having saved some money, Renoir entered the École des Beaux-Arts to study under the Swiss painter Charles Gleyre. This school taught the traditional style of painting that was popular at the time. In this style, paintings were supposed to be very realistic and depict historical and uplifting subjects; form, line, and composition were emphasized over color.

Renoir's teachers thought that he showed promise. But they warned him that if he didn't concentrate on drawing and pay less attention to color, he would become "another Delacroix." That must have pleased Renoir, for the Romantic painter Delacroix, known for his use of color, was one of the young student's favorites. He had discovered this artist's work at the Louvre museum, where he often spent his lunch hours studying and drawing from the works of the masters.

In 1863 one of Renoir's paintings was selected for the yearly Salon—an exhibition of traditional art governed by the powerful Academy of Fine Arts. This mark of approval meant that he was on his way to a commercially successful career—artists who were accepted by the Salon could almost always sell their works, while those who were rejected usually couldn't. Renoir would continue to submit works to the Salon off and on over the next 27 years, and a number were accepted. He liked the official recognition of the exhibit. But all the

same, he soon began to rebel against the restrictions of the formal, academic style that the Salon jury preferred.

### WITH THE IMPRESSIONISTS

In rebelling, Renoir joined a group of painters that included Édouard Manet, Edgar Degas, Claude Monet, Alfred Sisley, and Camille Pissarro. Beginning in 1866, they often met at the Café Guerbois in Paris to discuss art. Although their works differed in many ways, these artists shared a belief

On the Terrace *(1879). Renoir's paintings during this time were marked by soft contours, rainbow colors, warm light, and brushy surface textures.*

that paintings should portray nature and everyday scenes, and they were interested in capturing passing moments and the effects of natural light by using dabs and strokes of pure color. Renoir listened to the discussions, which often grew heated. But he found many of the arguments pointless. "Theories don't make good pictures," he is said to have remarked. When he painted, he said, "I simply let myself go."

In 1870 war broke out between France and Prussia (now part of Germany). Renoir enlisted in the cavalry, but his regiment didn't fight. When he returned to Paris after the war, he rejoined his old friends. In 1871 he settled in Argenteuil, a small town outside the city where he could live less expensively.

Renoir's more adventurous paintings, like those of his friends, were regularly turned down by the Salon. But the artists were eager for recognition. Thus, in 1874, thirty of them held their own exhibit. Critics denounced the works at the exhibit for their loose brushwork and lack of clarity and form. The paintings, said the critics, were more like sketches than finished works. One critic dismissed Claude Monet as an "impressionist." The name stuck, and soon the group adopted it with pride.

Renoir continued to paint Impressionist works—colorful, sun-filled landscapes and everyday scenes of people relaxing and enjoying themselves. He often painted outdoors, working from nature. And he was often joined by Monet and other Impressionists as he worked. But unlike the other Impressionists, who concentrated on painting landscapes, Renoir preferred painting the human figure—especially women and children. Even in his outdoor scenes, people were usually the center of activity. Some of Renoir's greatest paintings were done between 1874 and 1881. They are marked by soft contours, rainbow colors, warm light, and brushy surface textures. Although he found it difficult to sell these paintings, he managed to make a living by painting portraits and more traditional works as well.

In 1881, Renoir married Aline Charigot, and they set off on a honeymoon trip to Italy. The trip gave him a long-awaited chance to see some of the great works of art of the Italian Renaissance. Although he considered the traditional style of the French Salon dry and hollow, he had never lost his respect for the great art of the past. He was deeply impressed by his tour, and he returned to France feeling that he "had wrung Impressionism dry" and that he "knew neither how to paint nor draw."

## LATER YEARS

After his trip, Renoir began to change his style of painting. Some historians call this time his "harsh" or "dry" period. His figures became more solid, and he used harsher

Dance at Bougival (1883). As Renoir's style of painting changed, he concentrated more on line and composition, and his figures became more solid and detailed.

colors. He concentrated on line and composition, making careful drawings before he began to paint. He also began to choose more classical subjects, such as female nudes. And he worked less outdoors and more in his studio.

But he didn't completely abandon the ideals of Impressionism. Instead, he wanted to enrich Impressionism by bringing into it some of the traditions of classical art. In works from this period, Renoir often drew and painted the central figures carefully and in great detail. But the background and secondary figures are as freely done as his earlier works.

Renoir didn't fit the general picture of the Bohemian artist. His home life was respectable and traditional. He and Aline had three children, and he enjoyed spending time with his family and his friends. In fact, his wife and children were among his favorite painting subjects. And while he never grew wealthy from his art, his home was comfortable.

The artist came to depend on his family especially in his later years, when he suffered from crippling arthritis. It became difficult for him to hold a paintbrush, but he continued to work. His late works feature lush colors—golds, corals, reds, purples—flowing brushstrokes, and massive, rounded figures in relaxed poses.

Two Girls at the Piano (1893). Renoir's later works featured lush golds and reds, flowing brushstrokes, and softer, more relaxed figures.

In 1913 he took up sculpture. But by this time, he was too badly crippled to actually create the sculptures himself. Instead, he worked with a young Italian artist named Richard Guino. First, Renoir would choose a drawing or a section of a painting. Then, as he directed the work with a pointer, Guino would translate it into sculpture.

As the years went on, Renoir began to be recognized as the great artist that he was. But he remained as simple and direct about his art as he had always been. "I arrange my subject as I want it, then I go ahead and paint it, like a child," he told another painter. "I

have no rules and no methods." He still believed that art couldn't really be explained by theories. "The work of art must seize upon you, wrap you up in itself, carry you away," he said. "It is the means by which the artist conveys his passions."

Not long before his death, Renoir visited the Louvre in Paris for the last time. There he saw one of his own works, one that he had done around 1886 as a study for a larger painting. Thus, before he died on December 3, 1919, Renoir had found a place among the great masters that he had studied so many years before.

# PEOPLE, PLACES, EVENTS

The **National Gallery of Art** in Washington, D.C., celebrated its 50th birthday in 1991. To mark the event, the museum staged a special exhibit of works of art that were donated especially for the anniversary. The National Gallery is unusual among the world's major museums because it's so new. The museum was the idea of the wealthy philanthropist Andrew Mellon, who donated funds for the building and his entire collection of art, valued at $31 million. This encouraged others to

make gifts, and the museum's collection grew quickly. Today the National Gallery is a national treasure house of art. For the 50th anniversary, donors chipped in to provide $13 million and some 550 works of art. The exhibit, which ran from March to June, 1991, showcased 320 of these new works. They included paintings and drawings by old masters, works by famous American and European artists of the 19th and 20th centuries, and contemporary art. Among them were Paul Cézanne's *Boy in a Red Waistcoat* (1890; above) and Alberto Giacometti's *The Chariot* (1950; left). Like the other works that were donated for the anniversary, they became part of the National Gallery's permanent collection.

**Kevin Costner** achieved superstar status in 1991 when his film *Dances with Wolves* won the Academy Award as best motion picture. The actor starred in and directed the film, and he also won an Oscar for directing. Costner, who was born in 1955, began acting in films in the 1980's. He became well known for roles in such movies as *The Untouchables* and *Field of Dreams*. And he scored another box office hit in 1991 with *Robin Hood: Prince of Thieves*.

The year 1991 marked the 100th anniversary of the birth of one of America's most famous songwriters: **Cole Porter**. From the 1920's through the 1950's—a period sometimes called the golden age of American popular song—Porter, who died in 1964, wrote lyrics as well as music for Broadway musicals. His work included shows such as *Kiss Me Kate* and *Can-Can* and songs such as "Anything Goes," "Just One of Those Things," and "Love for Sale." In 1991 he was honored with a commemorative postage stamp, a gala concert at New York's Carnegie Hall, and celebrations in Peru, Indiana, where he was born.

Among the winners of the 1991 Tony Awards, for excellence in the theater, was Daisy Eagan (above, right, with John Cameron Mitchell). She was named best supporting actress in a musical for her role as Mary in **The Secret Garden,** an adaptation of the famous children's classic by Frances Hodgson Burnett. At the age of 11½, Eagan was the second youngest person ever to win a Tony. The award for best actress in a musical went to Lea Salonga (right), who starred in **Miss Saigon.** This musical tells of an ill-fated romance between a Vietnamese girl and an American soldier during the Vietnam War. With a production cost of $10 million, and $37 million in advance ticket sales, it was the year's most talked-about show.

The world of art met the world of high technology in 1990 and 1991 in a special exhibition that toured seven cities in the United States and Canada. Called **Information Art,** the exhibition was made up of working drawings for the designs of computer microchips—the tiny integrated circuits that enable computers to process information. These incredibly detailed drawings (one of which is shown here, along with a magnified segment) look like works of abstract art. But they have a completely practical purpose. To make the chips, the diagrams are reduced 100 to 200 times and then etched onto silicon, using photographic techniques. The different colors in the designs represent layers of circuitry to be laid down on the chips. Many of the designs themselves are drawn with computer plotters— they are too detailed to be drawn by hand.

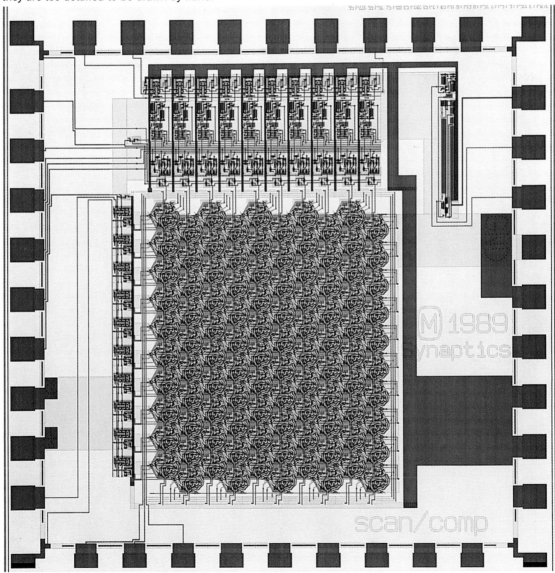

The days of the couch potato—a person who sits for hours, just passively watching television—may be numbered. During 1991, **interactive television** was being test-marketed in the United States and Canada. Interactive television lets the viewer control what appears on the screen. At the touch of a button, you can change camera angles, play (instead of just watch) game shows, or even pick a plot twist. In the mystery movie below, for example, viewers get to decide "who done it." In another interactive show, featuring singer Peter Gabriel, viewers could choose the lyrics sung and even the clothes worn by the star. So far, various interactive systems have been tested in communities in California and Massachusetts and in Montreal, Canada. One interactive network in Canada already has some 50,000 subscribers. But in the United States interactive TV isn't expected to become widely available for at least several years. If interactive TV catches on, it's likely to change television—and couch potatoes—forever.

Thirteen years of the television series *Dallas* came to an end when the show's final episode was aired in May, 1991. This prime-time soap opera, about a wealthy, double-dealing Texas family named the Ewings, was the third longest running TV series ever, after *Gunsmoke* and *Bonanza.* It was popular around the world. In the most famous episode, in May, 1980, lead character J.R. Ewing (played by Larry Hagman, below) was shot. Seventy-five percent of the U.S. TV viewing audience tuned in the following fall to find out who shot J.R.

One of 1991's hottest film directors was 34-year-old **Spike Lee**. Lee first drew attention as a director with *She's Gotta Have It* in 1986, his first feature film. After the success of his 1989 film *Do the Right Thing,* in which he also starred, he became the best known of a group of young black film-makers who address racial issues frankly, and sometimes controversially, in their work. His other films include *Mo' Better Blues* (1990) and *Jungle Fever* (1991). In 1991 he began work on a film biography of the black nationalist leader Malcolm X. Lee is also familiar to TV viewers for his work in commercials for well-known brands of jeans and athletic shoes.

# WINTER WONDERLANDS

If you live where winters are cold, you've probably tried your hand at sculpting snow. Working with snow is challenging and fun, so much so that snow sculpture contests have become popular events in many areas. A snow-sculpting contest was even included in the Olympic Arts Festival at the 1988 Winter Olympics in Calgary, Canada. And a similar contest will be part of the 1992 Winter Olympics in France.

Sculptures made of snow and ice range from simple snowmen to elaborate ice palaces, which are full-size buildings made from blocks of ice. In the late 1800's, ice palaces became very popular at winter carnivals. Montreal, Canada, set the pace by building

## A SPECIAL SNOW SHOW

One of the largest and most famous snow sculpture events is the annual Sapporo Snow Festival on Hokkaido, the northernmost island of Japan. It began in the early 1950's, when high-school students began building snowmen in a city park. Today the five-day festival draws people from all

ever more elaborate palaces for its winter sports carnival. A few years later, St. Paul, Minnesota, became the first U.S. city to follow suit. Some of the palaces built for these and other festivals had towering towers and were made of thousands of blocks of ice.

Ice palaces today are seldom that large, but they're still a feature of many winter carnivals. And along with them can be seen snow and ice sculptures in just about every form imaginable.

over the world. And the gigantic sculptures fill an area eleven blocks long and spill over into nearby streets.

A month before the festival, Japanese soldiers begin trucking in mounds of snow and ice. The soldiers carve many of the sculptures, but there are also teams from Japanese schools and even from other countries. From huge blocks of ice and snow,

the sculptors use axes, saws, spades, chisels, knives, and other tools to carve animals and characters from books, cartoons, movies, and television —and, of course, palaces and castles. There's even an area with snow slides and other attractions for children. At night, the sculptures glitter under floodlights.

As happens at other winter festivals, bulldozers knock the sculptures down after the festival ends. (If they were left to melt and tumble down on their own, someone might be hurt.) Photographs, like those shown on these pages, are all that are left of the artists' works—along with the memories of a wonderful time.

One of 1991's most popular rock groups was R.E.M., whose latest album, *Out of Time,* hit number one.

# THE MUSIC SCENE

*"Today's music ain't got the same soul.
I like that old-time rock and roll."*

Music fans who believed in the sentiments of that Bob Seger song could take heart in 1991. After more than a year of dominance by rap and dance music, rock and roll was making a comeback. A number of unmistakably rocking tunes were among the year's biggest hits. But the new rock and roll wasn't exactly the same as before. Rock musicians were borrowing elements from other kinds of music and coming up with new blends of sound.

### ROCK RULES!

A particularly thoughtful brand of rock was offered by R.E.M. Once familiar only to college-radio listeners, this Georgia-based quartet has increasingly moved into the mainstream. Their latest album, *Out of Time,* hit number one on the charts and soon went platinum, with more than a million copies sold. The record included unconventional love songs as well as songs about political and environmental concerns. The popular single "Losing My Religion" featured plaintive vocals by lead singer Michael Stipe over the appealing sounds of acoustic guitar and mandolin. The artful video for the song won six MTV video music awards, including best video of the year.

Another Georgia-based band, the Black Crowes, scored with their debut album, *Shake Your Money Maker,* which sold more than two million copies. The album's success was spurred by its hit single "She Talks to Angels." The group's guitar-driven sound reminded many listeners of "classic" rock bands of the early 1970's.

Other up-and-coming groups gave rock a new spin. On *The Reality of My Surroundings,* Los Angeles-based "funk and roll" band Fishbone came up with a wild mix of sounds, including metal, rap, and reggae. Three more bands who rocked on the wild side were Faith No More, the Red Hot Chili Peppers, and Jane's Addiction. Hot new British group Jesus Jones mixed guitar rock with dance music, along with psychedelic sounds of the 1960's. They also used digital sampling, a technique pioneered by rap artists, to electronically incorporate a variety of sounds—including bird songs—into their music. Their album *Doubt* produced a hit single, "Right Here, Right Now."

Perhaps the most dramatic event of the music scene in 1991 came toward the end of the year, when hard rock group Guns N' Roses released two new albums at once. The albums, *Use Your Illusion I* and *Use Your Illusion II,* immediately hit first and second place on the album chart and went gold, racking up sales of more than 500,000 each in the first week. The albums were the group's first release in several years and had been eagerly awaited by their fans. Non-fans have criticized Guns N' Roses songs for their sometimes violent and offensive lyrics. On the new albums, listeners found that the band had toned down its words somewhat, but not its electrifying sound.

Well-received albums were also released by rock-and-roll veterans Tom Petty (*Into the Great Wide Open*), Bob Seger (*The Fire Inside*), and John Mellencamp (*Whenever We Wanted*). And a 26-year-old rock band was the year's biggest success on the concert scene—the perennially popular Grateful Dead played sold-out shows throughout its 1991 tour.

The latest heartthrob on the music scene was Chris Isaak, who had a top-selling album, *Heart Shaped World*. His hit single, "Wicked Game," was a slow, haunting ballad sung in a style reminiscent of early rockers Roy Orbison and Elvis Presley. Isaak's '50's look—complete with pompadour haircut—added to this rockabilly connection.

### FRESH SOUNDS

Danceable pop music remained alive and well during the year. Singer-choreographer Paula Abdul returned after a year's absence with *Spellbound,* a collection of ballads and catchy dance tracks. The songs "Rush Rush" and "The Promise of a New Day" were number-one singles.

Pop singer Mariah Carey, whose 1990 debut album remained a top seller, released a follow-up. *Emotions* contained songs showcasing the singer's impressive vocal abilities. Former gospel star Amy Grant moved into the mainstream with *Heart in Motion* and its top-selling singles "Baby Baby" and "Every Heartbeat." And Michael Jackson launched his latest album, *Dangerous*, with a spectacular video of "Black or White," the album's first single.

C & C Music Factory blended rap and dance rhythms on *Gonna Make You Sweat*. The title track was a top-selling single, and it generated what was perhaps the year's most popular dance video. Swedish duo Roxette also made the charts with *Joyride* and its single "Fading Like a Flower (Every Time You Leave)." *Into the Light* was Gloria Estefan's latest LP, and it contained more of her Latin-flavored dance tunes.

One of the year's most unusual hits came from Natalie Cole. *Unforgettable* was a collection of pop standards originally performed by her father, the late Nat King Cole. Modern recording technology enabled Natalie to blend her vocals with those of her father for a "duet" on the title song.

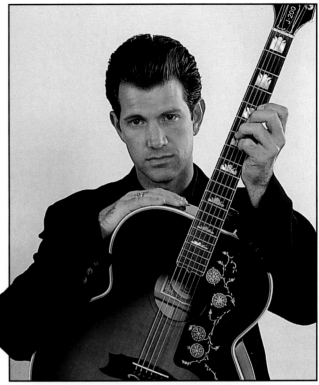

The latest musical heartthrob was Chris Isaak, who, with his '50's look, reminded fans of early rockers.

Soulful balladeer Michael Bolton had a number-one album, *Time, Love and Tenderness,* and a hit single, "Love Is a Wonderful Thing." Other soul providers included Luther Vandross, with his *Power of Love,* and Aaron Neville, with *Warm Your Heart.*

Australia's Crowded House released *Woodface.* British band Dire Straits tried for a comeback with *On Every Street,* their first album since 1985. Canada's Bryan Adams, also absent for several years, released *Waking Up the Neighbours.* The album's success was spurred by its number-one single, "(Everything I Do) I Do It For You," which was also found on the soundtrack of the 1991 movie *Robin Hood: Prince of Thieves.* Other movies that gave rise to successful soundtrack albums were *New Jack City, Boyz N the Hood, The Doors,* and *The Commitments.*

Many longtime stars were heard from during the year. Most proved that, when it comes to creating intelligent and highly listenable pop music, experience counts. Bon-

Pop singer Mariah Carey continued to demonstrate her vocal talents and walked off with two Grammy Awards.

second album, *Mama Said,* which harked back to the 1960's with a combination of soul and psychedelia. Saxophone player Candy Dulfer released *Saxuality,* an album of pop-jazz tunes. Although only 21, Dulfer had already played with many big names, including Prince and the Eurythmics.

### RAP AND HEAVY METAL

Several established rap stars offered new releases during the year. LL Cool J scored big with "Mama Said Knock You Out," which won an MTV video music award for best rap video. *Homebase* was the latest effort by the duo D. J. Jazzy Jeff and the Fresh Prince. (Fresh Prince also continued to star in the television sitcom *Fresh Prince of Bel Air*.) The album yielded a hit single, "Summertime."

M. C. Hammer (now known simply as "Hammer") followed up his top-selling 1990 album, *Please Hammer Don't Hurt 'Em,* with *Too Legit to Quit.* Hammer also debuted as the host of a new children's cartoon

C & C Music Factory blended rap and dance and made one of the year's most popular videos.

nie Raitt followed her 1989 Grammy-winning *Nick of Time* LP with *Luck of the Draw,* an album of songs—some bluesy, some rocking —about the ups and downs of romance. Another experienced singer-guitarist, Joni Mitchell, released the highly praised *Night Ride Home,* her first album in almost three years. *The Soul Cages* was Sting's latest effort. Written as a reflection on his father's death, the album's nine songs dealt mainly with father-son relationships. Albums with a more individual style were also released by England's Elvis Costello (*Mighty Like a Rose*), Richard Thompson (*Rumor and Sigh*), and Joe Jackson (*Laughter and Lust*).

Younger artists, too, made interesting contributions to the music year. A relatively unknown group, Extreme, had a surprise hit with "More Than Words," which featured mellow acoustic guitars and soft vocal harmonies. British group EMF attracted attention with their debut album, *Schubert Dip,* and its catchy dance/pop singles "Unbelievable" and "I Believe." Lenny Kravitz earned a place on the pop charts with his

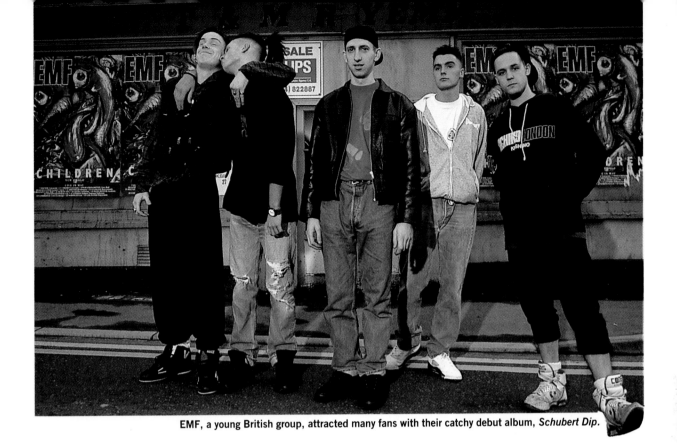

EMF, a young British group, attracted many fans with their catchy debut album, *Schubert Dip*.

show, *Hammerman,* that featured his music and dance. Veteran rappers Run-D.M.C., Ice Cube, and Public Enemy also released new rap albums during the year.

Since its beginnings, rap has been dominated by male performers, and some rap lyrics have been hostile to women. But recently, women rap artists have begun to talk back. Often their lyrics challenge the male rappers' negative stereotypes and urge women to respect themselves. On *Nature of a Sista',* her second album, Queen Latifah demonstrated vocal agility equal to the best of the male rappers. She also mixed in more tuneful sounds and used live musicians instead of digitally sampled tracks. Another female rapper, Yo-Yo, released a single, "Stompin' in the 90s," that reached number three on Billboard's rap singles chart.

Heavy metal was more popular than ever, with numerous releases making the charts. *Metallica,* by the group Metallica, was a number-one hit. Another favorite metal band, Queensrÿche, released *Empire;* the band's mellow single "Silent Lucidity" was made into a popular video. Albums by Skid Row, Scorpions, Cinderella, and Poison also racked up sales.

## COUNTRY AND BLUES

Country music continued to grow in popularity. Perhaps its combination of catchy melodies and grown-up subjects appealed to the many music fans approaching middle age. For the first time, a country music album—Garth Brooks's *Ropin' the Wind*—immediately hit the number-one spot on Billboard's pop album chart. (Two other Brooks albums—*Garth Brooks* and *No Fences*—also appeared on the charts during the year.) Brooks was one of a younger crop of male country vocalists, including Clint Black, Alan Jackson, and Mark Chesnutt, all of whom seemed to wear cowboy hats and sing with a soulful twang.

Standing in stark contrast to these smooth crooners were the Kentucky Headhunters, whose unkempt appearance and raucous sound unnerved some country music traditionalists. After releasing their debut album, *Pickin' on Nashville,* in 1990, the group won a Grammy in 1991 and released a second album, *Electric Barnyard.* Both albums appeared on Billboard's pop album chart during the year.

The blues, rock and roll's older relative, captured the spotlight in 1991 courtesy of a young jazz hero and some popular cartoon characters. Renowned jazz trumpeter Wynton Marsalis released *Soul Gestures in Southern Blue,* a three-album exploration of the blues form. Bandleader Marsalis also wrote most of the compositions. And in *Garfield—Am I Cool or What?,* an impressive lineup of artists musically expressed the philosophy of cartoon feline Garfield. Performers included guitar legend B. B. King, Patti LaBelle, and the Temptations. Popular cartoon family the Simpsons attempted their own vocals on *The Simpsons Sing the Blues,* a novelty album of mainly blues standards sung by the actors who provide the voices on *The Simpsons* television show.

### HAPPY BIRTHDAY, MTV

The year marked the tenth anniversary of MTV, the music video channel, which premiered on August 1, 1981. The occasion prompted an assessment of MTV's impact on popular music over the last decade. Most analysts agreed that the rise of music videos has focused attention on image—good looks and great dance moves have become at least as important as musical ability.

Some felt that this need for a perfect pack-

Renowned jazz trumpeter Wynton Marsalis released a three-album exploration of the blues form.

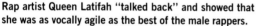

Rap artist Queen Latifah "talked back" and showed that she was as vocally agile as the best of the male rappers.

age had led to an increase in lip-syncing. Controversy over this issue had reached a boiling point in 1990 with the discovery that pop duo Milli Vanilli had done none of the singing on their Grammy-winning debut album. The two had lip-synced their way through music videos and concert appearances. (Their Grammy was taken back as a result.) The issue continued into 1991 when C & C Music Factory acknowledged that vocals "visualized" by Zelma Davis in their hit video "Gonna Make You Sweat" were actually sung by an unseen vocalist, Martha Wash. Despite such criticisms, the influence of MTV seemed certain to continue through the 1990's.

### MUSIC NOTES

Social activism by pop stars has become an important part of the music scene, as each year musicians join forces to support various

## 1991 GRAMMY AWARDS

| | | |
|---|---|---|
| Record of the Year | "Another Day in Paradise" | Phil Collins, artist |
| Album of the Year | *Back on the Block* | Quincy Jones, artist |
| Song of the Year | "From a Distance" | Julie Gold, songwriter |
| New Artist of the Year | | Mariah Carey |
| Pop Vocal Performance—female | "Vision of Love" | Mariah Carey, artist |
| Pop Vocal Performance—male | "Oh Pretty Woman (From a Black and White Night Live)" | Roy Orbison, artist |
| Pop Vocal Performance—group | "All My Life" | Linda Ronstadt, Aaron Neville, artists |
| Rock Vocal Performance—female | "Black Velvet" | Alannah Myles, artist |
| Rock Vocal Performance—male | "Bad Love" | Eric Clapton, artist |
| Rock Vocal Performance—group | "Janie's Got a Gun" | Aerosmith, artists |
| Country Vocal Performance—female | "Where've You Been" | Kathy Mattea, artist |
| Country Vocal Performance—male | "When I Call Your Name" | Vince Gill, artist |
| Country Vocal Performance—group | *Pickin' on Nashville* | The Kentucky Headhunters, artists |
| Rhythm and Blues Vocal Performance—female | *Compositions* | Anita Baker, artist |
| Rhythm and Blues Vocal Performance—male | "Here and Now" | Luther Vandross, artist |
| Rhythm and Blues Vocal Performance—group | "I'll Be Good to You" | Ray Charles, Chaka Khan, artists |
| Music Video Performance | "Opposites Attract" | Paula Abdul, artist |
| Score for a Motion Picture | *Glory* | James Horner, composer |
| Cast Show Album | *Les Misérables: The Complete Symphonic Recording* | David Caddick, producer |
| Classical Album | *Ives: Symphony No. 2; The Gong on the Hook and Ladder (Fireman's Parade on Main Street); Central Park in the Dark; The Unanswered Question* | Leonard Bernstein conducting the New York Philharmonic Orchestra |

causes. An increasingly popular fund-raising method is the "compilation album," to which several performers each contribute a song. Profits from album sales benefit a specified charity. The year saw the release of *Tame Yourself,* to benefit the animal rights group People for the Ethical Treatment of Animals, with performances by the Pretenders, k.d. lang, Belinda Carlisle, and the B-52s. Also released in 1991 was *For Our Children,* to benefit a foundation for children with AIDS. The album contained twenty songs for children, performed by such stars as Elton John, Sting, Paula Abdul, and James Taylor.

In May, some twenty performers on three continents performed in a televised concert to raise money for Kurdish refugees. The concert, called the Simple Truth, was broadcast in 37 countries and featured performances by, among others, Paul Simon, Sting, Gloria Estefan, Sinéad O'Connor, and Hammer.

The sixth annual Rock and Roll Hall of Fame Awards were held in January. Many of the 1991 inductees were early rhythm-and-blues performers, reflecting the important connection between R & B and rock and roll. Performers inducted were LaVern Baker, John Lee Hooker, Jimmy Reed, the Impressions, Wilson Pickett, Ike and Tina Turner, and the Byrds.

Legendary blues performer Howlin' Wolf was honored as an early influence on rock and roll. Also inducted were New Orleans songwriter Dave Bartholomew and record producer Ralph Bass. Meanwhile, delays continued in the construction of the Hall of Fame itself, scheduled to open in Cleveland in 1994.

Kirstie Alley (best actress, comedy series) and Ted Danson in *Cheers* (best comedy series).

# 1991 EMMY AWARDS

| CATEGORY | WINNER |
|---|---|
| Comedy Series | *Cheers* |
| Actor—comedy series | Burt Reynolds (*Evening Shade*) |
| Actress—comedy series | Kirstie Alley (*Cheers*) |
| Supporting Actor—comedy series | Jonathan Winters (*Davis Rules*) |
| Supporting Actress—comedy series | Bebe Neuwirth (*Cheers*) |
| Drama Series | *L.A. Law* |
| Actor—drama series | James Earl Jones (*Gabriel's Fire*) |
| Actress—drama series | Patricia Wettig (*thirtysomething*) |
| Supporting Actor—drama series | Timothy Busfield (*thirtysomething*) |
| Supporting Actress—drama series | Madge Sinclair (*Gabriel's Fire*) |
| Drama/Comedy Special or Miniseries | *Separate But Equal* |
| Variety, Music, or Comedy Program | *The 63rd Annual Academy Awards* |

Burt Reynolds (best actor, comedy series) and Marilu Henner in *Evening Shade.*

Moses Gunn and James Earl Jones (best actor, drama series) in *Gabriel's Fire.*

Beatrix Potter wrote *The Tale of Peter Rabbit*, one of the most popular children's books of all time. But Potter had another side to her talent—one that few people know of.

# THE TALE OF BEATRIX POTTER

*The Tale of Peter Rabbit* is one of the most popular children's books of all time. Ever since the book was published in 1902, the story of mischievous Peter and the charming illustrations that accompany it have been loved by young children.

The year 1991 marked the 125th anniversary of the birth of the author and illustrator of this well-known tale, Beatrix Potter. After *Peter Rabbit,* Potter produced more than twenty children's books featuring various animal characters. They made her famous. But there was another side to Potter's talent, one that few people know about.

### A PROPER YOUNG LADY

Helen Beatrix Potter was born in London, England, on July 28, 1866. She was raised as most upper-middle-class girls were at that time. This was the Victorian era, and women weren't expected to be educated or to have careers. So, while her younger brother Bertram went to school, Beatrix was taught at home. She had few friends and wasn't allowed to play sports—it wasn't ladylike.

Each summer, however, Beatrix had a taste of freedom. The Potter family took long vacations in Scotland and in England's Lake District. In these wild, scenic places, Beatrix discovered nature. She also discovered that she loved to draw, and she began to sketch the plants and animals she saw.

Nature fascinated her. Back in London, she spent hours in the British Museum of Natural History, one of the few places that she was allowed to visit alone. She also began to collect natural objects—shells, fossils, flowers—and a menagerie of small animals. Her pets included a hedgehog, snails, bats, mice, a lizard, and, of course, rabbits —including one named Peter.

By the time she was in her mid-twenties, Potter was an accomplished scientific illustrator. She completed more than 300 watercolors showing wild mushrooms and fungi, a subject in which she took a special interest. But when she showed her work to the authorities at the Royal Botanical Gardens at Kew, they dismissed it. They wouldn't take a young woman's scientific work seriously.

Potter wasn't put off easily. She submitted a paper on molds to an important scientific group—but she did so anonymously. The paper was accepted, proving that she was an expert in her subject. But she realized that, as a woman in what was then a man's field, she had little hope of gaining recognition.

### CHILDREN'S BOOKS

Instead, Beatrix Potter turned to children's books. For years, she had been entertaining the children of friends with made-up stories about her pets. *The Tale of Peter Rabbit* had begun as a letter to the son of her former governess, in which she illustrated the story with black-and-white sketches. She expanded the story and the illustrations and sent the results to a series of publishers. When all of them rejected it, she published the book herself in 1900.

The little book was immediately popular, and a major publisher agreed to take it if she would redo the illustrations in color. The book appeared in 1902 in the form that is so well known today. From then on, she turned out one story after another—*The Tailor of*

ceive some recognition. Her watercolors were used to illustrate a book on fungi in 1967. More were published in the 1980's, and they were also exhibited in London.

If Beatrix Potter had lived at another time, she very likely would have found a career in natural history. But she seems to have been happy to create children's books instead—and generations of young people have been glad that she did.

Before writing children's books, Potter was an accomplished nature artist. She did hundreds of watercolors of animals and plants. These included sketches of her pets Judy lizard and Peter rabbit. She especially liked drawing wild mushrooms and fungi, and after her death these scientific studies were used to illustrate several books.

*Gloucester, The Tale of Squirrel Nutkin, The Tale of Benjamin Bunny,* and more.

In 1905, Potter became engaged to her publisher, Norman Warne. Then, tragically, Warne suddenly died. As she was now earning a living from her books, Potter decided to leave London. She bought Hill Top, a farm in Sawrey, in northern England. And there she produced some of her best-known books. Her

characters—Jemima Puddle-duck, Jeremy Fisher, Mrs. Tittlemouse—were based on animals that were her pets or were on the farm. But they also had characteristics of people, often her friends and neighbors. And the settings were based on Potter's own house, garden, and farm and on the village nearby.

Beatrix Potter married William Heelis, a lawyer, in 1913. In her later years she became concerned about land development, which was taking over large areas of the English countryside. She bought a number of tracts of land in the Lake District to keep them from being developed. At her death, on December 22, 1943, this land and Hill Top were given to Britain's National Trust, so that they would be preserved forever.

It wasn't until years after her death that Potter's scientific illustrations began to re-

# FUN TO READ

*What did dinosaurs do after dark? They danced at a prehistoric party! That's the idea behind* Dinosaur Dances, *a book of fanciful verse by Jane Yolen and colorful pictures by Bruce Degen. Dinosaurs waltz in the moonlight and do the Stegosaurus Hop. Who's the best dancer? Tyrannosaurus, of course!*

# Thumbelina

There was once a woman who wanted to have a tiny child. So she went to an old witch and asked her what to do.

"Oh, I think I can help you," said the witch. "Plant this magical barleycorn in a flowerpot and watch what happens!"

The woman went home and planted the barleycorn, and a large beautiful flower bud immediately appeared.

"What a beautiful flower!" exclaimed the woman, and she kissed the red and yellow petals of the bud. As she kissed them, the flower burst open. And sitting in the middle of the velvety blossom was a tiny little girl. The lovely child was no bigger than a thumb, and so she was named Thumbelina.

Thumbelina was so tiny that she slept in a walnut shell. The blue petals of a violet were her mattress, and a rose petal was her blanket. During the day, the woman placed a bowl of water on a table. This miniature lake was ringed with white flowers, and in the middle was a large tulip petal. Thumbelina used this petal as a boat, and she would sit on it and sail from one side of the bowl to the other.

The years went by and Thumbelina grew into a lovely young woman. But she never grew bigger than a thumb.

One night, when Thumbelina was lying in her pretty walnut bed, an ugly toad crept in through a broken pane in the window. She hopped onto the table where Thumbelina was sleeping and gazed at the tiny girl.

"She would make a beautiful wife for my son," said the toad. And she took the walnut shell, with Thumbelina in it, and hopped out through the window into the garden.

Beyond the garden flowed a wide stream, with slippery and marshy banks. There the toad lived with her son. Ugh! He was as ugly and clammy as his mother. "Croak, croak, croak!" was all he could say when he saw the tiny girl in the walnut shell.

"Don't talk so loud or you will wake her," said the mother toad. "We must not allow her to escape. We will put her on a big water lily leaf in the stream. The leaf will be like an island, and she will never be able to reach shore." And that is where the toads left Thumbelina, still asleep in her walnut shell.

Morning came. Thumbelina woke up and looked around in great bewilderment and sadness. She saw water on every side of her and realized she could never escape.

Later that day, the old toad swam with her son to the leaf where Thumbelina was held captive. She said to Thumbelina in her low, rough voice: "Here is my son. You shall marry him tomorrow."

"Croak, croak, croak!" was all that the son could say. When the toads swam away, poor Thumbelina wept in despair.

The little fishes swimming in the water had heard the toad quite plainly, and they decided to help the tiny girl. They grouped together around the stalk that supported the leaf on which Thumbelina was sitting. And they nibbled away until the stalk was cut in two. Away floated the leaf down the stream, carrying Thumbelina far beyond the reach of the toads.

Thumbelina was delighted as she sailed past town after town. The sun shone on the water and made it sparkle like silver. Then a great insect came flying past. He caught sight of Thumbelina, lifted her off her lily leaf, and carried her to a tree. He placed the frightened girl on a large green leaf and gave her the honey from the flowers to eat. He told her that she was very pretty, although she was not in the least like an insect. Later on, all the other insects who lived in the same tree came to visit. They examined Thumbelina closely and remarked, "Why, she has only two legs! How very miserable!"

*The little fishes swimming in the water heard the toad, and they decided to help the tiny girl.*

"She has no feelers!" cried another.

"How ugly she is!" said the lady insects.

The insect who had stolen her thought that she was very pretty, but when he heard all the ladies saying she was ugly, he began to think so too. So he decided not to keep her. He flew down from the tree and placed Thumbelina on a daisy. There she sat and wept, because she was so ugly that the insects would have nothing to do with her—and yet she was really the most beautiful creature imaginable, like the loveliest rosebud.

The whole summer poor little Thumbelina lived alone in the woods. She wove a bed for herself of blades of grass and hung it up under a clover leaf so that she was protected from the rain. She gathered honey from the flowers for food, and drank the dew on the leaves every morning. Thus summer and autumn passed, but then came winter— the long, cold winter. All the birds who had sung so sweetly about her had flown away. The trees shed their leaves and the flowers died. The great clover leaf under which she had lived curled up and nothing remained of it but the withered stalk. She was terribly cold, for her clothes were ragged. It began to snow, and every snowflake that fell on her was like a whole shovelful because she was so tiny. Poor little Thumbelina.

Just outside the woods lay a great cornfield. But the corn had been gone a long time, and only the dry bare stubble was left standing in the frozen ground. This made a forest for Thumbelina to wander about in. One day she came upon the home of a field mouse, who had a little hole under a cornstalk. There the mouse lived warm and snug, with a storeroom full of corn. The tiny girl begged the field mouse for a little piece of barley.

"Poor little creature," said the field mouse, for she was a kind-hearted thing. "Come into my warm room and have some dinner with me." The field mouse was so enchanted with Thumbelina that she told the girl she could spend the entire winter in her home.

Thumbelina was very happy, and she kept the field mouse's house clean and neat and told all kinds of tales about her experiences in the outside world.

"Now I am expecting a visitor," announced the field mouse. "My neighbor, the mole, comes to call on me once a week. He is quite rich and has great big rooms and wears a fine black velvet coat. If you could only marry him, you would be well provided for. But he is blind, and he dislikes the sun and birds and flowers. So you must tell him some of your prettiest tales to amuse him."

Thumbelina made the visitor feel welcome. She sang to him and told him wonderful stories. And the mole fell in love with her. But Thumbelina was not at all pleased, for she had no desire to marry a mole.

276

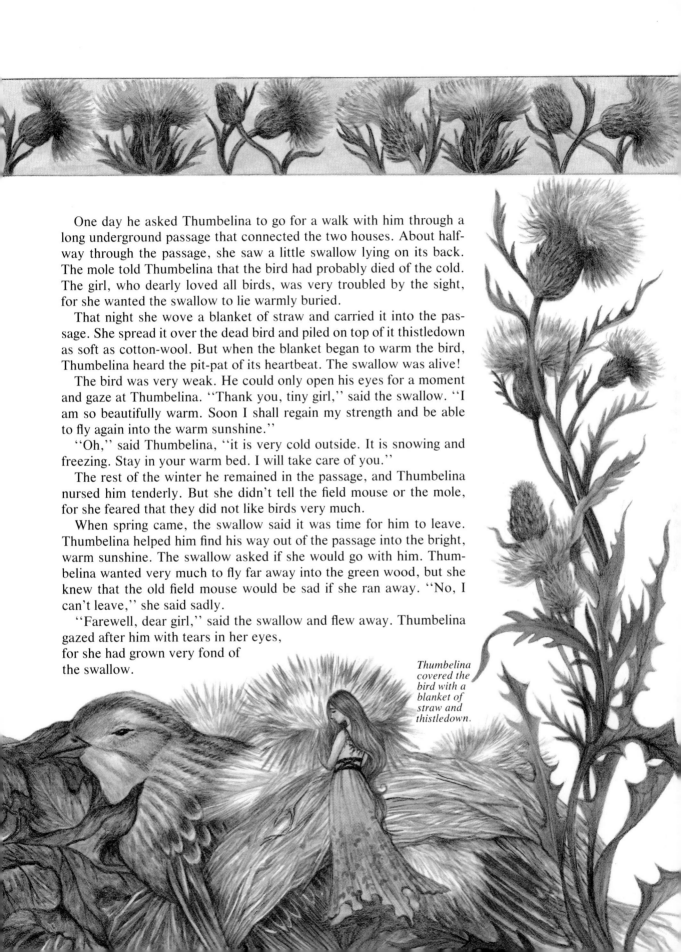

One day he asked Thumbelina to go for a walk with him through a long underground passage that connected the two houses. About halfway through the passage, she saw a little swallow lying on its back. The mole told Thumbelina that the bird had probably died of the cold. The girl, who dearly loved all birds, was very troubled by the sight, for she wanted the swallow to lie warmly buried.

That night she wove a blanket of straw and carried it into the passage. She spread it over the dead bird and piled on top of it thistledown as soft as cotton-wool. But when the blanket began to warm the bird, Thumbelina heard the pit-pat of its heartbeat. The swallow was alive!

The bird was very weak. He could only open his eyes for a moment and gaze at Thumbelina. "Thank you, tiny girl," said the swallow. "I am so beautifully warm. Soon I shall regain my strength and be able to fly again into the warm sunshine."

"Oh," said Thumbelina, "it is very cold outside. It is snowing and freezing. Stay in your warm bed. I will take care of you."

The rest of the winter he remained in the passage, and Thumbelina nursed him tenderly. But she didn't tell the field mouse or the mole, for she feared that they did not like birds very much.

When spring came, the swallow said it was time for him to leave. Thumbelina helped him find his way out of the passage into the bright, warm sunshine. The swallow asked if she would go with him. Thumbelina wanted very much to fly far away into the green wood, but she knew that the old field mouse would be sad if she ran away. "No, I can't leave," she said sadly.

"Farewell, dear girl," said the swallow and flew away. Thumbelina gazed after him with tears in her eyes, for she had grown very fond of the swallow.

*Thumbelina covered the bird with a blanket of straw and thistledown.*

A few days later, the field mouse said to Thumbelina: ''Now you are to be a bride! Our neighbor has proposed! What a wonderful piece of good fortune for a poor girl like you. Now you must prepare fine linens for your dowry.''

Thumbelina had to spin all day long. Every evening the mole visited her and told her that when summer was over and the sun was not shining so brightly, they would marry.

The tiny girl was very unhappy. She had no desire to marry the mole and live underground and never again see the sun or birds or flowers.

Soon it was winter, and the wedding day arrived. Before the mole came to fetch Thumbelina, she stole outside to say good-bye to the beautiful sun. ''Farewell, bright sun,'' she cried, stretching out her arms toward it. ''Farewell,'' she repeated, ''and give my love to the dear swallow when you see him.''

''Tweet, tweet!'' sounded in her ear all at once. She looked up, and there was the swallow flying past! As soon as he saw Thumbelina, he was very glad. She told him that it was her wedding day but how unwilling she was to marry the mole.

*The prince of the flowers placed a golden crown on Thumbelina's head and asked her to marry him.*

"The cold winter is coming," said the swallow. "I must fly away to warmer lands. Will you come with me this time? You can sit on my back and we will fly far away from the mole, over the mountains, to the warm countries where it is always summer and there are always beautiful flowers. Do come with me, dear little Thumbelina, who saved my life when I lay frozen in the dark tunnel!"

"Yes, I will go with you," said Thumbelina, and she hopped on the swallow's back. Higher and higher into the air flew the swallow, far above lakes and woods, over oceans and forests, above mountains so lofty their peaks were crested with snow. The air grew warmer and warmer. The sun was brighter. Below were vines filled with the lushest green and purple grapes. On the trees grew oranges and lemons, and the air was scented with myrtle and mint.

But the swallow flew on, and the lands became even more beautiful. Soon they flew over the most splendid green trees, encircling a sparkling blue lake. Beside the lake stood a glittering white marble castle. Winding vines climbed up the graceful slender pillars, and nestled in the vines were hundreds of swallows' nests. In one of these nests lived Thumbelina's swallow.

"Here is my house," he said. "And you can live in one of the lovely flowers that grow alongside the castle."

"That will be wonderful," Thumbelina said, clapping her little hands in joy.

The swallow set Thumbelina down in a garden filled with the most beautiful flowers. There, to her great astonishment, she found a tiny young man sitting in the middle of one of the flowers. On top of his head was a golden crown, and on his shoulders were the most delicate wings. And he was just as small as Thumbelina.

He bowed to Thumbelina and told her he was the prince of the flowers, and he thought that she was the most beautiful maiden he had ever seen. He took his golden crown from his head and put it on hers and asked if she would be his wife and princess of all the flowers.

Thumbelina was happier than she had ever been. "Yes, little prince," she said. "I shall be happy to be your princess."

Then out of each flower stepped tiny fairylike creatures, the lords and ladies of the flowers. Each presented Thumbelina with a gift and bowed before her. The most beautiful gift of all was a pair of tiny white wings, as delicate as gossamer. The wings were fastened to Thumbelina's shoulders, so that now she too could fly from flower to flower whenever she wished.

And so Thumbelina and the little prince were married. At the wedding the bridal song was sung in the sweetest music, by the best friend of both the bride and the groom—the swallow who had brought the tiny couple together.

# *A Proper Little Lady*

What would a proper little lady wear to go for a walk? Annabella Jones puts on her best blue dress, shiny black shoes, and a pretty hat. But Annabella is a tomboy at heart—and you can imagine what happens to her clothes when she goes outside! This humorous picture book was written by Nette Hilton, who is a teacher in Australia, and illustrated by Cathy Wilcox, an Australian artist and cartoonist.

# THE ORPHAN BOY

An ancient Masai tale of magic and betrayal is the basis for this story by Tololwa M. Mollel, who is from Tanzania, a country in East Africa. The mood-setting illustrations were created by Paul Morin, a Canadian artist. The story tells about a lonely old man who longs for a son and finds one when an orphan boy mysteriously appears at his home. But it soon becomes clear that the boy possesses unusual powers. Although the old man promises to let this be the boy's secret, he is overcome by curiosity—with disastrous results. In 1991 the book was awarded the Canadian Governor General's Children's Literature Award for illustration.

# Rosy's Garden

### A CHILD'S KEEPSAKE

### OF FLOWERS

Soft watercolor illustrations by Satomi Ichikawa, a Japanese artist, make this book a beautiful treasury of flowers. The story, by Elizabeth Laird, is about a little girl named Rosy who spends a summer with her grandmother and learns about her garden, from the first blooms of the season to the summer's last bouquet. Flower lore, flower facts, flower poems, and even flower games and crafts are woven into the text. Rosy learns that tulips originally came from Turkey and not Holland . . . that carnations were often used to make coronets in the Middle Ages . . . that delphinium comes from a Greek word meaning ''dolphin'' . . . that roses can be used to make a sweet-smelling face lotion. In addition to the fascinating information, pictures of beautiful flowers spill across the pages in profusion.

# BIRDS AND BEASTS

Cats, says poet William Jay Smith, are not at all like people: "Cats wear nothing: they lie by the fire / For twenty-four hours if they desire." Smith's witty poems combine with striking woodcuts by Jacques Hnizdovsky to make this an exceptional book. On each page is a poem about a different animal and an illustration that captures the essence of the beast in the artist's unique style. The subjects—there are 29 in all—range from familiar animals such as cats, dogs, sheep, and roosters to exotic creatures such as flamingos, tigers, peacocks, and llamas.

# MANIAC MAGEE

An orphan raised by his aunt and uncle in a hate-filled house, 11-year-old Jeffrey Lionel Magee runs away from home in this novel by Jerry Spinelli. As he searches for a new family, "Maniac" Magee becomes a local legend—people say he can outrun dogs and freight trains and untie any knot. In 1991 the book was awarded the John Newbery Medal, the highest American award for a book for young people.

# Black and White

This is a story about . . . well, it might be about some Holstein cows that escape from their field, or about a boy who is traveling on a train, or about some parents who behave very strangely, or about some impatient, newspaper-reading commuters. Or it might be about all these things. In this challenging picture book by David Macaulay, four stories are presented together—or perhaps they're four parts of the same story. The book won the 1991 Randolph Caldecott Medal as the best American picture book for children.

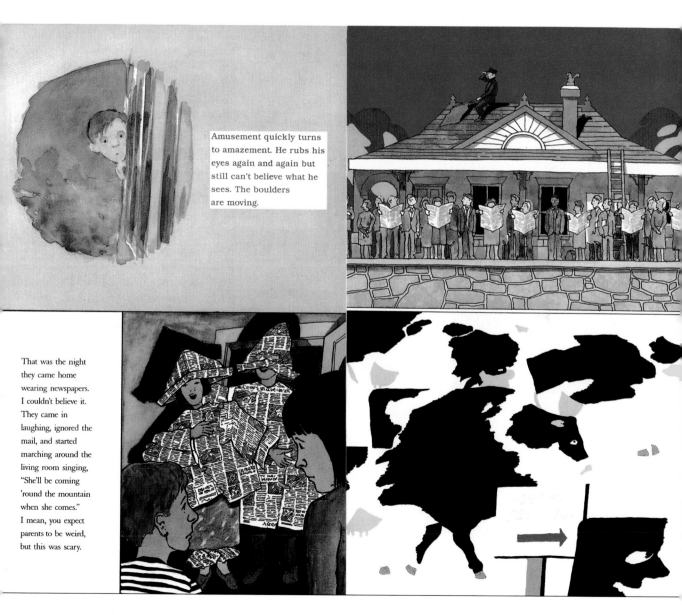

Amusement quickly turns to amazement. He rubs his eyes again and again but still can't believe what he sees. The boulders are moving.

That was the night they came home wearing newspapers. I couldn't believe it. They came in laughing, ignored the mail, and started marching around the living room singing, "She'll be coming 'round the mountain when she comes." I mean, you expect parents to be weird, but this was scary.

# LITTLE PARSLEY

This Italian folktale begins when a woman makes a great mistake: She eats parsley from a garden that belongs to five nasty witches—and the witches demand that the woman give them her daughter in return. Once the witches get their hands on the little girl, who is named Little Parsley, they give her one impossible task after another to do, always threatening to eat her if she fails. But with the help of a kind magician and some other unusual friends, clever Little Parsley is able to outwit the five old hags. The folktale is retold by Enzo Giannini, who also did the charming illustrations.

# A Hippopotamusn't

What musn't a hippo do? Among other things, "A hippopotamusn't roll / In gutters used by bowlers. / A hippopotamusn't fail / To floss his hippopotamolars." In clever nonsense rhymes and comical illustrations, this book presents members of the animal kingdom—from the lowly slug to the majestic elephant—usually in situations that would never be found in nature. The poems were written by J. Patrick Lewis, and the illustrations were done by Victoria Chess.

Just before 8 A.M., Hawaiian time, on the morning of December 7, 1941, Japanese war planes attacked the U.S. naval base at Pearl Harbor, Hawaii. U.S. naval and military commanders were taken completely by surprise. It was a Sunday morning, normally a quiet day at Pearl, and sailors, soldiers, and Marines were at breakfast or preparing for church services. Anti-aircraft batteries were lightly manned.

So well executed was the Japanese attack that U.S. forces were unable to put up an effective defense or launch a counterblow. The U.S. Pacific Fleet suffered terrible destruction. Eighteen U.S. warships were sunk, including the battleships Arizona, California, and West Virginia. In addition, nearly 190 American planes were destroyed on the ground, and another 160 were damaged. A total of 2,403 American servicemen lost their lives, and many others were wounded. By contrast, Japanese losses were light: 29 planes shot down and five midget submarines sunk, with a loss of fewer than 60 airmen and submarine crew members.

The surprise attack on Pearl Harbor was one of the worst military disasters in U.S. history. It was also a brilliant Japanese victory—a tribute to the careful planning of Japan's naval and air commanders and the skillful flying of Japanese pilots.

In 1991, as Americans commemorated the 50th anniversary of what President Franklin Roosevelt called "a date which will live in infamy," many still wondered how such a terrible disaster could have occurred.

Japan and the United States had been on a collision course since the early 1930's, when Japanese troops invaded Manchuria, then part of China. Later, in 1937, Japan launched a full-scale invasion of eastern China and quickly seized most of that country's coastal cities. By then, Japan's government was dominated by military officers who believed that expansion was the only way for Japan to solve its economic and overpopulation problems.

The United States reacted to Japanese military aggression by placing an embargo (a measure restricting trade) on certain military related items, such as oil, scrap iron, and gasoline used in airplanes. Angered by this, Japan developed closer ties with Nazi Germany and fascist Italy, already at war with Britain, France, and other European democracies. In 1940, Japan signed the Tripartite Pact and became (with Germany and Italy) one of the three Axis powers.

Cut off from U.S. oil, Japan began looking for other sources, particularly in the Dutch East Indies (now Indonesia). One major obstacle stood in the way of Japanese expansion south to Indonesia—the U.S. Pacific Fleet at Pearl Harbor. And so, in 1941, the Japanese secretly devised a plan to attack Pearl Harbor.

While Japanese military preparations continued, the United States and Japanese governments tried to solve their differences through diplomacy. Then, in November, 1941, American Secretary of State Cordell Hull demanded that Japan withdraw all its military forces from both China and Indochina. Japan's leaders regarded Hull's demands as unacceptable, and the final decision was made to attack Pearl Harbor. A long diplomatic note rejecting Hull's demands and breaking off negotiations was sent to the Japanese Embassy in Washington. It was to be delivered to Hull at one p.m. (7:30 A.M. Hawaiian time) on Sunday, December 7—one half hour before Japanese planes were scheduled to attack Pearl Harbor. Because of the time involved in decoding and typing the message at the Japanese embassy, the note wasn't delivered until more than an hour after the attack had begun.

Americans were outraged by this "sneak attack." They were also stunned by the Japanese success. Didn't government and military leaders know that an attack was imminent? Although U.S. intelligence officials had broken the Japanese diplomatic code many months earlier, messages concerning Pearl Harbor were considered low priority and were often left untranslated. Most U.S. naval and military experts didn't believe an attack on Pearl Harbor was likely. They also greatly underestimated the skill and daring of Japanese pilots and naval commanders.

The surprise attack on Pearl Harbor united Americans in their determination to defeat Japan and its Axis allies (who declared war on the United States a few days later). The day after Pearl Harbor, President Roosevelt denounced "the unprovoked and dastardly attack by Japan" and called on Congress for a formal declaration of war against Japan.

*"Remember Pearl Harbor!" became a rallying cry for Americans in the war that followed. After four years of fighting, the United States and its allies—including the Soviet Union, Britain, France, and China—emerged victorious in World War II. In the aftermath of that war, both Japan and Germany adopted democratic forms of govern-ment. Today they are among the world's great industrial democracies with strong ties to the United States.*

*The following story is a dramatized account of the tense final hours before the attack on Pearl Harbor, as seen through the eyes of a newspaper reporter in Washington, D.C.*

# PEARL HARBOR: A DAY OF INFAMY

"Taxi—hey, taxi!"

A gray and black Diamond cab screeched to a halt in front of Washington's Union Station, and a wavy-haired man jumped in.

"Where to, sir?" asked the driver.

Tommy Baxter, winded from the sprint to the cab, blurted, "First stop, the Willard Hotel. Then I'm going to the Navy Department building on Constitution Avenue."

Baxter settled back as the cab sped off, thinking about his various appointments for the day. Looking out the cab window, he could see the gleaming white dome of the Capitol Building. Only a few hours before, on this Saturday, December 6, 1941, the *New York Chronicle* reporter had hopped aboard an early morning train to Washington under special orders from city editor Barney Rice.

He could still hear the gruff, raspy-voiced Rice instructing him as he handed Baxter his train ticket. "Go on down and give the Washington crew a hand. This Pacific thing looks like it's ready to blow. I want a seasoned pro like you there when things begin to pop."

*A seasoned pro.* That's what his city editor had called him, and Baxter felt flattered. As the taxi turned into Pennsylvania Avenue, Baxter noticed a Marine Corps emblem tattooed on the driver's right hand. "You an ex-Marine?" the reporter asked. "Yeah," the driver replied, smiling. "I guess you noticed the tattoo."

Baxter found cab drivers good sounding boards. With isolationist and antiwar sentiment running high, he was curious about a veteran's view of the European war and Japanese expansion in the Pacific.

"What do you think of all these rumors about our getting involved in a war with Japan?"

The driver glanced over his shoulder, a look of annoyance on his face. "Listen pal, I don't think we have any business messing around with the Japanese or anyone else out there."

There was an angry edge in his voice as he pointed to a scar on his wrist. "See this? I was wounded at Belleau Wood in 1918, in the big war—you know, the one President Wilson said would be the war to end wars. A piece of German shrapnel took a chunk out of my forearm. No, sir, I don't want us getting into any more wars. There ain't nothing out in the Pacific worth getting American boys killed for."

"What about the war in Europe—can we afford to let the Nazis win?" queried Baxter.

"That's Europe's business!" the cab driver said emphatically.

Baxter thought to himself that this fellow's views were typical of the isolationist attitude of most Americans. He remembered the results of a recent poll that showed two-thirds of Americans opposed to the United States getting involved in the European war and in favor of strict neutrality. Only one out of twelve even favored giving aid to Britain and the other nations fighting against Nazi Germany.

Only four months earlier, Baxter recalled, Congress had just barely passed a law extending the military draft begun by Roosevelt in 1940. The vote in the House of Representatives was 203 to 202. He also remembered speeches in Congress denouncing President Roosevelt as a warmonger, and the frequent antiwar demonstrations at the White House. He had covered several of those two years earlier, when he had been assigned to the *Chronicle's* Washington Bureau.

The cab braked to a halt at the Willard Hotel. Baxter dashed in and left his bags with the bell captain. He made a quick call to the *Chronicle's* Washington office to let the desk editor know that he had arrived and to get any messages left for him. There were several, including one from a Japanese newspaper correspondent friend confirming an appointment later that afternoon at the Japanese Embassy.

Then it was back into the cab for the short trip to the Navy Department building on Constitution Avenue. As the cab cruised down the avenue, Baxter's eyes darted from the towering Washington Monument on his left to the imposing Greek columns of the Lincoln Memorial off in the distance beyond the great Reflecting Pool.

The cab pulled up in front of the Navy Building and the driver announced, "We're here, pal. That'll be 20 cents."

Baxter handed the man a quarter, jumped out of the taxi, and headed for the main entrance of the drab, three-story government building with the words "Navy Department" chiseled just below the roof. A

Marine guard checked the reporter's press pass before ushering him to a small, cluttered office. The furnishings consisted of a few desks and several file cabinets. Maps and charts covered the walls.

Baxter was warmly greeted at the door by Lieutenant Commander Frank Bailey. "Good to see you again, Tommy," the jovial, ruddy-faced officer said. Baxter had met Bailey while covering Atlantic naval maneuvers during his Washington stint. The two had become good friends, sharing a lively interest in sports. Bailey was now assigned to naval intelligence; he was a good starting point for a reporter trying to get inside information on the growing threat of a Pacific war.

Bailey nodded in the direction of two other navy officers seated at their desks. "Let me introduce you to Lieutenant Chuck Stafford. He's one of our hot-shot navy pilots." Stafford waved hello.

"And that surly looking fellow in the corner is Lieutenant Jimmy Peterson," Bailey continued. "We call him Grumpy—you know, like the dwarf in *Snow White*."

Baxter glanced at Peterson, who was the only one in full uniform, the two gold stripes of a lieutenant senior grade on his sleeves.

Baxter got right to the point. "I'd like to get your insight about the possibility of a war between the United States and Japan. There are lots of rumors flying around about negotiations with the Japanese breaking down. Some people seem to think that the Japanese may be getting ready to attack the Philippines—or possibly even Hawaii."

"Don't pay any attention to rumors," Bailey remarked. "Look, the Japanese would be fools to attack us. We're much too strong for them. We've got more ships and more planes . . ."

"Not to mention better pilots and sailors," interjected Stafford.

Baxter tossed out one of his information aces. "Well, if that's true, how come war alerts were sent out last week to Admiral Kimmel and General Short in Hawaii and MacArthur in the Philippines?"

Bailey looked surprised. "How the deuce did you find out about that —it's classified information!"

"It's a reporter's job to have good contacts," Baxter said with a wink.

"Don't worry about our bases in Hawaii and the Philippines," Bailey said testily, "they're well defended. I'll let you in on a little secret —but don't quote me. Our main concern right now is a Japanese naval task force heading south from Indochina waters. About thirty troop transports, eight cruisers, and twenty destroyers."

He pointed to a wall map. "We figure the Japanese are getting ready to hit the British in Singapore and Malaya."

Lieutenant Peterson, quiet until then, now spoke up. "That's all well and good Frank, but where are the Japanese aircraft carriers?"

"The last I heard they were still in Japanese waters," said Bailey.

Shaking his head, Peterson replied solemnly, "The fact is, we've lost track of them. For all we know they could be in striking distance of the Philippines—or even Pearl Harbor."

"We shouldn't be talking about this in front of a civilian," Stafford broke in.

Bailey waved him off. "Tommy's okay. He won't give away any secrets."

Then he turned back to the craggy-faced Peterson, who was stuffing tobacco into the blackened bowl of an old corncob pipe.

"The trouble with you, Jimmy, is that you're an eternal pessimist." Bailey paused to pull out a detailed map of the island of Oahu, which showed the various naval and air installations around Pearl Harbor. "Let's approach this little tactical problem like professional naval officers. Gather round, boys."

The four men grouped themselves around Bailey's desk as he spread out the map. "Now let's consider your worst case scenario—a Japanese attack on Pearl Harbor."

Bailey ran his finger from point to point on the map. "Gentlemen, Oahu is the Gibraltar of the Pacific. Pearl is ringed by air bases. We've got Bellows to the east, Wheeler to the north, Hickham on one side of the harbor, near the Navy Yard, and the Marine air base on the other side. Even if the Japanese could get close enough to launch an attack, we've got enough P-40 fighter planes, anti-aircraft batteries, and coastal defense guns—not to mention the firepower from our ships— to blow them out of the water and out of the sky."

Glancing at Peterson, Bailey concluded, "No, the Japanese wouldn't be crazy enough to attack Pearl. Anyway, we'd have plenty of time after a declaration of war to get our defenses up."

Peterson lit his pipe, took a puff, and pointed the stem at Bailey. "There won't be any declaration of war," he said, frowning. "The Japanese will do to us just what they did to the Russians at Port Arthur in 1904. They just sailed in with torpedo boats and wiped out a whole squadron of Russian ships—a well-executed surprise attack."

Peterson went back to his desk and placed a book and some photos in front of the others. "Let me show you something. This book was written in 1925 by a British naval expert—it's called *The Great Pacific War*. The author predicts that if war breaks out between Japan and the United States, it will start with a surprise attack on Pearl Harbor."

"Come on, Jimmy," blurted Bailey, "that's just a pet theory."

Peterson persisted. "Okay, now look at these recent aerial photos of Pearl Harbor." He pointed to an island in the middle of the harbor. "Here's Ford Island, and here, on the northeastern side, is Battleship Row. Look at those battlewagons sitting there like ducks in a pond."

Peterson looked over at Stafford. "You're a pilot. Wouldn't you agree that's a pretty juicy target for a few squadrons of bombers?"

Stafford nodded. "Sure, for the right pilots and planes. But we're talking about the Japanese—second rate in both departments."

Peterson took another puff on his pipe. "I'm not a Naval Academy graduate like you fellows. I'm just a ranker who made his way up from the engine room to the bridge. But I learned a long time ago never to underestimate an enemy—or a potential enemy. And let's be honest, fellows. Even some of the big brass were opposed to concentrating our entire Pacific Fleet at Pearl. Too inviting a target. C'mon Frank, why don't you tell your reporter friend what Admiral Stark said . . . "

Bailey put a finger over his lips. "That's enough, Jimmy. I think we've played this game out. Besides, I promised Tommy I'd treat him to lunch."

Later, over lunch, Baxter pressed Bailey for more information. He was curious about Peterson's reference to Admiral Stark, the chief of naval operations. "Why didn't you want me to hear what Peterson had to say about Stark?" he asked.

Hesitant at first, Bailey finally said, "Okay, but remember, it's off the record. Last January, Stark got a report that Pearl Harbor was vulnerable to air attack, especially by torpedo planes. You see, there's no practical way to place anti-torpedo nets around the battleships without messing up ship traffic in the harbor."

"That sounds a bit thorny," Baxter mused. "Maybe I should have a chat with Stark. Can you arrange it?"

"Sure, I don't see why not," replied Bailey. "But not before Monday afternoon. Everybody's gone for the weekend."

As they got up to leave the restaurant, Baxter said, "You've been a great help, Frank. If I can do you a favor some time . . . ."

Before he could finish, Bailey cut him short. "Glad you asked, pal. As a matter of fact you can do something for me. How about a couple of press passes to the Redskins game tomorrow? They're playing the Eagles. Should be quite a battle. Hey, why don't we both go?"

Baxter gave him a thumbs up. "You're on. I'll make arrangements for us to sit in the press box. Pick me up at my hotel at 10 A.M."

Then the reporter was off again, this time to the Japanese Embassy on Massachusetts Avenue. A Japanese official bowed the American reporter into the embassy foyer and escorted him to a comfortably furnished sitting room. Moments later, Baxter was joined by a slender Japanese man, neatly dressed in a gray tweed jacket and dark trousers.

The American rose and shook hands with his old friend Yoshio Sato —known to his press colleagues as Joe—a reporter for Japan's Domei News Agency. While they exchanged greetings, a woman in a kimono placed a tray with tea and rice cakes on a nearby table.

Noticing the strained look on Sato's face, Baxter observed, "You look upset, my friend. Are things as bad as they seem?"

In a troubled voice, Sato replied, "I'm afraid the signs are all bad. Really, I'm concerned that war between the United States and Japan could break out at any time."

Adjusting his horn-rimmed glasses, Sato pointed to a pile of Japanese newspapers. "Look at these headlines," he said, and then translated several from a Tokyo paper.

**"NEGOTIATIONS USELESS IN THE FACE OF AMERICAN ARROGANCE"**

**"WESTERN IMPERIAL POWERS ENCIRCLE JAPAN —WAR PREPARATIONS UNDERWAY"**

"Joe, do these headlines reflect Japanese public opinion?" asked Baxter. "Do the Japanese people really favor war with the United States?"

"No, I don't think any sensible Japanese

wants a war with America," responded Sato. "But yes, I do think that many Japanese people believe the American government is acting stubbornly and arrogantly. When President Roosevelt moved your Pacific fleet from California to Pearl Harbor, many Japanese felt that this was a direct threat to us."

"Well, Joe, speaking frankly," remarked Baxter, "a lot of Americans are concerned about Japanese aggression in China, and the movement of your forces into Indochina."

Sato acknowledged the remark with a nod. "I understand. You know how I feel. In my opinion, the Japanese military has too much power. Many of the generals are reckless fools. They think the Americans are cowards who will not fight. But I've lived here a long time and I know better.

"But you must understand that the Japanese are a proud people. We have a big population crowded into a small area—just a few islands. Most of the goods we need come from overseas. We see our expansion as necessary to our survival. When you threaten to cut off our oil supply if we don't give up territory we won with our blood, you are plunging a dagger into the heart of Japan."

A commotion in the hallway interrupted the conversation. Sato went out to investigate, while Baxter watched from the doorway. Across the hall, he could see diplomatic officials running in and out of a small room from which the sound of a wireless radio and the steady clackety-clack of typewriters could be heard.

Sato was talking to one of the embassy staff, when Baxter noticed Kichisaburo Nomura, the Japanese ambassador, approach them. After a short conversation, Sato motioned Baxter to join them.

Ambassador Nomura addressed Baxter in a friendly but formal manner. "I understand, Mr. Baxter, that you have expressed an interest in the current state of talks between the United States and Japan. Let me tell you that we intend to continue the talks with your government as long as negotiations are productive. But if your government continues to be unyielding in its demands, I cannot predict the outcome."

"What exactly is your view of the situation, Mr. Ambassador?" the reporter asked respectfully.

"As a diplomat I am hopeful that a peaceful solution may be worked out. But our two governments are very far apart on many important issues."

Before Baxter could ask another question, the ambassador bowed and walked away. Sato led Baxter out a rear door into the gardens behind the embassy building.

When they were out of earshot of embassy staffers, Sato told the American, "From what I just heard—and what I have been hearing for several days—I think we are close to the edge. The reason for all the bustle inside was an important message from Tokyo. It appears to take a tough stand against your government's demands."

Baxter listened attentively as Sato went on. "The other day I was speaking with special envoy Kurusu, who seemed very distraught. He

told me that he thought that the negotiations might just be a smoke-screen to cover some military action against your country."

"Did he really say that?" Baxter asked, a nervous edge in his voice.

"Yes. And I think matters may come to a head tomorrow. I heard one of the embassy staff mention that the message from Tokyo was to be delivered to Secretary of State Hull at 1 P.M. tomorrow."

As they spoke, spurts of flame suddenly erupted from another part of the garden. There was a popping sound, like firecrackers going off.

Puzzled, Baxter shot a glance at Sato, who informed him, "It's some of the staff burning documents. They have been doing it for several days. I think they are also destroying some of the code books as well. I'm afraid that's another ominous sign."

The pungent smell of burning paper flooded Baxter's nostrils. Sato gripped his hand. "I must go now, my friend. I hope that when we meet again we can still be friends."

The two journalists parted with a handshake, and Baxter went immediately to the *Chronicle*'s office to file his story. There, amid the clutter of back-dated newspapers and reams of wire-service copy, he typed out a lengthy account of the day's events. The *Chronicle*'s readers would have some thought-provoking news copy to chew on over Sunday breakfast, Baxter told himself. It was late evening by the time he cleared the story through rewrite. He returned to his hotel, had a light dinner, and turned in for the night.

While Baxter and the rest of Washington slept that night, a powerful Japanese naval task force was moving at full speed to a point 200 miles north of Hawaii. And at 9 A.M., Washington time, on the morning of December 7, while many Americans were at church or having breakfast, Japanese pilots on the six aircraft carriers in position off Hawaii were also up and about. It was then 3:30 A.M. Hawaiian time, and the Japanese pilots were eating a breakfast of red rice and *tai*—a fish served on special occasions. Soon dawn would break over the Pacific, and the red fireball of the morning sun would match the insignia on the planes taking off from the Japanese carriers.

At breakfast that Sunday morning, Baxter leafed through several newspapers. *The New York Times* carried a front-page article in which Secretary of the Navy Frank Knox proclaimed the U.S. Navy the best in the world. To make it even more powerful, he noted, 325 new ships and an additional 2,000 planes were under construction.

Very optimistic, thought Baxter. Such soothing statements would be reassuring reading for a quiet Sunday morning. Then he turned to a copy of his own newspaper. There, on the front page of the *Chronicle,* was his story under a boldface headline that blared:

**"U.S.–JAPAN WAR BELIEVED LIKELY, BUT NAVAL EXPERTS
ARE DIVIDED OVER WHERE JAPS WILL STRIKE FIRST"**

Baxter scanned the lead paragraph of his article. "As diplomatic efforts to prevent a U.S.-Japanese war appeared on the verge of collapse, American naval experts are divided over possible Pacific flash points. A well-placed source in the Navy Department believes that Japanese forces will probably first attack British bases in Malaya and Singapore before launching an assault on the Philippines. However, at

least
one U.S.
Navy officer be-
lieves that the American
Pacific Fleet at Pearl Harbor will be
the target of a Japanese first strike. 'There
will be no declaration of war,' this officer stated, 'just a
surprise attack, probably by air.'"

Promptly at 10 A.M. Bailey arrived, and the two set off for Griffith Stadium. The stadium was a rundown ball park, green paint peeling from the wood and steel grandstands. At full capacity it could hold 30,000 people. Baxter noticed that most of the seats were filling up. As the reporter and his friend settled into chairs in the press box, Baxter mentioned his conversation with Yoshio Sato and the reference to a 1 P.M. meeting with Secretary of State Hull.

"One P.M., did you say?" remarked Bailey. "That's interesting."

"Just out of curiosity," said Baxter, "given our conversation yesterday, what time will it be in Hawaii—at Pearl Harbor?"

Bailey thought for a moment. "Well, let's see. There's a five-and-a-half-hour difference. One P.M. here in Washington would be about 7:30 A.M. at Pearl." He hesitated. "I wonder . . . That's about the time crews go to breakfast. Oh c'mon, Tommy, let's forget about the world's problems and just enjoy the game."

And they did. The favored Redskins were in good form, and as the game went into the final minutes of play, they led the Philadelphia Eagles 20–14.

As Baxter focused on the game, an Associated Press reporter to his left suddenly nudged him in the ribs. "Can you beat this. I just got a wire from the main office saying that I should keep my story short, that the game isn't important."

"I guess your boss is an Eagles fan."

The AP man chuckled. "You could be right. Anyway, I wired back that this is the last game of the season and it's darn important."

Just then Baxter noticed people hurriedly leaving the stadium. Western Union messenger boys were scampering through the stands delivering telegrams to army and navy officers. Stadium loudspeakers blared messages calling for other officers to report to their units.

Baxter and Bailey looked at each other in bewilderment. "What's going on here?" Bailey wondered.

And then came the answer. The AP reporter next to Baxter jumped up, a teletype message in his hand. "Oh my God," he blurted. "The Japanese just attacked Pearl Harbor. We're at war!"

Most of the fans remained unaware of the Japanese attack and continued to watch the game. But pandemonium broke loose in the press box, and Baxter and Bailey rushed out of the stadium and headed for their car. Bailey was enraged. "Peterson was right! Those treacherous rats attacked us while talks were still going on!"

Bailey drove back to the center of town, dropping Baxter off near the White House. The rest of that Sunday, December 7, was a crazy

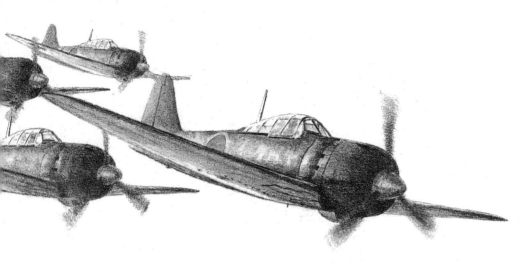

patchwork—a blur of government officials issuing statements that the *Chronicle* reporter hastily scrawled in his notebook. On his way to the White House, he ran into Secretary of State Hull, surrounded by other newsmen and press photographers.

Looking tired and a bit dazed by the day's events, the white-haired Hull managed to keep his composure as he told the reporters: "In my fifty years of public service, I have never been witness to such an outrageous act of treachery and deception. The Japanese government's message breaking off negotiations wasn't delivered until after 2 P.M., more than an hour after they began bombing Pearl Harbor."

The secretary walked quickly onto the White House grounds, a mob of reporters trailing behind. More government officials arrived, among them Congressional leaders and other members of the president's cabinet. From the harsh looks on their faces, Baxter reckoned that isolationism was a dead issue.

Later that evening, the president's press secretary told the reporters that Roosevelt would address a joint session of Congress the following afternoon.

Baxter was among the first of the reporters to arrive at the Capitol the next day, Monday, December 8. He observed that security was extremely tight. A line of Marines with fixed bayonets guarded the entrance. Behind them were lines of police and Secret Service men.

Hurrying inside to the House chamber, Baxter found a seat in the gallery press section. Not far away he caught sight of Eleanor Roosevelt, the president's wife, seated near the widow of President Woodrow Wilson. Mrs. Roosevelt appeared deep in thought. Baxter imagined she might be thinking of her four sons, all eligible for military service.

Shortly after noon, Speaker of the House Sam Rayburn called the House of Representatives into session. Soon after, members of the Senate filed in, Democrats and Republicans walking side by side in a display of solidarity.

When everyone was seated, Speaker Rayburn formally introduced the president, who then entered the chamber. Twenty years earlier, polio had crippled Roosevelt so that he could stand and walk only with the aid of metal braces. Now he slowly made his way to the podium on the arm of his son James, a captain in the U.S. Marine Corps Reserve.

Positioning himself at the rostrum, Roosevelt opened a notebook, adjusted his glasses, and began to speak.

"Yesterday, December 7, 1941—a date which will live in infamy—the United States of America was suddenly and deliberately attacked by the naval and air forces of the Empire of Japan . . ."

Baxter noted that the president spoke in a firm and resolute voice as he continued his address to Congress. "The attack yesterday on the Hawaiian islands has caused severe damage to American naval and military forces. . . . Many American lives have been lost."

His voice rising, Roosevelt declared, "No matter how long it may take us to overcome this premeditated invasion, the American people in their righteous might will win through to absolute victory . . ."

Applause broke out, exploding in great waves as everyone in the chamber stood and cheered the president.

Bringing his short address to a conclusion, Roosevelt called upon the Congress to declare "that since the unprovoked and dastardly attack by Japan on Sunday, December 7, a state of war has existed between the United States and the Japanese Empire."

Once again the hall erupted in applause and loud cheers. For a moment, Baxter set aside his role as a reporter. Emotion got the better of him as he leaped to his feet and joined in the cheering. He knew that the war would be a terrible time and that Americans and Japanese would both suffer greatly. But whatever the future might hold, Baxter also sensed that December 7, 1941—Pearl Harbor day—would remain etched forever in the minds of all Americans.

HENRY I. KURTZ
Author, *The Art of the Toy Soldier*

# POETRY

## SAILING HOMEWARD

Cliffs that rise a thousand feet
Without a break,
Lake that stretches a hundred miles
Without a wave.
Sands that are white through all the year,
Without a stain,
Pine-tree woods, winter and summer
Ever-green,
Streams that for ever flow and flow
Without a pause,
Trees that for twenty thousand years
Your vows have kept,
You have suddenly healed the pain of a traveler's heart,
And moved his brush to write a new song.

CHAN FANG-SHENG (4TH CENTURY)

## A WISE OLD OWL

A wise old owl lived in an oak;
The more he saw the less he spoke;
The less he spoke the more he heard:
Why can't we all be like that bird?

EDWARD HERSEY RICHARDS (dates unknown)

## THE KITTEN AT PLAY

See the kitten on the wall,
Sporting with the leaves that fall,
Withered leaves, one, two, and three
Falling from the elder-tree,
Through the calm and frosty air
Of the morning bright and fair.

See the kitten, how she starts,
Crouches, stretches, paws and darts;
With a tiger-leap half way
Now she meets her coming prey.
Lets it go as fast and then
Has it in her power again.

Now she works with three and four,
Like an Indian conjurer;
Quick as he in feats of art,
Gracefully she plays her part;
Yet were gazing thousands there,
What would little Tabby care?

WILLIAM WORDSWORTH (1770–1850)

## P'S AND Q'S

It takes a lot of letters to make up the alphabet,
And two or three of them are very easy to forget;
There's K—a funny letter—and X and Y and Z—
There's hardly any use at all for any of those three!
The vowels are the busy ones, A, E, I O, U—
They've twice the work that all the other letters have to do;
I don't know why it is that grown-up people always choose
To tell us children to be sure and mind our P's and Q's.

They're funny-looking letters, particularly Q,
It never goes around except in company with U;
P is much more important, it starts off pie and play,
It's not hard to remember if you think of it that way;
But lots of words begin with F and H and S and T,
They're just as worth remembering as any, seems to me;
Yet when we've strangers in the house, my parents always say,
"Be sure you don't forget to mind your P's and Q's today!"

RUPERT SARGENT HOLLAND (1878–1952)

## THE MOUSE AND THE CAKE

A mouse found a beautiful piece of plum cake,
The richest and sweetest that mortal could make;
'Twas heavy with citron and fragrant with spice,
And covered with sugar all sparkling as ice.

"My stars!" cried the mouse, while his eye beamed with glee,
"Here's a treasure I've found: what a feast it will be;
But, hark! there's a noise, 'tis my brothers at play;
So I'll hide with the cake, lest they wander this way.

"Not a bit shall they have, for I know I can eat
Every morsel myself, and I'll have such a treat."
So off went the mouse as he held the cake fast;
While his hungry young brothers went scampering past.

He nibbled, and nibbled, and panted, but still
He kept gulping it down till he made himself ill;
Yet he swallowed it all, and 'tis easy to guess,
He was soon so unwell that he groaned with distress.

His family heard him, and as he grew worse,
They sent for the doctor, who made him rehearse
How he'd eaten the cake to the very last crumb,
Without giving his playmates and relatives some.

"Ah me!" cried the doctor, "advice is too late;
You must die before long, so prepare for your fate.
If you had but divided the cake with your brothers,
'Twould have done you no harm, and been good for the others.

"Had you shared it, the treat had been wholesome enough;
But eaten by *one,* it was dangerous stuff;
So prepare for the worst—" and the word had scarce fled,
When the doctor turned round, and the patient was dead.

Now all little people the lesson may take,
And *some* large ones may learn from the mouse and the cake;
Not to be over-selfish with what we may gain,
Or the best of our pleasures may turn into pain.

ELIZA COOK (1818–1889)

## AUTUMN FIRES

In the other gardens
    And all up the vale,
From the autumn bonfires
    See the smoke trail!

Pleasant summer over
    And all the summer flowers,
The red fire blazes,
    The gray smoke towers.

Sing a song of seasons!
    Something bright in all!
Flowers in the summer,
    Fires in the fall!

ROBERT LOUIS STEVENSON (1850–1894)

## AN APPLE

First it was a pretty flower,
    dressed in pink and white,
Then it was a tiny ball,
    almost hid from sight.
Round and green and large it grew—
    then it turned to red.
It will make a splendid pie
    for your Thanksgiving Spread.

UNKNOWN

In 1904 the British writer Kenneth Grahame (1859–1932) began to tell a series of bedtime stories to his 4-year-old son, Alastair (known as Mouse). The stories were about a group of animals—a mole, a toad, a badger, a water rat—that lived in the English countryside. Over the next four years, the stories grew, and Grahame began to write them down. In 1908 they were published. The result was one of the most popular children's books of all time: The Wind in the Willows.

Grahame's animals aren't very animal-like. Instead, they are like people masquerading as animals. They drive cars, ride in trains, live in houses, and do all the other things that people do. And they are characters that would have been easily recognized in Grahame's day. Toad, for example, is a well-to-do fellow who lives on a country estate, Toad Hall. His constant pranks often get him in trouble. In the excerpt that follows, Toad has landed in jail for stealing a motorcar.

# THE WIND IN THE WILLOWS

## Toad's Adventures

When Toad found himself immured in a dank and noisome dungeon, and knew that all the grim darkness of a medieval fortress lay between him and the outer world of sunshine and well-metaled high roads where he had lately been so happy, disporting himself as if he had bought up every road in England, he flung himself at full length on the floor, and shed bitter tears, and abandoned himself to dark despair. "This is the end of everything," he said. "At least it is the end of the career of Toad, which is the same thing; the popular and handsome Toad, the rich and hospitable Toad, the Toad so free and careless and debonair! How can I hope to be ever set at large again," he said, "who have been imprisoned so justly for stealing so handsome a motorcar in such an audacious manner, and for such lurid and imaginative cheek, bestowed upon such a number of fat, red-faced policemen!" (Here his sobs choked him.) "Stupid animal that I was," he said, "now I must languish in this dungeon, till people who were proud to say they knew me, have forgotten the very name of Toad. O wise old Badger!" he said, "O clever, intelligent Rat and sensible Mole! What sound judgments, what a knowledge of men and matters you possess! O unhappy and forsaken Toad!" With lamentations such as these he passed his days and nights for several weeks, refusing his meals or intermediate light refreshments, though the grim and ancient jailer, knowing that Toad's pockets were well lined, frequently pointed out that many comforts, and indeed luxuries, could by arrangement be sent in—at a price —from outside.

Now the jailer had a daughter, a pleasant wench and good-hearted, who assisted her father in the lighter duties of his post. She was particularly fond of animals, and, besides her canary, whose cage hung on a nail in the massive wall of the keep by day, to the great annoyance of prisoners who relished an after-dinner nap, and was shrouded in an antimacassar on the parlor table at night, she kept several piebald mice and a restless revolving squirrel. This kind-hearted girl, pitying the misery of Toad, said to her father one day, "Father! I can't bear to see that poor beast so unhappy, and getting so thin! You let me have the managing of him. You know how fond of animals I am. I'll make him eat from my hand, and sit up, and do all sorts of things."

Her father replied that she could do what she liked with him. He was tired of Toad, and his sulks and his airs and his meanness. So that day she went on her errand of mercy, and knocked at the door of Toad's cell.

"Now, cheer up, Toad," she said coaxingly, on entering, "and sit up and dry your eyes and be a sensible animal. And do try and eat a bit of dinner. See, I've brought you some of mine, hot from the oven!"

It was bubble-and-squeak, between two plates, and its fragrance filled the narrow cell. The penetrating smell of cabbage reached the nose of Toad as he lay prostrate in his misery on the floor, and gave him the idea for a moment that perhaps life was not such a blank and desperate thing as he had imagined. But still he wailed, and kicked with his legs, and refused to be comforted. So the wise girl retired for the time, but, of course, a good deal of the smell of hot cabbage remained behind, as it will do, and Toad, between his sobs, sniffed and reflected, and gradually began to think new and inspiring thoughts: of chivalry, and poetry, and deeds still to be done; of broad meadows, and cattle browsing in them, raked by sun and wind; of kitchen gardens, and straight herb-borders, and warm snapdragon beset by bees; and of the comforting clink of dishes set down on the table at Toad Hall, and the scrape of chair legs on the floor as everyone pulled himself close up to his work. The air of the narrow cell took on a rosy tinge; he began to think of his friends, and how they would surely be

able to do something; of lawyers, and how they would have enjoyed his case, and what an ass he had been not to get in a few; and lastly, he thought of his own great cleverness and resource, and all that he was capable of if he only gave his great mind to it; and the cure was almost complete.

When the girl returned, some hours later, she carried a tray, with a cup of fragrant tea steaming on it; and a plate piled up with very hot buttered toast, cut thick, very brown on both sides, with the butter running through the holes in it in great golden drops, like honey from the honeycomb. The smell of that buttered toast simply talked to Toad, and with no uncertain voice; talked of warm kitchens, of breakfasts on bright frosty mornings, of cozy parlor firesides on winter evenings, when one's ramble was over and slippered feet were propped on the fender; of the purring of contented cats, and the twitter of sleepy canaries. Toad sat up on end once more, dried his eyes, sipped his tea and munched his toast, and soon began talking freely about himself, and the house he lived in, and his doings there, and how important he was, and what a lot his friends thought of him.

The jailer's daughter saw that the topic was doing him as much good as the tea, as indeed it was, and encouraged him to go on.

"Tell me about Toad Hall," said she. "It sounds beautiful."

"Toad Hall," said the Toad proudly, "is an eligible self-contained gentleman's residence, very unique; dating in part from the fourteenth century, but replete with every modern convenience. Up-to-date sanitation. Five minutes from church, post office, and golf-links. Suitable for—"

"Bless the animal," said the girl, laughing, "I don't want to *take* it. Tell me something *real* about it. But first wait till I fetch you some more tea and toast."

She tripped away, and presently returned with a fresh trayful; and Toad, pitching into the toast with avidity, his spirits quite restored to their usual level, told her about the boathouse, and the fishpond, and the old walled kitchen garden; and about the pigsties, and the stables, and the pigeon-house, and the hen-house; and about the dairy, and the wash-house, and the china cupboards, and the linen-presses (she liked that bit especially); and about the banquet hall, and the fun they had there when the other animals were gathered round the table and Toad was at his best, singing songs, telling stories, carrying on generally. Then she wanted to know about his animal friends, and was very interested in all he had to tell her about them and how they lived, and what they did to pass their time. Of course, she did not say she was fond of animals as *pets,* because she had the sense to see that Toad would be extremely offended. When she said good night, having filled his water jug and shaken up his straw for him, Toad was very much the same sanguine, self-satisfied animal that he had been of old. He sang a little song or two, of the sort he used to sing at his dinner parties, curled himself up in the straw, and had an excellent night's rest and the pleasantest of dreams.

They had many interesting talks together, after that, as the dreary days went on; and the jailer's daughter grew very sorry for Toad, and thought it a great shame that a poor little animal should be locked up in prison for what seemed to her a very trivial offense. Toad, of course, in his vanity, thought that her interest in him proceeded from a growing tenderness; and he could not help half regretting that the social gulf between them was so very wide, for she was a comely lass, and evidently admired him very much.

One morning the girl was very thoughtful, and answered at random, and did not seem to Toad to be paying proper attention to his witty sayings and sparkling comments.

"Toad," she said presently, "just listen, please. I have an aunt who is a washerwoman."

"There, there," said Toad graciously and affably, "never mind; think no more about it. I have several aunts who ought to be washerwomen."

"Do be quiet a minute, Toad," said the girl. "You talk too much, that's your chief fault, and I'm trying to think, and you hurt my head. As I said, I have an aunt who is a washerwoman; she does the washing for all the prisoners in this castle—we try to keep any paying business of that sort in the family, you understand. She takes out the washing on Monday morning, and brings it in on Friday evening. This is a Thursday. Now, this is what occurs to me: you're very rich—at least you're always telling me so—and she's very poor. A few pounds wouldn't make any difference to you, and it would mean a lot to her. Now, I think if she were properly approached—squared, I believe is the word you animals use—you could come to some arrangement by which she would let you have her dress and bonnet and so on, and you could escape from the castle as the official washerwoman. You're very alike in many respects—particularly about the figure."

"We're *not*," said the Toad in a huff. "I have a very elegant figure —for what I am."

"So has my aunt," replied the girl, "for what *she* is. But have it your own way. You horrid, proud, ungrateful animal, when I'm sorry for you, and trying to help you!"

"Yes, yes, that's all right; thank you very much indeed," said the Toad hurriedly. "But look here! you wouldn't surely have Mr. Toad, of Toad Hall, going about the country disguised as a washerwoman!"

"Then you can stop here as a Toad," replied the girl with much spirit. "I suppose you want to go off in a coach-and-four!"

Honest Toad was always ready to admit himself in the wrong. "You are a good, kind, clever girl," he said, "and I am indeed a proud and a stupid toad. Introduce me to your worthy aunt, if you will be so kind, and I have no doubt that the excellent lady and I will be able to arrange terms satisfactory to both parties."

Next evening the girl ushered her aunt into Toad's cell, bearing his week's washing pinned up in a towel. The old lady had been prepared beforehand for the interview, and the sight of certain golden sover-

eigns that Toad had thoughtfully placed on the table in full view practically completed the matter and left little further to discuss. In return
for his cash, Toad received a cotton print gown, an apron, a shawl,
and a rusty black bonnet; the only stipulation the old lady made being
that she should be gagged and bound and dumped down in a corner.
By this not very convincing artifice, she explained, aided by pictur-
esque fiction which she could supply herself, she hoped to retain her
situation, in spite of the suspicious appearance of things.

Toad was delighted with the suggestion. It would enable him to leave
the prison in some style, and with his reputation for being a desperate
and dangerous fellow untarnished; and he readily helped the jailer's
daughter to make her aunt appear as much as possible the victim of
circumstances over which she had no control.

"Now it's your turn, Toad," said the girl. "Take off that coat and
waistcoat of yours; you're fat enough as it is."

Shaking with laughter, she proceeded to "hook-and-eye" him into
the cotton print gown, arranged the
shawl with a professional fold, and
tied the strings of the rusty bonnet
under his chin.

"You're the very image of
her," she giggled, "only I'm
sure you never looked half
so respectable in all your
life before. Now, good-bye,
Toad, and good luck. Go
straight down the way
you came up; and if any

one says anything to you, as they probably will, being but men, you can chaff back a bit, of course, but remember you're a widow woman, quite alone in the world, with a character to lose.''

With a quaking heart, but as firm a footstep as he could command, Toad set forth cautiously on what seemed to be a most hare-brained and hazardous undertaking; but he was soon agreeably surprised to find how easy everything was made for him, and a little humbled at the thought that both his popularity, and the sex that seemed to inspire it, were really another's. The washerwoman's squat figure in its familiar cotton print seemed a passport for every barred door and grim getaway; even when he hesitated, uncertain as to the right turning to take, he found himself helped out of his difficulty by the warder at the next gate, anxious to be off to his tea, summoning him to come along sharp and not keep him waiting there all night. The chaff and the humorous sallies to which he was subjected, and to which, of course, he had to provide prompt and effective reply, formed, indeed, his chief danger; for Toad was an animal with a strong sense of his own dignity, and the chaff was mostly (he thought) poor and clumsy, and the humor of the sallies entirely lacking. However, he kept his temper, though with great difficulty, suited his retorts to his company and his supposed character, and did his best not to overstep the limits of good taste.

It seemed hours before he crossed the last courtyard, rejected the pressing invitations from the last guardroom, and dodged the outspread arms of the last warder, pleading with simulated passion for just one farewell embrace. But at last he heard the wicket gate in the great outer door click behind him, felt the fresh air of the outer world upon his anxious brow, and knew that he was free!

Dizzy with the easy success of his daring exploit, he walked quickly towards the lights of the town, not knowing in the least what he should do next, only quite certain of one thing, that he must remove himself as quickly as possible from a neighborhood where the lady he was forced to represent was so well known and so popular a character.

As he walked along considering, his attention was caught by some red and green lights a little way off, to one side of the town, and the sound of the puffing and snorting of engines and the banging of shunted trucks fell on his ear. ''Aha!'' he thought, ''this is a piece of luck! A railway station is the thing I want most in the whole world at this moment; and what's more, I needn't go through the town to get it, and shan't have to support this humiliating character by repartees which, though thoroughly effective, do not assist one's sense of self respect.''

He made his way to the station accordingly, consulted a time-table, and found that a train, bound more or less in the direction of his home, was due to start in half an hour. ''More luck!'' said Toad, his spirits rising rapidly, and went off to the booking-office to buy his ticket.

He gave the name of the station that he knew to be the nearest to the village of which Toad Hall was the principal feature, and mechanically put his fingers, in search of the necessary money, where his waistcoat pocket should have been. But here the cotton gown, which had nobly stood by him so far, and which he had basely forgotten, intervened, and frustrated his efforts. In a sort of nightmare he struggled with the strange uncanny thing that seemed to hold his hands,

turn all muscular strivings to water, and laugh at him all the time; while other travelers, forming up in a line behind, waited with impatience, making suggestions of more or less value and comments of more or less stringency and point. At last—somehow—he never rightly understood how—he burst the barriers, attained the goal, arrived at where all waistcoat pockets are eternally situated, and found —not only no money, but no pocket to hold it, and no waistcoat to hold the pocket!

To his horror he recollected that he had left both coat and waistcoat behind him in his cell, and with them his pocketbook, money, keys, watch, matches, pencil case—all that makes life worth living, all that distinguishes the many-pocketed animal, the lord of creation, from the inferior one-pocketed or no-pocketed productions that hop or trip about permissively, unequipped for the real contest.

In his misery he made one desperate effort to carry the thing off, and, with a return to his fine old manner—a blend of the Squire and the College Don—he said, "Look here! I find I've left my purse behind. Just give me that ticket, will you, and I'll send the money on tomorrow. I'm well known in these parts."

The clerk stared at him a moment, and then laughed. "I should think you were pretty well known in these parts," he said, "if you've tried this game on often. Here, stand away from the window, please, madam; you're obstructing the other passengers!"

An old gentleman who had been prodding him in the back for some moments here thrust him away, and, what was worse addressed him as his good woman, which angered Toad more than anything that had occurred that evening.

Baffled and full of despair, he wandered blindly down the platform where the train was standing, and tears trickled down each side of his nose. It was hard, he thought, to be within sight of safety and almost of home, and to be balked by the want of a few wretched shillings and by the pettifogging mistrustfulness of paid officials. Very soon his escape would be discovered, the hunt would be up, he would be caught, reviled, loaded with chains, dragged back again to prison and bread-and-water and straw; his guards and penalties would be doubled; and O, what sarcastic remarks the girl would make! What was to be done? He was not swift of foot; his figure was unfortunately recognizable. Could he not squeeze under the seat of a carriage? He had seen this method adopted by schoolboys, when the journey-money provided by thoughtful parents had been diverted to other and better ends. As he pondered, he found himself opposite the engine, which was being oiled, wiped, and generously caressed by its affectionate driver, a burly man with an oilcan in one hand and a lump of cotton-waste in the other.

"Hullo, mother!" said the engine driver, "what's the trouble? You don't look particularly cheerful."

"O, sir!" said Toad, crying afresh, "I am a poor unhappy washer-woman, and I've lost all my money, and can't pay for a ticket, and I *must* get home tonight somehow, and whatever I am to do I don't know. O dear. O dear!"

"That's a bad business, indeed," said the engine driver reflectively. "Lost your money—and can't get home—and got some kids, too, waiting for you, I dare say?"

"Any amount of 'em," sobbed Toad. "And they'll be hungry—and playing with matches—and upsetting lamps, the little innocents!—and quarreling, and going on generally. O dear, O dear!"

"Well, I'll tell you what I'll do," said the good engine driver. "You're a washerwoman to your trade, says you. Very well, that's that. And I'm an engine driver, as you may well see, and there's no denying it's terribly dirty work. Uses up a power of shirts, it does, till my missus is fair tired of washing 'em. If you'll wash a few shirts for me when you get home, and send 'em along, I'll give you a ride on my engine. It's against the Company's regulations, but we're not so very particular in these out-of-the-way parts."

The Toad's misery turned into rapture as he eagerly scrambled up into the cab of the engine. Of course, he had never washed a shirt in his life, and couldn't if he tried and, anyhow, he wasn't going to begin; but he thought: "When I get safely home to Toad Hall, and have money again, and pockets to put it in, I will send the engine driver enough to pay for quite a quantity of washing, and that will be the same thing, or better."

The guard waved his welcome flag, the engine driver whistled in cheerful response, and the train moved out of the station. As the speed increased, and the Toad could see on either side of him real fields and trees, and hedges, and cows, and horses, all flying past him, and as he thought how every minute was bringing him nearer to Toad Hall, and sympathetic friends, and money to chink in his pocket, and a soft bed to sleep in, and good things to eat, and praise and admiration at the recital of his adventures and his surpassing cleverness, he began to skip up and down and shout and sing snatches of song, to the great astonishment of the engine driver, who had come across washer-women before, at long intervals, but never one at all like this.

They had covered many and many a mile, and Toad was already considering what he would have for supper as soon as he got home, when he noticed that the engine driver, with a puzzled expression on his face was leaning over the side of the engine and listening hard. Then he saw him climb onto the coals and gaze out over the top of the train; then he returned and said to Toad: "It's very strange; we're the last train running in this direction tonight, yet I could be sworn that I heard another following us!"

Toad ceased his frivolous antics at once. He became grave and depressed, and a dull pain in the lower part of his spine, communicating itself to his legs, made him want to sit down and try desperately not to think of all the possibilities.

By this time the moon was shining brightly, and the engine driver, steadying himself on the coal, could command a view of the line behind them for a long distance.

Presently he called out, ''I can see it clearly now! It is an engine, on our rails, coming along at a great pace! It looks as if we were being pursued!''

The miserable Toad, crouching in the coal-dust, tried hard to think of something to do, with dismal want of success.

''They are gaining on us fast!'' cried the engine driver. ''And the engine is crowded with the queerest lot of people! Men like ancient warders, waving halberds; policemen in their helmets; waving truncheons; and shabbily dressed men in pot-hats, obvious and unmistakable plain-clothes detectives even at this distance, waving revolvers and walking-sticks; all waving, and all shouting the same thing—'Stop, stop, stop!' ''

Then Toad fell on his knees among the coals and, raising his clasped paws in supplication, cried, ''Save me, only save me, dear kind Mr. Engine driver, and I will confess everything! I am not the simple washerwoman I seem to be! I have no children waiting for me, innocent or otherwise! I am a toad—the well-known and popular Mr. Toad, a landed proprietor; I have just escaped, by my great daring and cleverness, from a loathsome dungeon into which my enemies had flung

me; and if those fellows on that engine recapture me, it will be chains and bread-and-water and straw and misery once more for poor, unhappy, innocent Toad!''

The engine driver looked down upon him very sternly, and said, "Now tell me the truth; what were you put in prison for?"

"It was nothing very much," said poor Toad, coloring deeply. "I only borrowed a motorcar while the owners were at lunch; they had no need of it at the time. I didn't mean to steal it, really; but people—especially magistrates—take such harsh views of thoughtless and high-spirited actions."

The engine driver looked very grave and said, "I fear that you have been indeed a wicked toad, and by rights I ought to give you up to offended justice. But you are evidently in sore trouble and distress, so I will not desert you. I don't hold with motorcars, for one thing; and I don't hold with being ordered about by policemen when I'm on my own engine, for another. And the sight of an animal in tears always makes me feel queer and soft-hearted. So cheer up, Toad! I'll do my best, and we may beat them yet!"

They piled on more coals, shoveling furiously; the furnace roared, the sparks flew, the engine leaped and swung, but still their pursuers slowly gained. The engine driver, with a sigh, wiped his brow with a handful of cotton-waste, and said, "I'm afraid it's no good, Toad. You see, they are running light, and they have the better engine. There's just one thing left for us to do, and it's your only chance, so attend very carefully to what I tell you. A short way ahead of us is a long tunnel, and on the other side of that the line passes through a thick wood. Now, I will put on all the speed I can while we are running through the tunnel, but the other fellows will slow down a bit, naturally, for fear of an accident. When we are through, I will shut off steam and put on brakes as hard as I can, and the moment it's safe to do so you must jump and hide in the wood, before they get through the tunnel and see you. Then I will go full speed ahead again, and they can chase me if they like, for as long as they like and as far as they like. Now mind and be ready to jump when I tell you!"

They piled on more coals, and the train shot into the tunnel, and the engine rushed and roared and rattled, till at last they shot out at the other end into fresh air and the peaceful moonlight, and saw the wood lying dark and helpful upon either side of the line. The driver shut off steam and put on brakes, the Toad got down on the step, and as the train slowed down to almost a walking pace he heard the driver call out, "Now, jump!"

Toad jumped, rolled down a short embankment, picked himself up unhurt, scrambled into the wood and hid.

Peeping out, he saw his train get up speed again and disappear at a great pace. Then out of the tunnel burst the pursuing engine, roaring and whistling, her motley crew waving their various weapons and shouting, "Stop! stop! stop!" When they were past, the Toad had a hearty laugh—for the first time since he was thrown into prison.

But he soon stopped laughing when he came to consider that it was now very late and dark and cold, and he was in an unknown wood, with no money and no chance of supper, and still far from friends and home; and the dead silence of everything, after the roar and rattle of the train, was something of a shock. He dared not leave the shelter of the trees, so he struck into the wood, with the idea of leaving the railway as far as possible behind him.

After so many weeks within walls, he found the wood strange and unfriendly and inclined, he thought, to make fun of him. Night-jars, sounding their mechanical rattle, made him think that the wood was full of searching warders, closing in on him. An owl, swooping noise-lessly towards him, brushed his shoulder with its wing, making him jump with the horrid certainty that it was a hand, then flitted off, mothlike, laughing its low ho! ho! ho! which Toad thought in very poor taste. Once he met a fox, who stopped, looked him up and down in a sarcastic sort of way, and said, "Hullo, washerwoman! Half a pair of socks and a pillowcase short this week! Mind it doesn't occur again!" and swaggered off, sniggering. Toad looked about for a stone to throw at him, but could not succeed in finding one, which vexed him more than anything. At last, cold, hungry, and tired out, he sought the shelter of a hollow tree, where with branches and dead leaves he made himself as comfortable a bed as he could, and slept soundly till the morning.

*You will have to read the rest of the book to find out about the further adventures of Toad, Mole, Badger, and Rat.*

# THE NEW BOOK OF KNOWLEDGE
# 1992

The following articles are from the 1992 edition of
*The New Book of Knowledge*. They are included
here to help you keep your encyclopedia up to date.

Large herds of zebras and wildebeests roam across the vast grasslands, or savannas, of Africa, grazing on the abundant plant life that includes a variety of grasses.

# BIOMES

The hot, humid rain forest, the dry desert, and the icy tundra all have something in common: Each one is a biome. A biome is a community of specific types of plants and animals that covers a large area of the earth's surface. Each biome is made up of many **habitats**—the places where a particular plant or animal normally lives and grows. The type of biome in a region is generally determined by the kind of climate in that region. Deserts cover dry regions. Rain forests cover hot, humid regions. Tundras cover cold and icy, dry regions.

Most of the different kinds of biomes can be found on every continent except Antarctica. Each place has unique species of plants and animals; but the plants and animals of a particular biome tend to be similar all around the world. For example, spine-covered cacti are common plants in the deserts of the American Southwest. In African deserts, plants called euphorbs grow in abundance. Euphorbs have fleshy, leafless stems and prickly spines, very much like the American cacti. Euphorbs and cacti have developed similar adaptations that allow them to live in the hot, dry desert biome. Similarities among plant species in biomes around the world allow scientists to identify the different kinds of biomes. Scientists also study a biome's **ecology**; that is, the interactions of living things with the environment and with each other.

▶ KINDS OF BIOMES

The major land biomes include the following: grasslands; deserts; chaparral; deciduous forests; coniferous forests; tundra; and tropical rain forests. Aquatic biomes also exist in rivers, lakes, ponds, and in the oceans. However, this article concentrates on the land biomes.

## Grasslands

Known as prairies in North America, savannas in central Africa, steppes in central Asia, and pampas in South America, grasslands are among the earth's richest biomes. The world's main agricultural crops, including corn, wheat, oats, and barley, were all bred from grasses—the main plants in the grassland environment.

Grasslands are found in climates slightly drier than the climates that support deciduous forests. Average rainfall in the grasslands varies from 10 to 40 inches (254 to 1,016 millimeters) annually. Fires, which can destroy deciduous forests, cause grasslands to thrive. Burned grasses enrich the soil and allow new plants to grow. Some grassland wildflowers cannot sprout unless their seeds are exposed to a fire's searing heat. Fires also keep certain plants from growing that would change the grassland environment, such as deciduous trees.

Grasslands that receive the most rain produce tall, dense grasses, as in America's tallgrass prairies. Grasses there can reach heights of 12 feet (3.7 meters). Early settlers riding through the grasslands had to stand up in the stirrups of their saddles to spot their cows grazing in these tall grasses. Grasslands that receive the least precipitation have short grasses. Short-grass prairies are dotted with clumps of grasses that grow less than 2 feet (0.6 meters) tall. Grasslands also include wildflowers, which add vibrant color to the green backdrop. An occasional shrub or tree dots the landscape, springing up in places where there is adequate moisture.

The dominant grassland animals are grazers. In Africa, millions of gazelles, zebras, and wildebeests migrate across the savannas, each grazing on a different part of the grass plant. Predators, including lions, tigers, and hyenas, stalk the old and sick grazing animals. Vultures feed on the decaying carcasses while insects strip the bones clean. In their natural state, grasslands support the largest herds of animals in the world.

## Deserts

Regions that receive less than 10 inches (254 millimeters) of rain each year are generally classified as deserts. Desert rains are infrequent. Sometimes it will rain only once or twice a year. When it does rain, a great quantity of rain may fall so rapidly that a quick, heavy flood (called a flash flood) occurs. Deserts also tend to have extreme variations in temperatures. Days are very hot, but temperatures plummet at night, sometimes dipping down below freezing. Desert plants and animals have to be quite hardy to adapt to these difficult conditions.

Succulents, plants that store water in their leaves or stems, are among the major plants of the deserts. Cacti and euphorbs are two different types of succulents. Shrubs with small leathery or waxy leaves also thrive in some desert environments. These plants may shed their leaves and remain dormant through the desert's harshest seasons. Some desert plants live short lives, sprouting, flowering, setting seed, and dying in the few days during and after a heavy rain. The seeds of these plants lie dormant in the sand for months or years until adequate rain once again falls.

Desert animals must also find ways to adapt to the extreme dryness and heat. Many rest in their underground burrows during the day and come out only at night. Others, such as certain iguanas and other types of lizards, are active during the day. They spend most of their time out of the sun, venturing from the shade of one plant only to scurry to the shade of another. Some animals can survive with very little water. The kangaroo rat is one animal that does not need water to drink. It gets its water from the seeds and leaves it eats.

## Chaparral

Scattered along certain coastal areas is the chaparral biome. The Mediterranean coast, the coast of southern California, the coast of central Chile, the southern tip of Africa, and the southern coast of Australia all are covered by chaparral. Like the desert, the chaparral gets little rainfall. Some regions average as little as 10 inches (254 millimeters) of rain a year, all of which falls during the winter months. However, warm, moist air from the oceans helps balance the chaparral environment and prevents conditions from being as severe as those in the desert.

The main plants of the chaparral are tough evergreen shrubs with small leathery leaves. Animals adapted to a dry climate, including lizards, rodents, rabbits, hawks, and owls, inhabit the chaparral. Deer and songbirds migrate to the chaparral during the wet winters, when food is more plentiful.

The scattered evergreen shrubs of the chaparral, which are the plants found most often in this dry coastal biome, help prevent soil erosion.

During the hot, rainless summers, brush-fires often rage across the chaparral. However, chaparral plants are well adapted to what would be a disaster in other places. Many species produce fire-resistant seeds. Others send shoots from the base of charred stumps. It takes as little as ten years for a burned area of chaparral to recover completely.

## Deciduous Forests

Spanning eastern North America, central Europe, eastern China, and the southeast coast of Australia, deciduous forests grace the land. Such forests are made up of trees that grow and shed their leaves in a distinct seasonal pattern. In spring the trees bud, in summer they grow, in autumn they lose their leaves, and in winter they stand dormant. Ample rain falls throughout the year, averaging about 40 inches (1,016 millimeters) annually. In this constantly changing environment, many different types of plants and animals flourish.

Deciduous forests, such as the maple-beech forests of North America, tend to have rich soil that supports numerous types of plants. Shrubs grow in the shade of the leafy maple and birch trees. Ferns, flowers, and mosses carpet the floor of the deciduous forest. Mushrooms and other fungi grow on rotting leaves and logs.

Animal life, too, is quite abundant in these woods. Earthworms and insects tunnel through the dark, moist soil. Songbirds flit among the tree branches and on the ground. Amphibians, such as newts and salamanders, scurry through the thick cover of fallen leaves. Deer browse and rodents burrow. Predators, such as foxes, weasels, and bobcats, stalk their prey. Such activity, especially during the summer months, makes deciduous forests inviting places in which to study wildlife.

In the winter, when the trees have shed their leaves and the woods stand under a blanket of snow, life in the forest slows down. Many living things adapt to the cold by becoming dormant. Some mammals hibernate, burrowing in dens for a long

Snowy owl

Pronghorn antelope

Black bear

American elk

Raccoon

Rufus hummingbird

Bell's vireo

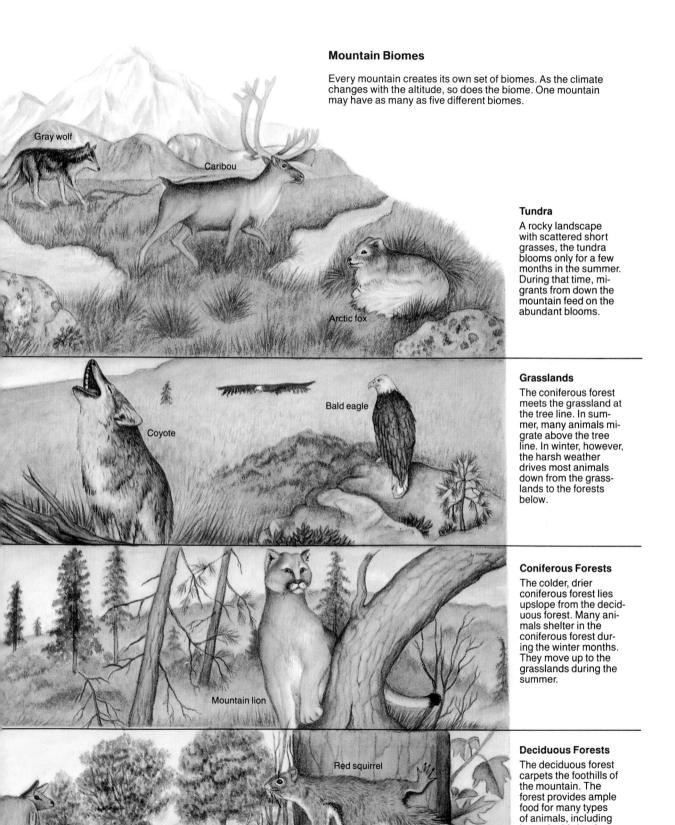

## Mountain Biomes

Every mountain creates its own set of biomes. As the climate changes with the altitude, so does the biome. One mountain may have as many as five different biomes.

Gray wolf

Caribou

### Tundra

A rocky landscape with scattered short grasses, the tundra blooms only for a few months in the summer. During that time, migrants from down the mountain feed on the abundant blooms.

Arctic fox

### Grasslands

The coniferous forest meets the grassland at the tree line. In summer, many animals migrate above the tree line. In winter, however, the harsh weather drives most animals down from the grasslands to the forests below.

Coyote

Bald eagle

### Coniferous Forests

The colder, drier coniferous forest lies upslope from the deciduous forest. Many animals shelter in the coniferous forest during the winter months. They move up to the grasslands during the summer.

Mountain lion

### Deciduous Forests

The deciduous forest carpets the foothills of the mountain. The forest provides ample food for many types of animals, including hummingbirds, vireos, deer, raccoons, and squirrels.

Red squirrel

Black-tailed deer

period of inactivity. Others, including most birds, migrate, spending the winter in warmer climates. A few, including sparrows, raccoons, and rabbits, stay through the winter, searching out food as best they can.

### Coniferous Forests

Coniferous forests are forests that are largely made up of cone-bearing trees. There are two distinct types of coniferous forest biomes: the temperate coniferous forest and the northern coniferous, or boreal, forest.

The temperate coniferous forest is found in moist, coastal environments, including the northern Pacific coast of North America and the eastern coast of Australia. These forests contain the largest trees in the world—the giant sequoia trees of California (redwoods) and the towering eucalyptus trees of Australia. The boreal forests are much more extensive than the temperate coniferous forests. They stretch across the northern reaches of North America, Europe, and Asia. In these regions, winters are long and cold. The short, cool summers allow only a brief growing season.

Pine, spruce, hemlock, and fir trees are the most common trees in the boreal forests. All have needle-like leaves that help prevent water loss in the cold, dry winter air. The soil in coniferous forests tends to be acidic, and few

During the summer months, a wide variety of animals—elk, moose, birds, rabbits, and insects—populate the coniferous forest, feeding on tree leaves and grasses.

types of plants can grow in it. Blueberry shrubs and heather plants, however, thrive in the acidic soil.

Many different types of animals live in the boreal forests, especially in the warmer summer months. Moose, elk, and deer browse on tree leaves. Migratory birds eat the plentiful insects, which hatch in the late spring and summer. Porcupines gnaw on pine bark. Snowshoe hares, whose coats change from brown to white to blend in with both summer's fallen leaves and winter's blanket of snow, dart from under cover. Wolverines and bears stalk their prey.

### Tundra

North of the boreal forest lies the tundra. Under this treeless region is a layer of frozen ground more than 1,000 feet (305 meters) thick, called permafrost. The soil on top of the permafrost thaws for only eight weeks during the short Arctic summer. The small flowering plants and dwarf trees of the tundra have to grow, bloom, and set seed quickly to survive. The outburst of growth in the tundra during the summer creates a colorful carpet of low-lying flowers that dazzles the eye. Adding to the colorful display are the numerous types of lichens, which are really a combination of algae and fungi living and growing together, that cover the rocky landscape.

Not many animals spend the long winter months in the tundra. Some small rodents, such as lemmings, have adapted to the harsh winter environment. Arctic foxes, wolves, and polar bears also stay, feeding on whatever they can find during the quiet winter months.

When summer comes, the tundra once again teems with life. Herds of caribou and also reindeer graze on the tundra's quick-growing grasses. Flocks of migrating birds make the tundra their destination. Many birds feed on the numerous insects that hatch in the ponds and puddles of the tundra's soggy ground. As summer fades away, the caribou and many other mammals travel to the forests and the birds fly south. The tundra again becomes a snowy, silent world.

### Tropical Rain Forests

Tropical rain forests are damp, humid places where lush, leafy plants abound. In most tropical rain forests, annual rainfall averages between 80 and 200 inches (2,032 and

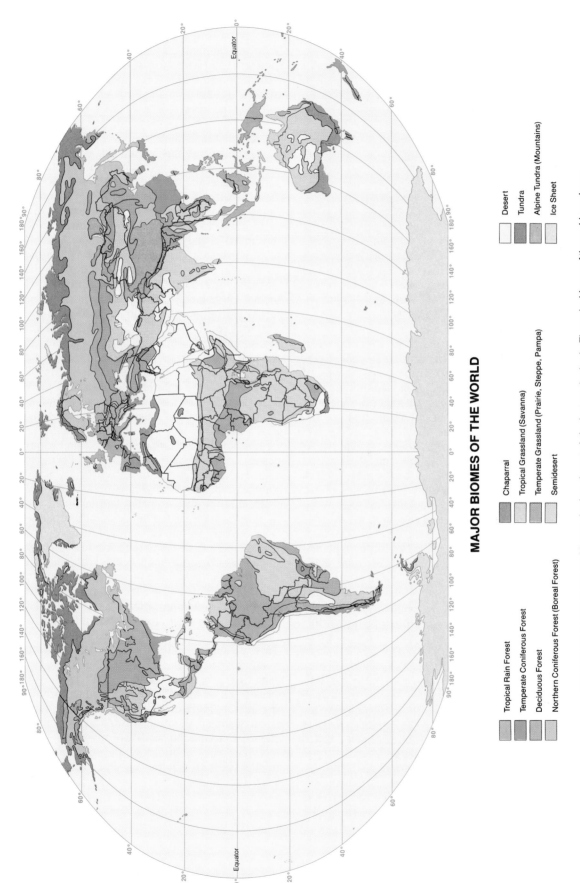

# MAJOR BIOMES OF THE WORLD

Tropical Rain Forest

Temperate Coniferous Forest

Deciduous Forest

Northern Coniferous Forest (Boreal Forest)

Chaparral

Tropical Grassland (Savanna)

Temperate Grassland (Prairie, Steppe, Pampa)

Semidesert

Desert

Tundra

Alpine Tundra (Mountains)

Ice Sheet

A biome includes a large geographic area that has characteristic plants and animals. The major biomes of the world are shown on the map above. Each biome has a certain type of climate and soil to which plants and animals of the region have adapted.

The continued destruction of the rain forest may contribute to dramatic climate changes that could threaten life in all the other biomes around the world.

5,080 millimeters). The rain falls evenly year-round. Temperatures hardly vary, hovering just below 80°F (27°C) day and night. This steady environment has the greatest variety of plant and animal species of all the biomes.

The leafy branches of tall trees, 75 to 100 feet (23 to 30 meters) in height, spread out to form a canopy that shades and shelters the tropical rain forest. Beneath the canopy, lower trees form leafy umbrellas 40 to 60 feet (12 to 18 meters) tall. A few smaller trees grow 20 to 30 feet (6 to 9 meters) above a shrub layer that is at most 10 feet (3 meters) tall. The floor of the rain forest receives so little light that only plants able to grow in almost total shade can live there. Thick jungle growth occurs only along river edges or other places where light easily penetrates to the ground.

The most lively part of the tropical rain forest is the canopy and upper layers of trees. Colorful flowers use the higher tree branches as platforms to reach the sun. These plants, called epiphytes, send no roots into the soil. They get their nutrients from the small amounts of dirt and dust that collect in the forks of tree branches. They gather moisture from the misty air. Some epiphytes, called bromeliads, have overlapping leaves that form a cup at their base. The bromeliad cup can hold several quarts of water to nourish the plant. These miniature ponds are the breeding grounds for snails, insects, and tiny frogs.

Larger animals, including lizards, birds, monkeys, and leopards, inhabit the rain forest. Although a few rain forest animals search for roots and seeds on the ground, most dwell solely in the trees.

▶ THE CHANGING BIOMES

These descriptions of biomes apply to regions that have not been disturbed by human activity. But in many places throughout the world, nature's biomes have been altered. Forests are cut down for farms. Domestic animals are set loose on grasslands, crowding out the animals that naturally live there. Desert land is irrigated to grow crops. Oil rigs in the Arctic tundra destroy large patches of the slow-growing plants. Such activities upset the natural balance of the biomes.

The disruption of the biomes can cause tremendous problems for people living in the regions. In the dry grasslands of the Sahel, in western Africa, domestic goats and sheep have overgrazed the land. The thin layer of topsoil has blown away, and the Sahel is becoming a desert. This process, called desertification, threatens other parts of the world where people have pushed the land to its limits.

In other places, disturbing the biomes may cause serious problems in the future. People in Central America, South America, and Southeast Asia have been burning down the tropical rain forests to make farmland and cutting down the trees for lumber. Each year millions of acres of rain forest are destroyed. The loss of these lush lands may seriously disrupt the global climate. Plants need carbon dioxide to grow, and they take this gas from the air. Without the rain forests, the amount of carbon dioxide in the air will increase tremendously. This gas holds heat close to the earth, warming the atmosphere and the earth's surface. This warming is called the **greenhouse effect**. With the destruction of the tropical rain forests, the greenhouse effect could cause our planet to heat up at an unhealthy rate—resulting in many problems.

Environmental groups and government agencies around the world are working to protect the world's biomes. In this way, the earth's precious natural resources can be preserved for future life.

ELIZABETH KAPLAN
Author, *Biology Bulletin Monthly*

Originally nomads of the desert, most Arabs today live in cities such as Cairo (*left*)—the capital of Egypt and the most populous city in the Arab world. Only a relatively few Arabs, like these Bedouins in Qatar (*below*), still follow the nomadic way of life, traveling over age-old routes, seeking pasture and water for their livestock.

# ARABS

The name "Arab" refers to the peoples who speak Arabic as their native language. The Arabs originated in the deserts of what is now Saudi Arabia, which occupies most of the vast Arabian Peninsula. However, the impression that Arabs are still people of the desert—that is, Bedouins or nomads—is inaccurate. Most Arabs today are city dwellers. Nomads make up less than 10 percent of the Arab population, which numbers nearly 200 million.

**The Arab World.** Geographically, the Arab world stretches across North Africa and includes most of the countries of the Middle East, except for Iran, Turkey, Israel, and Cyprus. The nations of the Arab world are Algeria, Bahrain, Egypt, Iraq, Jordan, Kuwait, Lebanon, Libya, Morocco, Oman, Qatar, Saudi Arabia, Sudan, Syria, Tunisia, the United Arab Emirates, and Yemen.

In addition, about 1.8 million Palestinian Arabs live on the West Bank of the Jordan River and in the Gaza Strip, territories occupied by Israel since the 1967 Arab-Israeli War. Nearly 800,000 Arabs live in Israel itself. Arabs from Lebanon and Syria, in particular, have also emigrated to many parts of the world, especially North and South America.

The Arabs are a diverse people, but there are basic elements that link most of them. The most important of these are the Islamic religion and the Arabic language, and the culture and history associated with them.

**Religion.** The great majority of Arabs are Muslims, or followers of the religion of Islam. There are also significant numbers of Christian Arabs, particularly in Egypt, Lebanon, Syria, and among the Palestinians. In Lebanon, Christians of various denominations make up about 40 percent of the population.

Islam originated in the Arabian Peninsula more than 1,300 years ago. It spread rapidly through much of Asia and Africa, so that today some of the largest Muslim countries and communities are outside the Arab world.

Islam, whether Arab or non-Arab, has two major branches—Sunni Islam and Shi'i Islam. Sunni Islam is the larger branch, and most Arabs are Sunnis. However, Shi'ites are a majority in Iraq and make up the single largest religious community in Lebanon. Bahrain's population is about 70 percent Shi'ite, while some other small Persian Gulf states have important Shi'ite minorities.

**The Arabic Language.** Arabic belongs to the Semitic group of languages, which also in-

Young Arabs (*left*) study the Koran, the sacred book of Islam. Islam originated in the Arabian Peninsula in the 600's and spread to much of Asia and Africa. A miniature painting of the 1200's (*right*) depicts a caravan of Arab pilgrims on the way to Mecca, the holiest city of Islam. Muslims are expected to make at least one pilgrimage (*hajj*) to Mecca in a lifetime.

cludes Hebrew. The languages of Arabs and Jews thus are closely related. More broadly, Arabic is a part of the Hamito-Semitic family, which can be traced back to ancient Egyptian and includes some languages of Ethiopia.

The Arabic alphabet has 28 characters, which are written from right to left. Arabic script has two main forms—Kufic and Nashki. Kufic is angular in shape. Nashki is rounded and flowing with the letters joined. A modified Arabic alphabet is also used in the languages of some non-Arab Muslim countries.

Arabic developed among the Bedouins of the Arabian desert. Its growth was greatly encouraged by a tradition of poetry that was highly elaborate in its oral (spoken) form before being written down. With the coming of Islam in the A.D. 600's, the Koran (Quran), the sacred book of Islam, became the model for the future use of the language. It was the one text that all Arab (and later all non-Arab) Muslims learned. Educated Muslims memorized the Koran completely, and it became the standard for classical Arabic.

As the Koran accompanied the Arab conquests, its message and style spread across the Islamic world. Eventually, variations in the spoken language developed. Today, certain dialects, especially the Moroccan, are difficult for other Arabs to understand, but all share a common written language. Arabs also can communicate orally by speaking in the classical Arabic used for writing.

**Arab History and Civilization.** References to Arabs as nomads and camel herders of northern Arabia appear in writings as early as the 800's B.C. The name was later applied to all inhabitants of the Arabian Peninsula.

Arabs were then a tribal society. They were grouped together according to family heritage, tracing their origins back to a common ancestor. But tribal society in the Arabian Peninsula was always fragmented because of the harsh desert conditions. Tribes broke up into smaller clans, who roamed the desert, stopping at oases (fertile areas) and wells for food and water. No great Arab state appeared until the coming of Islam.

**Mohammed.** Islam originated in the city of Mecca, in what is now western Saudi Arabia. Mecca was the birthplace, in about A.D. 570, of the prophet of Islam, Mohammed ibn Abdullah. Mohammed preached a monotheistic religion—a belief in one God—like that of Christians and Jews. When faced with opposition from the people of Mecca, he fled north to Medina. The Muslim calendar begins with this migration, called the Hegira, in A.D. 622, because it marked the beginning of a separate Muslim community. Mecca and Medina today are the two holiest cities of Islam.

**The Spread of Islam.** At the time of Mohammed's death in 632, Mecca and most of the tribes of the Arabian Peninsula had accepted Islam. A century later an Islamic empire, under Arab leadership, ranged from Spain across North Africa and most of the present-day Middle East to Central Asia and northern India. Spain, conquered by Arabs from North Africa in 711, was the center of a great Arab-Islamic civilization, with major contributions by Jews, until the end of the 1400's.

Islam was the motivating force behind this conquest, but non-Muslims were not forcibly converted to Islam. Different religions were tolerated. Christians and Jews were permitted to practice their faiths as long as special taxes were paid to Muslim rulers.

**The Caliphates.** The Muslim rulers who succeeded to the political leadership of Islam first held by the Prophet Mohammed were known as caliphs. There were two great caliphates or dynasties of Arab origin—the Umayyad and the Abbasid. Umayyad rule lasted from 661 to 750 and was centered in Damascus (the present capital of Syria). The Abbasids ruled between 750 and 1258 from their capital of Baghdad (the modern-day capital of Iraq).

**Arab Achievements.** Islamic civilization, including both Arab and Persian (Iranian) influences, flourished under the Abbasids. Its accomplishments included advances in literature, philosophy, and medicine. Greek philosophy, including the works of Plato and Aristotle, was translated into Arabic as well. The translations passed, by way of Muslim Spain, to European Christian scholars, thus preserving one of the great heritages of Western civilization. Islamic medical texts were used in Europe until the 1600's.

Arab scholars also made important contributions in mathematics. What we call Arabic numerals (the symbols we use for our numbers) actually originated in India and were modified by the Arabs. But Muslim mathematicians invented algebra, which comes from the Arabic *al-Jabr*.

Some words from Arabic literature have also come down to us. Probably the best known is "genie," from the Arabic *jinn*, a spirit that appears in "Aladdin and the Wonderful Lamp" and other tales, part of the collection of stories most commonly known as *The Arabian Nights.*

**Arab Decline.** At the height of its power, the Abbasid Caliphate was immensely wealthy, dominating trade between Europe

Arabs are united by their use of the Arabic language, shown here in a page from the Koran. The many faces of the Arab world include a Syrian man (*right*); a Bedouin chief (*far right*); a woman from Sudan in traditional dress (*below*); and Egyptian schoolchildren (*below right*).

and Asia. But the collapse of the dynasty in 1258 meant the end of Arab leadership of the Islamic world. Its later rulers were the Ottoman Turks, whose empire, centered in Constantinople (present-day Istanbul), included most of the Arab lands.

As the Ottoman Empire itself declined in the 1800's, many of the Arab lands were taken over as colonies by European powers. At the start of World War I in 1914, all of North Africa was under European control. Algeria, Tunisia, and Morocco were ruled by France; Libya was an Italian colony; and Egypt was dominated by Britain. By 1918, when the war ended, what was left of the Ottoman Empire had fallen apart.

At the 1919 peace conference, Britain and France were awarded the remaining Arab lands, with the understanding that they would foster the development of the peoples of these regions toward self-government. Syria and Lebanon went to France, and Iraq and Palestine went to Britain.

**The Palestine Question.** Palestine represented a special case. During World War I, British officials had suggested to Arab leaders

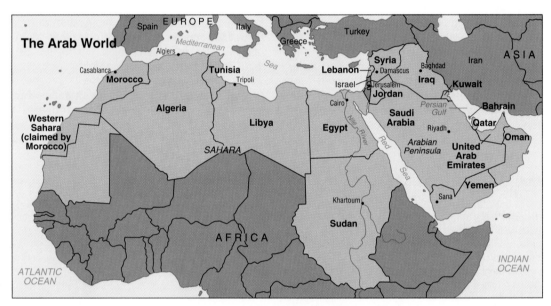

The Arab World

The landscape of the Arab world is as varied as its people. An Iraqi farmer (*below*) plows a fertile area in the upper valley of the Tigris and Euphrates rivers. By contrast, most of the Arabian Peninsula (*right*) is made up of desert.

that Palestine would be included in areas to be granted Arab self-determination. The British then promised Palestine to leaders of the Zionist movement, which called for a Jewish state in Palestine. The origin of the Arab-Israeli conflict lies in the history of these conflicting promises as well as Palestinian Arab opposition to Jewish claims in the region.

**Recent History.** Most of the Arab lands won their independence in stages after World War II ended in 1945. Some did so peacefully, others after a struggle. The creation of the Jewish state of Israel in part of Palestine in 1948 set off hostilities that led to five Arab-Israeli wars —in 1948, 1956, 1967, 1973, and 1982. The conflict continues today, particularly over the claims of the Palestinian Arabs to their own state in the West Bank and Gaza.

In addition to Arab-Israeli hostility, there have been clashes between Arab regimes or within the countries themselves because of territorial ambitions or ideological differences. The civil war that wracked Lebanon from the mid-1970's to late 1990 (and may erupt again) reflected the struggle for political power between different religious communities. The conflict was intensified by the aims of surrounding nations and the Palestine Liberation Organization (PLO), which most Palestinian Arabs look to for leadership.

Iraq's invasion of Kuwait in 1990 was caused by its desire to gain more shoreline on the Persian Gulf as well as control of Kuwait's

vast oil reserves. The quick defeat of Iraq in a short war in 1991, by a coalition led by the United States, ended this threat, but the long-term results of the war still remain to be seen.

**Arab Society Today.** In spite of political conflicts and differences among them, the Arab peoples have many things that continue to unite them. In addition to a common written language and values rooted for the most part in Islam, Arabs also have a sense of a shared history. This includes both greatness under past Muslim dynasties and forced submission to foreign rulers in more recent times.

Traditional Arab cultural values stress family ties and unity, which can be important in forming political factions. Such relationships have become less common in the large cities, where the growth of modern professions has created new political and economic alliances. Many educated young people now marry as they choose, whereas once it was assumed that marriages would be arranged by families. Some Arab countries demand stricter allegiance to traditional ways. Saudi Arabia, for example, is an extremely conservative society.

**Resources.** Arab countries vary greatly in economic development. Except for oil, most have little in the way of natural resources. Saudi Arabia and the small Persian Gulf states, once home only to small numbers of nomadic peoples, now have incredible wealth due to oil. At the same time, countries with rich historical pasts are poor today.

Kuwait, for example, a country the size of New Jersey, has the world's second largest oil reserves (Saudi Arabia has the largest) and a per capita (per person) income of about $15,000 a year. By contrast, Egypt, a center of Arab and Islamic culture with a large population, has a per capita income of only about $710 a year. This disparity has led educated people from the poorer Arab nations to seek work in the wealthy Persian Gulf states.

Agricultural productivity is high in Arab lands, but good farm land is often scarce because of a limited water supply. Population growth, which is much too high in countries such as Egypt, is another important factor in the future of the Arab world.

CHARLES D. SMITH
San Diego State University
Author, *Islam and the Search for Social
Order in Modern Egypt*

**Workers drill for offshore oil in the Red Sea. Oil is the most valuable resource in the Arab world, with the largest deposits found in Saudi Arabia.**

Bounding gracefully across the plains of Africa, impalas (*above*) can jump as high as 8 feet (2.4 meters) in a single leap. Safe within the protective camouflage of tall grasses, a baby Grant's gazelle (*left*) is nuzzled by its mother.

# ANTELOPES

Antelopes are usually slender, graceful mammals that have two-hoofed toes on each foot and hollow horns. Although they are sometimes thought to be part of the deer family, antelopes are actually more closely related to cattle. Antelopes, cattle, and other animals such as bison, buffaloes, goats, and sheep all belong to the same family, called Bovidae.

Most antelopes live in Africa. There are also several species, or kinds, of antelopes found in Asia. While there are no true antelopes in North America, a close relative of the antelopes, the mountain goat, makes its home in the Rocky Mountains of North America.

▶ CHARACTERISTICS OF ANTELOPES

There is great variety in the size of antelopes. The smallest, the royal antelope of Africa's western coast, is about the size of a rabbit. It measures about 10 inches (25 centimeters) high at the shoulder and weighs about 8 pounds (3.8 kilograms). The largest antelope, the giant eland of West Africa, is about the size of a large cow. It measures 6 feet (1.8 meters) high at the shoulder and can weigh more than 1,200 pounds (544 kilograms).

The appearance of the various species of antelopes seems to vary as much as their size does. Their smooth coat of hair is generally colored with variations of white, gray, or brown. Several species have more distinctive coloring, such as the bongo, which is red with vertical white stripes, and the male sable antelope, which is nearly all black with white markings on its face, belly, and rump.

In some kinds of antelopes, both males and females have horns; in others only males have horns. Antelopes keep the horns all their life, unlike the antlers of deer, which are shed each year. The horns can be many different shapes and sizes—long and curved, short and ringed, spiral, or lyre-shaped.

The strong slender legs of the antelope enable them to leap high and run fast. The impala can jump 8 feet (2.4 meters) high, and the black buck of India can reach speeds of about 60 miles (97 kilometers) per hour.

Plants, such as leaves and grasses, make up the diet of the antelope. The antelope must tear its food from the plant by pressing the front teeth in the lower jaw against a hard pad in the upper jaw. The food is only slightly chewed before it is swallowed. After the food

Although actual fights between antelopes are rare, these greater kudu males have locked horns in a pushing match to resolve a territorial conflict. One of the males will eventually give in and withdraw from the match with head lowered and tail tucked between his legs.

passes to the stomach, it is called cud. At a later time, the cud is forced back into the mouth to be chewed thoroughly with the back molars before it is swallowed again. Antelopes and other animals, such as deer, cattle, sheep, and goats, that eat in this manner are called cud-chewers, or **ruminants**.

▶ ANTELOPES AND THEIR YOUNG

Some male and female antelopes mate throughout the year, while others mate at a certain time of the year. The time between mating and the birth of the offspring varies from about five and a half months to about nine months, depending on the kind of antelope. Usually, only one baby is born at a time.

Most females living in herds leave the herd and find a secluded area in which to give birth. After giving birth, the mother licks the baby antelope, or calf, to rouse it. Within minutes, the calf is able to stand on its own.

In the first few months of life, the mother antelope may hide the calf in tall grass or bush when she feeds. Because calves, as well as sick and old antelopes, are easy catches for predators, many do not reach adulthood.

▶ THE LIFE OF THE ANTELOPE

Antelopes, which live in herds, alone, or in pairs, can be found in a variety of habitats, or environments: grassy plains, dense tropical forests, hot deserts, high mountains, and even swamplands. The antelope spends much of the day, except for the hot afternoon, feeding, drinking, and ruminating (chewing its cud). During the afternoon, when the sun is at its hottest, the antelope rests.

Many kinds of antelopes are territorial. This means that males mark an area as their own and guard it against other males. Although males spend much of their time defending their territory from other males, females are allowed to enter the territory to mate.

Hyenas, wild dogs, and large cats (such as lions and leopards) prey on antelopes. The smaller antelopes are also threatened by eagles, small cats, and pythons. These shy creatures often protect themselves by running away from predators. Some antelopes that live in herds use signals to warn others of danger; the springbok is one antelope that alerts others by leaping high into the air when it senses an enemy is near.

▶ ANTELOPES AND THEIR ENVIRONMENT

For at least 2 million years, humans have hunted antelopes for food. The beauty of some antelopes has made them a target for hunters who desire their skins or horns. Others have hunted them solely for sport.

The long years of hunting have left some antelopes, such as the bontebok and the giant sable, scarce; others, such as the bluebuck, have been completely wiped out. Recent efforts have been made to protect some antelopes in parks and in private reserves. Additional efforts have focused on preserving the wild antelopes by establishing game ranches where antelopes would be raised, much like cattle, for meat. With commercial antelope meat available, it would be less likely that the wild antelopes would be hunted as a food source.

LYNN MARCINKOWSKI WOOLF
Science Writer

Reviewed by JAMES DOHERTY
Curator of Mammals
The Bronx Zoo

By joining together to voice their demands, union members hope to persuade employers to increase wages and improve working conditions.

# LABOR MOVEMENT

Labor is a word that generally describes the work people are hired to perform for others. Workers, or laborers, are paid for their labor in the form of salaries and wages, which they use to pay for food, clothing, shelter, and other necessities of life.

The word labor also is used to describe the workers themselves taken together as a group. So when we speak of "labor's goals," we actually mean the goals of the workers. Likewise, when we speak of the labor movement, we refer to the sequence of historical events and efforts through which labor has sought to improve overall working conditions. The most significant outcome of the modern labor movement has been the development and evolution of labor unions.

## ▶ THE PURPOSE OF LABOR UNIONS

Before labor unions existed, employers had a great deal of power. Some employers, in order to increase their profits, took advantage of their workers, paying them extremely low wages and working them long hours. There were no laws to protect workers from unsafe work environments; if they got sick or were injured on the job, no insurance programs existed to help support them or their families while they recovered. In order to gain more power and control over their work environments, workers began grouping together to form unions.

A labor union is an organization of workers, who work in a specific trade or closely related trades. Membership dues pay for operating expenses and aid members during illness, old age, strikes, and periods of unemployment.

The primary purpose of a union is to prevent employers from taking unfair advantage of their employees. Through a process called **collective bargaining**, union representatives protect workers' rights by negotiating contracts with employers that are favorable to the workers.

## ▶ HOW THE LABOR MOVEMENT BEGAN

Prior to the modern era, most people did not work for wages. In ancient Greece and Rome, slaves performed much of the labor. Food and shelter were provided by their masters in return. Later, during the Middle Ages, serfs were required to do agricultural work for lords in return for protection against enemy invaders. These serfs did not earn wages.

As trade slowly began to develop, people began moving into towns, where they produced food, clothing, and utensils by hand. Artisans and other crafts people worked at home or in small shops that became known as cottage industries. Artisans who made similar crafts organized themselves into associations called guilds. Guilds existed for almost every type of crafts person, such as blacksmiths (ironworkers) and cordwainers (shoemakers).

### The Industrial Revolution

Many centuries later in England, toward the end of the 1700's, methods of production changed dramatically with the invention of several crude machines. These machines, used chiefly for spinning and weaving, revolutionized England's textile industry.

Machinery soon began to appear in other industries. Much of it was powered by steam engines, which had been developed by a Scottish instrument maker named James Watt (1736–1819). Machinery could produce more goods in less time than could an individual person working by hand. New methods of transportation and distribution also created a wider demand for goods.

This economic and industrial upheaval became known as the Industrial Revolution. It soon spread to the rest of western Europe and to the United States. By the beginning of the 1800's, it had almost completely changed the way in which people in the Western world lived. Small shops gave way to factories, which were required to house the large machines. Both the factories and the machines were expensive, and only people with sufficient capital—wealth in money or goods—could afford to own them. These owners became known as capitalists.

The Industrial Revolution divided society into two new classes—the capitalists (owners) and the workers (wage earners). Factory workers were dependent on the owners who paid them wages. The owners rarely worked alongside the workers as they had once done in the days of cottage industries. As a result, workers did not feel close to their employers, and when their work caused them problems, they felt that there was no one to whom they could turn.

In the early factory days, job conditions were often bad, particularly in the early English cotton mills. Before the Industrial Revolution, workers had craft guilds to aid them, but no agencies now existed to protect factory workers. So they began grouping together to form unions. By acting together, they hoped to place themselves in a stronger position to deal with their grievances and complaints.

These trade unions were mostly founded in the workers' social clubs. However, the British Parliament soon passed laws making trade unions illegal. The workers' status did not improve until 1868 when Parliament passed the Trade Union Act and the workers formed the Trade Unions Congress (TUC).

## ▶ THE LABOR MOVEMENT GROWS IN THE UNITED STATES

One of the greatest difficulties that early American unions had to overcome was the public's unfavorable opinion of them. American society generally stressed individualism and scorned the actions of organized labor groups. Workers were thought of as servants, who were meant only to obey the orders of their employers. Many workers who formed unions and made demands on their employers were arrested and tried for the "crime" of trying to improve their conditions. In 1806, for example, a group of Philadelphia cordwainers was found guilty of a "conspiracy to raise their own wages." Despite the cultural and legal obstacles to organized labor, by the 1820's American workers began to form city-wide trade associations.

### The Rise of National Federations of Labor Unions

In the 1850's the number of union organizations began to grow. Craft unions were formed by printers, stonecutters, and others.

During and immediately following the Civil War (1861–65), business boomed. With labor in such high demand, more unions flourished.

The first important national labor federation—or group of labor unions—was formed in 1866 to give a more powerful voice to the individual labor unions. This federation,

The Industrial Revolution gave rise to "sweatshops." Workers, desperate to earn a living, were crowded into unsafe, makeshift factories, where they labored for insignificant wages and received no benefits.

Child labor was the cruelest consequence of unchecked employment practices. These "breaker boys" sorted lumps of coal in the mines ten hours a day.

called National Labor Unions (NLU), favored an eight-hour workday and putting an end to child labor. By 1872, however, the NLU had ceased to exist.

In the 1870's, strikes among the anthracite coal miners of Pennsylvania and eastern railway workers resulted in violence, and in the latter case federal troops were sent to maintain law and order. The violence made labor organizations very unpopular with the public at large and limited their credibility.

### The Knights of Labor

In 1869 several Philadelphia garment cutters under the leadership of Uriah S. Stephens founded the Noble Order of the Knights of Labor. Employers at that time were very unfriendly toward unions, so the Knights began as a secret organization. In 1878 it became a national federation. The Knights favored farmers' and producers' co-operatives, public ownership of utilities, and other reform measures. Many workers were attracted by labor's group dedication. Membership skyrocketed to more than 700,000 by 1886.

The Knights then became involved in quarrels, strikes, and other difficulties with the national craft unions. On May 4, 1886, strikers from the McCormick Harvester Works in Chicago held a meeting at Haymarket Square. One group, not related to the Knights, exploded a bomb, killing a number of people, including several policemen. Again there was a sharp public reaction against labor, even

---

though the unions played no part in the riot. Terence V. Powderly, Grand Master Workman of the Knights, was a reformer rather than an organizer. He was not able to hold the Knights together, and it finally went out of existence.

### American Federation of Labor (AFL)

A rival organization to the Knights of Labor was launched in Pittsburgh in 1881. Called the Federation of Organized Trades and Labor

The Great Railroad Strike of 1877 was among the first of many strikes against the powerful railroad industry. Angry workers, dissatisfied with the corrupt business practices of the railroad tycoons, vandalized railroad property (*above*) from Pittsburgh to Chicago. In Baltimore, U.S. troops were called in to control violent street rioters (*right*).

ment. In 1886 he was elected the first president of the American Federation of Labor (AFL), and, except for one year (1895), he served in that position until his death.

**William Dudley (Big Bill) Haywood** (1869–1928), born Salt Lake City, Utah. Haywood was one of the most feared labor leaders in

William D. (Big Bill) Haywood

U.S. history. He left school at an early age, became a miner to help support his family, and later joined a union called the Western Federation of Miners. In 1905 Haywood chaired the founding convention of the Industrial Workers of the World (IWW). The following year he was arrested and charged with conspiracy in the murder of Frank

Steunenberg, a former governor of Idaho. Haywood was acquitted of the charge and went on to become the top official of the IWW (1915–17), at which time he was labeled "the most dangerous man in America." In 1918 he was convicted of spying under wartime espionage laws along with 100 other IWW leaders. Haywood jumped bail and fled to the Soviet Union.

**Sidney Hillman** (1887–1946), born Zagare, Lithuania. During his career as a union official, Hillman promoted labor-management cooperation. He served as president (1915–46) of the Amalgamated Clothing Workers of America and as vice president (1938–46) of the Congress of Industrial Organizations (CIO). He was

one of President Franklin D. Roosevelt's key labor advisers and helped develop

**Profiles**

New Deal policies during the Great Depression of the 1930's. As chairman (1943–46) of the CIO's Political Action Committee, he established close ties between the CIO and the Democratic Party. In 1946 he helped found the World Federation of Trade Unions (WFTU).

**James R. (Jimmy) Hoffa** (1913–75?), born Brazil, Ind. The son of a coal miner, Hoffa left school after the ninth grade and became a stockboy and freight handler in Detroit. In 1931 he founded a local union, which he later brought into the International Brotherhood of Teamsters (IBT). As president (1957–71) of the IBT, Hoffa built the truckers' union into one of the largest and most powerful in the country. However, during federal investi-

The International Ladies' Garment Workers' Union (*top*) and the Women's Trade Union League (*above*) protested on behalf of immigrants, women, and children—the three most oppressed segments of the work force.

Unions (FOOTALU), its purpose was to promote the interests of the craft unions. The group was reorganized in 1886 and renamed the American Federation of Labor (AFL). One of the group's founders and its first president was Samuel Gompers, the leader of the Cigarmakers' Union.

The federation was weakened by two violent strikes. In 1892, steelworkers went on strike at the Carnegie Company plant in Homestead, Pennsylvania. Several hundred private police from the Pinkerton Detective Agency battled them. Plant manager Henry C. Frick was determined to crush the union—"If it takes all summer . . . Yes, even my life itself." The strike collapsed. In 1894, federal troops put down another strike, this time by workers against the Pullman Company in Chicago. This strike was led by Eugene V. Debs, leader of American Railway Union.

The function of the AFL was to charter national unions. Its leaders, believing that the federation should not become too involved in politics, devoted their energies to achieving results through collective bargaining.

### Industrial Workers of the World

Some labor groups felt that the AFL was too conservative. Among those dissatisfied were Eugene Debs, William D. (Big Bill) Haywood, and Daniel De Leon. In 1905, these men founded a revolutionary group called the Industrial Workers of the World (IWW), whose members were nicknamed

---

**Profiles**

gations of union corruption by organized crime in the 1950's, Hoffa and the Teamsters figured prominently. In 1964 he was convicted on several different criminal charges, including misuse of union funds, and in 1967 he began serving a 13-year prison term. President Richard Nixon lifted Hoffa's prison term in 1971 under the condition that he not participate in union affairs until 1980. Hoffa disappeared, however, in 1975. It is presumed that he was the victim of a gangland murder.

**Joseph Lane Kirkland** (1922–    ), born Camden, S.C. Kirkland joined the AFL staff in 1948 and for many years was chief assistant to AFL-CIO president George Meany, whom he succeeded as president in 1979. Kirkland vigorously criticized the economic policies of President Ronald Reagan's administration and led union support for Democratic presidential candidates.

**John L. Lewis** (1880–1969), born Lucas, Ia. Lewis had a fifty-year career as a union official. In 1920, he became president of the United Mine Workers (UMW), a position he held until his retirement in 1960. In 1935 he formed the Committee for Industrial Organization (CIO). As president of the CIO (1935–40), Lewis became the most powerful labor leader in the United States and a major force in national politics. During World War II and afterward, Lewis led the miners in a series of controversial strikes. These strikes won the miners substantial medical and retirement benefits.

**George Meany** (1894–1980), born Bronx, N.Y. A plumber by trade, Meany was a union official most of his life. He served as vice president of the New York State Federation of Labor (1934–39). Later he was elected secretary-treasurer of the American Federation of Labor (AFL) and became its president in 1952. Meany successfully engineered the merger of the AFL and CIO in 1955 and served as president of the combined AFL-CIO until his retirement in 1979. A dedicated anti-Communist, Meany played an active role in politics and was a strong influence in the Democratic Party.

**Philip Murray** (1886–1952), born Blantyre, Scotland. In 1902 he immigrated to western Pennsylvania, where he began working in the coal mines. In 1919 he was elected vice president of the United Mine Workers (UMW). He held that position for twenty years, working closely with UMW president John L. Lewis. In 1935 he helped Lewis form the Committee for Industrial Organization. He served as chair-

Wobblies. Their ultimate goal was to force an overthrow of the capitalist system, because they believed that the workers themselves should own the means of production, not a handful of wealthy capitalists. The Wobblies were thus associated politically with the Socialist Party.

The Wobblies favored strikes and sabotage instead of collective bargaining. To their ranks they drew mainly unskilled labor from the West and political radicals from eastern textile mills. After 1920, the IWW lost members to the Communist Party and other left-wing political groups. Other organized labor groups

opposed the Wobblies, and the IWW gradually lost its influence.

## Congress of Industrial Organizations (CIO)

By the 1930's the American economy was dominated by mass-production industries. The AFL, which organized primarily on a craft basis, failed to organize the mass-production industries because the industries used un-

The Industrial Workers of the World organized unskilled laborers into a revolutionary union of industries. Known as Wobblies, the group's members were feared political radicals, who preached class warfare against employers.

**Walter P. Reuther** (1907–70), born Wheeling, W. Va. As a young man, Reuther went to Detroit to work in automobile factories. He played a prominent role in the sit-down strikes of the 1930's that established the United Automobile Workers (UAW). As president (1946–70) of the UAW, he succeeded in obtaining for union members such benefits as cost-of-living wage increases and health and pension benefits. In 1952, Reuther succeeded Philip Murray as president of the CIO and helped plan its 1955 merger with the AFL. As vice president (1955–68) of the AFL-CIO, he ran the Industrial Union Department. Reuther was an anti-Communist and a founder of Americans for Democratic Action (ADA). He was a staunch supporter of civil rights.

**Rose Schneiderman** (1884–1972), born Sarin, Poland. She immigrated to the United States in 1890. She left school at the age of 13 and found work in the hat industry. In 1903 she helped organize a local of the United Cloth Hat and Cap Makers' Union and became the first woman to serve on its executive board. In 1905 she joined the Women's Trade Union League (WTUL), serving as vice president (1919–26) and president (1918–19 and 1926–47). She actively participated in the reforms of President Franklin D. Roosevelt's New Deal programs.

man (1936–42) of the Steelworkers Organizing Committee and later as president (1942–52) of the United Steelworkers of America. Murray replaced Lewis as president of the CIO in 1940, serving until his death in 1952.

skilled labor—workers who were not indentified with a particular craft. Some leaders in the AFL, including John L. Lewis of the United Mine Workers (UMW), thought that a new kind of organization was required to represent all of the workers in an entire industry. Lewis created such a union in 1935, called the Committee for Industrial Organization, but it was soon forced out of the AFL.

In 1937 the Committee for Industrial Organization launched a successful sit-down strike against General Motors and organized the automobile industry. That same year, under the leadership of Philip Murray, it also organized the steel industry. In 1938 the group changed its name to Congress of Industrial Organizations (CIO).

Many workers flocked to join the AFL and the CIO during the 1940's. At the end of World War II, the government lifted the wage and price controls that had benefited the workers. The removal of this safeguard resulted in many strikes. This, in turn, led to the passage of the Labor-Management Relations Act (or Taft-Hartley Act) of 1947, which placed restrictions on strikes that were considered by the government to endanger the nation's safety, health, or welfare.

John L. Lewis, "the roaring lion of labor," led the United Mine Workers (UMW) for forty years. This 1940's caricature pictures him addressing his union members.

### The AFL-CIO

The Taft-Hartley Act was a setback for labor, and some people believed that the AFL and CIO should join forces to strengthen labor's position and influence. The two organizations finally merged in 1955, and George Meany became the first president of the combined AFL-CIO.

In addition to negotiating contracts for labor union members, the AFL-CIO established departments to handle government legislation, legal matters, and international concerns; to fight for civil rights, social security benefits, occupational safety and health, veterans' benefits, and full-time employment; and to promote projects to improve education, housing, and community services. However, in spite of all of its efforts, union membership continued to decline over the next three decades.

Today the AFL-CIO is recognized as the voice of organized labor in the United States, but not all union members are associated with it. Some belong to two minor organizations—the Confederated Unions of America and the National Independent Union Council. Still others, such as the National Education Association (NEA), operate entirely independently. However, three major unions that had long been independent rejoined the AFL-CIO in the 1980's—the United Auto Workers (UAW); the International Brotherhood of Teamsters, Chauffeurs, Warehousemen, and Helpers of America (truck drivers and others); and the United Mine Workers (UMW).

### ▶ POLITICS AND LABOR IN THE UNITED STATES

Unions usually work for reforms through established political parties, although they have occasionally tried to develop parties of their own. The first labor party, the Workingmen's Party, appeared in 1828. The ten-hour day and free public schools were major issues in its political campaigns.

After the Civil War, labor continued to feel that the government was unfriendly to its aims. Workers and farmers joined to form the Greenback-Labor Party in 1878. They supported wider use of paper currency, the eight-hour day, and votes for women.

Many leaders of the various socialist groups supported the economic aims of the unions. But they hoped eventually to transform America's capitalist society into a socialist workers' society, wherein the means of production would be owned by workers instead of by a private individual or corporation.

Several small labor parties sprang up in the 1930's. Most important of these was the American Labor Party. It supported progressive candidates of the major parties and in some cases nominated its own.

Today the AFL-CIO is closely linked with the Democratic Party, although no formal relationship exists. The voting power of union members is strongest in largely industrial areas, and the "labor vote" is highly prized, especially in U.S. presidential elections.

### ▶ ORGANIZED LABOR AROUND THE WORLD

In many parts of the world there are more agricultural than industrial workers in the labor force. Because unions usually form around industries, the labor movement is strongest in industrialized nations.

In Canada the labor movement is closely associated with labor in the United States. Most union members belong to the Canadian Labour Congress (CLC), which was formed in 1956. In the province of Quebec there are Roman Catholic labor syndicates, which are similar to unions. These syndicates belong to the Confederation of National Trade Unions (CNTU).

### Outside North America

In most countries outside North America the labor movement is associated with a political party. The Trades Union Congress (TUC) in Great Britain, for example, is politically allied with the Labour Party. Japan and Mexico have several large federations of unions, each representing a different opinion. Various unions in France and Italy represent Roman Catholic concerns as well as socialist and Communist viewpoints.

The Communist labor unions in the Soviet-controlled nations of Eastern Europe are very different from those in Western industrial nations because their right to strike or bargain with management has been limited. However, when the Communist structure began to crumble in the late 1980's, independent labor unions began to emerge everywhere, even within the Soviet Union itself.

Labor movements in Africa, Asia, and Latin America have existed since the early

Solidarity, a federation of Polish trade unions led by Lech Walesa (right), was the first independent labor union permitted by a Communist government.

1900's, but as the economies of these areas are largely based on agriculture, the power of organized labor is limited in these regions. Since World War II, industry has made rapid gains in such countries as Japan, India, South Korea, Taiwan, Singapore, South Africa, and Brazil. Today union activities in these countries are a part of everyday life.

### ▶ INTERNATIONAL ORGANIZATIONS

Internationally there are two dominant labor organizations—the World Federation of Trade Unions (WFTU) and the International Confederation of Free Trade Unions (ICFTU), to which the AFL-CIO belongs. Rivalry between these two groups has encouraged the growth of unions in less-developed countries. The International Labor Organization (ILO), founded in 1919, became a specialized agency of the United Nations in 1945. Its aims are to promote collective bargaining and improve working conditions around the world.

Prepared with the cooperation of
LOUIS HOLLANDER
Former Vice President
Amalgamated Clothing Workers of America

Reviewed by MELVYN DUBOFSKY
State University of New York at Binghamton

335

# BERLIN

The city of Berlin has long been a center of German political, economic, cultural, and intellectual life. Twice during the course of history it has served as the capital of a unified Germany.

Berlin first became the national capital in 1871, when the various German states were united into a single country. However, in the years that followed the defeat of the Nazi German regime in World War II (1939–45), Berlin—like Germany itself—was divided into two parts. East Berlin became the capital of East Germany (the German Democratic Republic), while West Berlin became one of the federal states of West Germany (the Federal Republic of Germany). During these years, the small university town of Bonn served as the capital of West Germany.

With the reunification of East and West Germany in 1990, however, Berlin once again became the official capital.

**Location, Area, and Population.** Berlin is situated in northeastern Germany, on the Spree and Havel rivers. Its location has made it a traditional crossroads of trade between eastern and western and northern and southern Europe. Lying on the great sandy plain of the North German lowlands, the city has an average elevation of only about 112 feet (34 meters) above sea level.

Berlin makes up an urban area of about 441 square miles (1,142 square kilometers). With a population of nearly 3.5 million, it is the largest city in Germany and one of the ten largest cities in Europe. Yet the city's numerous parks, forests, lakes and other waterways give some of its districts a rustic, or country-like, setting.

**Places of Interest.** In the center of the former West Berlin the ruined tower of the Kaiser Wilhelm Memorial Church stands as a stark reminder of the destruction of World War II. Next to it is the new, modernistic church building, completed in 1961. The two structures are situated at the eastern end of the Kurfürstendamm, an elegant avenue of fashionable shops, restaurants, and theaters.

The reconstructed Reichstag, the old parliament building, is a landmark of historical importance. The original building was burned in 1933, soon after the Nazis took power. The present German parliament (or legislature) meets there on festive public occasions. Nearby is a Soviet war memorial, the Tiergarten, and the new Congress Hall. The Tiergarten, a park near the center of the city with a zoo and aquarium, is especially popular with Berliners. Other new buildings include the Berlin Philharmonic concert hall, the opera house, and several museums.

For years the wall that divided the city attracted millions of visitors. It was torn down in 1990, and all that remains of this relic of the Cold War is a swath of open space.

A sunny day draws Berliners to an outdoor café. In the background, the ruins of the old Kaiser Wilhelm Memorial Church stand as a stark reminder of the destruction of World War II.

The Brandenburg Gate, one of Berlin's best-known monuments, is situated in the historic center of the city, in what was formerly East Berlin. Because of its closeness to the Berlin Wall, the Gate was a symbol of the division of the city. A triumphal arch some 85 feet (26 meters) high, the Gate faces the Tiergarten and stands at the western end of a tree-lined boulevard, Unter den Linden ("Under the Linden Trees"). This thoroughfare was once the site of military parades and the funeral processions of German rulers. Most of the government buildings, palaces, and foreign embassies that at one time lined the avenue were destroyed during World War II, but those that could be saved were restored.

At the eastern end of Unter den Linden is a giant square, which the East Germans named Marx-Engels-Platz, after the two major figures in the founding of Communism. It is also the site of the former royal palace. The huge Palace of the Republic, which once housed the East German parliament, stands nearby. Numerous museums are located on the appropriately named Museum Island.

**Cultural Life.** Berlin has been a cultural center of Germany for much of its modern history. During the Weimer period (1919–33), it was the entertainment capital of the world. Its cabarets, theaters, and motion pictures enjoyed an international reputation, lost during the Nazi era that followed.

*Right:* A poster for the silent film classic *Metropolis* dates from 1926, when Berlin was famed for its popular entertainment. *Below:* This war memorial is dedicated to the nearly 5,000 Soviet soldiers killed in the 1945 battle for Berlin.

East German border guards at the Brandenburg Gate calmly looked on in 1989 as West Berliners celebrated the coming reunification of the long-divided city.

The city's division into eastern and western sectors from 1949 to 1990 meant that each developed its own distinct cultural life. Attempts were made, however, to preserve a common heritage. The great pre-war museum collections, for example, were divided between East and West Berlin's museums.

Berlin has recaptured some of its past glory through its Philharmonic Orchestra concerts, opera houses, theater groups, a yearly cultural festival, and jazz and rock performances. The Free University and Humboldt University play an important role in the city's intellectual life. Its many museums include the world-famous Pergamon Museum, noted for its collection of classical art.

**The Economy.** Before World War II, Berlin was a center of commerce and banking as well as an important industrial city. By the 1950's, West Berlin had recovered from the war's destruction and was in the midst of an economic boom. At the same time, East Berlin was integrated into the Communist economic system of East Germany. The standard of living was considerably higher in the West than in the East.

The major industries in the Greater Berlin area involve the production of electrical and electronic equipment, machinery and motor vehicles, engineering products, processed foods, chemicals, and clothing. The city also has the largest number of scientific and technological research institutions in the country.

Since the reunification of Germany in 1990, the federal government has provided substantial economic assistance to the former eastern sector.

**The City's Origins.** The city of Berlin developed out of two small trading settlements, Kölln and Berlin, which are first mentioned in documents of the 1200's. The two settlements merged in the 1300's. In 1486, Berlin became the seat of the electors (or rulers) of what was then the small state of Brandenburg. The Thirty Years' War (1618–48) laid waste to the city, but it was rebuilt by the Great Elector Frederick William.

**Capital.** In 1701, Berlin became the capital of the kingdom of Prussia, which had grown out of the original core of Brandenburg. In spite of military occupation by foreign armies during the wars of the 1700's and 1800's, Berlin, along with Prussia, grew steadily in importance. When the German states united around Prussia to form the German Empire in 1871, Berlin became its capital.

During World War II, much of Berlin was destroyed by bombing and in the

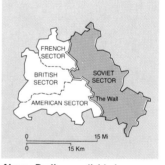

*Above:* Berlin was divided among the four victorious Allied powers in 1945, at the end of World War II. In 1949 the U.S., British, and French sectors were joined to form West Berlin. The Soviet sector became East Berlin. The city remained divided until 1989–90. *Left:* When the Soviet Union blockaded West Berlin in 1948–49, cutting off all land access to that part of the city, its people were supplied through a massive airlift by U.S. and British planes.

heavy ground fighting that took place at the end of the war in Europe. On May 2, 1945, Soviet armies captured the city. U.S., British, French, and Soviet forces each occupied a sector of Berlin. Germany as a whole was divided along the same lines. The United States, Britain, and France occupied the western part of the country (which later became West Germany). The Soviet Union controlled the eastern part (later to become East Germany). Berlin itself lay within the Soviet area of occupation of Germany. An inter-Allied governing authority administered the city jointly.

**The City Divided.** In 1949 separate East and West Germanys were established. The U.S., British, and French sectors of Berlin were joined to form West Berlin; the Soviet sector became East Berlin. But the four Allied powers still had final control over the city.

In 1953 a revolt by workers in East Berlin against the East German government was crushed by Soviet tanks. Increasing numbers of East Berliners fled to West Berlin in subsequent years, until 1961, when the East German authorities erected a fortified wall, physically separating the two parts of the city.

As onlookers cheer, a young Berliner adds his own blows to the crumbling wall that for nearly thirty years had physically divided the city. Erected in 1961, the Berlin Wall was designed to stop the flood of Germans escaping from Communist East Germany to West Germany, which had become a drain on the East German economy. The wall was also a symbol of the division of Germany itself, which lasted until 1990, when both Germany and Berlin were again united.

**Blockade and Airlift.** In 1948, Berlin became a focal point of the Cold War, the period of hostility that developed between the Soviet Union and the nations of the West after the war. The Soviets informally withdrew from the governing authority and tried to force the Western powers to end controls over their three sectors. When this failed, the Soviets cut off all land and water communications between western Germany and the three western sectors of Berlin in an effort to gain control over the entire city.

In response, the Western Allies launched a massive airlift of food and other supplies to the isolated western sectors. The blockade lasted eleven months, until May 1949, when the Soviets, not having gained their objective, lifted it.

**Reunification.** The easing of political tensions and a new agreement between the Western Allies and the Soviet Union in 1971 eased travel restrictions for Germans. Nevertheless, the Berlin Wall remained a symbol of a divided city and nation for nearly twenty more years. In November 1989, however, following widespread protests by its own people, the East German government opened the guarded crossing points of the wall.

As East Berliners poured into West Berlin in celebration, the dismantling of the wall and of a divided Germany was already underway. On October 3, 1990, the two Germanys were united and a separate West and East Berlin ceased to exist.

GERARD BRAUNTHAL
University of Massachusetts, Amherst

The ruins of Machu Picchu, an ancient Inca city, still stand in Peru. The cultures of native peoples are a key element of Latin American art and architecture.

# LATIN AMERICAN ART AND ARCHITECTURE

The art of Latin America is remarkably varied due to the many different kinds of populations and traditions found in its main regions: Mexico and Central America, the Caribbean, and South America. In fact, Latin America consists of more than thirty countries, each of which has its own historical and cultural experiences.

Although this diversity makes Latin American art difficult to define, one common trait that can be identified is the presence of three distinct cultural heritages: Indian, European, and African. Before colonization, Mexico, Central America, and the Andean region of South America contained large numbers of native Indian peoples whose sophisticated cultures were later blended with the traditions brought by the Europeans. On the other hand, in the Caribbean and eastern South America, where native populations were small or de-

stroyed by the invaders and colonizers, European traditions were imposed with little resistance. The culture of these two areas was also greatly affected by Africans brought there as slaves by the Europeans.

This blending of cultures is an important characteristic of Latin American art. To the initial mix of Indian, African, and European traditions, other elements were added during the 1800's and 1900's. European immigrants and Latin American artists studying abroad brought in newer international artistic trends. These were combined with the arts of the various nations and transformed at the local level into something new and original. Difficult economic and political conditions have often limited the work of Latin American artists; nevertheless, they have continuously made significant contributions to world art.

## ▶ COLONIAL ART AND ARCHITECTURE

The occupation of present-day Latin America by the Spanish and Portuguese began at the end of the 1400's. After the Spanish subdued the native peoples, they divided the conquered lands into four colonies, or viceroyalties: New Spain (present-day Mexico and Central America) and the viceroyalties of New Granada, Peru, and Río de la Plata (Spanish territories south of Panama). At the same time, the Portuguese founded the viceroyalty of Brazil. All the Spanish and Portuguese colonies became independent during the 1800's.

In order to control the native populations and convert them to Christianity, the Spanish destroyed many of the Indians' cultural landmarks. Churches were built on the ruins of native temples, taking advantage of the spiritual importance of these sites for the Indians. This led to associations between Christian saints and native gods; churches were often decorated with figures that combined pagan and Christian characteristics.

**The Plateresque Style.** The forced conversions of large numbers of native peoples led to a need for bigger churches. A solution was found in a Latin American version of the Spanish Renaissance style called plateresque. This style has elegant exterior decoration that looks like the work of silversmiths (*plateros*).

Plateresque forms were combined with Gothic vaults—high arched ceilings suitable for large buildings—and open chapels facing on spacious courtyards, from which large congregations could hear Mass.

One of the best examples of this style is the Church of San Augustín in Acolman, Mexico, built about 1560. The inside walls are decorated with a series of magnificent frescoes (paintings done on wet plaster) of religious subjects. The themes and styles of the frescoes followed European models.

**Baroque Architecture.** During the 1600's and 1700's, the baroque, a new style brought from Europe, was successfully adopted throughout Latin America. The baroque style, with its lavish decoration and dramatic effects, inspired new ways of expressing the blend of the native and European heritages.

Latin American builders modified the baroque style to suit the environment of the New World: Areas plagued by earthquakes needed thicker walls, and tropical regions required wood ceilings to provide better ventilation. Other regional traits were painted plaster and tile work, as well as lavishly decorated facades (fronts) and interiors. In coastal areas, European baroque models were followed more closely, while Indian and local influences grew stronger in the more isolated inland cities. Similarly, cathedrals and parish churches tended to be more plain, while churches built by religious orders reflected in their splendor the monks' efforts to capture the imagination of the native peoples.

In New Spain, the somber European style of the Cathedral of Mexico City was abandoned in smaller urban centers in favor of more expressive styles. For example, the interior of the magnificent Rosary Chapel in the Monastery Church of Santo Domingo in Puebla, Mexico, is covered with brightly painted plasterwork. In New Granada, where native influence was weaker, baroque building styles were more closely linked with those of Europe. The Church of the Jesuits in Quito, Ecuador, was built following Italian models for the plan and facade. But the interior shows a strong Arabic influence in the geometric patterns of its stucco decoration. This decoration is also an example of the use of gold ornamentation on red background, characteristic of Quito artists.

Baroque architecture of the viceroyalty of Peru had special modifications designed to withstand earthquakes, such as the cane-and-wood roofing known as *quincha* and the use of thick old Inca walls for the foundations of buildings. In the Church of the Jesuits in Cuzco, the facade is protected from tremors by two flanking bell towers, whose massiveness is balanced by elegant decoration.

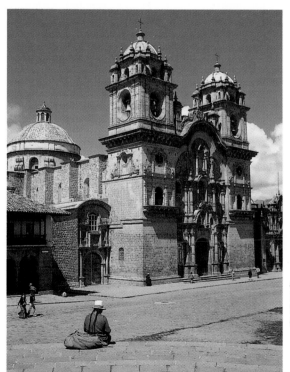

*Above:* Santo Domingo Cathedral (1512–41), on the island of Hispaniola, was the first cathedral built in the New World. *Left:* The Church of the Jesuits (1651–68) in Cuzco, Peru, features two massive bell towers.

341

Unlike Peru, Brazil is not threatened by earthquakes. Baroque architects there did not have to design quake-proof buildings and thus were free to experiment with more inventive forms. An interesting regional style developed in Minas Gerais, a wealthy gold-mining area. Several churches were built in Ouro Preto, a city in the region. One, the church of Nossa Senhora do Rosário (1785), shows the typical tendency of that region toward curving forms. In Bahia, the capital of the viceroyalty of Brazil, facades were patterned after Portuguese models, but interiors, such as that of Bahia's cathedral, exploded in dazzling displays of gold decoration.

**Baroque Painting and Sculpture.** With the exception of the School of Cuzco in Peru, which developed a more unique style, colonial painters of the baroque era closely followed European models. Portraits were popular among wealthy members of the colonial nobility, who posed for formal likenesses dressed in their best finery. Important painters included Cristóbal de Villalpando of Mexico, Miguel de Santiago of Ecuador, and Melchor Pérez de Holguín of Peru.

Sculptors, on the other hand, worked in more independent styles. Most of them carved images in wood and either gilded them (coated them with a layer of gold) or covered them with plaster, which was later painted. Often, the figures were designed to be dressed in rich cloth costumes. Among the most important baroque sculptors were Jerónimo Balbás, who created many monumental altarpieces in Mexico; Alonso de la Paz, a Guatemalan who made high-quality painted sculptures; and Manuel Chili (called Capiscara) of the School of Quito, who based his sculptural groups on Spanish and Italian models. Sculptors in inland regions, rather than imitating European works, emphasized flattened forms. A notable example is the Virgin of Guadalupe in the Cathedral of Sucre, Bolivia.

An outstanding colonial sculptor was Brazil's Antonio Francisco Lisboa, known as O Aleijadinho ("The Little Cripple"). His painted-wood figures (1797–99) in the church of Bom Jesus, Congonhas do Campo, and his dramatic stone statues of the twelve prophets (1800–1805) outside the same church mark the peak of Brazilian baroque sculpture.

▶ 1800'S

During the first half of the 1800's, most Spanish-American colonies gained independence and formed into separate republics. Brazil became independent from Portugal in 1822, but it was ruled by the Portuguese royal family until the late 1800's. With indepen-

In addition to native artists, many European and North American artists traveled through Latin America painting scenes of everyday life. Styles and techniques were learned from them, as well as from foreign artists and architects hired to teach at newly founded academies and schools of fine arts. Soon, local

dence came a rejection of Spanish and Portuguese traditions in favor of French cultural models.

**Architecture.** The most important trend in architecture of the early 1800's was **neoclassicism.** This style, which originated in France, used columned facades and other forms inspired by the classical architecture of ancient Greece and Rome. In Brazil, the French architect Grandjean de Montigny designed the Imperial Academy of Fine Arts and other official buildings in the neoclassic style.

**Painting.** The 1800's produced few sculptors in Latin America. Painting was the most important of the arts. Many young republics defined their national identities through images of heroes and battles, landscapes, and portraits, painted in the styles of French artists. The Mexican landscape painter José Maria Velasco specialized in views of the Valley of Mexico, while the Venezuelan Arturo Michelena portrayed the national heroes of his country's war of independence. Juan Manuel Blanes of Uruguay and Prilidiano Pueyrredón of Argentina worked on portraits of important people as well as of gauchos (cowboys).

artists began to travel to European cities for training. By the turn of the century, there had emerged in Latin America a wealthy cultural elite, who showed a strong preference for French styles in art and architecture.

▶ 1900'S

The first two decades of the 1900's saw the rise of three important modern art movements in Latin America: muralism, modernism, and martinfierrism. The **muralists,** centered in Mexico, included Diego Rivera, David Alfaro Siqueiros, and José Clemente Orozco. Brazil's **modernists** included Anita Malfatti, Lasar Segal, and Tarsila do Amaral. The **martinfierrists,** based in Argentina, took their name from the famous Argentine epic poem *Martín Fierro.* They included Norah Borges, Emilio Pettoruti, and Xul Solar. All these artists, except Orozco, had been active in various European modern art movements. When they returned to their native countries, they rejected the styles of the late 1800's, still popular in Latin America, in favor of modern trends.

Artists like Rivera and Amaral turned to the native and popular cultures of their own countries as a source of artistic inspiration. Pettoruti and Xul Solar used the modern styles of cubism and futurism to express the urban experience of the rapidly growing Latin American cities.

The Mexican muralists painted large-scale frescoes that commented on contemporary events. Their realistic style was well suited to their purpose of conveying the ideals of the Mexican Revolution. Muralism had a major impact in both North and South America. During the 1930's, it inspired the work of socially active artists such as Candido Portinari in Brazil and Antonio Berni in Argentina. The muralists' dignified representations of native peoples also influenced many artists in the Andean region.

**Surrealism.** During the 1930's and 1940's, the modern art movement known as surrealism became popular in many Latin American countries. Surrealist artists tried to portray the world of dreams and the unconscious by painting images from their imagination. The Chilean painter Roberto Matta developed a highly personal version of surrealism, and his work had a significant influence on the art of the United States. In Mexico, artists such as Rufino Tamayo, Leonora Carrington, Juan O'Gorman, and Frida Kahlo favored themes that ranged from the dreamlike to the personal and autobiographical. Another surrealist, Wilfredo Lam, successfully combined European styles with cultural elements from his Afro-Cuban background.

*Above:* The murals of Diego Rivera comment on Mexican history. *Below: Mundo* (1925), by Argentine painter Xul Solar. *Below left:* Works by Colombian artist Fernando Botero often feature comically plump figures.

The Foreign Ministry Building is one of many structures designed by architect Oscar Niemeyer for Brasília, the capital of Brazil. The plan for the capital and its buildings was one of the most ambitious architectural projects of modern Latin America.

**Abstract Movements.** The abstract art movement began to grow in Latin America during the 1930's. Abstract art usually consists of lines, colors, and shapes that do not represent any real object. An early figure in the abstract movement was Uruguayan artist Joaquín Torres-García. His paintings and sculptures, although not completely abstract, combined simplified figures with geometric shapes. His art and teachings were highly influential throughout Latin America, particularly in Uruguay and Argentina.

Torres-García paved the way for younger artists who developed purely geometric and abstract styles. In Argentina in the 1940's, artists of the Concrete Invention and Madi groups, such as Tomás Maldonado and Gyula Kosice, made irregularly shaped paintings of basic geometric forms and color planes, as well as mobile abstract sculptures. In Brazil, the Neo-Concrete artists of São Paulo, such as Helio Oiticica and Lygia Clark, transformed simple geometric shapes and color planes into playful sculptures and intensely colored installations.

Many Latin American artists worked in abstract styles after the 1950's. Among them were the painters Fernando de Szyszlo (Peru), María Luisa Pacheco (Bolivia), and Gunther Gerzso (Mexico) and the sculptors Jesús Rafael Soto (Venezuela), Edgar Negret (Colombia), and Julio LeParc (Argentina).

**Figure Painting.** After the 1960's, many Latin American artists turned to the human figure as a way to express the widespread suffering of contemporary life. In the following decades, different styles of figure painting existed side by side. For example, Brazil's Antonio H. Amaral painted realistic images with hidden political commentaries, and Colombia's Fernando Botero painted satirical works featuring comically plump figures, while the paintings of Puerto Rico's Rafael Ferrer have an expressionistic quality.

**Conceptual Art.** Latin American artists such as Luis Camnitzer (Uruguay) and Catalina Parra (Chile) began to work with conceptual art in the 1960's. Conceptual artworks have two parts: an idea or concept, and a written or visual explanation of that concept. Photographs, texts, sound and video recordings, maps, and diagrams are among the techniques used to explain or document the concept.

**Architecture.** Several large building projects were undertaken in different parts of Latin America during the 1900's. The University of Mexico was designed in 1950–53 by a group of more than 150 architects, including Juan O'Gorman and Félix Candela. It combines modern architecture with the work of Mexican muralists. Similarly, the University City in Caracas, Venezuela, built in 1950–57 by Carlos Raul Villanueva, integrates modern buildings with works by artists. Perhaps the most daring large-scale architectural project in Latin America was that for Brasília. The new capital of Brazil was planned by Lúcio Costa in 1957, and most of its buildings were designed after 1960 by Oscar Niemeyer. The city's spacious layout and graceful buildings were designed to bring the life of Brazil inland from the old coastal cities.

FLORENCIA BAZZANO NELSON
Rochester Institute of Technology

**345**

# NORTHWEST PASSAGE

The Northwest Passage is a route that connects the Atlantic and Pacific oceans by way of the icy Arctic waters of North America. For centuries European explorers who sought a faster trade route to Asia imagined that such a route must exist, and many devoted their lives to finding it.

The search for the fabled Northwest Passage, which began soon after Christopher Columbus's voyage of 1492, reveals tales of extraordinary courage and determination. When Columbus sailed westward across the Atlantic Ocean and landed on an island in the Bahamas, he believed that he had reached Asia, his intended destination. The European explorers who followed him, however, soon realized that Columbus had not reached Asia at all, but had approached the shores of two unknown continents. At first they considered this New World little more than an obstacle in their journey to the Orient, and they immediately began looking for a way to sail through it.

The first attempts to find the Northwest Passage were made by John Cabot (1497) for Britain and Giovanni da Verrazano (1524) and Jacques Cartier (1534) for France. However, the British began the search in earnest after 1576, when Sir Martin Frobisher discovered what is now Baffin Island. About nine years later, John Davis explored the western coast of Greenland and sailed into the strait that now bears his name.

In the 1600's, the search for the Northwest Passage centered around Hudson Bay, discovered by Henry Hudson in 1610. Then William Baffin explored Hudson Strait, Hudson Bay, and the shores of Baffin Bay between 1612 and 1616. Baffin sailed almost as far north as 78 degrees north latitude. This achievement was not equaled for another 200 years because after 1631 exploration efforts in the north focused on finding furs, which could be sold in Europe for enormous profit.

It was not until 1818 that Commander John Ross renewed Britain's search for a continuous westward route to the Pacific Ocean. Ross followed the course Baffin had taken some 200 years earlier, and he charted much of the coastline along the way.

The most famous voyage of this period, however, was Sir John Franklin's tragic expedition of 1845. Franklin and his men disappeared and dozens of rescue parties searched for them in the following years. Unfortunately, Franklin and his men were never found alive, but consequently, the rescue missions contributed about 6,000 miles (9,560 kilometers) of newly explored coastline to the map of Canada's Arctic Islands.

From 1850 to 1854, Captain Robert McClure traveled, partly by sea and partly by sled

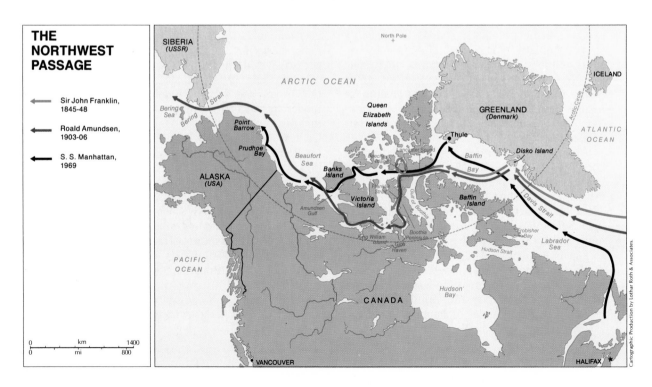

**THE NORTHWEST PASSAGE**

← Sir John Franklin, 1845-48

← Roald Amundsen, 1903-06

← S. S. Manhattan, 1969

**Amundsen, Roald** (1872–1928), Norwegian explorer, b. Borge. Amundsen achieved many firsts in exploration, including the first successful voyage through the Northwest Passage (1903–06). Then, concentrating his efforts on the other side of the world, he led an expedition to the South Pole. He reached the pole on December 14, 1911, beating the ill-fated British explorer, Robert Scott, by just five weeks. In 1920, Amundsen returned to the Arctic and completed a voyage through the Northeast Passage. He thus became the first person to sail both the Northwest and Northeast passages. In 1928, Amundsen disappeared in the Arctic while searching for Italian explorer Umberto Nobile.

**Franklin, Sir John** (1786–1847), British rear admiral, b. Lincolnshire. Franklin went in search of the Northwest Passage in 1845, having previously explored the mouth of the Coppermine River (1819) and other Arctic regions (1825–26). It is now known that Franklin discovered the passage on his third Arctic expedition, but he disappeared during the course of it. His ships, *Erebus* and *Terror*, were last seen in Baffin Bay in July 1845. Over the years, no fewer than forty expeditions were sent to find him. In 1859, a search party sponsored by Franklin's wife found a cairn (memorial of piled rocks) on King William Island, revealing Franklin had died on June 11, 1847. Others apparently had died trying to make it back on foot to

the Canadian mainland. An earlier search expedition in 1850 had found the graves of three sailors on Beechey Island. More than a century later, in 1984, scientists examined two of the bodies. (See photo below.)

**Frobisher, Sir Martin** (1535–94), British navigator and explorer, b. Yorkshire. Frobisher made three voyages in search of the Northwest Passage. On his first voyage in 1576, he discovered what is now Frobisher Bay, an inlet in Baffin Island. He returned to England with some ore that was mistakenly identified as gold. Investors hoping to find more of the precious metal sponsored Frobisher's next two voyages (1577 and 1578). Frobisher did not find gold, but he did discover what later became known as the Hudson Strait. He went on to serve as vice admiral in Sir Francis Drake's 1585–86 expedition to the West Indies, and in 1588 he was knighted for fighting against the Spanish Armada. He was fatally wounded in 1594 while fighting the Spanish on the coast of France.

**Ross, Sir John** (1777–1856), British explorer, b. Wigtownshire, Scotland. From 1818 to 1834, he led several Arctic expeditions specifically to find the Northwest Passage, and an 1850 expedition to find Sir John

Roald Amundsen

Sir John Franklin

Franklin. John Ross explored Boothia Peninsula, the Gulf of Boothia, and King William Land. His nephew, **Sir James Clark Ross** (1800–1862), b. London, joined his uncle's 1829–33 expedition, during which he discovered the North Magnetic Pole. In 1848 he also commanded an unsuccessful, two-year expedition in search of Sir John Franklin. But James Clark Ross is best known for exploring Antarctica.

The body of John Torrington, a crew member of Sir John Franklin's ill-fated 1845 expedition, was found perfectly preserved in the Arctic permafrost.

and on foot, from the Bering Sea eastward to the Atlantic. McClure's travels, along with the findings of the Franklin search expeditions, showed that no practical water route existed through the Arctic islands. The ice floes (sheets of floating ice) simply made the route impassable through much of the year.

The historic first crossing of the Northwest Passage by sea finally was made by a Norwegian explorer, Roald Amundsen, in a 47-ton herring boat named the *Gjoa*. Sailing east to west, Amundsen's three-year voyage (1903–06) ran through Lancaster Sound and then south and west to the Beaufort Sea and the Bering Strait.

The first successful west-to-east voyage was begun in 1940 by Henry A. Larsen of the Royal Canadian Mounted Police. He sailed from Vancouver, British Columbia, on the 80-

ton schooner *St. Roch* and reached Halifax, Nova Scotia, two years later. In 1944, Larsen made the return voyage from Halifax to Vancouver, and the *St. Roch* distinguished itself as the first vessel to make the trip in a single season.

In 1960 the first undersea voyage was accomplished by the U.S. nuclear submarine *Seadragon,* and in 1969 the U.S. icebreaking oil tanker *Manhattan* became the first commercial vessel to break through.

More recent exploration has been aided by advancements in radar and aerial photography. Because of its treacherous conditions, however, the Northwest Passage has yet to become a commercially practical route between the Atlantic and Pacific oceans.

C. CECIL LINGARD
Director, *Canada Year Book*

Land is a limited resource in Hong Kong. Many families in its large population, faced with the scarcity of land, are forced to live on boats in Hong Kong harbor.

# ECONOMICS

Why is it difficult to satisfy everyone's wants? Why are some people richer than others? Why do people sometimes have trouble finding jobs? Why do the prices of things increase? For centuries people have pondered these questions and many others like them. The science that deals with such questions is called economics, and the scientists who study these questions are called economists.

## ▶ SCARCITY, GOODS, AND SERVICES

One of the basic concerns of economics is the relation between resources and wants. More specifically, economists study how individuals and societies use limited resources to satisfy their needs and wants. Unfortunately, the earth does not have enough resources to satisfy everyone. If it did, everything would be available to everyone, and no one would be in need.

The problem of trying to meet unlimited wants with limited resources (such things as land, labor, and factories) is the most basic of all economic problems. Economists call it the problem of **scarcity**. There are simply not enough resources in any society to provide its people with everything they want. In a world of limited resources, only so many cars, shoes, electronic games, movies, bushels of grain, and other things can be produced in any given year. There will not be nearly enough of these things to satisfy everyone.

Although it is not possible to satisfy everyone's wants, most societies try to satisfy as much as possible through the production of economic goods and services. Economic **goods** are things of value that can be seen and touched, such as bicycles, automobiles, clothing, and television sets. Economic goods also include such things as factories, stores, machines, and tools. Economic **services** are things that have value but often cannot be seen or touched, such as entertainment, medical care, legal advice, and national defense.

## ▶ LAWS OF SUPPLY AND DEMAND

Perhaps the most basic laws in the science of economics are the laws of supply and demand. These laws play a major role in almost all economic issues.

The law of demand says that as the price of a good or service rises (and other factors remain unchanged), the demand for that item will fall. As the price of the good or service falls, the demand for the item will rise. In other words, people will buy more of an item if the price is low than if the price is high.

The law of supply is the opposite of the law of demand. It says that as the price of an item rises (and other factors remain unchanged), the supply of the item will rise. As the price of the item falls, the supply will also fall. It is only natural that as prices rise, the people providing goods and services will be willing to supply larger quantities of those goods and services.

The interaction of supply and demand determines the prices of goods and services. An increase in demand tends to make prices higher. A decrease in demand tends to make prices lower. Similarly, an increase in supply tends to make prices lower, while a decrease in supply tends to make them higher.

The basic resources an economy needs for the production of goods and services are called factors of production. Economists usually divide the factors of production into three basic categories: natural resources, capital goods, and labor. Many economists add a fourth factor of production—entrepreneurship.

## Natural Resources

Natural resources are things provided by nature, such as land, air, water, forests, oil, coal, iron ore, and other minerals. Natural resources are the starting point of all production. As such they represent the most basic limitation on how much any economy can produce. No matter how much labor, capital goods, and technological knowledge an economy has, it simply cannot produce goods without natural resources.

## Capital Goods

Capital goods are human-made resources used for the production of other goods and services. Factories, machines, tools, and office buildings are all examples of capital goods. Such capital goods are necessary for using natural resources. For example, sawmills, chain saws, and other capital goods are needed to convert timber into usable products.

## Labor

Labor, which is sometimes called human resources, is any kind of human effort used for production. For economists, labor includes not only physical work but also intellectual work and the use of human knowledge, talents, and skills. The work of truck drivers, factory workers, lawyers, doctors, and public officials are all examples of labor. Labor is essential to production because natural resources and capital goods are of no value unless they can be put to use by the work of people.

## Entrepreneurship

Natural resources, capital goods, and labor must be combined and organized before production can take place. This process is known as entrepreneurship. An **entrepreneur** is a person who takes the initiative to bring the three factors of production together in order to produce a good or service. He or she provides money, time, and effort to buy raw materials, hire labor, and buy machinery to produce a particular good or service. In return, the entrepreneur receives a profit for his or her efforts. The cheaper the cost of producing the good or service, the greater the profit.

In deciding how to use limited resources to satisfy people's wants, a society must consider three basic questions: What goods and services will be produced? How will those goods and services be produced? For whom will the goods and services be produced?

## What Goods and Services Will Be Produced?

This is a difficult and complex question. A portion of a nation's limited resources must be used by the government to provide government services, including such things as national defense. The remaining resources are available for use in producing other goods and

Trees are a valuable natural resource. In this Arkansas forest, trees are cut and prepared for shipment to mills for the production of goods such as paper and lumber.

services. Some of these resources will be used to produce capital goods, such as factories, machines, and tools. The rest will be available for the production of consumer goods and services, such as food, medical care, bicycles, automobiles, and movies.

**Consumer Sovereignty.** In some countries the government decides how many, and what kinds of, consumer goods and services will be produced. But in the United States and Canada, the people (consumers) decide what will be produced—a process called consumer sovereignty. People ''vote'' (with their money) for the goods and services they want produced. If consumers do not buy a product in sufficient quantity to make its production profitable, producers will discontinue making the product. If people demand more of a product than is available, production will be increased.

### How Will Goods and Services Be Produced?

There is often more than one way to produce a particular good or service. For example, suppose a construction company has been hired to dig a large basement for a new building. The basement could perhaps be dug by fifty workers using shovels and wheelbarrows, or by one worker using a giant crane. The construction company, in competition with other companies for the job, must choose the most efficient and least costly method of digging the basement. In this case, it would probably mean using one worker and the giant crane rather than fifty workers equipped with shovels and wheelbarrows.

Competition forces producers to use the least costly methods of production. It allows consumers to buy goods and services at lower prices than would be possible if less efficient, higher-cost methods of production were used.

### For Whom Will Goods and Services Be Produced?

No nation can produce enough goods and services to satisfy all its citizens' wants. It is necessary, therefore, to have some way of deciding who gets the things that are produced.

In the United States, goods and services are distributed on the basis of wealth. The people with the most money get the most goods and services. While this may be an efficient way of deciding who gets what, it is not necessarily a fair way. People with the most money may not be the most deserving or the ones with the

greatest need. Nor do they necessarily work the hardest. Some people who work very hard earn a small income. Although some wealthy people have worked hard to get their money, others have inherited much of it.

**Providing Basic Goods and Services.** If the distribution of goods and services were based entirely on personal wealth, some people might be without food, clothing, and shelter through no fault of their own. The fact that a person is willing and able to work does not guarantee that he or she will be able to find a good job. Some people are so disabled that they are unable to work. For these reasons, governments and private organizations sponsor various programs for the purpose of helping the very poor obtain some basic goods and services.

## ▶ KINDS OF ECONOMIC SYSTEMS

Every society has an organized set of procedures for answering the three basic economic questions. This set of procedures determines a nation's economic system. There are basically three kinds of economic systems in the world: traditional economies, command economies, and market economies.

### Traditional Economies

In some rural, nonindustrial areas of the world, there is no national economy. Instead, there are many small economies centered around families or tribal units, each of which produces almost everything it consumes. In

The crops being harvested by the Otavalo Indian tribe are part of a traditional economy in Ecuador, South America.

these economies, the basic questions of "what," "how," and "for whom" are answered directly by the people involved. Because the answers to these questions are usually based on tradition, these economies are called traditional economies.

### Command Economies

In some societies, answers to the three basic economic questions are determined by the government. Individuals have little control or influence over economic questions and issues. They are told what to produce, how to produce it, and what they will receive. Economies in which the government makes most or all economic decisions are called command economies. The economy of China is an example of a command economy.

### Market Economies

In many Western societies, the answers to basic economic questions are determined primarily by individuals and businesses. Buyers and sellers in the marketplace have a great deal of economic freedom, and the economy functions largely through the laws of supply and demand. Because economic decisions are made by individuals in a free marketplace, such economies are called market economies. The economies of the United States, Canada, and Japan are examples of market economies.

**Maintaining Freedom of Choice.** There are steps a government sometimes takes to make sure the market allows consumers freedom of choice. Often the government passes laws that require producers to give correct information about their products. Other laws forbid dishonest advertising. Still others try to equalize the uneven power of producers. For example, if one large producer provides almost all of a certain good or service, it is called a **monopoly**. If only a few large producers provide all of a certain good or service, it is called an **oligopoly**. Laws in some countries limit the power of monopolies and oligopolies so that they cannot control the market unfairly.

### Mixed Economies

Almost no economies in the world are exclusively command or market economies that rely solely on government decisions or on free markets to answer basic economic questions. Instead, most major economies are mixed economies in which some decisions are made by individuals in the marketplace and others are made by the government.

### Capitalism, Socialism, and Communism

Economies are also categorized on the basis of who owns most of the means of production (such as factories, natural resources, and machinery). Economies in which the means of production are owned primarily by individuals or private companies are called **capitalist** systems. The United States has a capitalist economic system. Economies in which the government owns some or all of the means of production are called **socialist** systems. There

The weavers in this carpet factory in Inner Mongolia, China (*top*), work in a command economy. The variety of vegetables in this Idaho supermarket (*left*) is one result of the market economy in the United States.

is a great variation among socialist systems. In some socialist systems, the government may own only certain key industries, such as steel or energy. In others it may own almost everything. A **communist** system is a type of socialist system in which the government controls virtually all industries and makes all economic decisions.

### Economic Goals

Every society tries to attain certain economic objectives. Four goals that are fundamental to all economic systems are efficiency, equity, stability, and growth.

**Efficiency.** Because of the problem of scarcity, it is very important that limited resources be used as efficiently as possible. This means that all workers who want to work should be able to get jobs, and other productive resources should be fully used. This is not always the case. Sometimes business activity slows down, and factories and workers become idle. During such times, the government may make decisions in an attempt to stimulate the economy and get it running more efficiently again.

Full utilization of productive resources is only one part of efficiency. In addition to producing the largest possible output with available resources, an economy should also be producing combinations of goods and services that best meet the preferences of the people.

**Equity.** Equity refers to economic fairness or justice, and it involves the distribution of a society's total production of goods and services among its citizens. The question of who gets how much is determined primarily by the distribution of income among the members of

---

## WONDER QUESTION

### What is the amazing "invisible hand"?

Consider life in a major city with millions of inhabitants who require huge amounts of various goods and services to meet their wants and needs. Do people lie awake at night worrying that the goods and services they need might be unavailable when they need or want them? In market economies such as the United States and Canada, people take it for granted that the things they need or want will be available. But if you think about it, the fact that most things are usually available when people want them is a remarkable accomplishment.

Suppose you decide that you want to have fish and sliced tomatoes for dinner. You can be almost certain you will find them at the nearest supermarket. The fish may have come from a faraway ocean or lake, and the tomatoes from a distant farm—and all shipped to your local supermarket at just the right time for eating. None of the many people involved in producing and marketing these products knew you were going to want them on a particular day, yet they were there at the very time you needed them.

As amazing as it may seem, there is no government agency, business, or individual responsible for ensuring that the economic needs and wants of people are met. It is the American economic system—its market economy—that sees to it that products of the right type and in the right quantity are available when most people want them. Some economists say that the economy works like an "invisible hand" in meeting the needs of the people.

The principle of the invisible hand was first reported by the economist Adam Smith in 1776 in his book *Inquiry Into the Nature and Causes of the Wealth of Nations*. Smith said that in a market economy, if individuals were allowed to pursue their own self-interests without government interference, they would be led, as if by an invisible hand, to achieve what is best for the society. The idea of letting economic problems work themselves out with no government interference is known as *laissez-faire*, a French term meaning "let do" or "let things alone." Although the U.S. economy today is very different from the type of economy described by Adam Smith, the principle of the invisible hand still applies to some extent.

The actions of most people are aimed at getting the greatest amount of satisfaction for the least amount of cost. Businesses work to maximize their profits, workers seek higher wages, and consumers attempt to get the maximum value for their money. To maximize their profits, businesses must provide the goods and services that most consumers want at the right time and in the right places. In this way, the American economy operates as if it were regulated by an "invisible hand."

society. Those with the most income get the most goods and services.

Most societies try to achieve an equitable distribution of income. It is important to understand, however, that equitable means "fair" or "just," not "equal." What seems fair and just to some people may seem unfair and unjust to others. The terms "fair" and "just" involve value judgments, and there is no scientific way of determining what is a fair or just distribution of income.

**Stability.** A goal of every society is to achieve price stability for its goods and services. This does not mean that all prices should be fixed. It means that the average level of prices should be stable. When average prices rise substantially, an economy experiences what is known as **inflation**. Inflation can be very harmful to a society. If average prices fall substantially, it is known as **deflation**, which can also be harmful to an economy.

**Growth.** Another goal of every society is economic growth—an increase in the quantity of goods and services produced per person. If economic production does not grow when the population is growing, the standard of living will decline. If production grows at the same rate as the population growth, the standard of living will remain constant. If production grows more rapidly than the population growth, the standard of living will rise.

▶ **ECONOMIC PROBLEMS**

All nations face many economic problems, including the inability to satisfy all wants, unemployment, inflation, recession or depression, budget deficits and a national debt.

### Inability to Satisfy All Wants

Because all nations have limited resources and unlimited wants, they all face the problem of scarcity. There is no way to eliminate this problem, but certain things can be done to increase the production obtained from a given amount of resources. One way to increase production, and thus narrow the gap between limited resources and unlimited wants, is to increase **productivity**—to produce more goods and services with less material and in a shorter time. Increased productivity results in increased output per person.

One way to achieve greater productivity is through specialization. Both individuals and nations can become more productive by spe-

The "robots" in this garment factory in the United States are programmed to sew pieces of fabric into articles of clothing.

cializing in the production of the things they can produce most efficiently.

Another way to increase productivity and economic output is through the use of new technology. New machines and new techniques have played a very important role in increasing economic productivity throughout history. They continue to do so today.

### Unemployment and Inflation

Unemployment and inflation are both very serious problems for a nation. Unemployment, of course, means that people who could be productive are out of work and are not contributing to the health of the economy.

Inflation causes a decline in the purchasing power of money, which means that consumers can purchase less with the money they have. The most commonly used measure of the inflation rate is the **consumer price index**. This measure, sometimes referred to as the "cost-of-living index," is used to determine the average increase in the prices of goods and services commonly purchased by consumers. Unemployment and inflation are interrelated in such a way that efforts to reduce one usually make the other worse.

### Recession or Depression

A period of reduced economic activity and increased unemployment is called a recession.

Adam Smith

John Maynard Keynes

**Adam Smith** (1723–90) is generally considered to be the founder of economics. Born in Scotland, Smith became a professor of logic and moral philosophy at the University of Glasgow at age 28. His studies led him to the conclusion that people always act in their own best interest. He argued that if individuals were allowed to pursue their interests free from government interference, they would promote what was best for society as a whole.

Smith revolutionized economics with the publication of *Inquiry Into the Nature and Causes of the Wealth of Nations* (1776). Because of the ideas in this book, Smith is given credit for promoting the economic freedom, the industrialization, and the prosperity that characterized the Western world during the 1800's.

**John Maynard Keynes** (1883–1946), a British economist, revolutionized economic thinking in the 1900's. With the publication of *The General Theory of Employment, Interest and Money* (1936), Keynes became one of the most influential economists of all time. In this book, he set forth a theory that became known as Keynesian economics.

Keynes argued that insufficient spending in an economy can cause continued high unemployment. He thus argued that government should use its powers to tax and spend to influence the nation's level of spending. By the 1950's, Keynesian economics had become the dominant economic theory in the Western world. By the 1960's, Keynes's ideas had become the basis for economic policy in the United States and in most other Western nations.

**Paul Samuelson** (1915– ), the first American to receive the Nobel prize for economics (1970), is one of the world's best-known economists. During his career, which includes a professorship at the Massachusetts Institute of Technology, Samuelson has produced an extraordinary range of scientific economic work. His first book, *Foundations of Economic Analysis* (1947), helped break new ground by making economics a more precise and scientific discipline.

Samuelson has been a leading supporter of Keynesian economics and a leading critic of the economic theory of monetarism—the idea that control of the

Economists define recession as a period when the gross national product (GNP)—the total market value of all goods and services produced during a year—is declining and unemployment is rising. If the gross national product, or GNP, falls to a very low level and remains there for a prolonged period while large numbers of people are unemployed, the situation is called a depression. Depressions are times of severe economic crisis for every nation.

## Budget Deficits and the National Debt

Most countries prepare an annual national budget—a plan outlining income and spending for the nation. Any time a government

During a severe recession or depression when large numbers of people are out of work, the lines at unemployment insurance offices get very long. These are times when such people need help in supplying basic needs such as food and shelter for their families.

Paul Samuelson

Milton Friedman

John Kenneth Galbraith

money supply is the primary determining factor of a nation's economic performance. He believes the government should use its power to tax and spend in order to influence spending and control unemployment and inflation.

**Milton Friedman** (1912– ), a recipient of the Nobel prize for economics (1976), is a well-known contemporary economist. A critic of Keynesian economics, he is a leading spokesman for monetarism. Friedman opposes the use of monetary policy (changes in credit availability and interest rates) and fiscal policy (changes in government taxing and spending) to influence spending. Instead, he favors a policy designed to increase the money supply by a given amount each year.

Friedman is also known for his opposition to government intervention in the economy. He feels that many government programs designed to help the disadvantaged or to protect consumers do more harm than good. His consistent support for free markets is reflected in the titles of his books, *Capitalism and Freedom* (1962) and *Free to Choose* (1980).

**John Kenneth Galbraith** (1908– ), an American economist, is best known for his skillfully written books on economic topics, including *American Capitalism* (1952), *Economic Development in Perspective* (1962), *The Affluent Society* (1958), and *The New Industrial State* (1967). His books have sparked widespread interest in economic issues.

Born in Canada, Galbraith became a United States citizen in 1937. He was a professor of economics at Harvard University from 1949 to 1975. In addition to his career in economics, Galbraith served as U.S. ambassador to India from 1961 to 1969.

---

spends more than its total revenue, or income, it has a budget deficit. One of the most serious problems facing the United States in recent years has been its large budget deficit. Throughout the 1980's and into the early 1990's, the United States government had annual deficits averaging approximately $200 billion.

When a government borrows money to finance a deficit, it causes an increase in the national debt. In early 1981, the national debt of the United States reached $1 trillion. It had taken the nation more than two hundred years to accumulate this first $1 trillion of debt. By 1986 the national debt had doubled to $2 trillion. And by the end of the 1980's the national debt was more than $3 trillion. The rapid rise in the national debt and the huge budget deficits of recent years are considered very serious problems by many economists.

### ▶ CAREERS IN ECONOMICS

Economists are employed in many different job settings. About half of all economists work in government agencies at the federal, state, and local levels. They collect and analyze information about economic conditions and about possible changes in government economic policies. They and other economists often utilize **econometrics**—the application of mathematical analysis to the development of economic theory. This analysis can show relationships between different forms of economic activity and help predict the results of different economic policies.

Many other economists work for private businesses, such as insurance companies, banks, investment companies, manufacturing firms, economic research firms, and management consulting firms. Also, many economists teach and often do research at colleges and universities.

The amount of training required to become an economist depends on the type of job. A college or university bachelor's degree with a major in economics is adequate for many entry-level jobs. Most jobs for economists, however, require advanced training, with either a master's degree or a doctorate in economics.

ALLEN SMITH
Author, *Understanding Economics*

# BIOLOGICAL CLOCK

As the sun rises on a warm, sunny day, the trumpet-shaped flowers of the morning glory unfold. It is in the afternoon, as the morning glories close, that the buds of moss roses uncurl. When darkness comes, moss roses curl shut. Only then do evening primrose flowers open, pale and ghostly in the night. In the morning, before daylight, they close again.

The opening and closing of the flowers is one of the natural cycles, called **biological rhythms**, that occur in living things. The biological rhythms of the morning glories, moss roses, and evening primroses occur within a single day. Such rhythms are called *circadian rhythms*, from the Latin words *circa* and *diem*, meaning "about a day." But not all biological rhythms are based on a day. Some, such as the beating of the heart, occur every few seconds. Other rhythms are repeated each month, and still others are repeated each year.

Scientists use the term **biological clock** to describe the internal timing mechanism that controls biological rhythms. Where is this biological clock and what is it? In animals, the brain is thought to play a role; however, plants, fungi, and microscopic organisms lack brains and still exhibit biological rhythms. There is increasing evidence that chemicals produced by living things trigger the cycles. These chemicals, in turn, are controlled by factors outside the living organism, including the light-dark cycle of a day and the changing seasons of a year. Yet, even if an organism is shut off from all clues in the environment, it will still display biological rhythms.

▶ **BIOLOGICAL CLOCKS IN NATURE**

The biological rhythms of seashore organisms are often linked to the rise and fall of the ocean's tides. Clams, mussels, and barnacles feed by filtering food from the water. When the tide is in, their shells open and they feed. As the tides go out, the shells close and the animals are protected from the drying air.

The migration of animals is an event that is triggered by a signal from an animal's biological clock. One of the most dramatic examples of a migration is the journey some birds make in spring and autumn. These migrations are associated with changes in day length. As days grow longer, birds leave their winter feeding grounds in the south. By the time they reach their northern destination, the plants they depend on for food are flourishing there. When the birds reach their summer feeding grounds, another biological rhythm is triggered: They are ready to mate and raise young. As autumn approaches, days shorten, temperatures drop, and plants begin to die. Birds' biological clocks signal the return to the south where there is food and warmth.

Like flowers, birds, and other animals, humans have biological clocks that control their biological rhythms. Humans have daily, weekly, monthly, and seasonal biological rhythms. Body temperature, blood pressure,

The jimsonweed, which blooms at night, is a desert flower with a biological rhythm opposite that of most flowers. *Far left:* Throughout the hours of daylight, the flower of the jimsonweed remains tightly closed. *Left:* After the sun has set, the funnel-shaped flower slowly opens.

sleeping and waking, and the levels of many chemicals in the body have a 24-hour rhythm. Many illnesses appear to have a yearly rhythm. Colds, flu, and pneumonia are most common in autumn and winter. Outbreaks of childhood diseases such as measles most often occur in spring and summer.

### ▶ CHANGES IN BIOLOGICAL CLOCKS

More is known about circadian rhythms in humans than about any other kind of biological rhythm. When people travel by plane across several time zones, their internal clocks are no longer in tune with where they are. This is called jet lag. The effects of jet lag are worse when people travel to a place with a later time (that is, west to east) than it is when they travel to a place with an earlier time (east to west). People with jet lag feel cranky and tired. Their hand-eye coordination is not as good as usual and they may be forgetful. It takes several days for the body's biological clock to reset to the new time zone.

People who work night shifts also experience problems with their biological clocks. They are generally not as productive or alert as people who work during the day, and they have more accidents on the job. They also have more health and sleep problems than

At a signal from their biological clocks, monarch butterflies gather in huge swarms to make a yearly migration that covers thousands of miles.

people who work day shifts. Scientists studying this problem found a possible solution by conducting a test study. At night, people worked under very bright lights. When they went home to sleep, they slept in totally darkened bedrooms. After three days, the workers' biological clocks had been reset. Their temperature cycles were the same as day workers: highest when they were at work, and lowest when they were sleeping.

### ▶ ADVANCES AND DISCOVERIES

Exciting breakthroughs are being made with new medical treatments. Certain medical problems are associated with different times of the day. Heart attacks, strokes, and sudden death happen most often during the waking hours before noon. Asthma and ulcer attacks occur most often between midnight and 8 A.M. This information can be used in treatment. Heart medication taken right after waking may help protect a person with heart disease. Medication for asthma and ulcers is available in time-release tablets. When these tablets are taken at night, an individual is helped most during the high-risk time.

Biological clocks control the biological rhythms that make the world a familiar place. As scientists learn more about these rhythms, especially those in humans, new solutions can be found to make travel more comfortable, working conditions safer, and medical treatment more effective.

KARIN L. RHINES
Co-author, *Discover Science*

Workers who switch between day and night shifts, such as these firefighters, experience problems with their biological clocks similar to the effects of jet lag.

Beetles vary greatly, not only in appearance but also in lifestyle. While the dung beetle (*left*) busily forms a dung ball to use as a nest for its eggs, the locust borer beetle (*above*) lays its eggs on plentiful goldenrod.

# BEETLES

Wherever you look, on the ground, in the air, or in lakes and ponds, they can be found. They go busily about their daily tasks—whether it is nibbling on plant leaves, chewing wood from rotting logs, or cleaning the bones of dead animals. They are beetles, the most common of all the insects. In North America alone, there are more than 30,000 different kinds, or species, of beetles. Throughout the world, about 300,000 species of beetles can be found; and every year, new species are being discovered.

Beetles make up the insect order, or group, called Coleoptera. It is the largest order of the animal kingdom. The name Coleoptera, which means "sheath wing" in Greek, refers to the beetle's pair of hard, inflexible outer wings. The wings, called **elytra**, lock together down the beetle's back to provide a protective shell for the beetle.

Sometimes called the armored tank of the insect world, the beetle owes much of its ability to survive to the leathery elytra. With this tough outer shell, the beetle can live under stones and in other sheltered areas that insects with soft bodies cannot use, because they would be crushed. The beetle's shell also makes it resistant to dryness. This allows the beetle to live in places that are drier than the habitats of many other insects.

## ▶ THE CHARACTERISTICS OF BEETLES

There is a great variety in the appearance of beetles. Some beetles are dark brown so that they blend in with the soil. Other beetles have bright colors or complex patterns on their elytra. Still others are iridescent, changing color in the sunlight. Although beetles vary greatly in size, shape, and color, they all share the same body plan. Like that of other insects, the beetle's body is divided into three main parts: the head, the thorax, and the abdomen.

**Body Parts.** The **head**, at the front of the body, holds the main sense organs (eyes and antennae), chewing mouthparts, and a primitive brain. Projecting from the head, the beetle's two antennae are covered with tiny hairs. The hairs are special sense organs that help the beetle detect sounds and odors. A pair of compound eyes, one on each side of the head, gives the beetle a well-developed sense of sight.

The chewing mouthparts of most beetles are designed to crush or break food into small pieces before the food actually enters the

## The External Body Structures of a Beetle

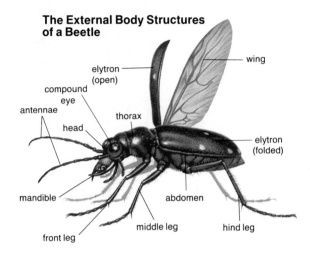

Labels: wing, elytron (open), compound eye, antennae, head, thorax, elytron (folded), mandible, abdomen, front leg, middle leg, hind leg

mouth. Plant-eating beetles have mouthparts that allow them to slice leaves, cut stems, bore under bark, or crush seeds. Beetles that eat other insects or animals have mouthparts that allow them to pierce, stab, or crush their prey. Some of these beetles can cause painful bites to an inexperienced insect collector.

The **thorax** forms the middle part of the body and holds the beetle's three pairs of legs as well as the elytra and a pair of hind wings. Different kinds of beetles have different kinds of legs. Many predatory beetles have long, slender legs that enable them to pursue their prey swiftly. Beetles that dig through the soil have legs that are flattened with toothed edges,

allowing the beetles to sweep large amounts of soil behind them.

The **abdomen** houses the organs that help the beetle digest food, get rid of waste, and produce offspring. The beetle does not have special organs, like our lungs, to help it breathe. Instead, holes called **spiracles** pierce the abdomen. Air enters the beetle's body through the spiracles and passes through tubes into open spaces in the abdomen and the rest of the body.

**Locomotion.** If the beetle needs to fly, it unlocks the elytra and the hind wings unfold. Only the hind wings are used for flight. When the beetle is not flying, the elytra cover and protect the thin, delicate hind wings.

Some beetles spend most of their life in water. An aquatic beetle has flattened legs that are used for paddles as it pushes through the water. A built-in air tank helps the beetle swim and dive underwater. The space between the elytra and the soft body underneath fills up with air. While the beetle is under water, it breathes using the stored air.

**Behavior.** Most beetles, unlike many types of bees, ants, wasps, and termites, are solitary insects. They live alone rather than in large nests or hives. Different types of beetles have

Two behaviors that are important to a beetle's survival are its ability to defend itself and its ability to reproduce. The bombardier beetle (*below*) effectively repels its enemies with a hot pulsing jet of chemicals. The mating blister beetle (*right*) provides for its offspring by laying its eggs near a larval food source.

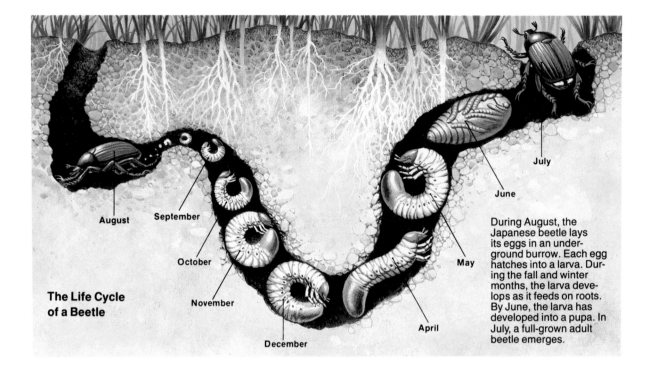

**The Life Cycle of a Beetle**

August
September
October
November
December
April
May
June
July

During August, the Japanese beetle lays its eggs in an underground burrow. Each egg hatches into a larva. During the fall and winter months, the larva develops as it feeds on roots. By June, the larva has developed into a pupa. In July, a full-grown adult beetle emerges.

different types of behavior that allow them to adapt to their environment, feed, defend themselves from predators, and breed.

People have been interested in some of the more unusual beetles for hundreds, even thousands, of years. In ancient Egypt, people were fascinated by the scarab, or dung beetle. This insect makes a ball of dung to lay its eggs in. Often the ball is as large or larger than the scarab itself. Some beetles make dung balls as big as softballs.

The Egyptians considered the ball of dung and the life of the scarab to be symbols for the world and the cycles of nature. So important was the scarab that it was used as a seal on many important Egyptian documents.

Another beetle with unusual behavior is the tortoise beetle. As it grows, it is protected by a collection of its own waste and shed skins. Stuck to its body, this material helps camouflage, or hide, the young beetle from predators. It also serves as a defense, because the foul odor of the pile of wastes discourages other insects and animals from coming close for an attack. Nicknamed the trash peddler, the young tortoise beetle develops into a brilliant, shiny metallic adult.

The bombardier beetle has an even more dramatic defense against predators. When an attacking animal approaches, the bombardier beetle raises its rear end into the air and shoots out a hot spray of burning liquid at the attacker. The spray is released with an explosion that is quite loud. The combination of the surprising sound and harmful spray wards off most animals that would prey on this beetle.

▶ **THE LIFE CYCLE OF THE BEETLE**

Beetles, like many other insects, have a life cycle during which they pass through several different stages before becoming an adult. This process of growth and change is called **metamorphosis**.

**The Egg.** Most beetles begin the first stage of life as an egg. Beetle eggs are generally oval in shape with a tough but flexible outer shell. Inside the egg, the growing beetle feeds on the large yolk. The first stage ends when the developing beetle cuts its way through the shell, hatching into a beetle larva.

**The Larva.** The larval stage is the only one in which the beetle grows in size. Because beetles lay eggs on or in a food source, a newly emerged larva does not have to hunt for food. The larva, also called a grub, spends most of its time eating. When the larva grows too large for the hard shell (called an exoskeleton) that covers its body, the shell splits. The soft grub that emerges will quickly grow a new, larger exoskeleton. The new covering

# Some Common Beetle Families

**Firefly**
**Family:** Lampyridae
**Common name:** lightning bug or firefly
  The name *Lampyridae* means "shining fire" in Latin. In some species, the eggs, larvae, pupae (plural of pupa), and adult fireflies all emit a glowing light.

**Two-spotted Ladybug**
**Family:** Coccinellidae
**Common name:** ladybird beetle or ladybug
  The name *ladybug* originated in the Middle Ages. Named the beetle of Our Lady, this insect was dedicated to the Virgin Mary.

**Colorado Potato Beetle**
**Family:** Chrysomelidae
**Common name:** leaf beetle
  There are more than 25,000 species of leaf beetles in the world. Both the larvae (plural of larva) and the adult leaf beetles feed on leaves. This makes many leaf beetles serious crop pests.

**Dung Beetle**
**Family:** Scarabaeidae
**Common name:** scarab
  The scarab beetles are one of the largest families of beetles, with almost 1,300 North American species and 20,000 species in the world.

**Striped Blister Beetle**
**Family:** Meloidae
**Common name:** blister beetle
  When a predator attacks a blister beetle, the beetle discharges a drop of blood containing an oily chemical. This chemical causes severe blistering of the skin.

**Fiery Searcher Ground Beetle**
**Family:** Carabidae
**Common name:** ground beetle
  Almost all ground beetles are nocturnal, so they hide during the day and search for food at night. They are very aggressive predators, even climbing trees to get their prey.

**Boll Weevil**
**Family:** Curculionidae
**Common name:** snout beetle or weevil
  With 40,000 species of snout beetles, this is the largest family of beetles in the world. These beetles get their name because they have a long snout, with their mouthparts attached at the farthest end.

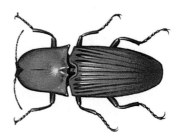

**Click Beetle**
**Family:** Elateridae
**Common name:** click beetle or snapping beetle
  When attacked, the click beetle falls backward and plays dead. To right itself, the beetle bends at the thorax and hooks a long spine into an abdominal groove. It unhooks the spine with a click, throwing itself in the air and flipping end over end.

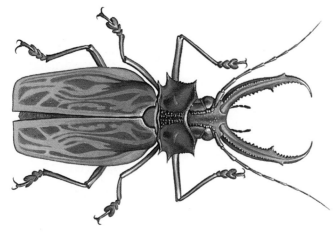

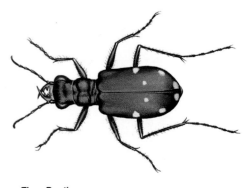

**Tiger Beetle**
**Family:** Cicindelidae
**Common name:** tiger beetle
  Tiger beetle larvae wait for prey at the entrance of their vertical burrows. They attach themselves to the burrow wall with a hooklike spine on the abdomen that prevents them from being pulled out of the burrow when capturing large prey.

**Giant Longhorn Beetle**
**Family:** Cerambycidae
**Common name:** long-horned or wood-boring beetle
  Larvae of this family are wood borers. They are easy to capture because they can be picked out of the wood with hooked sticks. Partly for this reason, the larvae are used as food in many parts of the world.

will also be shed as the larva continues to eat and grow. This process of growing and shedding the outer layer is called **molting**. A larva may molt three to seven times before it enters the next stage.

**The Pupa.** As it enters the pupal stage, the beetle buries itself underground or in a tree trunk or a plant so that it will not be attacked by predators. It usually forms a hard casing around itself for protection. Then it stops all movement for several days or weeks. On the outside it looks as if nothing is happening. But inside its case, the insect is transforming itself. The pupa forms legs, wings, and elytra. Its digestive system changes, and its reproductive

system develops. When its development is complete, an adult beetle emerges and crawls or flies away.

**The Adult.** Although long-lived compared with most other insects, adult beetles live for less than a month. During this time they must mate, and the females must find a suitable place to lay their eggs. These ends accomplished, the adult beetle dies.

▶ **BEETLES AND THEIR ENVIRONMENT**

Many plant-eating beetles are considered serious pests because they feed on farm crops, trees, bushes, and other plants. One of the most destructive of these beetles is the boll weevil. Until 1843 the boll weevil lived only in Mexico, where it fed on a wild relative of the cotton plant. By 1892 the boll weevil had reached the southern tip of Texas, where there were vast fields of domesticated cotton. The boll weevil was able to spread quickly through the acres and acres of cropland, spreading northward into the southern United States at a rate of about 60 miles per year. Nothing the farmers could do prevented the expansion of this beetle's range.

One reason the boll weevil was able to spread so quickly is that a female boll weevil can lay as many as 300 eggs in her lifetime. The entire life cycle of the boll weevil takes only two or three weeks. Therefore, several generations of boll weevils can hatch in one summer, quickly increasing the population. Today, cotton farmers use a variety of methods to control the spread of the boll weevil, from insecticides and fertilizers to the introduction of sterile boll weevils that prevent the beetle from breeding successfully. But the boll weevil is a very adaptable insect. No method has enabled farmers to get rid of the boll weevil completely.

Other beetles are considered important in controlling insect pests on farm crops and in gardens. Ladybugs, or ladybird beetles, attack and eat aphids, scale insects, mites, and other pests. They have been used commercially since 1888 to control these insects in greenhouses and orchards. Many gardeners use ladybugs today to try to get rid of unwanted insects without using pesticides.

As a larva and an adult, the plant-eating Mexican bean beetle (*below*) is considered a pest. Carrion beetles (*bottom*) provide a beneficial service by feeding on animal wastes and dead animals.

GAIL M. TERZI
Forest Biologist
Contributor, *Insect Biochemistry* journal

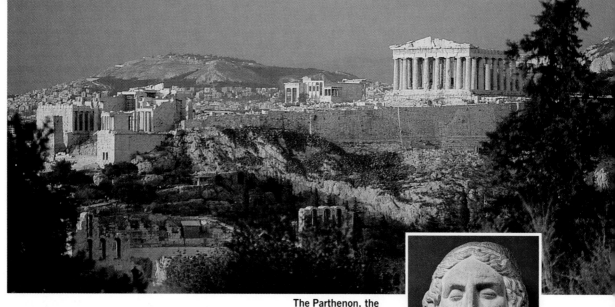

# GREECE, ANCIENT

The civilization of ancient Greece centered in the islands of the Aegean Sea and the lands bordering both sides of the Aegean, a region that includes most of present-day Greece and the western coast of Turkey. The people who inhabited these areas never numbered more than 1½ to 2 million, yet they produced a culture that is generally considered to be the foundation of Western civilization. The accomplishments of the Greeks (or Hellenes, as they called themselves) in architecture, sculpture, literature, philosophy, science, and politics were often imitated by later cultures, and they continue to dazzle us today. Few peoples have made such lasting contributions to human thought and art.

**The Land and People: An Overview.** The land that gave rise to Greek civilization is a rugged one, with few natural resources. It is largely mountainous, and only about one fifth of the land supports farming or the pasturing of livestock. The climate of the coastal areas, where most of the people live, is warm, sunny, and dry for most of the year. Winter rains make cultivation of the soil possible.

Most places in Greece are close to the sea, and the irregular coastline provides many fine harbors. The sea, traditionally, has played an important role in the lives of Greeks. The ancient Greeks were skilled sailors; they were equally at home on ships of war or on merchant vessels trading goods across the Mediterranean Sea.

The Parthenon, the most famous symbol of ancient Greece, overlooks Athens. Little is known about the blind poet Homer (*right*), long associated with the Greek epics the *Iliad* and the *Odyssey*.

Aside from malaria, which was a serious disease for the very young or the very old, the ancient Greeks were a healthy people. The basic food crops, including olives, cereal grains, and fruits and vegetables, provided a simple but nutritious diet. (Olive oil was also used as fuel for lamps.) Goats were a source of milk, and sheep yielded wool and, occasionally, meat. The surrounding waters teemed with fish.

In general, the Greeks of ancient times, even in their cities, lived close to the land and to nature. This may help explain the richness of their art and architecture, which depended so much on the use of natural materials and an appreciation of color and light.

**Early Greece: The Mycenaeans.** The definition of a "Greek," according to the Greeks themselves, was a person whose native language was Greek. Archaeologists and language scholars believe that sometime after about 1900 B.C. there was a movement of peoples speaking an Indo-European language into the Greek peninsula. Their interaction with the peoples already living there produced the Greek language.

the Minoans. The Minoans (named after their legendary king, Minos) were a non-Greek people who had created a wealthy and advanced civilization. The Minoans eventually came into conflict with the more warlike Mycenaeans. The Mycenaeans conquered Crete but, in doing so, adopted many aspects of Minoan art, architecture, and writing into Mycenaean culture.

**A Dark Age.** The Mycenaean civilization collapsed in a violent upheaval in about 1050 B.C. At one time it was thought that the Mycenaeans had been overrun by a new group of Greek-speaking invaders, the Dorians. However, most archaeologists and historians believe that the Mycenaean kingdoms fell victim to internal rebellion and disorder. Whatever happened, by about 1000 B.C., Greece had been plunged into a Dark Age, which lasted for more than two centuries.

**The Polis, or City-State.** By about 750 B.C., a new type of Greek community, the *polis*, or city-state, was beginning to take shape. The city-state consisted of a town surrounded by the territory needed to support it. The town and its lands formed an independent state. There were perhaps as many as a thousand different city-states. Most had only a few thousand inhabitants.

Greek city-states were also established as colonies of older cities. They were founded along the coastal areas of the Black Sea, southern Italy, the island of Sicily, and what are today France and Spain. These colonies were, like their mother-cities, independent states. They were settled for agricultural and commercial reasons and as a relief from overpopulation at home.

The colonies also spread Greek culture throughout the Mediterranean world. The Greeks believed themselves superior to non-Greek-speaking peoples. A non-Greek man, for example, was called a *barbaros*, because to a Greek his language sounded like *bar-bar*, or nonsense. This is the origin of the English word "barbarian," meaning "uncivilized."

The Lion Gate at Mycenae and gold burial mask date from the Mycenaean Greek period, which reached its height about 1250 B.C.

These early Greeks eventually founded a number of small kingdoms, which were independent of each other, while sharing a common culture. This culture is called Mycenaean, named after one of the leading kingdoms of the time, Mycenae. A typical Mycenaean settlement consisted of a large fortified palace and administrative center, surrounded by villages and farmland. During times of war and disorder, the palace was a place of refuge for the local people, most of whom were farmers.

The king's scribes kept records of taxes paid, written on clay tablets. From the surviving tablets we know that the language of the Mycenaeans was an early form of Greek.

The power of the Mycenaean kings grew, and by about 1250 B.C., they were involved in military expeditions overseas. The famous Trojan War may have been just such an expedition, an attempt by the Mycenaeans to conquer the Asian coastal city of Troy.

**The Minoans.** To the south of Mycenaean Greece lay the large island of Crete, home of

One of the virtues of the polis system was also one of its failings. The Greeks' fierce love of independence made it impossible for the city-states to unite. They were highly competitive and often at war with one another. This lack of unity also made the Greek cities vulnerable to foreign invasion.

**Life in the Polis: Athens.** With a total population of about 250,000, Athens was one of the largest of the city-states. The city itself was surrounded by heavily fortified walls. Outside the walls lay the countryside, with its olive orchards, farmland, and grazing areas. More than three quarters of all Athenians lived in such rural areas. Those who lived close enough would visit the city often, to buy and sell goods, take part in major religious festivals, and participate in politics.

Inside the walls, whose gates were locked at night, Athens was a town of winding streets and low one-story buildings. Private homes were modest, since the home was not the central part of an Athenian citizen's life. Socially, Athenian men (only men could be citizens) preferred the company of other men. Wives, who had no public life, raised the children and managed the household affairs.

Dominating the center of Athens was the Acropolis ("high city"), a fortified rocky hill on which the city's major temples were built. Just below was the *agora*, the public marketplace, which also served as a political arena. The *agora* hummed with activity, as both farmers and townspeople mixed to argue over the price of goods or to debate politics.

**Slavery.** Slavery was a feature of life in most Greek cities and was considered a part of the natural order of things. Most slaves had been captured in war. Domestic slaves assisted in household tasks. Those with special skills worked as metalsmiths, pottery makers, or in other crafts. Domestic slaves were relatively well-treated, and some managed to save enough money to buy their freedom. This was not the case for those who worked in the silver mines of Athens or at similar labors. Their lives were harsh and short.

**Forms of Government.** The ancient Greeks had various forms of government, whose names are often familiar to us today. Some city-states were oligarchies—that is, governed by a relatively few wealthy and powerful individuals. Some were ruled by tyrants, who had seized power by force. And some were governed by large groups of citizens. The Greek word for people is *demos*. Thus, a city-state that was governed by the people was called a democracy.

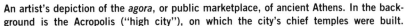

An artist's depiction of the *agora*, or public marketplace, of ancient Athens. In the background is the Acropolis ("high city"), on which the city's chief temples were built.

The religion of the ancient Greeks included the worship of numerous gods and goddesses, among them Poseidon, the god of the seas.

Athens was the most famous of the democratic city-states. No more than 30,000 to 40,000 of its inhabitants, however, were entitled to full rights as citizens, including the right to vote and hold office. Athenian women, children, slaves, and resident foreigners had no political rights.

When an Athenian boy reached the age of 18, he received military training and eventually assumed the rights of citizenship. He became a member of an assembly, made up of all Athenian citizens. The assembly elected officials, passed laws, set taxes, and supervised foreign policy, including matters of peace and war.

**Sparta: City of Soldiers.** The Greeks of the city-state of Sparta developed an altogether different way of life. Always suspicious of outsiders and constantly fearful of invasion, the Spartans had one single goal—the creation of the finest type of soldier. Only native Spartans could qualify for citizenship. Spartan boys spent only their first six years at home, after which they were enrolled in military training schools. They received training until they were in their 20's and served on active military duty until they were 30. Only then were they permitted to marry, establish homes, and raise families.

Spartan girls were given extensive physical training, so that they could produce strong, healthy babies who would one day take their fathers' places in the army. The result was a superb Spartan army that was widely admired (and often feared) throughout ancient Greece.

**Religion.** The ancient Greeks believed in numerous gods and goddesses who controlled the world. The gods resembled the Greeks themselves, even including some of their faults. But they were more powerful as well as immortal (able to live forever). These beliefs most likely originated with the first Greek-speaking peoples, who also adopted some of

At the battle of Plataea in 479 B.C., a combined force of Athenian and Spartan infantry (on the left) crushed a Persian army that had invaded European Greece. The victory ended the Persian Wars and allowed the Greek city-states the freedom to seek their own destinies.

366

the religious ideas of the earlier, non-Greek inhabitants. Although the Greeks were very religious, religion never interfered with their need to experiment, explore, and think freely for themselves.

**The Persian Wars.** The city-states faced a serious threat to their freedom in the early 400's B.C. from the huge Persian Empire. The Greek cities in Asia Minor (modern Turkey) had earlier fallen to the Persians, who then turned to the cities of European Greece. In 490 B.C. an army sent by the Persian king Darius attacked Athens. The Persians were met at Marathon by the outnumbered Athenian citizen-soldiers, who won a stunning victory.

Ten years later, in 480 B.C., King Xerxes led an enormous Persian army in a full-scale invasion of Greece. In the face of this danger, most of the city-states abandoned their traditional independence to form an alliance. At the pass of Thermopylae, the Spartan king Leonidas sacrificed himself and three hundred fellow Spartans to delay the Persian march on Athens and permit the other Greeks to complete their military preparations. That same year, in a great battle off the island of Salamis, near Athens, the Athenian navy defeated a larger Persian fleet. In 479 B.C. a combined force of Athenians and Spartans crushed the Persian army at Plataea. The Persians retreated from Europe, leaving the city-states free to seek their own destinies.

**The Golden Age.** The years from about 500 to 323 B.C. are considered the Golden Age (or Classical Age) of Greek civilization. One of the Greeks' greatest achievements was the invention of philosophy, meaning "love of wisdom." The Greeks were the first people to attempt to explain the origin and composition of the universe in scientific terms. They believed that, since there were laws regulating the physical universe, there must also be laws to govern human relations. Great schools of philosophy were established in Athens, led by Plato and his student Aristotle. Plato had been inspired by his own teacher, Socrates, who taught his students to ask "What is good?" "How can one live well?" and "How can I find out the answer to these questions?"

Greek philosophy continued to grow over the next few centuries. It had enormous influence on Western thought and the development of Christianity. The Greeks also advanced the study of mathematics. The rules and proofs of geometry (meaning "to measure the earth") were first compiled by Euclid in the 300's B.C.

The Greeks were especially creative in literature. Greek is a rich language, and the Greeks used it to describe how they felt about themselves and their gods. Their ability to express human emotions and to relate the facts of their history resulted in a heritage of drama and poetry among the greatest ever written. The Greeks also invented the writing of history. Herodotus has left us an account of the Persian wars, and Thucydides a retelling of the Peloponnesian War.

The Greeks built marble monuments of enduring beauty. Temples like the Parthenon (dedicated to the goddess Athena Parthenos) in Athens remind us of the grandeur of ancient Greece. Sculptors created statues of such grace and vitality that artists still study and imitate them.

**Athletics.** The ancient Greeks strove for physical as well as intellectual excellence. Several panhellenic ("all-Greek") festivals provided them with the opportunity to compete peacefully in athletics, both for their cities and for individual glory. The most famous of these was the Olympic Games, from which our modern Olympics are derived. Originating as a religious festival in honor of Zeus, the king of the gods, they were held every four years. Truces were declared in times of war, so that the athletes could travel safely.

## GREECE IN THE PELOPONNESIAN WAR

Sparta and Allies   Athens and Allies

THRACE
Byzantium
MACEDONIA
THASOS
CHALCIDICE
EPIRUS
LEMNOS
(TURKEY)
CORCYRA
THESSALY
AEGEAN SEA
Mytilene
LEUCAS
LESBOS
PERSIAN EMPIRE
AETOLIA
BOEOTIA
EUBOEA
CHIOS
CEPHALLENIA
ACHAEA
Corinth
Thebes
Notium
ZACYNTHUS
ELIS
ARGOS
Athens
SAMOS
Ephesus
PELOPONNESUS
Miletus
Pylos
Sparta
NAXOS
RHODES
MEDITERRANEAN SEA
CRETE

**The Peloponnesian War.** Athens had emerged from the Persian Wars as the most formidable naval power in Greece. Still fearful of the Persians, nearly two hundred city-states formed a defensive league under Athenian leadership. But by the 450's B.C. the Athenians had converted this voluntary league into an Athenian empire. The Spartans were suspicious of this growth of Athenian power. The unity that had developed against the Persian threat was replaced by two hostile alliances, led by Athens and Sparta.

In 431 B.C. war broke out between Athens and Sparta. It was called the Peloponnesian War because Sparta and most of its allies were located in the southern part of Greece, or Peloponnesus. The war lasted on and off until 404 B.C. For part of this period Athens was led by its great statesman Pericles. Although the Spartan army was usually supreme on land, the Athenians were protected by their navy and strong walls. The defeat of an Athenian expedition against the Greek city of Syracuse, in Sicily, in 413 B.C was a turning point in the war. Eventually, the Spartans defeated the Athenian fleet, which had protected the shipments of food into Athens from overseas colonies. With the failure of their navy, the Athenians were starved into submission.

**The Rise of Macedon.** North of the Greek cities lay the kingdom of Macedon, which had played only a minor role in Greek history. In 360 B.C., however, Philip II came to the Macedonian throne. Philip's aim was to attack the Persian Empire and seize the riches of Asia. However, he could not risk leaving an unsettled Greece behind him. When the Greeks, led by the brilliant Athenian orator (public speaker) Demosthenes, rejected Philip's offer of an alliance under Macedon, Philip went to war against them.

The matter was settled at the battle of Chaeronea in 338 B.C., during which Philip's young son Alexander distinguished himself. The Greeks were defeated and forced to accept Philip's terms. He returned to Macedon to prepare for the invasion of Asia, but was assassinated by one of his own bodyguards. The 20-year-old Alexander was hailed as king.

**Alexander the Great.** The career of Alexander III, called the Great, was one of the most extraordinary in history. Before his death at age 32, he had conquered the Persian Empire and founded his own empire, which stretched from Macedon and Greece to Egypt and across Asia to the borders of India. His conquests permitted the spread of Greek culture into western Asia, where it remained an important cultural force until the rise of the Arabs and the Islamic religion some 900 years later.

**The Hellenistic Age.** The centuries following Alexander's death are known as the Hellenistic Age. His empire, now divided into several independent kingdoms, was ruled by his former generals and their descendants. In Egypt, Ptolemy I founded a dynasty, or royal family, that lasted for three centuries. In Syria, the Seleucid kingdom, named after Seleucus I, controlled much of what we now call the Middle East. And in Macedon itself, a new dynasty, the Antigonids, replaced the family of Philip and Alexander.

Greek culture was dominant among the Macedonians and Greeks who ruled the Hellenistic kingdoms, but it did not penetrate deeply into the native traditions of these lands. Thus two cultures, Greek and native, existed side by side, but with little influence on one another.

**Rome and Later Greek Culture.** The rising power of Rome marked the end of the Hellenistic kingdoms, which fell to Roman armies in a series of wars. The last to succumb was Egypt, led by its queen Cleopatra VII, who killed herself in 30 B.C., rather than become a captive of Rome.

Roman conquest did not mean the end of Greek civilization. Many educated Romans spoke and wrote the Greek language, imitated Greek authors, admired Greek philosophy, and collected Greek art. In A.D. 330, the Roman emperor Constantine I, the Great, rebuilt the old Greek city of Byzantium, which was renamed Constantinople (that is, the city, or *polis*, of Constantine). After the collapse of the Western Roman Empire in the A.D. 400's, Constantinople remained the capital of the Eastern Roman, or Byzantine, Empire. The surviving part of the Roman Empire thus was the Greek part. Centered in Constantinople (modern Istanbul), it lasted, with a few interruptions, for another thousand years.

EUGENE N. BORZA
The Pennsylvania State University
Author, *The Classical Tradition*

# SUPPLEMENT

# DEATHS

**Arthur, Jean.** American actress; died on June 19, at the age of 90. Arthur began her career in silent movies and starred in such classics as *Mr. Smith Goes to Washington* (1939) and *Shane* (1953).

**Ashcroft, Dame Peggy.** British actress; died on June 14, at the age of 83. Dame Peggy starred in stage, film, and television. She won a 1985 Academy Award for her performance in the movie *A Passage to India*.

**Bardeen, John.** American physicist; died on January 30, at the age of 82. Bardeen was a co-inventor of the transistor, which revolutionized the electronics industry. He won the Nobel Prize in Physics twice—in 1956 for the transistor, and in 1972 for research on low-temperature superconductivity.

**Bellamy, Ralph.** American actor; died on November 29, at the age of 87. Bellamy appeared in more than 100 movies and starred in a number of television shows. He also gained fame for his roles in Broadway plays, particularly for his portrayal of Franklin D. Roosevelt in *Sunrise at Campobello* (1958).

**Capra, Frank.** Italian-born movie director; died on September 3, at the age of 94. Capra's films included such classics as *It Happened One Night* (1934), *Mr. Smith Goes to Washington* (1939), and *It's a Wonderful Life* (1946).

Frank Capra

Colleen Dewhurst

**Convy, Bert.** American actor and television game-show host; died on July 15, at the age of 57. Convy, who appeared on stage, film, and television, was best known as host of the TV game shows *Tattletales, Win, Lose or Draw,* and *Super Password.*

**Davis, Miles.** American jazz trumpeter and composer; died on September 28, at the age of 65. Davis was one of the most innovative musicians of the 20th century. He helped to establish such styles as cool jazz, hard bop, and jazz-rock.

**Dewhurst, Colleen.** Canadian-born actress; died on August 22, at the age of 67. Dewhurst performed on stage, screen, and television for over 40 years. She was best known for her portrayals of tragic heroines in the plays of Eugene O'Neill.

**Durocher, Leo.** American baseball manager and player; died on October 7, at the age of 86. Durocher played major league baseball for seventeen seasons. He later managed the Brooklyn Dodgers, New York Giants, Chicago Cubs, and Houston Astros, earning the nickname "The Lip" for his combative style.

**Fonteyn, Dame Margot.** British ballet dancer; died on February 21, at the age of 71. Dame Margot's career as a prima ballerina spanned several decades. In the 1960's and 1970's, she dazzled audiences when she danced with Soviet-born dancer Rudolf Nureyev—they were considered one of the greatest ballet partnerships in history.

**Ford, Tennessee Ernie.** American country-and-western singer and television personality; died on October 17, at the age of 72. Ford's hit songs included "Mule Train" and "The Ballad of Davy Crockett." His 1955 recording of "16 Tons" became one of the best-selling records of all time.

**Foxx, Redd.** American comedian; died on October 11, at the age of 68. Foxx was best known for his role as the feisty junk dealer on the 1970's television series *Sanford and Son.*

**Franciscus, James.** American actor; died on July 8, at the age of 57. Franciscus appeared in both films and television. He was best known for his roles in three TV series during the 1950's and 1960's—*Naked City*, *Mr. Novak*, and *Longstreet*.

**Gandhi, Rajiv.** Indian politician; assassinated on May 21, at the age of 46. Gandhi, who was prime minister from 1984 to 1989, was the son of Prime Minister Indira Gandhi and the grandson of Prime Minister Jawaharlal Nehru.

**Geisel, Theodor Seuss (Dr. Seuss).** American author and illustrator; died on September 24, at the age of 87. Geisel wrote and illustrated nearly 50 books, many of which have become children's classics. His stories were noted for their nonsense words, whimsy, and rhyme, and they featured such characters as Yertle the Turtle, the Lorax, and the Cat in the Hat.

**Getz, Stan.** American jazz saxophonist; died on June 6, at the age of 64. Getz was noted for his improvisations and for pioneering such jazz movements as the cool school of jazz of the 1950's and the bossa nova style of the 1960's.

**Gobel, George.** American comedian; died on February 24, at the age of 71. Gobel began his career at the age of 11, singing on a radio program. He had his own television show in the 1950's and later appeared regularly on the game show *The Hollywood Squares*.

**Theodor Geisel (Dr. Seuss)**

**Martha Graham**

**Goren, Charles.** American contract-bridge expert; died on April 3, at the age of 90. Goren popularized the point-count system that is used to evaluate and bid a bridge hand. He wrote extensively on the game and hosted the first successful television show about bridge.

**Graham, Martha.** American dancer and choreographer; died on April 1, at the age of 96. Graham was considered one of the greatest artists of the 20th century. She was the creator of modern dance, which was a revolutionary departure from traditional ballet.

**Grange, Harold "Red."** American football player; died on January 28, at the age of 87. Known as the "Galloping Ghost," Grange became famous as a running back for the University of Illinois in the 1920's. In 1925 he joined the Chicago Bears, where his exploits on the playing field continued.

**Greene, Graham.** British author; died on April 3, at the age of 86. Greene's best-known works included the novels *The Power and the Glory* (1940), *The Third Man* (1950), *The Quiet American* (1956), and *Our Man in Havana* (1958).

**Heinz, John, III.** U.S. Senator from Pennsylvania; died on April 4, at the age of 52. Heinz, a Republican, was a member of the House of Representatives from 1971 to 1976, and a senator since 1977. He was noted for his efforts to help workers and the elderly.

Edwin Land

**Honda, Soichiro.** Japanese automaker; died on August 5, at the age of 84. In 1948, he founded Honda Motor Company, which today is one of the world's leading car manufacturers.

**Land, Edwin.** American scientist and inventor; died on March 1, at the age of 81. Land, who received more than 500 patents during his lifetime, founded the Polaroid Corporation in 1937 to market his inventions. He conceived the idea of the instant camera, which was introduced to the public in 1947.

**Landon, Michael.** American actor; died on July 1, at the age of 54. Landon was best known for his roles in the television series *Bonanza* (1959–73), *Little House on the Prairie* (1974–82), and *Highway to Heaven* (1984–89).

**Lean, David.** British film director; died on April 16, at the age of 83. Lean's sixteen films, which won a total of 28 Academy Awards, included *Bridge on the River Kwai* (1957), *Lawrence of Arabia* (1962), and *Dr. Zhivago* (1965).

**Luke, Keye.** Chinese-born actor; died on January 12, at the age of 86. Luke's best-known roles included Number-One Son in the Charlie Chan films of the 1930's and 1940's and the martial arts instructor in the *Kung Fu* television series of the 1970's.

**MacMurray, Fred.** American actor; died on November 5, at the age of 83. MacMurray appeared in almost 80 movies, including *Double Indemnity* (1944), *The Apartment* (1960), and *The Absent-Minded Professor* (1961). He was especially known for his portrayal of the father in the popular television series *My Three Sons,* which ran from 1960 to 1972.

**Maxwell, Robert.** Czechoslovakian-born British publisher; died on November 5, at the age of 68. Maxwell headed one of the world's largest publishing empires, presiding over newspapers, book companies, and other investments.

**Montand, Yves.** Italian-born French actor and singer; died on November 9, at the age of 70. Noted for his elegance and charm, Montand appeared in more than 50 films, including *The Crucible* (1956), *Z* (1969), and *Manon of the Spring* (1986).

**Motherwell, Robert.** American artist; died on July 16, at the age of 76. Motherwell was one of the originators of the Abstract Expressionist movement and was noted for his large paintings, bold compositions, and strong colors. His best-known work was the series *Elegies to the Spanish Republic.*

**Murray, Arthur.** American dance instructor; died on March 3, at the age of 95. Murray, who founded a chain of more than 300 dance studios, used diagrams to teach people how to move their feet during a waltz, rumba, or other dance.

Michael Landon

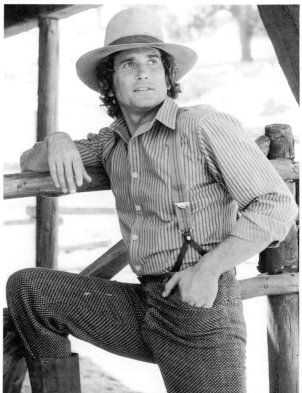

**Olav V.** King of Norway; died on January 17, at the age of 87. As Crown Prince, Olav was a symbol of resistance to Nazi Germany's occupation of Norway in World War II. He became monarch in 1957 and was fondly called *folke konge* ("The People's King") by his subjects.

**Porter, Sylvia.** American financial columnist; died on June 5, at the age of 77. Porter was noted for her ability to present complex economic information in easy-to-understand language. In addition to writing a syndicated newspaper column, she was the author of more than twenty books.

**Ray, Aldo.** American actor; died on March 27, at the age of 64. The gravel-voiced actor's best-remembered film roles were as soldiers in *Battle Cry* (1955), *The Naked and the Dead* (1958), and *Green Berets* (1968).

**Reasoner, Harry.** American television newscaster; died on August 6, at the age of 68. Reasoner was particularly noted for his work at CBS, where he was one of the original anchors of *60 Minutes*.

**Remick, Lee.** American actress; died on July 2, at the age of 55. Remick starred in many films, television miniseries, and stage plays. Her most acclaimed performances were in the films *Anatomy of a Murder* (1959) and *Days of Wine and Roses* (1962).

**Serkin, Rudolf.** Austrian-born concert pianist and teacher; died on May 8, at the age of 88. Serkin,

Lee Remick

one of the most admired pianists of his time, made his concert debut in 1915, at the age of 12. He was also a founder of the Marlboro Festival for chamber music in Vermont.

**Singer, Isaac Bashevis.** Polish-born writer; died on July 24, at the age of 87. Many of Singer's novels and short stories, which were written in Yiddish, focused on Jewish life in Eastern Europe before World War II. He was awarded the 1978 Nobel Prize in literature.

**Snelling, Richard.** Governor of Vermont; died on August 14, at the age of 64. Snelling, a Republican, served nearly nine years in office, from 1977 to 1985 and in 1991.

**Thomas, Danny.** American comedian, actor, and producer; died on February 6, at the age of 79. Thomas was best-known as the star of the television series *Make Room for Daddy* (later called *The Danny Thomas Show*), which ran from 1953 to 1964. In 1962 he founded the St. Jude Children's Research Hospital in Memphis, Tennessee.

**Tierney, Gene.** American movie actress; died on November 6, at the age of 70. Tierney's best-known films included *Laura* (1944), *Leave Her to Heaven* (1945), and *The Ghost and Mrs. Muir* (1947).

**Tower, John.** American politician; died on April 5, at the age of 65. Tower, a Republican, was a U.S. senator from Texas from 1961 to 1984. He was an influential and powerful legislator and an expert on military affairs.

**Wagner, Robert.** American politician; died on February 12, at the age of 80. Wagner was the Democratic mayor of New York City from 1954 to 1965. He later served as U.S. Ambassador to Spain and as U.S. envoy to the Vatican.

Fred MacMurray

# INDEPENDENT NATIONS OF THE WORLD

| NATION | CAPITAL | AREA (in sq mi) | POPULATION (estimate) | GOVERNMENT |
|---|---|---|---|---|
| Afghanistan | Kabul | 250,000 | 16,100,000 | Najibullah—communist party secretary and president |
| Albania | Tirana | 11,100 | 3,250,000 | Ramiz Alia—president<br>Ylli Bufi—premier |
| Algeria | Algiers | 919,595 | 25,000,000 | Chadli Benjedid—president |
| Angola | Luanda | 481,354 | 10,000,000 | José Eduardo dos Santos—president |
| Antigua and Barbuda | St. John's | 171 | 77,000 | C. Vere Bird—prime minister |
| Argentina | Buenos Aires | 1,068,297 | 32,300,000 | Carlos Saúl Menem—president |
| Australia | Canberra | 2,967,895 | 17,000,000 | Paul Keating—prime minister |
| Austria | Vienna | 32,374 | 7,700,000 | Kurt Waldheim—president<br>Franz Vranitzky—chancellor |
| Bahamas | Nassau | 5,380 | 253,000 | Lynden O. Pindling—prime minister |
| Bahrain | Manama | 240 | 503,000 | Isa ibn Salman al-Khalifa—head of state |
| Bangladesh | Dhaka | 55,598 | 115,600,000 | Shahabuddin Ahmed—president<br>Khaleda Zia—prime minister |
| Barbados | Bridgetown | 168 | 255,000 | Lloyd Erskine Sandiford—prime minister |
| Belgium | Brussels | 11,781 | 9,800,000 | Baudouin I—king<br>Wilfried Martens—premier |
| Belize | Belmopan | 8,867 | 188,000 | George Price—prime minister |
| Benin (Dahomey) | Porto-Novo | 43,484 | 4,700,000 | Nicephore Soglo—president |
| Bhutan | Thimbu | 18,147 | 1,500,000 | Jigme Singye Wangchuck—king |
| Bolivia | La Paz<br>Sucre | 424,165 | 7,400,000 | Jaime Paz Zamora—president |
| Botswana | Gaborone | 231,804 | 1,300,000 | Quett Masire—president |
| Brazil | Brasília | 3,286,478 | 150,400,000 | Fernando Collor de Mello—president |
| Brunei Darussalam | Bandar Seri Begawan | 2,226 | 266,000 | Hassanal Bolkiah—head of state |
| Bulgaria | Sofia | 42,823 | 9,000,000 | Zhelyu Zhelev—president<br>Filip Dimitrov—premier |
| Burkina Faso (Upper Volta) | Ouagadougou | 105,869 | 9,000,000 | Blaise Compaoré—president |
| Burma (Myanmar) | Rangoon | 261,218 | 41,700,000 | Saw Maung—head of government |
| Burundi | Bujumbura | 10,747 | 5,500,000 | Pierre Buyoya—president |

| NATION | CAPITAL | AREA (in sq mi) | POPULATION (estimate) | GOVERNMENT |
|---|---|---|---|---|
| Cambodia (Kampuchea) | Pnompenh | 69,898 | 8,200,000 | Heng Samrin—communist party secretary<br>Norodom Sihanouk—president |
| Cameroon | Yaoundé | 183,569 | 11,800,000 | Paul Biya—president |
| Canada | Ottawa | 3,851,809 | 27,000,000 | Martin Brian Mulroney—prime minister |
| Cape Verde | Praia | 1,557 | 370,000 | Antonio Monteiro Mascarenhas—president |
| Central African Republic | Bangui | 240,535 | 3,000,000 | André Kolingba—president |
| Chad | N'Djemena | 495,754 | 5,700,000 | Idriss Deby—president |
| Chile | Santiago | 292,257 | 13,200,000 | Patricio Aylwin—president |
| China | Beijing | 3,705,390 | 1,140,000,000 | Jiang Zemin—communist party secretary<br>Li Peng—premier |
| Colombia | Bogotá | 439,736 | 33,000,000 | César Gaviria Trujillo—president |
| Comoros | Moroni | 838 | 600,000 | Mohammed Djohar—president |
| Congo | Brazzaville | 132,047 | 2,300,000 | Denis Sassou-Nguesso—president |
| Costa Rica | San José | 19,575 | 3,000,000 | Rafael Calderón Fournier—president |
| Cuba | Havana | 44,218 | 10,600,000 | Fidel Castro—president |
| Cyprus | Nicosia | 3,572 | 702,000 | George Vassiliou—president |
| Czechoslovakia | Prague | 49,370 | 15,700,000 | Vaclav Havel—president<br>Marian Calfa—premier |
| Denmark | Copenhagen | 16,629 | 5,100,000 | Margrethe II—queen<br>Poul Schlüter—premier |
| Djibouti | Djibouti | 8,494 | 409,000 | Hassan Gouled Aptidon—president |
| Dominica | Roseau | 290 | 83,000 | Mary Eugenia Charles—prime minister |
| Dominican Republic | Santo Domingo | 18,816 | 7,200,000 | Joaquín Balaguer—president |
| Ecuador | Quito | 109,483 | 10,800,000 | Rodrigo Borja Cevallos—president |
| Egypt | Cairo | 386,660 | 53,200,000 | Mohammad Hosni Mubarak—president<br>Atef Sedky—premier |
| El Salvador | San Salvador | 8,124 | 5,300,000 | Alfredo Cristiani—president |
| Equatorial Guinea | Malabo | 10,831 | 348,000 | Obiang Nguema Mbasogo—president |
| Estonia | Tallinn | 17,458 | 1,600,000 | Arnold F. Ruutel—president |
| Ethiopia | Addis Ababa | 471,777 | 49,200,000 | Meles Zenawi—president |
| Fiji | Suva | 7,055 | 765,000 | Ratu Sir Penaia Ganilau—president |
| Finland | Helsinki | 130,120 | 5,000,000 | Mauno Koivisto—president<br>Esko Aho—premier |
| France | Paris | 211,207 | 56,400,000 | François Mitterrand—president<br>Edith Cresson—premier |
| Gabon | Libreville | 103,346 | 1,200,000 | Omar Bongo—president |
| Gambia | Banjul | 4,361 | 861,000 | Dawda K. Jawara—president |
| Germany | Berlin | 137,744 | 79,500,000 | Richard von Weizäcker—president<br>Helmut Kohl—chancellor |

| NATION | CAPITAL | AREA (in sq mi) | POPULATION (estimate) | GOVERNMENT |
|---|---|---|---|---|
| Ghana | Accra | 92,099 | 15,000,000 | Jerry Rawlings—head of government |
| Greece | Athens | 50,944 | 10,000,000 | Constantine Karamanlis—president<br>Constantine Mitsotakis—premier |
| Grenada | St. George's | 133 | 85,000 | Nicholas Brathwaite—prime minister |
| Guatemala | Guatemala City | 42,042 | 9,200,000 | Jorge Serrano Elias—president |
| Guinea | Conakry | 94,926 | 5,800,000 | Lansana Conté—president |
| Guinea-Bissau | Bissau | 13,948 | 965,000 | João Bernardo Vieira—president |
| Guyana | Georgetown | 83,000 | 796,000 | Hugh Desmond Hoyte—president |
| Haiti | Port-au-Prince | 10,714 | 6,500,000 | Joseph Nerette—president |
| Honduras | Tegucigalpa | 43,277 | 5,100,000 | Rafael Leonardo Callejas—president |
| Hungary | Budapest | 35,919 | 10,600,000 | Arpad Goncz—president<br>Jozsef Antall—premier |
| Iceland | Reykjavik | 39,768 | 255,000 | Vigdis Finnbogadottir—president<br>David Oddsson—premier |
| India | New Delhi | 1,269,340 | 827,100,000 | Ramaswamy Venkataraman—president<br>P. V. Narasimha Rao—prime minister |
| Indonesia | Jakarta | 735,358 | 179,300,000 | Suharto—president |
| Iran | Teheran | 636,294 | 54,600,000 | Ayatollah Ali Khamenei—religious leader<br>Ali Hashemi Rafsanjani—president |
| Iraq | Baghdad | 167,925 | 18,900,000 | Saddam Hussein—president |
| Ireland | Dublin | 27,136 | 3,500,000 | Mary Robinson—president<br>Charles Haughey—prime minister |
| Israel | Jerusalem | 8,019 | 4,700,000 | Chaim Herzog—president<br>Yitzhak Shamir—prime minister |
| Italy | Rome | 116,303 | 57,700,000 | Francesco Cossiga—president<br>Giulio Andreotti—premier |
| Ivory Coast | Yamoussoukro | 124,503 | 12,000,000 | Félix Houphouët-Boigny—president |
| Jamaica | Kingston | 4,244 | 2,400,000 | Michael Manley—prime minister |
| Japan | Tokyo | 143,751 | 123,500,000 | Akihito—emperor<br>Kiichi Miyazawa—premier |
| Jordan | Amman | 35,475 | 4,000,000 | Hussein I—king<br>Sherif Zeid ibn Shaker—premier |
| Kenya | Nairobi | 224,959 | 24,000,000 | Daniel arap Moi—president |
| Kiribati | Tarawa | 264 | 66,000 | Teatao Teannaki—president |
| Korea (North) | Pyongyang | 46,540 | 21,800,000 | Kim Il Sung—president<br>Yon Hyong Muk—premier |
| Korea (South) | Seoul | 38,025 | 42,800,000 | Roh Tae Woo—president<br>Chung Won Shik—premier |
| Kuwait | Kuwait | 6,880 | 2,100,000 | Jabir al-Ahmad al-Sabah—head of state |
| Laos | Vientiane | 91,429 | 4,100,000 | Kaysone Phomvihan—president<br>Khamtai Siphandon—premier |
| Latvia | Riga | 24,600 | 2,700,000 | Anatolijs V. Gorbunovs—president |
| Lebanon | Beirut | 4,015 | 2,700,000 | Elias Hrawi—president<br>Omar Karami—premier |

| NATION | CAPITAL | AREA (in sq mi) | POPULATION (estimate) | GOVERNMENT |
|---|---|---|---|---|
| Lesotho | Maseru | 11,720 | 1,800,000 | Letsie III—king<br>Elias P. Ramaema—prime minister |
| Liberia | Monrovia | 43,000 | 2,600,000 | Amos Sawyer—president |
| Libya | Tripoli | 679,362 | 4,500,000 | Muammar el-Qaddafi—head of government |
| Liechtenstein | Vaduz | 61 | 29,000 | Hans Adam—prince |
| Lithuania | Vilnius | 25,200 | 3,900,000 | Vytautas Landsbergis—president |
| Luxembourg | Luxembourg | 999 | 373,000 | Jean—grand duke<br>Jacques Santer—premier |
| Madagascar | Antananarivo | 226,657 | 11,200,000 | Didier Ratsiraka—president |
| Malawi | Lilongwe | 45,747 | 8,300,000 | H. Kamuzu Banda—president |
| Malaysia | Kuala Lumpur | 127,317 | 17,900,000 | Azlan Muhibuddin Shah—king<br>Mahathir Mohammad—prime minister |
| Maldives | Male | 115 | 215,000 | Maumoon Abdul Gayoom—president |
| Mali | Bamako | 478,765 | 8,200,000 | Soumana Sacko—head of government |
| Malta | Valletta | 122 | 354,000 | Vincent Tabone—president<br>Eddie Fenech Adami—prime minister |
| Marshall Islands | Majuro | 70 | 43,000 | Amata Kabua—president |
| Mauritania | Nouakchott | 397,954 | 2,000,000 | Maouya Ould Sidi Ahmed Taya—president |
| Mauritius | Port Louis | 790 | 1,100,000 | Anerood Jugnauth—prime minister |
| Mexico | Mexico City | 761,602 | 86,200,000 | Carlos Salinas de Gortari—president |
| Micronesia | Colonia | 271 | 105,000 | Bailey Olter—president |
| Monaco | Monaco-Ville | 0.6 | 29,000 | Rainier III—prince |
| Mongolia | Ulan Bator | 604,248 | 2,200,000 | Gombojavyn Ochirbat—communist party secretary |
| Morocco | Rabat | 172,413 | 25,100,000 | Hassan II—king<br>Azzedine Laraki—premier |
| Mozambique | Maputo | 309,494 | 15,700,000 | Joaquím A. Chissano—president |
| Namibia | Windhoek | 318,260 | 1,800,000 | Sam Nujoma—president |
| Nauru | Yaren District | 8 | 10,000 | Bernard Dowiyogo—president |
| Nepal | Katmandu | 54,362 | 18,900,000 | Birendra Bir Bikram Shah Deva—king<br>Girija Prasad Koirala—prime minister |
| Netherlands | Amsterdam | 15,770 | 14,900,000 | Beatrix—queen<br>Ruud Lubbers—premier |
| New Zealand | Wellington | 103,736 | 3,300,000 | Jim Bolger—prime minister |
| Nicaragua | Managua | 50,193 | 3,900,000 | Violeta Barrios de Chamorro—president |
| Niger | Niamey | 489,190 | 7,700,000 | Ali Saibou—president |
| Nigeria | Abuja | 356,667 | 108,500,000 | Ibrahim Babangida—president |
| Norway | Oslo | 125,056 | 4,200,000 | Harald V—king<br>Gro Harlem Brundtland—premier |
| Oman | Muscat | 82,030 | 1,500,000 | Qabus ibn Said—sultan |

| NATION | CAPITAL | AREA (in sq mi) | POPULATION (estimate) | GOVERNMENT |
|---|---|---|---|---|
| Pakistan | Islamabad | 310,404 | 112,000,000 | Gulam Ishaq Khan—president<br>Nawaz Sharif—prime minister |
| Panama | Panama City | 29,761 | 2,400,000 | Guillermo Endara—president |
| Papua New Guinea | Port Moresby | 178,260 | 3,700,000 | Rabbie Namaliu—prime minister |
| Paraguay | Asunción | 157,047 | 4,300,000 | Andrés Rodríguez Pedotti—president |
| Peru | Lima | 496,222 | 22,300,000 | Alberto Fujimori—president |
| Philippines | Manila | 115,830 | 61,500,000 | Corazon C. Aquino—president<br>Salvador H. Laurel—vice-president |
| Poland | Warsaw | 120,725 | 38,200,000 | Lech Walesa—president<br>Jan Olszewski—premier |
| Portugal | Lisbon | 35,553 | 10,500,000 | Mário Alberto Soares—president<br>Aníbal Cavaco Silva—premier |
| Qatar | Doha | 4,247 | 368,000 | Khalifa ibn Hamad al-Thani—head of state |
| Rumania | Bucharest | 91,700 | 23,200,000 | Ion Iliescu—president<br>Theodor Stolojon—premier |
| Rwanda | Kigali | 10,169 | 7,200,000 | Juvénal Habyarimana—president |
| St. Christopher and Nevis | Basseterre | 105 | 44,000 | Kennedy Simmonds—prime minister |
| St. Lucia | Castries | 238 | 151,000 | John Compton—prime minister |
| St. Vincent and the Grenadines | Kingstown | 150 | 116,000 | James F. Mitchell—prime minister |
| São Tomé and Príncipe | São Tomé | 372 | 121,000 | Miguel Trovoada—premier |
| Saudi Arabia | Riyadh | 830,000 | 14,900,000 | Fahd ibn Abdul-Aziz—king |
| Senegal | Dakar | 75,750 | 7,300,000 | Abdou Diouf—president |
| Seychelles | Victoria | 107 | 67,000 | France Albert René—president |
| Sierra Leone | Freetown | 27,700 | 4,200,000 | Joseph Momoh—president |
| Singapore | Singapore | 224 | 3,000,000 | Wee Kim Wee—president<br>Go Chok Tong—prime minister |
| Solomon Islands | Honiara | 10,983 | 321,000 | Solomon Mamaloni—prime minister |
| Somalia | Mogadishu | 246,200 | 7,500,000 | Ali Mahdi Mohammed—president |
| South Africa | Pretoria<br>Cape Town<br>Bloemfontein | 471,444 | 35,300,000 | F. W. de Klerk—president |
| Soviet Union | Moscow | 8,582,254 | 280,400,000 | Reorganized into Commonwealth of Independent States |
| Spain | Madrid | 194,897 | 39,000,000 | Juan Carlos I—king<br>Felipe González Márquez—premier |
| Sri Lanka (Ceylon) | Colombo | 25,332 | 17,000,000 | Ranasinghe Premadasa—president |
| Sudan | Khartoum | 967,500 | 25,200,000 | Omar Hasan Ahmad al-Bashir—prime minister |

| NATION | CAPITAL | AREA (in sq mi) | POPULATION (estimate) | GOVERNMENT |
|---|---|---|---|---|
| Suriname | Paramaribo | 63,037 | 422,000 | Ronald Venetiaan—president |
| Swaziland | Mbabane | 6,704 | 768,000 | Mswati III—king |
| Sweden | Stockholm | 173,731 | 8,600,000 | Carl XVI Gustaf—king<br>Carl Bildt—premier |
| Switzerland | Bern | 15,941 | 6,700,000 | René Felber—president |
| Syria | Damascus | 71,498 | 12,100,000 | Hafez al-Assad—president<br>Mahmoud Zubi—premier |
| Taiwan | Taipei | 13,885 | 20,500,000 | Lee Teng-hui—president<br>Hao Po-tsun—premier |
| Tanzania | Dar es Salaam | 364,898 | 25,600,000 | Ali Hassan Mwinyi—president |
| Thailand | Bangkok | 198,457 | 57,200,000 | Bhumibol Adulyadej—king<br>Anand Panyarachun—premier |
| Togo | Lomé | 21,622 | 3,500,000 | Gnassingbe Eyadema—president |
| Tonga | Nuku'alofa | 270 | 95,000 | Taufa'ahau Tupou IV—king<br>Prince Tu'ipelehake—prime minister |
| Trinidad & Tobago | Port of Spain | 1,980 | 1,200,000 | Noor Hassanali—president<br>Patrick Manning—prime minister |
| Tunisia | Tunis | 63,170 | 8,200,000 | Zine el-Abidine Ben Ali—president |
| Turkey | Ankara | 301,381 | 58,700,000 | Turgut Ozal—president<br>Suleyman Demirel—prime minister |
| Tuvalu | Funafuti | 10 | 10,000 | Bikenibeu Paeniu—prime minister |
| Uganda | Kampala | 91,134 | 18,800,000 | Yoweri Museveni—president |
| United Arab Emirates | Abu Dhabi | 32,278 | 1,600,000 | Zayd ibn Sultan al-Nuhayan—president |
| United Kingdom | London | 94,226 | 57,200,000 | Elizabeth II—queen<br>John Major—prime minister |
| United States | Washington, D.C. | 3,618,467 | 250,000,000 | George H. Bush—president<br>James Danforth Quayle—vice-president |
| Uruguay | Montevideo | 68,037 | 3,100,000 | Luis Alberto Lacalle—president |
| Vanuatu | Vila | 5,700 | 147,000 | Walter Lini—prime minister |
| Venezuela | Caracas | 352,143 | 19,700,000 | Carlos Andrés Pérez—president |
| Vietnam | Hanoi | 128,402 | 66,200,000 | Do Muoi—communist party secretary<br>Vo Van Kiet—premier |
| Western Samoa | Apia | 1,097 | 164,000 | Malietoa Tanumafili II—head of state |
| Yemen (Sana) | Sana | 203,849 | 11,300,000 | Ali Abdullah Saleh—president<br>Haider Abu Bakr al-Attas—premier |
| Yugoslavia | Belgrade | 98,766 | 23,800,000 | Stipe Mesic—president |
| Zaire | Kinshasa | 905,565 | 35,600,000 | Mobutu Sese Seko—president |
| Zambia | Lusaka | 290,585 | 8,100,000 | Frederick Chiluba—president |
| Zimbabwe | Harare | 150,333 | 9,400,000 | Robert Mugabe—executive president |

# THE CONGRESS OF THE UNITED STATES

## UNITED STATES SENATE

### (57 Democrats, 43 Republicans)

**Alabama**
Howell T. Heflin (D)
Richard C. Shelby (D)

**Alaska**
Ted Stevens (R)
Frank H. Murkowski (R)

**Arizona**
Dennis DeConcini (D)
John S. McCain III (R)

**Arkansas**
Dale Bumpers (D)
David H. Pryor (D)

**California**
Alan Cranston (D)
John F. Seymour (R)**

**Colorado**
Timothy E. Wirth (D)
Hank Brown (R)

**Connecticut**
Christopher J. Dodd (D)
Joseph I. Lieberman (D)

**Delaware**
William V. Roth, Jr. (R)
Joseph R. Biden, Jr. (D)

**Florida**
Bob Graham (D)
Connie Mack (R)

**Georgia**
Sam Nunn (D)
Wyche Fowler, Jr. (D)

**Hawaii**
Daniel K. Inouye (D)
Daniel K. Akaka (D)

**Idaho**
Steve Symms (R)
Larry E. Craig (R)

**Illinois**
Alan J. Dixon (D)
Paul Simon (D)

**Indiana**
Richard G. Lugar (R)
Dan Coats (R)

**Iowa**
Charles E. Grassley (R)
Thomas R. Harkin (D)

**Kansas**
Robert J. Dole (R)
Nancy Landon Kassebaum (R)

**Kentucky**
Wendell H. Ford (D)
Mitch McConnell (R)

**Louisiana**
J. Bennett Johnston (D)
John B. Breaux (D)

**Maine**
William S. Cohen (R)
George J. Mitchell (D)

**Maryland**
Paul S. Sarbanes (D)
Barbara A. Mikulski (D)

**Massachusetts**
Edward M. Kennedy (D)
John F. Kerry (D)

**Michigan**
Donald W. Riegle, Jr. (D)
Carl Levin (D)

**Minnesota**
David F. Durenberger (R)
Paul Wellstone (D)

**Mississippi**
Thad Cochran (R)
Trent Lott (R)

**Missouri**
John C. Danforth (R)
Christopher S. Bond (R)

**Montana**
Max Baucus (D)
Conrad Burns (R)

**Nebraska**
J. James Exon, Jr. (D)
J. Robert Kerrey (D)

**Nevada**
Harry Reid (D)
Richard H. Bryan (D)

**New Hampshire**
Warren B. Rudman (R)
Robert C. Smith (R)

**New Jersey**
Bill Bradley (D)
Frank R. Lautenberg (D)

**New Mexico**
Pete V. Domenici (R)
Jeff Bingaman (D)

**New York**
Daniel P. Moynihan (D)
Alfonse M. D'Amato (R)

**North Carolina**
Jesse Helms (R)
Terry Sanford (D)

**North Dakota**
Quentin N. Burdick (D)
Kent Conrad (D)

**Ohio**
John H. Glenn, Jr. (D)
Howard M. Metzenbaum (D)

**Oklahoma**
David L. Boren (D)
Donald L. Nickles (R)

**Oregon**
Mark O. Hatfield (R)
Bob Packwood (R)

**Pennsylvania**
Harris Wofford (D)*
Arlen Specter (R)

**Rhode Island**
Claiborne Pell (D)
John H. Chafee (R)

**South Carolina**
Strom Thurmond (R)
Ernest F. Hollings (D)

**South Dakota**
Larry Pressler (R)
Thomas A. Daschle (D)

**Tennessee**
James R. Sasser (D)
Albert Gore, Jr. (D)

**Texas**
Lloyd Bentsen (D)
Phil Gramm (R)

**Utah**
Jake Garn (R)
Orrin G. Hatch (R)

**Vermont**
Patrick J. Leahy (D)
James M. Jeffords (R)

**Virginia**
John W. Warner (R)
Charles S. Robb (D)

**Washington**
Brock Adams (D)
Slade Gorton (R)

**West Virginia**
Robert C. Byrd (D)
John D. Rockefeller IV (D)

**Wisconsin**
Robert W. Kasten, Jr. (R)
Herbert H. Kohl (D)

**Wyoming**
Malcolm Wallop (R)
Alan K. Simpson (R)

(D) Democrat
(R) Republican

*elected in 1991
**appointed to fill P. Wilson's seat

# UNITED STATES HOUSE OF REPRESENTATIVES

## (268 Democrats, 166 Republicans, 1 Independent)

**Alabama**
1. H. L. Callahan (R)
2. W. L. Dickinson (R)
3. G. Browder (D)
4. T. Bevill (D)
5. B. Cramer (D)
6. B. Erdreich (D)
7. C. Harris, Jr. (D)

**Alaska**
D. Young (R)

**Arizona**
1. J. J. Rhodes III (R)
2. E. Pastor (D)*
3. B. Stump (R)
4. J. L. Kyl (R)
5. J. Kolbe (R)

**Arkansas**
1. W. V. Alexander, Jr. (D)
2. R. Thornton (D)
3. J. P. Hammerschmidt (R)
4. B. F. Anthony, Jr. (D)

**California**
1. F. Riggs (R)
2. W. W. Herger (R)
3. R. T. Matsui (D)
4. V. Fazio (D)
5. N. Pelosi (D)
6. B. Boxer (D)
7. G. Miller (D)
8. R. V. Dellums (D)
9. F. H. Stark, Jr. (D)
10. D. Edwards (D)
11. T. P. Lantos (D)
12. T. Campbell (R)
13. N. Y. Mineta (D)
14. J. Doolittle (R)
15. G. Condit (D)
16. L. E. Panetta (D)
17. C. Dooley (D)
18. R. H. Lehman (D)
19. R. J. Lagomarsino (R)
20. W. M. Thomas (R)
21. E. W. Gallegly (R)
22. C. J. Moorhead (R)
23. A. C. Beilenson (D)
24. H. A. Waxman (D)
25. E. R. Roybal (D)
26. H. L. Berman (D)
27. M. Levine (D)
28. J. C. Dixon (D)
29. M. Waters (D)
30. M. G. Martinez, Jr. (D)
31. M. M. Dymally (D)
32. G. M. Anderson (D)
33. D. Dreier (R)
34. E. E. Torres (D)
35. J. Lewis (R)
36. G. E. Brown, Jr. (D)
37. A. A. McCandless (R)
38. R. K. Dornan (R)
39. W. E. Dannemeyer (R)
40. C. C. Cox (R)
41. W. D. Lowery (R)
42. D. Rohrabacher (R)
43. R. Packard (R)
44. R. Cunningham (R)
45. D. L. Hunter (R)

**Colorado**
1. P. Schroeder (D)
2. D. Skaggs (D)
3. B. N. Campbell (D)
4. W. Allard (R)
5. J. M. Hefley (R)
6. D. Schaefer (R)

**Connecticut**
1. B. B. Kennelly (D)
2. S. Gejdenson (D)
3. R. DeLauro (D)
4. C. Shays (R)
5. G. Franks (R)
6. N. L. Johnson (R)

**Delaware**
T. R. Carper (D)

**Florida**
1. E. Hutto (D)
2. P. Peterson (D)
3. C. E. Bennett (D)
4. C. T. James (R)
5. B. McCollum, Jr. (R)
6. C. B. Stearns (R)
7. S. M. Gibbons (D)
8. C. W. B. Young (R)
9. M. Bilirakis (R)
10. A. Ireland (R)
11. J. Bacchus (D)
12. T. Lewis (R)
13. P. J. Goss (R)
14. H. A. Johnston (D)
15. E. C. Shaw, Jr. (R)
16. L. J. Smith (D)
17. W. Lehman (D)
18. I. Ros-Lehtinen (R)
19. D. B. Fascell (D)

**Georgia**
1. R. L. Thomas (D)
2. C. F. Hatcher (D)
3. R. B. Ray (D)
4. B. Jones (D)
5. J. R. Lewis (D)
6. N. Gingrich (R)
7. G. B. Darden (D)
8. J. R. Rowland (D)
9. E. L. Jenkins (D)
10. D. Barnard, Jr. (D)

**Hawaii**
1. N. Abercrombie (D)
2. P. Mink (D)

**Idaho**
1. L. LaRocco (D)
2. R. H. Stallings (D)

**Illinois**
1. C. A. Hayes (D)
2. G. Savage (D)
3. M. Russo (D)
4. G. E. Sangmeister (D)
5. W. O. Lipinski (D)
6. H. J. Hyde (R)
7. C. Collins (D)
8. D. Rostenkowski (D)
9. S. R. Yates (D)
10. J. E. Porter (R)
11. F. Annunzio (D)
12. P. M. Crane (R)
13. H. W. Fawell (R)
14. J. D. Hastert (R)
15. T. W. Ewing (R)*
16. J. Cox, Jr. (D)
17. L. Evans (D)
18. R. H. Michel (R)
19. T. L. Bruce (D)
20. R. Durbin (D)
21. J. F. Costello (D)
22. G. Poshard (D)

**Indiana**
1. P. J. Visclosky (D)
2. P. R. Sharp (D)
3. T. Roemer (D)
4. J. Long (D)
5. J. P. Jontz (D)
6. D. L. Burton (R)
7. J. T. Myers (R)
8. F. McCloskey (D)
9. L. H. Hamilton (D)
10. A. Jacobs, Jr. (D)

**Iowa**
1. J. Leach (R)
2. J. Nussle (R)
3. D. R. Nagle (D)
4. N. Smith (D)
5. J. R. Lightfoot (R)
6. F. L. Grandy (R)

**Kansas**
1. C. P. Roberts (R)
2. J. C. Slattery (D)
3. J. Meyers (R)
4. D. Glickman (D)
5. D. Nichols (R)

**Kentucky**
1. C. Hubbard, Jr. (D)
2. W. H. Natcher (D)
3. R. L. Mazzoli (D)
4. J. Bunning (R)
5. H. D. Rogers (R)
6. L. J. Hopkins (R)
7. C. C. Perkins (D)

**Louisiana**
1. R. L. Livingston, Jr. (R)
2. W. Jefferson (D)
3. W. J. Tauzin (D)
4. J. McCrery (R)
5. T. J. Huckaby (D)
6. R. H. Baker (R)

**Maine**
1. T. Andrews (D)
2. O. J. Snowe (R)

**Maryland**
1. W. Gilchrest (R)
2. H. Delich Bentley (R)
3. B. L. Cardin (D)
4. C. T. McMillen (D)
5. S. H. Hoyer (D)
6. B. B. Byron (D)
7. K. Mfume (D)
8. C. A. Morella (R)

**Massachusetts**
1. J. Olver (D)*
2. R. E. Neal (D)
3. J. D. Early (D)
4. B. Frank (D)
5. C. G. Atkins (D)
6. N. Mavroules (D)
7. E. J. Markey (D)
8. J. P. Kennedy II (D)
9. J. J. Moakley (D)
10. G. E. Studds (D)
11. B. J. Donnelly (D)

**Michigan**
1. J. Conyers, Jr. (D)
2. C. D. Pursell (R)
3. H. E. Wolpe (D)
4. F. S. Upton (R)
5. P. B. Henry (R)
6. B. Carr (D)
7. D. E. Kildee (D)
8. B. Traxler (D)
9. G. Vander Jagt (R)
10. D. Camp (R)
11. R. W. Davis (R)
12. D. E. Bonior (D)
13. B. Collins (D)
14. D. M. Hertel (D)
15. W. D. Ford (D)
16. J. D. Dingell (D)
17. S. M. Levin (D)
18. W. S. Broomfield (R)

**Minnesota**
1. T. J. Penny (D)
2. V. Weber (R)
3. J. Ramstad (R)
4. B. F. Vento (D)
5. M. O. Sabo (D)
6. G. Sikorski (D)
7. C. Peterson (D)
8. J. L. Oberstar (D)

**Mississippi**
1. J. L. Whitten (D)
2. M. Espy (D)
3. G. V. Montgomery (D)
4. M. Parker (D)
5. G. Taylor (D)

**Missouri**
1. W. L. Clay (D)
2. J. K. Horn (D)
3. R. A. Gephardt (D)
4. I. Skelton (D)
5. A. D. Wheat (D)
6. E. T. Coleman (R)
7. M. D. Hancock (R)
8. W. Emerson (R)
9. H. L. Volkmer (D)

**Montana**
1. P. Williams (D)
2. R. C. Marlenee (R)

**Nebraska**
1. D. Bereuter (R)
2. P. Hoagland (D)
3. B. Barrett (R)

**Nevada**
1. J. H. Bilbray (D)
2. B. Farrell Vucanovich (R)

**New Hampshire**
1. B. Zeliff (R)
2. D. Swett (D)

**New Jersey**
1. R. Andrews (D)
2. W. J. Hughes (D)
3. F. Pallone, Jr. (D)
4. C. H. Smith (R)
5. M. S. Roukema (R)
6. B. J. Dwyer (D)
7. M. J. Rinaldo (R)
8. R. A. Roe (D)
9. R. G. Torricelli (D)
10. D. M. Payne (D)
11. D. A. Gallo (R)
12. R. A. Zimmer (R)
13. H. J. Saxton (R)
14. F. J. Guarini (D)

**New Mexico**
1. S. Schiff (R)
2. J. R. Skeen (R)
3. W. B. Richardson (D)

**New York**
1. G. J. Hochbrueckner (D)
2. T. J. Downey (D)
3. R. J. Mrazek (D)
4. N. F. Lent (R)
5. R. J. McGrath (R)
6. F. H. Flake (D)
7. G. L. Ackerman (D)
8. J. H. Scheuer (D)
9. T. J. Manton (D)
10. C. E. Schumer (D)
11. E. Towns (D)
12. M. R. O. Owens (D)
13. S. J. Solarz (D)
14. S. Molinari (R)
15. B. Green (R)
16. C. B. Rangel (D)
17. T. Weiss (D)
18. J. Serrano (D)
19. E. L. Engel (D)
20. N. M. Lowey (D)
21. H. Fish, Jr. (R)
22. B. A. Gilman (R)
23. M. R. McNulty (D)
24. G. B. Solomon (R)
25. S. L. Boehlert (R)
26. D. O. Martin (R)
27. J. T. Walsh (R)
28. M. F. McHugh (D)
29. F. Horton (R)
30. L. M. Slaughter (D)
31. B. Paxon (R)
32. J. J. LaFalce (D)
33. H. J. Nowak (D)
34. A. Houghton, Jr. (R)

**North Carolina**
1. W. B. Jones (D)
2. T. Valentine (D)
3. H. M. Lancaster (D)
4. D. E. Price (D)
5. S. L. Neal (D)
6. H. Coble (R)
7. C. Rose (D)
8. W. G. Hefner (D)
9. J. A. McMillan (R)
10. C. Ballenger (R)
11. C. Taylor (R)

**North Dakota**
B. L. Dorgan (D)

**Ohio**
1. C. Luken (D)
2. W. D. Gradison, Jr. (R)
3. T. P. Hall (D)
4. M. G. Oxley (R)
5. P. E. Gillmor (R)
6. B. McEwen (R)
7. D. Hobson (R)
8. J. Boehner (R)
9. M. C. Kaptur (D)
10. C. E. Miller (R)
11. D. E. Eckart (D)
12. J. R. Kasich (R)
13. D. J. Pease (D)
14. T. C. Sawyer (D)
15. C. P. Wylie (R)
16. R. Regula (R)
17. J. A. Traficant, Jr. (D)
18. D. Applegate (D)
19. E. F. Feighan (D)
20. M. R. Oakar (D)
21. L. Stokes (D)

**Oklahoma**
1. J. M. Inhofe (R)
2. M. Synar (D)
3. B. Brewster (D)
4. D. McCurdy (D)
5. M. H. Edwards (R)
6. G. English (D)

**Oregon**
1. L. AuCoin (D)
2. R. F. Smith (R)
3. R. L. Wyden (D)
4. P. A. DeFazio (D)
5. M. Kopetski (D)

**Pennsylvania**
1. T. M. Foglietta (D)
2. L. Blackwell (D)*
3. R. A. Borski, Jr. (D)
4. J. P. Kolter (D)
5. R. T. Schulze (R)
6. G. Yatron (D)
7. W. C. Weldon (R)
8. P. H. Kostmayer (D)
9. B. Shuster (R)
10. J. M. McDade (R)
11. P. E. Kanjorski (D)
12. J. P. Murtha (D)
13. L. Coughlin (R)
14. W. J. Coyne (D)
15. D. L. Ritter (R)
16. R. S. Walker (R)
17. G. W. Gekas (R)
18. R. Santorum (R)
19. W. F. Goodling (R)
20. J. M. Gaydos (D)
21. T. J. Ridge (R)
22. A. J. Murphy (D)
23. W. F. Clinger, Jr. (R)

**Rhode Island**
1. R. K. Machtley (R)
2. J. Reed (D)

**South Carolina**
1. A. Ravenel, Jr. (R)
2. F. D. Spence (R)
3. B. C. Derrick, Jr. (D)
4. E. J. Patterson (D)
5. J. M. Spratt, Jr. (D)
6. R. M. Tallon, Jr. (D)

**South Dakota**
T. Johnson (D)

**Tennessee**
1. J. H. Quillen (R)
2. J. J. Duncan, Jr. (R)
3. M. Lloyd (D)
4. J. H. S. Cooper (D)
5. B. Clement (D)
6. B. J. Gordon (D)
7. D. K. Sundquist (R)
8. J. S. Tanner (D)
9. H. E. Ford (D)

**Texas**
1. J. Chapman (D)
2. C. Wilson (D)
3. S. Johnson (R)*
4. R. M. Hall (D)
5. J. W. Bryant (D)
6. J. L. Barton (R)
7. B. Archer (R)
8. J. M. Fields (R)
9. J. Brooks (D)
10. J. J. Pickle (D)
11. C. Edwards (D)
12. P. M. Geren (D)
13. B. Sarpalius (D)
14. G. Laughlin (D)
15. E. de la Garza (D)
16. R. D. Coleman (D)
17. C. W. Stenholm (D)
18. C. Washington (D)
19. L. E. Combest (R)
20. H. B. Gonzalez (D)
21. L. S. Smith (R)
22. T. D. DeLay (R)
23. A. G. Bustamante (D)
24. M. Frost (D)
25. M. A. Andrews (D)
26. R. K. Armey (R)
27. S. P. Ortiz (D)

**Utah**
1. J. V. Hansen (R)
2. D. W. Owens (D)
3. W. Orton (D)

**Vermont**
B. Sanders (I)

**Virginia**
1. H. H. Bateman (R)
2. O. B. Pickett (D)
3. T. J. Bliley, Jr. (R)
4. N. Sisisky (D)
5. L. F. Payne, Jr. (D)
6. J. R. Olin (D)
7. G. F. Allen (R)*
8. J. Moran (D)
9. F. C. Boucher (D)
10. F. R. Wolf (R)

**Washington**
1. J. R. Miller (R)
2. A. Swift (D)
3. J. Unsoeld (D)
4. S. W. Morrison (R)
5. T. S. Foley (D)
6. N. D. Dicks (D)
7. J. McDermott (D)
8. R. Chandler (R)

**West Virginia**
1. A. B. Mollohan (D)
2. H. O. Staggers, Jr. (D)
3. R. E. Wise, Jr. (D)
4. N. J. Rahall II (D)

**Wisconsin**
1. L. Aspin (D)
2. S. Klug (R)
3. S. C. Gunderson (R)
4. G. D. Kleczka (D)
5. J. Moody (D)
6. T. E. Petri (R)
7. D. R. Obey (D)
8. T. Roth (R)
9. F. J. Sensenbrenner, Jr. (R)

**Wyoming**
C. Thomas (R)

(D) Democrat
(R) Republican
(I) Independent

*elected in 1991

## UNITED STATES SUPREME COURT

**Chief Justice:** William H. Rehnquist (1986)
**Associate Justices:**
Byron R. White (1962)
Harry A. Blackmun (1970)
John Paul Stevens (1975)
Sandra Day O'Connor (1981)
Antonin Scalia (1986)
Anthony M. Kennedy (1988)
David H. Souter (1990)
Clarence Thomas (1991)

## UNITED STATES CABINET

**Secretary of Agriculture:** Edward R. Madigan
**Attorney General:** William P. Barr
**Secretary of Commerce:** vacant
**Secretary of Defense:** Richard B. Cheney
**Secretary of Education:** Lamar Alexander
**Secretary of Energy:** James D. Watkins
**Secretary of Health and Human Services:**
Louis W. Sullivan
**Secretary of Housing and Urban Development:**
Jack F. Kemp
**Secretary of the Interior:** Manuel Lujan, Jr.
**Secretary of Labor:** Lynn Martin
**Secretary of State:** James A. Baker III
**Secretary of Transportation:** vacant
**Secretary of the Treasury:** Nicholas F. Brady
**Secretary of Veteran Affairs:** Edward J. Derwinski

Louisiana's election for governor: In a contest that gained national attention, former Governor Edwin Edwards (*left*) defeated ex-Klansman David Duke (*right*).

## STATE GOVERNORS

| State | Governor | State | Governor |
|---|---|---|---|
| **Alabama** | Guy Hunt (R) | **Montana** | Stanley G. Stephens (R) |
| **Alaska** | Walter J. Hickel (I) | **Nebraska** | Ben Nelson (D) |
| **Arizona** | J. Fife Symington III (R)* | **Nevada** | Bob Miller (D) |
| **Arkansas** | Bill Clinton (D) | **New Hampshire** | Judd Gregg (R) |
| **California** | Pete Wilson (R) | **New Jersey** | James J. Florio (D) |
| **Colorado** | Roy Romer (D) | **New Mexico** | Bruce King (D) |
| **Connecticut** | Lowell P. Weicker, Jr. (I) | **New York** | Mario M. Cuomo (D) |
| **Delaware** | Michael N. Castle (R) | **North Carolina** | James G. Martin (R) |
| **Florida** | Lawton Chiles (D) | **North Dakota** | George Sinner (D) |
| **Georgia** | Zell Miller (D) | **Ohio** | George V. Voinovich (R) |
| **Hawaii** | John Waihee (D) | **Oklahoma** | David Walters (D) |
| **Idaho** | Cecil D. Andrus (D) | **Oregon** | Barbara Roberts (D) |
| **Illinois** | Jim Edgar (R) | **Pennsylvania** | Robert P. Casey (D) |
| **Indiana** | Evan Bayh (D) | **Rhode Island** | Bruce Sundlun (D) |
| **Iowa** | Terry E. Branstad (R) | **South Carolina** | Carroll A. Campbell, Jr. (R) |
| **Kansas** | Joan Finney (D) | **South Dakota** | George S. Mickelson (R) |
| **Kentucky** | Brereton C. Jones (D)* | **Tennessee** | Ned R. McWherter (D) |
| **Louisiana** | Edwin Edwards (D)* | **Texas** | Ann Richards (D) |
| **Maine** | John R. McKernan, Jr. (R) | **Utah** | Norman H. Bangerter (R) |
| **Maryland** | William Donald Schaefer (D) | **Vermont** | Howard B. Dean (D)** |
| **Massachusetts** | William F. Weld (R) | **Virginia** | L. Douglas Wilder (D) |
| **Michigan** | John Engler (R) | **Washington** | Booth Gardner (D) |
| **Minnesota** | Arne Carlson (R) | **West Virginia** | Gaston Caperton (D) |
| **Mississippi** | Kirk Fordice (R)* | **Wisconsin** | Tommy G. Thompson (R) |
| **Missouri** | John Ashcroft (R) | **Wyoming** | Mike Sullivan (D) |

*elected in 1991   **appointed to succeed R. A. Snelling, who died in August       (D) Democrat   (R) Republican   (I) Independent

# THE 1990 UNITED STATES CENSUS
## FINAL FIGURES

The Constitution of the United States requires that a census be taken every ten years, so that membership in the House of Representatives may be fairly apportioned (divided up) among the states.

The table below provides the final 1990 census figures for the resident population of the United States, and it indicates the representation of each state in the House of Representatives. The population figures include people living in the District of Columbia and the 50 states; they exclude citizens living outside the United States. The changes in representation in the House of Representatives takes effect in January, 1993, following the elections of 1992. (The Census Bureau has stated that about 5.3 million people weren't counted in the 1990 census. It nevertheless has rejected a revision of the census count. As a result, a number of cities and states have filed suit to bring about an adjustment to the census.)

| STATE | RESIDENT POPULATION | | | | REPRESENTATIVES | | |
|---|---|---|---|---|---|---|---|
| | 1990 | 1980 | Change | % | 1990 | 1980 | Change |
| Alabama | 4,040,587 | 3,893,888 | +146,699 | +3.8 | 7 | 7 | 0 |
| Alaska | 550,043 | 401,851 | +148,192 | +36.9 | 1 | 1 | 0 |
| Arizona | 3,665,228 | 2,718,215 | +947,013 | +34.8 | 6 | 5 | +1 |
| Arkansas | 2,350,725 | 2,286,435 | +64,290 | +2.8 | 4 | 4 | 0 |
| California | 29,760,021 | 23,667,902 | +6,092,119 | +25.7 | 52 | 45 | +7 |
| Colorado | 3,294,394 | 2,889,964 | +404,430 | +14.0 | 6 | 6 | 0 |
| Connecticut | 3,287,116 | 3,107,576 | +179,540 | +5.8 | 6 | 6 | 0 |
| Delaware | 666,168 | 594,338 | +71,830 | +12.1 | 1 | 1 | 0 |
| Dist. of Columbia | 606,900 | 638,333 | −31,433 | −4.9 | * | | |
| Florida | 12,937,926 | 9,746,324 | +3,191,602 | +32.7 | 23 | 19 | +4 |
| Georgia | 6,478,216 | 5,463,105 | +1,015,111 | +18.6 | 11 | 10 | +1 |
| Hawaii | 1,108,229 | 964,691 | +143,538 | +14.9 | 2 | 2 | 0 |
| Idaho | 1,006,749 | 943,935 | +62,814 | +6.7 | 2 | 2 | 0 |
| Illinois | 11,430,602 | 11,426,518 | +4,084 | 0.0 | 20 | 22 | −2 |
| Indiana | 5,544,159 | 5,490,224 | +53,935 | +0.1 | 10 | 10 | 0 |
| Iowa | 2,776,755 | 2,913,808 | +137,053 | −4.7 | 5 | 6 | −1 |
| Kansas | 2,477,574 | 2,363,679 | +113,895 | +4.8 | 4 | 5 | −1 |
| Kentucky | 3,685,296 | 3,660,777 | +24,519 | +0.7 | 6 | 7 | −1 |
| Louisiana | 4,219,973 | 4,205,900 | +14,073 | +0.3 | 7 | 8 | −1 |
| Maine | 1,227,928 | 1,124,660 | +103,268 | +9.2 | 2 | 2 | 0 |
| Maryland | 4,781,468 | 4,216,975 | +564,493 | +13.4 | 8 | 8 | 0 |
| Massachusetts | 6,016,425 | 5,737,037 | +279,388 | +4.9 | 10 | 11 | −1 |
| Michigan | 9,295,297 | 9,262,078 | +33,219 | +0.4 | 16 | 18 | −2 |
| Minnesota | 4,375,099 | 4,075,970 | +299,129 | +7.3 | 8 | 8 | 0 |
| Mississippi | 2,573,216 | 2,520,638 | +52,578 | +2.1 | 5 | 5 | 0 |
| Missouri | 5,117,073 | 4,916,686 | +200,387 | +4.1 | 9 | 9 | 0 |
| Montana | 799,065 | 786,690 | +12,375 | +1.6 | 1 | 2 | −1 |
| Nebraska | 1,578,385 | 1,569,825 | +8,560 | +0.5 | 3 | 3 | 0 |
| Nevada | 1,201,833 | 800,493 | +401,340 | +50.1 | 2 | 2 | 0 |
| New Hampshire | 1,109,252 | 920,610 | +188,642 | +20.5 | 2 | 2 | 0 |
| New Jersey | 7,730,188 | 7,364,823 | +365,365 | +5.0 | 13 | 14 | −1 |
| New Mexico | 1,515,069 | 1,302,894 | +212,175 | +16.3 | 3 | 3 | 0 |
| New York | 17,990,455 | 17,558,072 | +432,383 | +2.5 | 31 | 34 | −3 |
| North Carolina | 6,628,637 | 5,881,766 | +746,871 | +12.7 | 12 | 11 | +1 |
| North Dakota | 638,800 | 652,717 | −13,917 | −2.1 | 1 | 1 | 0 |
| Ohio | 10,847,115 | 10,797,630 | +49,485 | +0.5 | 19 | 21 | −2 |
| Oklahoma | 3,145,585 | 3,025,290 | +120,295 | +4.0 | 6 | 6 | 0 |
| Oregon | 2,842,321 | 2,633,105 | +209,216 | +7.9 | 5 | 5 | 0 |
| Pennsylvania | 11,881,643 | 11,863,895 | +17,748 | +0.1 | 21 | 23 | −2 |
| Rhode Island | 1,003,464 | 947,154 | +56,310 | +5.9 | 2 | 2 | 0 |
| South Carolina | 3,486,703 | 3,121,820 | +364,883 | +11.7 | 6 | 6 | 0 |
| South Dakota | 696,004 | 690,768 | +5,236 | +0.8 | 1 | 1 | 0 |
| Tennessee | 4,877,185 | 4,591,120 | +286,065 | +6.2 | 9 | 9 | 0 |
| Texas | 16,986,510 | 14,229,191 | +2,757,319 | +19.4 | 30 | 27 | +3 |
| Utah | 1,722,850 | 1,461,037 | +261,813 | +17.9 | 3 | 3 | 0 |
| Vermont | 562,758 | 511,456 | +51,302 | +10.0 | 1 | 1 | 0 |
| Virginia | 6,187,358 | 5,346,818 | +840,540 | +15.7 | 11 | 10 | +1 |
| Washington | 4,866,692 | 4,132,156 | +734,536 | +17.8 | 9 | 8 | +1 |
| West Virginia | 1,793,477 | 1,949,644 | −156,167 | −8.0 | 3 | 4 | −1 |
| Wisconsin | 4,891,769 | 4,705,767 | +186,002 | +4.0 | 9 | 9 | 0 |
| Wyoming | 453,588 | 469,557 | −15,969 | −3.4 | 1 | 1 | 0 |
| **TOTAL U.S.** | **248,709,873** | **226,545,805** | **22,164,068** | **+9.8** | **435** | **435** | **0** |

* The District of Columbia sends one nonvoting representative to the House of Representatives but is excluded from the apportionment process.

# PLACES WITH POPULATIONS OF 25,000 OR MORE

In the following tables, final figures are shown for incorporated places with populations of 25,000 or more, except in the New England states and Hawaii, for which all places of 25,000 or more are listed.

Abbreviations used in these tables are: B (borough); C (city); T (town or township); and V (village).

## ALABAMA

| | |
|---|---|
| Anniston C | 26,623 |
| Auburn C | 33,830 |
| Bessemer C | 33,497 |
| Birmingham C | 265,968 |
| Decatur C | 48,761 |
| Dothan C | 53,589 |
| Florence C | 36,426 |
| Gadsden C | 42,523 |
| Hoover C | 39,788 |
| Huntsville C | 159,789 |
| Mobile C | 196,278 |
| Montgomery C | 187,106 |
| Phenix City C | 25,312 |
| Prichard C | 34,311 |
| Tuscaloosa C | 77,759 |

## ALASKA

| | |
|---|---|
| Anchorage C | 226,338 |
| Fairbanks C | 30,843 |
| Juneau C | 26,751 |

## ARIZONA

| | |
|---|---|
| Chandler C | 90,533 |
| Flagstaff C | 45,857 |
| Gilbert T | 29,188 |
| Glendale C | 148,134 |
| Mesa C | 288,091 |
| Peoria C | 50,618 |
| Phoenix C | 983,403 |
| Prescott C | 26,455 |
| Scottsdale C | 130,069 |
| Sierra Vista C | 32,983 |
| Tempe C | 141,865 |
| Tucson C | 405,390 |
| Yuma C | 54,923 |

## ARKANSAS

| | |
|---|---|
| Conway C | 26,481 |
| Fayetteville C | 42,099 |
| Fort Smith C | 72,798 |
| Hot Springs C | 32,462 |
| Jacksonville C | 29,101 |
| Jonesboro C | 46,535 |
| Little Rock C | 175,795 |
| North Little Rock C | 61,741 |
| Pine Bluff C | 57,140 |
| Springdale C | 29,941 |
| West Memphis C | 28,259 |

## CALIFORNIA

| | |
|---|---|
| Alameda C | 76,459 |
| Alhambra C | 82,106 |
| Anaheim C | 266,406 |
| Antioch C | 62,195 |
| Apple Valley T | 46,079 |
| Arcadia C | 48,290 |
| Azusa C | 41,333 |
| Bakersfield C | 174,820 |
| Baldwin Park C | 69,330 |
| Bell C | 34,365 |
| Bellflower C | 61,815 |
| Bell Gardens C | 42,355 |
| Berkeley C | 102,724 |
| Beverly Hills C | 31,971 |
| Brea C | 32,873 |
| Buena Park C | 68,784 |
| Burbank C | 93,643 |
| Burlingame C | 26,801 |
| Camarillo C | 52,303 |
| Campbell C | 36,048 |
| Carlsbad C | 63,126 |
| Carson C | 83,995 |
| Cathedral City C | 30,085 |
| Ceres C | 26,314 |
| Cerritos C | 53,240 |
| Chico C | 40,079 |
| Chino C | 59,682 |
| Chula Vista C | 135,163 |
| Claremont C | 32,503 |
| Clovis C | 50,323 |
| Colton C | 40,213 |
| Compton C | 90,454 |
| Concord C | 111,348 |
| Corona C | 76,095 |
| Coronado C | 26,540 |
| Costa Mesa C | 96,357 |
| Covina C | 43,207 |
| Culver City C | 38,793 |
| Cupertino C | 40,263 |
| Cypress C | 42,655 |
| Daly City C | 92,311 |
| Dana Point C | 31,896 |
| Danville C | 31,306 |
| Davis C | 46,209 |
| Diamond Bar C | 53,672 |
| Downey C | 91,444 |
| El Cajon C | 88,693 |
| El Centro C | 31,384 |
| El Monte C | 106,209 |
| Encinitas C | 55,386 |
| Escondido C | 108,635 |
| Eureka C | 27,025 |
| Fairfield C | 77,211 |
| Folsom C | 29,802 |
| Fontana C | 87,535 |
| Foster City C | 28,176 |
| Fountain Valley C | 53,691 |
| Fremont C | 173,339 |
| Fresno C | 354,202 |
| Fullerton C | 114,144 |
| Gardena C | 49,847 |
| Garden Grove C | 143,050 |
| Gilroy C | 31,487 |
| Glendale C | 180,038 |
| Glendora C | 47,828 |
| Hanford C | 30,897 |
| Hawthorne C | 71,349 |
| Hayward C | 111,498 |
| Hemet C | 36,094 |
| Hesperia C | 50,418 |
| Highland C | 34,439 |
| Huntington Beach C | 181,519 |
| Huntington Park C | 56,065 |
| Imperial Beach C | 26,512 |
| Indio C | 36,793 |
| Inglewood C | 109,602 |
| Irvine C | 110,330 |
| Laguna Niguel C | 44,400 |
| La Habra C | 51,266 |
| Lakewood C | 73,557 |
| La Mesa C | 52,931 |
| La Mirada C | 40,452 |
| Lancaster C | 97,291 |
| La Puente C | 36,955 |
| La Verne C | 30,897 |
| Lawndale C | 27,331 |
| Livermore C | 56,741 |
| Lodi C | 51,874 |
| Lompoc C | 37,649 |
| Long Beach C | 429,433 |
| Los Altos C | 26,303 |
| Los Angeles C | 3,485,398 |
| Los Gatos T | 27,357 |
| Lynwood C | 61,945 |
| Madera C | 29,281 |
| Manhattan Beach C | 32,063 |
| Manteca C | 40,773 |
| Marina C | 26,436 |
| Martinez C | 31,808 |
| Maywood C | 27,850 |
| Menlo Park C | 28,040 |
| Merced C | 56,216 |
| Milpitas C | 50,686 |
| Mission Viejo C | 72,820 |
| Modesto C | 164,730 |
| Monrovia C | 35,761 |
| Montclair C | 28,434 |
| Montebello C | 59,564 |
| Monterey C | 31,954 |
| Monterey Park C | 60,738 |
| Moorpark C | 25,494 |
| Moreno Valley | 118,779 |
| Mountain View C | 67,460 |
| Napa C | 61,842 |
| National City C | 54,249 |
| Newark C | 37,861 |
| Newport Beach C | 66,643 |

| | | | | | | |
|---|---|---|---|---|---|---|
| Norwalk C | 94,279 | Santa Clarita C | 110,642 | Thornton C | 55,031 |
| Novato C | 47,585 | Santa Cruz C | 49,040 | Westminster C | 74,625 |
| Oakland C | 372,242 | Santa Maria C | 61,284 | Wheat Ridge C | 29,419 |
| Oceanside C | 128,398 | Santa Monica C | 86,905 | | |
| Ontario C | 133,179 | Santa Paula C | 25,062 | **CONNECTICUT** | |
| Orange C | 110,658 | Santa Rosa C | 113,313 | Branford T | 27,603 |
| Oxnard C | 142,216 | Santee C | 52,902 | Bridgeport C | 141,686 |
| Pacifica C | 37,670 | Saratoga C | 28,061 | Bristol C | 60,640 |
| Palmdale | 68,842 | Seal Beach C | 25,098 | Cheshire T | 25,684 |
| Palm Springs C | 40,181 | Seaside C | 38,901 | Danbury C | 65,585 |
| Palo Alto C | 55,900 | Simi Valley C | 100,217 | East Hartford T | 50,452 |
| Paradise T | 25,408 | South Gate C | 86,284 | East Haven T | 26,144 |
| Paramount C | 47,669 | South San Francisco C | 54,312 | Enfield T | 45,532 |
| Pasadena C | 131,591 | Stanton C | 30,491 | Fairfield T | 53,418 |
| Petaluma C | 43,184 | Stockton C | 210,943 | Glastonbury T | 27,901 |
| Pico Rivera C | 59,177 | Sunnyvale C | 117,229 | Greenwich T | 58,441 |
| Pittsburg C | 47,564 | Temecula C | 27,099 | Groton T | 45,144 |
| Placentia C | 41,259 | Temple City C | 31,100 | Hamden T | 52,434 |
| Pleasant Hill C | 31,585 | Thousand Oaks C | 104,352 | Hartford C | 139,739 |
| Pleasanton C | 50,553 | Torrance C | 133,107 | Manchester T | 51,618 |
| Pomona C | 131,723 | Tracy C | 33,558 | Meriden C | 59,479 |
| Porterville C | 29,563 | Tulare C | 33,249 | Middletown C | 42,762 |
| Poway C | 43,516 | Turlock C | 42,198 | Milford C | 49,938 |
| Rancho Cucamonga C | 101,409 | Tustin C | 50,689 | Naugatuck B | 30,625 |
| Rancho Palos Verdes C | 41,659 | Union City C | 53,762 | New Britain C | 75,491 |
| Redding C | 66,462 | Upland C | 63,374 | New Haven C | 130,474 |
| Redlands C | 60,394 | Vacaville C | 71,479 | Newington T | 29,208 |
| Redondo Beach C | 60,167 | Vallejo C | 109,199 | New London C | 28,540 |
| Redwood City C | 66,072 | Victorville C | 40,674 | Norwalk C | 78,331 |
| Rialto C | 72,388 | Visalia C | 75,636 | Norwich C | 37,391 |
| Richmond C | 87,425 | Vista C | 71,872 | Shelton C | 35,418 |
| Ridgecrest C | 27,725 | Walnut C | 29,105 | Southington T | 38,518 |
| Riverside C | 226,505 | Walnut Creek C | 60,569 | Stamford C | 108,056 |
| Rohnert Park C | 36,326 | Watsonville C | 31,099 | Stratford T | 49,389 |
| Rosemead C | 51,638 | West Covina C | 96,086 | Torrington C | 33,687 |
| Roseville C | 44,685 | West Hollywood C | 36,118 | Trumbull T | 32,016 |
| Sacramento C | 369,365 | Westminster C | 78,118 | Vernon T | 29,841 |
| Salinas C | 108,777 | West Sacramento C | 28,898 | Wallingford T | 40,822 |
| San Bernardino C | 164,164 | Whittier C | 77,671 | Waterbury C | 108,961 |
| San Bruno C | 38,961 | Woodland C | 39,802 | West Hartford T | 60,110 |
| San Buenaventura | | Yorba Linda C | 52,422 | West Haven C | 54,021 |
| (Ventura) C | 92,575 | Yuba City C | 27,437 | Wethersfield T | 25,651 |
| San Carlos C | 26,167 | Yucaipa C | 32,824 | Windsor T | 27,817 |
| San Clemente C | 41,100 | | | | |
| San Diego C | 1,110,549 | **COLORADO** | | **DELAWARE** | |
| San Dimas C | 32,397 | Arvada C | 89,235 | Dover C | 27,630 |
| San Francisco C | 723,959 | Aurora C | 222,103 | Newark C | 25,098 |
| San Gabriel C | 37,120 | Boulder C | 83,312 | Wilmington C | 71,529 |
| San Jose C | 782,248 | Colorado Springs C | 281,140 | | |
| San Juan Capistrano C | 26,183 | Denver C | 467,610 | **FLORIDA** | |
| San Leandro C | 68,223 | Englewood C | 29,387 | Altamonte Springs C | 34,879 |
| San Luis Obispo C | 41,958 | Fort Collins C | 87,758 | Boca Raton C | 61,492 |
| San Marcos C | 38,974 | Grand Junction C | 29,034 | Boynton Beach C | 46,194 |
| San Mateo C | 85,486 | Greeley C | 60,536 | Bradenton C | 43,779 |
| San Pablo C | 25,158 | Lakewood C | 126,481 | Cape Coral C | 74,991 |
| San Rafael C | 48,404 | Littleton C | 33,685 | Clearwater C | 98,784 |
| San Ramon C | 35,303 | Longmont C | 51,555 | Coconut Creek C | 27,485 |
| Santa Ana C | 293,742 | Loveland C | 37,352 | Coral Gables C | 40,091 |
| Santa Barbara C | 85,571 | Northglenn C | 27,195 | Coral Springs C | 79,443 |
| Santa Clara C | 93,613 | Pueblo C | 98,640 | Davie T | 47,217 |

| | | | | | | |
|---|---|---|---|---|---|
| Daytona Beach C | 61,921 | Marietta C | 44,129 | Harvey C | 29,771 |
| Deerfield Beach C | 46,325 | Rome C | 30,326 | Highland Park C | 30,575 |
| Delray Beach C | 47,181 | Roswell C | 47,923 | Hoffman Estates V | 46,561 |
| Dunedin C | 34,012 | Savannah C | 137,560 | Joliet C | 76,836 |
| Fort Lauderdale C | 149,377 | Smyrna C | 30,981 | Kankakee C | 27,575 |
| Fort Myers C | 45,206 | Valdosta C | 39,806 | Lansing V | 28,086 |
| Fort Pierce C | 36,830 | Warner Robins C | 43,726 | Lombard V | 39,408 |
| Gainesville C | 84,770 | | | Maywood V | 27,139 |
| Hallandale C | 30,996 | **HAWAII** | | Moline C | 43,202 |
| Hialeah C | 188,004 | Hilo C | 37,808 | Mount Prospect V | 53,170 |
| Hollywood C | 121,697 | Honolulu C | 365,272 | Naperville C | 85,351 |
| Homestead C | 26,866 | Kailua (Oahu) C | 36,818 | Niles V | 28,284 |
| Jacksonville C | 672,971 | Kaneohe C | 35,488 | Normal T | 40,023 |
| Kissimmee C | 30,050 | Mililani Town C | 29,359 | Northbrook V | 32,308 |
| Lakeland C | 70,576 | Pearl City C | 30,993 | North Chicago C | 34,978 |
| Lake Worth C | 28,564 | Waimalu C | 29,967 | Oak Forest C | 26,203 |
| Largo C | 65,674 | Waipahu C | 31,435 | Oak Lawn V | 56,182 |
| Lauderdale Lakes C | 27,341 | | | Oak Park V | 53,648 |
| Lauderhill C | 49,708 | **IDAHO** | | Orland Park V | 35,720 |
| Margate C | 42,985 | Boise City C | 125,738 | Palatine V | 39,253 |
| Melbourne C | 59,646 | Idaho Falls C | 43,929 | Park Ridge C | 36,175 |
| Miami C | 358,548 | Lewiston C | 28,082 | Pekin C | 32,254 |
| Miami Beach C | 92,639 | Nampa C | 28,365 | Peoria C | 113,504 |
| Miramar C | 40,663 | Pocatello C | 46,080 | Quincy C | 39,681 |
| North Lauderdale C | 26,506 | Twin Falls C | 27,591 | Rockford C | 139,426 |
| North Miami C | 49,998 | | | Rock Island C | 40,552 |
| North Miami Beach C | 35,359 | **ILLINOIS** | | Rolling Meadows C | 22,591 |
| Oakland Park C | 26,326 | Addison V | 32,058 | Schaumburg V | 68,586 |
| Ocala C | 42,045 | Alton C | 32,905 | Skokie V | 59,432 |
| Orlando C | 164,693 | Arlington Heights V | 75,460 | Springfield C | 105,227 |
| Ormond Beach C | 29,721 | Aurora C | 99,581 | Streamwood V | 30,987 |
| Palm Bay C | 62,632 | Belleville C | 42,785 | Tinley Park V | 37,121 |
| Panama City C | 34,378 | Berwyn C | 45,426 | Urbana C | 36,344 |
| Pembroke Pines C | 65,452 | Bloomington C | 51,972 | Waukegan C | 69,392 |
| Pensacola C | 58,165 | Bolingbrook V | 40,843 | Wheaton C | 51,464 |
| Pinellas Park C | 43,426 | Buffalo Grove V | 36,427 | Wheeling V | 29,911 |
| Plantation C | 66,692 | Burbank C | 27,600 | Wilmette V | 26,690 |
| Pompano Beach C | 72,411 | Calumet City C | 37,840 | Woodridge V | 26,256 |
| Port Orange C | 35,317 | Carbondale C | 27,033 | | |
| Port St. Lucie C | 55,866 | Carol Stream V | 31,716 | **INDIANA** | |
| Riviera Beach C | 27,639 | Champaign C | 63,502 | Anderson C | 59,459 |
| St. Petersburg C | 238,629 | Chicago C | 2,783,726 | Bloomington C | 60,633 |
| Sanford C | 32,387 | Chicago Heights C | 33,072 | Carmel C | 25,380 |
| Sarasota C | 50,961 | Cicero T | 67,436 | Columbus C | 31,802 |
| Sunrise C | 64,407 | Danville C | 33,828 | East Chicago C | 33,892 |
| Tallahassee C | 124,773 | Decatur C | 83,885 | Elkhart C | 43,627 |
| Tamarac C | 44,822 | De Kalb C | 34,925 | Evansville C | 126,272 |
| Tampa C | 280,015 | Des Plaines C | 53,223 | Fort Wayne C | 173,072 |
| Titusville C | 39,394 | Downers Grove V | 46,858 | Gary C | 116,646 |
| West Palm Beach C | 67,643 | East St. Louis C | 40,944 | Greenwood C | 26,265 |
| | | Elgin C | 77,010 | Hammond C | 84,236 |
| **GEORGIA** | | Elk Grove Village V | 33,429 | Indianapolis C | 741,952 |
| Albany C | 78,122 | Elmhurst C | 42,029 | Kokomo C | 44,962 |
| Athens C | 45,734 | Evanston C | 73,233 | Lafayette C | 43,764 |
| Atlanta C | 394,017 | Freeport C | 25,840 | Lawrence C | 26,763 |
| Augusta C | 44,639 | Galesburg C | 33,530 | Marion C | 32,618 |
| Columbus C | 179,278 | Glendale Heights V | 27,973 | Merrillville T | 27,257 |
| East Point C | 34,402 | Glenview V | 37,093 | Michigan City C | 33,822 |
| La Grange C | 25,597 | Granite City C | 32,862 | Mishawaka C | 42,608 |
| Macon C | 106,612 | Hanover Park V | 32,895 | Muncie C | 71,035 |

| | | | | | | |
|---|---|---|---|---|---|---|
| New Albany C | 36,322 | New Iberia C | 31,828 | Newton C | 82,585 |
| Portage C | 29,060 | New Orleans C | 496,938 | Northampton C | 29,289 |
| Richmond C | 38,705 | Shreveport C | 198,525 | North Attleborough T | 25,038 |
| South Bend C | 105,511 | | | Norwood T | 28,700 |
| Terre Haute C | 57,483 | **MAINE** | | Peabody C | 47,039 |
| West Lafayette C | 25,907 | Bangor C | 33,181 | Pittsfield C | 48,622 |
| | | Lewiston C | 39,757 | Plymouth T | 45,608 |
| **IOWA** | | Portland C | 64,358 | Quincy C | 84,985 |
| Ames C | 47,198 | | | Randolph T | 30,093 |
| Bettendorf C | 28,132 | **MARYLAND** | | Revere C | 42,786 |
| Burlington C | 27,208 | Annapolis C | 33,187 | Salem C | 38,091 |
| Cedar Falls C | 34,298 | Baltimore C | 736,014 | Saugus T | 25,549 |
| Cedar Rapids C | 108,751 | Bowie C | 37,589 | Somerville C | 76,210 |
| Clinton C | 29,201 | Frederick C | 40,148 | Springfield C | 156,983 |
| Council Bluffs C | 54,315 | Gaithersburg C | 39,542 | Stoughton T | 26,777 |
| Davenport C | 95,333 | Hagerstown C | 35,445 | Taunton C | 49,832 |
| Des Moines C | 193,187 | Rockville C | 44,835 | Tewksbury T | 27,266 |
| Dubuque C | 57,546 | | | Waltham C | 57,878 |
| Fort Dodge C | 25,894 | **MASSACHUSETTS** | | Watertown T | 33,284 |
| Iowa City C | 59,738 | Agawam T | 27,323 | Wellesley T | 26,615 |
| Marshalltown C | 25,178 | Amherst T | 35,228 | Westfield C | 38,372 |
| Mason City C | 29,040 | Andover T | 29,151 | West Springfield T | 27,537 |
| Sioux City C | 80,505 | Arlington T | 44,630 | Weymouth T | 54,063 |
| Waterloo C | 66,467 | Attleboro C | 38,383 | Woburn C | 35,943 |
| West Des Moines C | 31,702 | Barnstable T | 40,949 | Worcester C | 169,759 |
| | | Beverly C | 38,195 | | |
| **KANSAS** | | Billerica T | 37,609 | **MICHIGAN** | |
| Emporia C | 25,512 | Boston C | 574,283 | Allen Park C | 31,092 |
| Hutchinson C | 39,308 | Braintree T | 33,836 | Ann Arbor C | 109,592 |
| Kansas City C | 149,767 | Brockton C | 92,788 | Battle Creek C | 53,540 |
| Lawrence C | 65,608 | Brookline T | 54,718 | Bay City C | 38,936 |
| Leavenworth C | 38,495 | Cambridge C | 95,802 | Burton C | 27,617 |
| Lenexa C | 34,034 | Chelmsford T | 32,383 | Dearborn C | 89,286 |
| Manhattan C | 37,712 | Chelsea C | 28,710 | Dearborn Heights C | 60,838 |
| Olathe C | 63,352 | Chicopee C | 56,632 | Detroit C | 1,027,974 |
| Overland Park C | 111,790 | Dartmouth T | 27,244 | East Detroit C | 35,283 |
| Salina C | 42,303 | Dracut T | 25,594 | East Lansing C | 50,667 |
| Shawnee C | 37,993 | Everett C | 35,701 | Farmington Hills C | 74,652 |
| Topeka C | 119,883 | Fall River C | 92,703 | Ferndale C | 25,084 |
| Wichita C | 304,011 | Falmouth T | 27,960 | Flint C | 140,761 |
| | | Fitchburg C | 41,194 | Garden City C | 31,846 |
| **KENTUCKY** | | Framingham T | 64,989 | Grand Rapids C | 189,126 |
| Bowling Green C | 40,641 | Gloucester C | 28,716 | Holland C | 30,745 |
| Covington C | 43,264 | Haverhill C | 51,418 | Inkster C | 30,772 |
| Frankfort C | 25,968 | Holyoke C | 43,704 | Jackson C | 37,446 |
| Henderson C | 25,945 | Lawrence C | 70,207 | Kalamazoo C | 80,277 |
| Hopkinsville C | 29,809 | Leominster C | 38,145 | Kentwood C | 37,826 |
| Lexington-Fayette C | 225,366 | Lexington T | 28,974 | Lansing C | 127,321 |
| Louisville C | 269,063 | Lowell C | 103,439 | Lincoln Park C | 41,832 |
| Owensboro C | 53,549 | Lynn C | 81,245 | Livonia C | 100,850 |
| Paducah C | 27,256 | Malden C | 53,884 | Madison Heights C | 32,196 |
| | | Marlborough C | 31,813 | Midland C | 38,053 |
| **LOUISIANA** | | Medford C | 57,407 | Muskegon C | 40,283 |
| Alexandria C | 49,188 | Melrose C | 28,150 | Novi C | 32,998 |
| Baton Rouge C | 219,531 | Methuen T | 39,990 | Oak Park C | 30,462 |
| Bossier City C | 52,721 | Milford T | 25,355 | Pontiac C | 71,166 |
| Kenner C | 72,033 | Milton T | 25,725 | Portage C | 41,042 |
| Lafayette C | 94,440 | Natick T | 30,510 | Port Huron C | 33,694 |
| Lake Charles C | 70,580 | Needham T | 27,557 | Rochester Hills C | 61,766 |
| Monroe C | 54,909 | New Bedford C | 99,922 | Roseville C | 51,412 |

388

Royal Oak C . . . . . . . . . . . . 65,410
Saginaw C . . . . . . . . . . . . . 69,512
St. Clair Shores C . . . . . . . 68,107
Southfield C . . . . . . . . . . . 75,728
Southgate C . . . . . . . . . . . 30,771
Sterling Heights C . . . . . . 117,810
Taylor C . . . . . . . . . . . . . . 70,811
Troy C . . . . . . . . . . . . . . . . 72,884
Warren C . . . . . . . . . . . . . 144,864
Westland C . . . . . . . . . . . . 84,724
Wyandotte C . . . . . . . . . . . 30,938
Wyoming C . . . . . . . . . . . 63,891

## MINNESOTA
Apple Valley C . . . . . . . . . 34,598
Blaine C . . . . . . . . . . . . . . 38,975
Bloomington C . . . . . . . . . 86,335
Brooklyn Center C . . . . . . 28,887
Brooklyn Park C . . . . . . . . 56,381
Burnsville C . . . . . . . . . . . . 51,288
Coon Rapids C . . . . . . . . . 52,978
Duluth C . . . . . . . . . . . . . 85,493
Eagan C . . . . . . . . . . . . . . 47,409
Eden Prairie C . . . . . . . . . 39,311
Edina C . . . . . . . . . . . . . . 46,070
Fridley C . . . . . . . . . . . . . 28,335
Mankato C . . . . . . . . . . . . 31,477
Maple Grove C . . . . . . . . . 38,736
Maplewood C . . . . . . . . . 30,954
Minneapolis C . . . . . . . . . 368,383
Minnetonka C . . . . . . . . . 48,370
Moorhead C . . . . . . . . . . . 32,295
Plymouth C . . . . . . . . . . . 50,889
Richfield C . . . . . . . . . . . 35,710
Rochester C . . . . . . . . . . . 70,745
Roseville C . . . . . . . . . . . . 33,485
St. Cloud C . . . . . . . . . . . 48,812
St. Louis Park C . . . . . . . . 43,787
Saint Paul C . . . . . . . . . . 272,235
Winona C . . . . . . . . . . . . . 25,399

## MISSISSIPPI
Biloxi C . . . . . . . . . . . . . . 46,319
Greenville C . . . . . . . . . . . 45,226
Gulfport C . . . . . . . . . . . . 40,775
Hattiesburg C . . . . . . . . . . 41,882
Jackson C . . . . . . . . . . . . . 196,637
Meridian C . . . . . . . . . . . . 41,036
Pascagoula C . . . . . . . . . . 25,899
Tupelo C . . . . . . . . . . . . . 30,685

## MISSOURI
Blue Springs C . . . . . . . . . 40,153
Cape Girardeau C . . . . . . . 34,438
Chesterfield C . . . . . . . . . 37,991
Columbia C . . . . . . . . . . . 69,101
Florissant C . . . . . . . . . . . 51,206
Gladstone C . . . . . . . . . . . 26,243
Independence C . . . . . . . . 112,301
Jefferson City C . . . . . . . . 25,481

Joplin C . . . . . . . . . . . . . . 40,961
Kansas City C . . . . . . . . . . 435,146
Kirkwood C . . . . . . . . . . . 27,291
Lee's Summit C . . . . . . . . 46,418
Maryland Heights C . . . . . 25,407
Raytown C . . . . . . . . . . . . 30,601
St. Charles C . . . . . . . . . . 54,555
St. Joseph C . . . . . . . . . . . 71,852
St. Louis C . . . . . . . . . . . . 396,685
St. Peters C . . . . . . . . . . . 45,779
Springfield C . . . . . . . . . . 140,494
University City C . . . . . . . . 40,087

## MONTANA
Billings C . . . . . . . . . . . . . 81,151
Butte-Silver Bow C . . . . . . 33,941
Great Falls C . . . . . . . . . . 55,097
Missoula C . . . . . . . . . . . . 42,918

## NEBRASKA
Bellevue C . . . . . . . . . . . . 30,982
Grand Island C . . . . . . . . . 39,386
Lincoln C . . . . . . . . . . . . . 191,972
Omaha C . . . . . . . . . . . . . 335,795

## NEVADA
Carson City C . . . . . . . . . 40,443
Henderson C . . . . . . . . . . 64,942
Las Vegas C . . . . . . . . . . . 258,295
North Las Vegas C . . . . . . 47,707
Reno C . . . . . . . . . . . . . . . 133,850
Sparks C . . . . . . . . . . . . . 53,367

## NEW HAMPSHIRE
Concord C . . . . . . . . . . . . 36,006
Derry T . . . . . . . . . . . . . . 29,603
Dover C . . . . . . . . . . . . . . 25,042
Manchester C . . . . . . . . . 99,567
Nashua C . . . . . . . . . . . . . 79,662
Portsmouth C . . . . . . . . . 25,925
Rochester C . . . . . . . . . . . 26,630
Salem T . . . . . . . . . . . . . . 25,746

## NEW JERSEY
Altantic City C . . . . . . . . . 37,986
Bayonne C . . . . . . . . . . . . 61,444
Camden C . . . . . . . . . . . . 87,492
Clifton C . . . . . . . . . . . . . 71,742
East Orange C . . . . . . . . . 73,552
Elizabeth C . . . . . . . . . . . 110,002
Fair Lawn B . . . . . . . . . . . 30,548
Fort Lee B . . . . . . . . . . . . 31,997
Garfield C . . . . . . . . . . . . 26,727
Hackensack C . . . . . . . . . 37,049
Hoboken C . . . . . . . . . . . . 33,397
Jersey City C . . . . . . . . . . 228,537
Kearny T . . . . . . . . . . . . . 34,874
Linden C . . . . . . . . . . . . . 36,701
Long Branch C . . . . . . . . . 28,658
Millville C . . . . . . . . . . . . 25,992

Newark C . . . . . . . . . . . . . 275,221
New Brunswick C . . . . . . . 41,711
Paramus B . . . . . . . . . . . . 25,067
Passaic C . . . . . . . . . . . . . 58,041
Paterson C . . . . . . . . . . . . 140,891
Perth Amboy C . . . . . . . . 41,967
Plainfield C . . . . . . . . . . . 46,567
Rahway C . . . . . . . . . . . . . 25,325
Sayreville B . . . . . . . . . . . 34,986
Trenton C . . . . . . . . . . . . . 88,675
Union City C . . . . . . . . . . 58,012
Vineland C . . . . . . . . . . . . 54,780
Westfield T . . . . . . . . . . . . 28,870
West New York T . . . . . . . 38,125

## NEW MEXICO
Alamogordo C . . . . . . . . . 27,596
Albuquerque C . . . . . . . . . 384,736
Clovis C . . . . . . . . . . . . . . 30,954
Farmington C . . . . . . . . . . 33,997
Hobbs C . . . . . . . . . . . . . . 29,115
Las Cruces C . . . . . . . . . . 62,126
Rio Rancho C . . . . . . . . . . 32,505
Roswell C . . . . . . . . . . . . . 44,654
Santa Fe C . . . . . . . . . . . . 55,859

## NEW YORK
Albany C . . . . . . . . . . . . . 101,082
Auburn C . . . . . . . . . . . . . 31,258
Binghamton C . . . . . . . . . 53,008
Buffalo C . . . . . . . . . . . . . 328,123
Elmira C . . . . . . . . . . . . . . 33,724
Freeport V . . . . . . . . . . . . 39,894
Hempstead V . . . . . . . . . . 49,453
Ithaca C . . . . . . . . . . . . . . 29,541
Jamestown C . . . . . . . . . . 34,681
Lindenhurst V . . . . . . . . . 26,879
Long Beach C . . . . . . . . . . 33,510
Mount Vernon C . . . . . . . . 67,153
Newburgh C . . . . . . . . . . . 26,454
New Rochelle C . . . . . . . . 67,265
New York C . . . . . . . . . 7,322,564
Niagara Falls C . . . . . . . . . 61,840
North Tonawanda C . . . . . 34,989
Poughkeepsie C . . . . . . . . 28,844
Rochester C . . . . . . . . . . . 231,636
Rome C . . . . . . . . . . . . . . 44,350
Saratoga Springs C . . . . . . 25,001
Schenectady C . . . . . . . . . 65,566
Syracuse C . . . . . . . . . . . . 163,860
Troy C . . . . . . . . . . . . . . . 54,269
Utica C . . . . . . . . . . . . . . . 68,637
Valley Stream V . . . . . . . . 33,946
Watertown C . . . . . . . . . . 29,429
White Plains C . . . . . . . . . 48,718
Yonkers C . . . . . . . . . . . . 188,082

## NORTH CAROLINA
Asheville C . . . . . . . . . . . 61,607
Burlington C . . . . . . . . . . . 39,498

| | | |
|---|---|---|
| Cary T | 43,858 | |
| Chapel Hill T | 38,719 | |
| Charlotte C | 395,934 | |
| Concord C | 27,347 | |
| Durham C | 136,611 | |
| Fayetteville C | 75,695 | |
| Gastonia C | 54,732 | |
| Goldsboro C | 40,709 | |
| Greensboro C | 183,521 | |
| Greenville C | 44,972 | |
| Hickory C | 28,301 | |
| High Point C | 69,496 | |
| Jacksonville C | 30,013 | |
| Kannapolis C | 29,696 | |
| Kinston C | 25,295 | |
| Raleigh C | 207,951 | |
| Rocky Mount C | 48,997 | |
| Wilmington C | 55,530 | |
| Wilson C | 36,930 | |
| Winston-Salem C | 143,485 | |

## NORTH DAKOTA

| | |
|---|---|
| Bismarck C | 49,256 |
| Fargo C | 74,111 |
| Grand Forks C | 49,425 |
| Minot C | 34,544 |

## OHIO

| | |
|---|---|
| Akron C | 223,019 |
| Barberton C | 27,623 |
| Beavercreek C | 33,626 |
| Bowling Green C | 28,176 |
| Brunswick C | 28,230 |
| Canton C | 84,161 |
| Cincinnati C | 364,040 |
| Cleveland C | 505,616 |
| Cleveland Heights C | 54,052 |
| Columbus C | 632,910 |
| Cuyahoga Falls C | 48,950 |
| Dayton C | 182,044 |
| East Cleveland C | 33,096 |
| Elyria C | 56,746 |
| Euclid C | 54,875 |
| Fairborn C | 31,300 |
| Fairfield C | 39,729 |
| Findlay C | 35,703 |
| Gahanna C | 27,791 |
| Garfield Heights C | 31,739 |
| Hamilton C | 61,368 |
| Huber Heights C | 38,696 |
| Kent C | 28,835 |
| Kettering C | 60,569 |
| Lakewood C | 59,718 |
| Lancaster C | 34,507 |
| Lima C | 45,549 |
| Lorain C | 71,245 |
| Mansfield C | 50,627 |
| Maple Heights C | 27,089 |
| Marion C | 34,075 |
| Massillon C | 31,007 |

| | |
|---|---|
| Mentor C | 47,358 |
| Middletown C | 46,022 |
| Newark C | 44,389 |
| North Olmsted C | 34,204 |
| Parma C | 87,876 |
| Reynoldsburg C | 25,748 |
| Sandusky C | 29,764 |
| Shaker Heights C | 30,831 |
| Springfield C | 70,487 |
| Stow C | 27,702 |
| Strongsville C | 35,308 |
| Toledo C | 332,943 |
| Upper Arlington C | 34,128 |
| Warren C | 50,793 |
| Westerville C | 30,269 |
| Westlake C | 27,018 |
| Youngstown C | 95,732 |
| Zanesville C | 26,778 |

## OKLAHOMA

| | |
|---|---|
| Bartlesville C | 34,256 |
| Broken Arrow C | 58,043 |
| Edmond C | 52,315 |
| Enid C | 45,309 |
| Lawton C | 80,561 |
| Midwest City C | 52,267 |
| Moore C | 40,318 |
| Muskogee C | 37,708 |
| Norman C | 80,071 |
| Oklahoma City C | 444,719 |
| Ponca City C | 26,359 |
| Shawnee C | 26,017 |
| Stillwater C | 36,676 |
| Tulsa C | 367,302 |

## OREGON

| | |
|---|---|
| Albany C | 29,462 |
| Beaverton C | 53,310 |
| Corvallis C | 44,757 |
| Eugene C | 112,669 |
| Gresham C | 68,235 |
| Hillsboro C | 37,520 |
| Lake Oswego C | 30,576 |
| Medford C | 46,951 |
| Portland C | 437,319 |
| Salem C | 107,786 |
| Springfield C | 44,683 |
| Tigard C | 29,344 |

## PENNSYLVANIA

| | |
|---|---|
| Allentown C | 105,090 |
| Altoona C | 51,881 |
| Bethel Park B | 33,823 |
| Bethlehem C | 71,428 |
| Chester C | 41,856 |
| Easton C | 26,276 |
| Erie C | 108,718 |
| Harrisburg C | 52,376 |
| Johnstown C | 28,134 |
| Lancaster C | 55,551 |

| | |
|---|---|
| McKeesport C | 26,016 |
| Monroeville B | 29,169 |
| New Castle C | 28,334 |
| Norristown B | 30,749 |
| Philadelphia C | 1,585,577 |
| Pittsburgh C | 369,879 |
| Plum B | 25,609 |
| Reading C | 78,380 |
| Scranton C | 81,805 |
| State College B | 38,923 |
| Wilkes-Barre C | 47,523 |
| Williamsport C | 31,933 |
| York C | 42,192 |

## RHODE ISLAND

| | |
|---|---|
| Coventry T | 31,083 |
| Cranston C | 76,060 |
| Cumberland T | 29,038 |
| East Providence C | 50,380 |
| Johnston T | 26,542 |
| Newport C | 28,227 |
| North Providence T | 32,090 |
| Pawtucket C | 72,644 |
| Providence C | 160,728 |
| Warwick C | 85,427 |
| West Warwick T | 29,268 |
| Woonsocket C | 43,877 |

## SOUTH CAROLINA

| | |
|---|---|
| Anderson C | 26,184 |
| Charleston C | 80,414 |
| Columbia C | 98,052 |
| Florence C | 29,813 |
| Greenville C | 58,282 |
| Mount Pleasant T | 30,108 |
| North Charleston C | 70,218 |
| Rock Hill C | 41,643 |
| Spartanburg C | 43,467 |
| Sumter C | 41,943 |

## SOUTH DAKOTA

| | |
|---|---|
| Rapid City C | 54,523 |
| Sioux Falls C | 100,814 |

## TENNESSEE

| | |
|---|---|
| Bartlett T | 26,989 |
| Chattanooga C | 152,466 |
| Clarksville C | 75,494 |
| Cleveland C | 30,354 |
| Columbia C | 28,583 |
| Germantown C | 32,893 |
| Hendersonville C | 32,188 |
| Jackson C | 48,949 |
| Johnson City C | 49,381 |
| Kingsport C | 36,365 |
| Knoxville C | 165,121 |
| Memphis C | 610,337 |
| Murfreesboro C | 44,922 |
| Nashville–Davidson C | 510,784 |
| Oak Ridge C | 27,310 |

## TEXAS

| | |
|---|---|
| Abilene C | 106,654 |
| Amarillo C | 157,615 |
| Arlington C | 261,721 |
| Austin C | 465,622 |
| Baytown C | 63,850 |
| Beaumont C | 114,323 |
| Bedford C | 43,762 |
| Brownsville C | 98,962 |
| Bryan C | 55,002 |
| Carrollton C | 82,169 |
| College Station C | 52,456 |
| Conroe C | 27,610 |
| Corpus Christi C | 257,453 |
| Dallas C | 1,006,877 |
| Deer Park C | 27,652 |
| Del Rio C | 30,705 |
| Denton C | 66,270 |
| DeSoto C | 30,544 |
| Duncanville C | 35,748 |
| Edinburg C | 29,885 |
| El Paso C | 515,342 |
| Euless C | 38,149 |
| Fort Worth C | 447,619 |
| Galveston C | 59,070 |
| Garland C | 180,650 |
| Grand Prairie C | 99,616 |
| Grapevine C | 29,202 |
| Haltom City C | 32,856 |
| Harlingen C | 48,735 |
| Houston C | 1,630,553 |
| Huntsville C | 27,925 |
| Hurst C | 33,574 |
| Irving C | 155,037 |
| Killeen C | 63,535 |
| Kingsville C | 25,276 |
| La Porte C | 27,910 |
| Laredo C | 122,899 |
| League City C | 30,159 |
| Lewisville C | 46,521 |
| Longview C | 70,311 |
| Lubbock C | 186,206 |
| Lufkin C | 30,206 |
| McAllen C | 84,021 |
| Mesquite C | 101,484 |
| Midland C | 89,443 |
| Mission C | 28,653 |
| Missouri City C | 36,176 |
| Nacogdoches C | 30,872 |
| New Braunfels C | 27,334 |
| North Richland Hills C | 45,895 |
| Odessa C | 89,699 |
| Pasadena C | 119,363 |
| Pharr C | 32,921 |
| Plano C | 128,713 |
| Port Arthur C | 58,724 |
| Richardson C | 74,840 |
| Round Rock C | 30,923 |
| San Angelo C | 84,474 |
| San Antonio C | 935,933 |
| San Marcos C | 28,743 |
| Sherman C | 31,601 |
| Temple C | 46,109 |
| Texarkana C | 31,656 |
| Texas City C | 40,822 |
| Tyler C | 75,450 |
| Victoria C | 55,076 |
| Waco C | 103,590 |
| Wichita Falls C | 96,259 |

## UTAH

| | |
|---|---|
| Bountiful C | 36,659 |
| Layton C | 41,784 |
| Logan C | 32,762 |
| Murray C | 31,282 |
| Ogden C | 69,909 |
| Orem C | 67,561 |
| Provo C | 86,835 |
| St. George C | 28,502 |
| Salt Lake City C | 159,936 |
| Sandy C | 75,058 |
| West Jordan C | 42,892 |
| West Valley City C | 86,976 |

## VERMONT

| | |
|---|---|
| Burlington C | 39,127 |

## VIRGINIA

| | |
|---|---|
| Alexandria C | 111,183 |
| Blacksburg T | 34,590 |
| Charlottesville C | 40,341 |
| Chesapeake C | 151,976 |
| Danville C | 53,056 |
| Hampton C | 133,793 |
| Harrisonburg C | 30,707 |
| Lynchburg C | 66,049 |
| Manassas C | 27,957 |
| Newport News C | 170,045 |
| Norfolk C | 261,229 |
| Petersburg C | 38,386 |
| Portsmouth C | 103,907 |
| Richmond C | 203,056 |
| Roanoke C | 96,397 |
| Suffolk C | 52,141 |
| Virginia Beach C | 393,069 |

## WASHINGTON

| | |
|---|---|
| Auburn C | 33,102 |
| Bellevue C | 86,874 |
| Bellingham C | 52,179 |
| Bremerton C | 38,142 |
| Edmonds C | 30,744 |
| Everett C | 69,961 |
| Kennewick C | 42,155 |
| Kent C | 37,960 |
| Kirkland C | 40,052 |
| Longview C | 31,499 |
| Lynnwood C | 28,695 |
| Olympia C | 33,840 |
| Redmond C | 35,800 |
| Renton C | 41,688 |
| Richland C | 32,315 |
| Seattle C | 516,259 |
| Spokane C | 177,196 |
| Tacoma C | 176,664 |
| Vancouver C | 46,380 |
| Walla Walla C | 26,478 |
| Yakima C | 54,827 |

## WEST VIRGINIA

| | |
|---|---|
| Charleston C | 57,287 |
| Huntington C | 54,844 |
| Morgantown C | 25,879 |
| Parkersburg C | 33,862 |
| Wheeling C | 34,882 |

## WISCONSIN

| | |
|---|---|
| Appleton C | 65,695 |
| Beloit C | 35,573 |
| Brookfield C | 35,184 |
| Eau Claire C | 56,856 |
| Fond du Lac C | 37,757 |
| Green Bay C | 96,466 |
| Greenfield C | 33,403 |
| Janesville C | 52,133 |
| Kenosha C | 80,352 |
| La Crosse C | 51,003 |
| Madison C | 191,262 |
| Manitowoc C | 32,520 |
| Menomonee Falls V | 26,840 |
| Milwaukee C | 628,088 |
| New Berlin C | 33,592 |
| Oshkosh C | 55,006 |
| Racine C | 84,298 |
| Sheboygan C | 49,676 |
| Superior C | 27,134 |
| Waukesha C | 56,958 |
| Wausau C | 37,060 |
| Wauwatosa C | 49,366 |
| West Allis C | 63,221 |

## WYOMING

| | |
|---|---|
| Casper C | 46,742 |
| Cheyenne C | 50,008 |
| Laramie C | 26,687 |

# CANADA

**Capital:** Ottawa
**Head of State:** Queen Elizabeth II
**Governor General:** Ramon Hnatyshyn
**Prime Minister:** Martin Brian Mulroney (Progressive Conservative)
**Leader of the Opposition:** Jean Chrétien (Liberal)
**Population:** 27,023,100
**Area:** 3,851,809 sq mi (9,976,185 km²)

## PROVINCES AND TERRITORIES

### Alberta
Capital: Edmonton
Lieutenant Governor: Gordon Towers
Premier: Donald R. Getty (Progressive Conservative)
Leader of the Opposition: Ray Martin (New Democratic Party)
Entered Confederation: Sept. 1, 1905
Population: 2,525,200
Area: 255,285 sq mi (661,188 km²)

### British Columbia
Capital: Victoria
Lieutenant Governor: David C. Lam
Premier: Michael F. Harcourt (New Democratic Party)
Leader of the Opposition: Gordon Wilson (Liberal)
Entered Confederation: July 20, 1871
Population: 3,218,900
Area: 366,255 sq mi (948,600 km²)

### Manitoba
Capital: Winnipeg
Lieutenant Governor: George Johnson
Premier: Gary Filmon (Progressive Conservative)
Leader of the Opposition: Sharon Carstairs (Liberal)
Entered Confederation: July 15, 1870
Population: 1,097,000
Area: 251,000 sq mi (650,090 km²)

### New Brunswick
Capital: Fredericton
Lieutenant Governor: Gilbert Finn
Premier: Frank McKenna (Liberal)
Leader of the Opposition: Danny Cameron, interim leader
  (Confederation of Regions)
Entered Confederation: July 1, 1867
Population: 727,300
Area: 28,354 sq mi (73,436 km²)

### Newfoundland
Capital: St. John's
Lieutenant Governor: Frederik W. Russell
Premier: Clyde Wells (Liberal)
Leader of the Opposition: Leonard Simms
  (Progressive Conservative)
Entered Confederation: March 31, 1949
Population: 574,300
Area: 156,185 sq mi (404,517 km²)

### Nova Scotia
Capital: Halifax
Lieutenant Governor: Lloyd Crouse
Premier: Donald W. Cameron (Progressive
  Conservative)
Leader of the Opposition: Vincent J. MacLean (Liberal)
Entered Confederation: July 1, 1867
Population: 900,800
Area: 21,425 sq mi (55,491 km²)

### Ontario
Capital: Toronto
Lieutenant Governor: Hal Jackman
Premier: David Peterson (Liberal)
Leader of the Opposition Party: Murray Elston (Liberal)
Entered Confederation: July 1, 1867
Population: 9,919,400
Area: 412,582 sq mi (1,068,582 km²)

### Prince Edward Island
Capital: Charlottetown
Lieutenant Governor: Lloyd G. MacPhail
Premier: Joseph A. Ghiz (Liberal)
Leader of the Opposition: Leone Bagnall (Progressive
  Conservative)
Entered Confederation: July 1, 1873
Population: 130,100
Area: 2,184 sq mi (5,657 km²)

### Quebec

Capital: Quebec City
Lieutenant Governor: Gilles Lamontagne
Premier: Robert Bourassa (Liberal)
Leader of the Opposition: Jacques Parizeau (Parti Québécois)
Entered Confederation: July 1, 1867
Population: 6,850,900
Area: 594,860 sq mi (1,540,700 km²)

### Saskatchewan

Capital: Regina
Lieutenant Governor: Sylvia Fedoruk
Premier: Roy Romanow (New Democratic Party)
Leader of the Opposition: Grant Devine (Progressive Conservative)
Entered Confederation: Sept. 1, 1905
Population: 997,400
Area: 251,700 sq mi (651,900 km²)

### Northwest Territories

Capital: Yellowknife
Commissioner: Daniel L. Norris
Government Leader: Nellie Cournoyea
Reconstituted as a Territory: Sept. 1, 1905
Population: 54,800
Area: 1,304,896 sq mi (3,379,684 km²)

### Yukon Territory

Capital: Whitehorse
Commissioner: J. Kenneth McKinnon
Premier: Tony Penikett (New Democratic Party)
Leader of the Opposition: Dan Lang (Progressive Conservative)
Organized as a Territory: June 13, 1898
Population: 27,000
Area: 186,299 sq mi (482,515 km²)

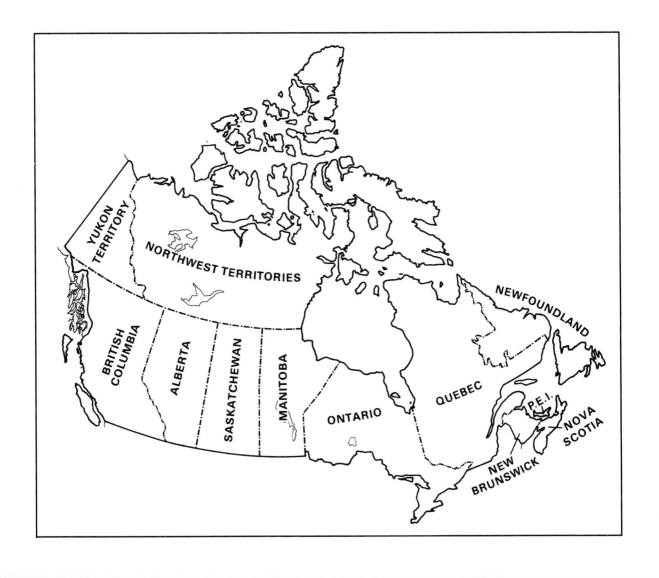

# INDEX

## A

**Abstract art,** nonrepresentational art 345
**Academy Awards,** movies 248; pictures 249, 255
**Accidents and disasters**
 cyclone, Bangladesh 22
 drought, California 19
 earthquake, India 35
 earthquake, Pakistan and Afghanistan 18
 fire, California 34
 flood, China 28
 flood and landslide, Philippines 36
 oil spill, Antarctica 120
 oil spill, Persian Gulf 46, 96
 oil wells, Kuwait 44, 46; picture 12–13
 ship collision, Pacific Ocean 28
 volcanic eruption, Japan 27
 volcanic eruption, Pacific Ocean Ring of Fire 27
 volcanic eruption, Philippines 27, 133
**Adamson, James C.,** American astronaut 30
**Afansev, Viktor,** Soviet astronaut 128–29
**Afghanistan** 374
 earthquake 18
**Africa**
 antelopes 326–27
**African National Congress (ANC),** South African black-
  rights party 54–55
**Agriculture**
 country fairs 190–93
 crop circles 124–25
 plant-eating beetles 362
 scarecrows 212–15
**Agriculture, United States Department of**
 secretary nomination 17
**Aho, Esko,** premier of Finland
 named 22
**AIDS (acquired immune deficiency syndrome),** disease
 *For Our Children,* record album to benefit foundation
  for child victims 267
**Air pollution** 23
 burning Kuwaiti oil wells, picture 12–13
 national parks, U.S. 31
**Akbulut, Yildirim,** prime minister of Turkey
 resigned 35
**Alabama**
 census figures 384, 385
**Alaska**
 anniversary of U.S. purchase 39
 census figures 384, 385

**Albania** 374
 elections 20, 63
 Warsaw Pact membership 18
**Alberta,** province, Canada 392
**Algae,** underwater plant
 coral reef pollution 95
**Algeria** 374
 Islamic fundamentalism 52
**Alia, Ramiz,** president of Albania
 resigned as Communist Party leader 20
***Alice's Adventures in Wonderland,*** book by Lewis Carroll
 virtual reality system 103; picture 100
**Alley, Kirstie,** American actress, picture 268
**Allison, Emily,** American photography contest winner,
  picture 236
**Amundsen, Roald,** Norwegian explorer 347
**Anand Panyarachun,** premier of Thailand
 named 18
**Anatomy,** body parts
 animal faces 74–75
 beetle 358–59
**Anderson, Terry,** American hostage in Lebanon
 freed 38, 53; picture 38
**Anderson, Ottis,** American athlete 172, 173
**Angola** 374
 civil war end 24
**Animals**
 animals in the news, pictures 88–91
 Antarctica 118, 119, 121
 antelopes 326–27
 behavior during solar eclipse 133
 biomes 314–20
 *Birds and Beasts,* book by William Jay Smith, picture
  283
 coelacanth, water-dwelling ancestor 25
 coral polyps 92–97
 endangered 70–73, 75, 83, 88, 89, 90, 327
 faces, pictures 74–75
 lizards 76–83; pictures 69–70
 mystery creatures 202–03
 pandas 70–73, 159
 Potter, Beatrix, illustrations of 270–71
 puzzles 152, 153
 record album to benefit animal rights group 267
 stamps 145
 Westminster Kennel Club dog show winner, picture 91
 *Wind in the Willows, The,* book by Kenneth Grahame
  302–12
 *see also* specific animals
**Anniversaries** 39
 Columbus, Christopher, arrival in New World 34, 39,
  159, 194–201

# C

397

# F

# G

**Gandhi, Rajiv,** prime minister of India
 assassinated 24, 371
**Gardening**
 wildflowers 112–13
*Garfield—Am I Cool or What?,* record album 266
**Gaza Strip,** Israeli-occupied territory 50, 51
**Gecko,** lizard 76, 78, 79, 82, 83; picture 69–70
**Geisel, Theodor Seuss (Dr. Seuss),** American author and
 illustrator 371
**Gemar, Charles D.,** American astronaut 32
**Geography**
 puzzle 147
**Georgia,** U.S. state
 census figures 384, 387
 Stone Mountain 206
**Georgia,** Soviet republic
 independence move 60
**Geostationary Operational Environmental Satellites
 (GOES),** weather satellites
 cloud-movement measurement, picture 131
**German Democratic Republic (East Germany)**
 Warsaw Pact membership 18
**Germany** 375
 Berlin 336–39
 economic summit participation 28
 economy 49
 hostages in Lebanon 38, 53
 Nobel Prize for Physiology or Medicine 35
 Yugoslavian Civil War 62
**Getz, Stan,** American musician 371
**Ghali, Boutros,** secretary general of the United Nations
 named 36
**Ghana** 376
*Ghost,* movie, picture 249
**Giacometti, Alberto,** Swiss artist 254
**Giannini, Enzo,** American writer and illustrator
 *Little Parsley,* book, picture 286
**Gila monster,** lizard 76, 81
*Glasnost,* Soviet openness policy 57–58
**Glass lizard,** reptile 77, 81
**Gleyre, Charles,** Swiss painter 251
**Global warming,** atmospheric buildup of carbon dioxide
 and other gases 23, 94–95, 320
**Gobel, George,** American comedian 371
**Godwin, Linda M.,** American astronaut 22
**Goetz-Adlerstein, Eva,** American artist
 toy design, picture 229
**Golan Heights,** Israel
 settlements 51
**Goldberg, Whoopi,** American actress, picture 249
**Golf,** sport 175
**Goods, economic,** tangible things of value 348, 349–50
**Gorbachev, Mikhail S.,** president of Soviet Union
 coup attempt against 30, 57–58, 59; picture 58
 nuclear arms reduction treaty 32, 61; picture 28
 restructuring and openness policies 28, 57–58
 Soviet Union dissolution 39
**Gordimer, Nadine,** South African writer 35
**Goren, Charles,** American bridge (card game) expert 371
**Governors of the states of the United States** 383
 Edwards, Edwin, election, picture 383
 Snelling, Richard, death of 373
**Graham, Martha,** American dancer and choreographer
 371
**Graham, Sylvester,** American doctor and nutritionist
 whole-grain advocacy 160
**Grahame, Kenneth,** English writer
 *Wind in the Willows, The,* book 302–12
**Grammy Awards,** music 267

**Grange, Harold "Red",** American football player 371
**Grasslands,** prairie
 biome 314–15, 317, 319
**Graves' disease,** overactive thyroid gland 24
**Great Barrier Reef,** Australia 96, 97
**Great Britain** *see* United Kingdom
**Great mullein,** wildflower 112
**Greece** 376
 history 363–68
 membership in European Community 48
**Greece, ancient** 363–68
 beliefs about emotions 211
 scarecrows 213
**Greene, Graham,** English writer 371
**Greenhouse effect,** global warming trend 23, 94–95,
 320
**Green iguana,** lizard 79, 80
**Greenpeace International,** environmental group
 Antarctica 123
**Green with envy,** expression of speech 211
**Gregory, Frederick D.,** American astronaut 38
**Grenada** 376
**Gretzky, Wayne,** Canadian athlete 176, 177
**Gross national product (GNP),** total market value of all
 goods and services produced during a year 354
**Guatemala** 376
 election 16
**Guinea** 376
**Guinea-Bissau** 376
**Guino, Richard,** Italian artist 253
**Gulf War** *see* Persian Gulf War
**Gunn, Moses,** American actor, picture 269
**Gutierrez, Sidney M.,** American astronaut 26
**Guyana** 376

# H

**Habitat,** natural environment of animal or plant
 biome 314–20
 Biosphere II simulation 33
 Texas State Aquarium 90
**Hagman, Larry,** American actor, picture 259
**Hair-raising experience,** expression of speech 208
**Haiti** 376
 military coup 32
 Pan American Games 164
**Hammond, L. Blaine., Jr.,** American astronaut 24
**Harald,** king of Norway
 succession 17
**Harbaugh, Gregory J.,** American astronaut 24
**Harding, Tonya,** American athlete, picture 178
**Havel, Vaclav,** president of Czechoslovakia 63
**Hawaii**
 census figures 384, 387
 Pearl Harbor attack 288–99
 solar eclipse 133
**Health** *see* Medicine and health
**Heifetz, Jascha,** Russian-American violinist
 child prodigy 223; picture 223
**Heinz, John,** American politician 371
**Heisman Trophy,** football 172, 173
**Hennen, Thomas J.,** American astronaut 38
**Henner, Marilu,** American actress, picture 269

**Literature**
Geisel, Theodor Seuss (Dr. Seuss), death of 371
Greene, Graham, death of 371
Nobel Prize 35
Singer, Isaac Bashevis, death of 373
*see also* Young people's literature
**Lithuania** 377
independence movement 16, 32, 57, 59; picture 17
United Nations admission 32
**Little League baseball,** sport 169; picture 231
*Little Parsley,* book by Enzo Giannini, picture 286
**Lizards,** reptiles 76–83; pictures 69–70
**Loch Ness monster,** mysterious creature 202–03
**Loci method,** mnemonic device
memory sharpening 117
**Louisiana**
census figures 384, 388
gubernatorial election, picture 383
**Low, G. David,** American astronaut 30
**Lucid, Shannon W.,** American astronaut 30
**Luge,** sport 186–87; picture 186
**Luke, Keye,** Chinese-American actor 372
**Luxembourg** 377
European Community membership 48
**Ly, Chanthou,** American photography contest winner, picture 239

# M

**Maazel, Lorin,** American conductor
child prodigy 224; picture 224
**Macaulay, David,** American writer
*Black and White,* book, picture 285
**MacMurray, Fred,** American actor 372
**Madagascar** 377
*Madame Charpentier and Her Children,* painting by Pierre Auguste Renoir, picture 240–41
**Madigan, Edward,** American secretary of agriculture
nominated and confirmed 17
**Magellan,** space probe 127–28
**Magellan, Ferdinand,** Portuguese navigator and explorer 127
*Magic Flute, The,* opera by Wolfgang Amadeus Mozart 245; picture 245
**Maine**
census figures 384, 388
**Malawi** 377
**Malaysia** 377
**Maldives** 377
**Mali** 377
military coup 20
**Mallon, Meg,** American athlete, picture 175
**Malta** 377
**Manarov, Musa,** Soviet astronaut 128–29
**Mandela, Nelson,** South African black leader 54, 55
**Mandela, Winnie,** South African black activist 55
**Mandrill,** baboon, picture 75
*Maniac Magee,* book by Jerry Spinelli, picture 284
**Manitoba,** province, Canada 392
**Mann, Jack,** British hostage in Lebanon 53
**Maps**
Columbus's first voyage 200
Northwest Passage 346

Old World and New World 201
Soviet republics 60
topographic, for orienteering 136–39
**Maria Theresa,** empress of Austria 244
**Marie Antoinette,** queen of France 244
**Marine iguana,** reptile 82
**Marine life**
Antarctica 121
coelacanth 25
coral reefs 92–97
fish 25; picture 74
Texas State Aquarium, Corpus Christi, picture 90
**Maris, Roger,** American athlete 186
**Market economy,** economy determined by buyers and sellers 351, 352
Eastern European countries' changeover to 63
**Marsalis, Wynton,** American musician 266
**Marshall, Thurgood,** American Supreme Court justice retirement 26, 28; picture 66
**Marshall Islands** 377
United Nations admission 32
**Martin, Lynn,** American secretary of labor
appointment confirmed, picture 67
**Maryland**
census figures 384, 388
**Masri, Taher,** premier of Jordan
named 26
**Massachusetts**
census figures 384, 388
Salem witchcraft trials anniversary 39
**Mauna Kea,** Hawaii
solar eclipse 133
**Mauritania** 377
**Mauritius** 377
dodo bird 91
**Maxwell, Robert,** Czechoslovakian–British publisher 372
**Mazowiecki, Tadeusz,** premier of Poland 16
**McCarthy, John,** British hostage in Lebanon 53
**McClure, Mike,** American photography contest winner, picture 238
**McClure, Robert**
British explorer 346–47
**McMonagle, Donald R.,** American astronaut 24
**Medicine and health**
balanced diet benefits 104–09
biological clock 356–57
Nobel Prize 35
sports medicine 232–33
use of virtual reality 103
zero gravity problems 127
**Mellon, Andrew,** American philanthropist 254
**Memory,** brain function for recalling past events and information 114–17
**Mengistu Haile-Mariam,** president of Ethiopia
resigned 24
**Menuhin, Yehudi,** American violinist
child prodigy 222–23; picture 222
**Meteorology,** science of weather and climate
weather satellites, picture 131
**Mexico** 377
Pan American Games 164
**Michigan**
census figures 384, 388–89
**Microchips,** integrated circuits for computers
Information Art exhibit 257
**Micronesia** 377
United Nations admission 32

# N

# P

# T

# Z

# ILLUSTRATION CREDITS AND ACKNOWLEDGMENTS

The following list credits or acknowledges, by page, the source of illustrations and text excerpts used in this work. Illustration credits are listed illustration by illustration—left to right, top to bottom. When two or more illustrations appear on one page, their credits are separated by semicolons. When both the photographer or artist and an agency or other source are given for an illustration, they are usually separated by a slash. Excerpts from previously published works are listed by inclusive page numbers.

12– © Peter Turnley/Black Star
13
16 © Steve Liss/*Time* magazine
17 © Gedrius Pocius/Sygma
18 © 1991 John Trever/*Albuquerque (N.M.) Journal*
19 © Douglas Burrows/Gamma-Liaison
21 © Patrick Downs/DOD Pool-*Los Angeles Times*
22 © Reuters/Bettmann
23 © Rob Mustard
25 © Peter Scoones/Planet Earth Pictures
26 © Giordano/Saba
27 © Philippe Bouseiller/*Figaro* magazine
28 © Wojtek Laski/Sipa
29 © Chiasson/Gamma-Liaison
30 © Alexandra Avakian/Contact Press Images/Woodfin Camp & Associates
31 © Carr Clifton
33 © Peter Menzel; © AP/Wide World Photos
34– © Maggie Hallahan/Network Images
35
36 AP/Wide World Photos
37 © Darryl Heikes/U.S. News & World Report
38 AP/Wide World Photos
40 © Andrew Popper/*U.S. News & World Report*
41 © Gamma-Liaison
42 Illustration adapted from *Newsweek*, 1/28/91, P. 20, staff artist; © Eyup Coskun/Sipa Press
43 © AP/Wide World Photos; © Alfred/Sipa Press
44 © Delahaye/Sipa Press
45 © Arai/Sipa Press
46 © Alex/Sipa Press; © Chamussy Laurent/Sipa Press
47 © A. Tannenbaum/Sygma
48 © B. Jaubert/Sipa Image; © Persuy/Sipa Press
50 © M. Milner/Sygma
51 © Peterson/Gamma-Liaison
53 AP/Wide World Photos
54 © Louise Gubb/J.B. Pictures
56 © Hernandez/Sipa Press
58 © Klaus Reisinger/Black Star; © URSS Gamma/Gamma-Liaison
59 AP/Wide World Photos
62 © Filip Horvat/Saba
63 © Antonello Nusca/Gamma-Liaison
64 © Dennis Brack/Black Star; © Terry Ashe/*Time* magazine
65 © Klaus Reisinger/Black Star; © A. Gyori/Sygma
66 © Terry Ashe/*Time* magazine; © Robert Trippet/Sipa Press
67 © Rolf-Finn Hestoft/Saba; The Granger Collection
68– © Dwight R. Kuhn
69
70 © Michael George/Bruce Coleman, Inc.
71 © Norman Meyers/Bruce Coleman, Inc.
72 Gerry Ellis/Ellis Wildlife Collection
73 © R. Norman Metheny/*Christian Science Monitor*
74 © Wilf Schurig/Animals Animals; © Stephen Dalton/Animals Animals; © Mike Bacon
75 © Michael Habicht/Animals Animals; © Grant Heilman/Grant Heilman Photography; © Frans Lanting/Minden Pictures
76 © Gail Shumway
77 © T. A. Wiewandt
78 © Edward S. Ross; © Dwight R. Kuhn; © Dwight R. Kuhn
79 © Brian Parker/Tom Stack & Associates

80 © A. Blank/Bruce Coleman, Inc.; © Belinda Wright/DRK Photo
81 © T. A. Wiewandt
82– © Stephen Dalton/Photo Researchers, Inc.
83
82 © Dwight R. Kuhn
84 © Gary Vestal
86 © Kjell B. Sandved; © Kjell B. Sandved; © Paulette Brunner/Tom Stack & Associates; © Kjell B. Sandved
87 Artist, Michèle A. McLean
88 © Ron Garrison/Zoological Society of San Diego; © Jett Britnell/DRK Photo
89 © Ron Garrison/Zoological Society of San Diego
90 © 1990 Helen Swetman/Courtesy of Texas State Aquarium
91 © Robert Maass/*Sports Illustrated*; National Museums of Scotland
92– © Carl Roessler
93
93 © Larry Tackett/Tom Stack & Associates; © Brian Parker/Tom Stack & Associates; © Stephen Frink/The Waterhouse
94 © Carl Roessler
95 © Stephen Frink/The Waterhouse; Oxford Scientific Films/Animals Animals
97 © Mike Bacon
98– © Gordon Wiltsie/Peter Arnold, Inc.
99
100 © George Steinmetz
102 © 1989 by The New York Times Company. Adapted by permission
103 © Peter Menzel
108– Artist, Michèle A. McLean
109
110 © Jeff Lepore/Photo Researchers, Inc.; © Dave Muench
111 © Stephen Krasemann/Photo Researchers, Inc.; © G. C. Kelley/Photo Researchers, Inc.; © Hal Horwitz/Photo/Nats
112 © L. L. Rue III/Earth Scenes; © Richard L. Carlton/Photo Researchers, Inc.
113 © Jeff Lepore/Photo Researchers, Inc.; © Ron Austing/Photo Researchers, Inc.
115 © John Pack
118– © Tim Gibson/envision
119
120 © Joyce Photograhics/Photo Researchers, Inc.
121 © Gordon Wiltsie/Peter Arnold, Inc.
122– © Wolfgang Kaehler
123
123 © Art Wolfe
124 © Frederick C. Taylor/Fortean Picture Library
124– © Terence Meaden/Sipa Press
125
125 © Maxine Hicks; © Frederick C. Taylor/Fortean Picture Library
126– NASA
127
128 © Ray Fairall/Photo-Reporters
130 Hughes Aircraft Company; NASA
131 Earth Observation Satellite Company; Hughes Aircraft Company
132 © Frank Zullo/Sipa Press
133 © J. Cachero/Sygma
134– Designed and created by Jenny Tesar
135
136 © Lane Stewart/*Sports Illustrated for Kids*
137 © Andy Dappen

139 © Lane Stewart/*Sports Illustrated for Kids*
140 SOLUTION: Mount Rushmore
141 Designed and created by Jenny Tesar
148– Most of the hats designed and created by Jenny
151 Tesar; expandable hatrack courtesy Country Lane Interiors Etcetera, Danbury, Connecticut
153 Artist, Sharon Holm
154– Courtesy, *Crafts 'n Things* magazine. For more
157 detailed instructions on these craft projects, write to Crafts 'n Things, Dept. GL, 701 Lee Street, Suite 100, Des Plaines, IL 60016
158– Courtesy, Krause Publications, Inc.
159
160 From *Many Hands Cooking: An International Cookbook for Boys and Girls.* © 1974 by Terry Touff Cooper and Marilyn Ratner. Reprinted by permission of Harper & Row, Publishers, Inc.
161 From *Many Friends Cooking: An International Cookbook for Boys and Girls.* Text © 1980 by Terry Touff Cooper and Marilyn Ratner. Illustrations © 1980 by Tony Chen. Used by permission from Philomel Books, a division of the Putnam Publishing Group
162– Focus on Sports
163
164 © David Leah/Allsport
165 © Rick Stewart/Allsport
166 © Focus on Sports
167 © John Swart/Allsport
169 © Manny Millan/*Sports Illustrated*
170 © Focus on Sports
172– © Focus on Sports
173
174 Allsport
175 © Sportschrome East/West
176 © Paul Bereswill/*Sports Illustrated*
178 © Heinz Kluetmeiser/*Sports Illustrated*; © Tim DeFrisco/Allsport
179 © Simon Bruty/Allsport; © Reuters/Bettmann
180 © Mitchell B. Reibel/Sportschrome East/West
181 © Dan Smith/Allsport
182 © Mike Powell/Allsport
183 © Bob Martin/Allsport; © Gray Mortimore/Allsport
184 Courtesy of Bloom Public Relations
185 The Bettmann Archive; Cosmo-Sileo, New York
186 © Melanie S. Freeman/*Christian Science Monitor*
187 © Simon Bruty/Allsport
188– The Granger Collection
189
190 © Doris Brookes/Telephoto; © Martha McBride/Unicorn Stock Photos
190– © Jonathan A. Meyers/Amwest
191
191 © Anthony Nicholls/Amwest
192 © H. H. Thomas III/Unicorn Stock Photos
193 © Dick Keen/Unicorn Stock Photos
194 © Giraudon/Art Resource
195 © Scala/Art Resource
196 North Wind Picture Archives
197 The Granger Collection; North Wind Picture Archives
198 The Granger Collection
199 © Scala/Art Resource; The Granger Collection
200 © Scala/Art Resource
201 The Granger Collection
202 © Anthony Shiels/Fortean Picture Library; © International Society of Cryptozoology

## Acknowledgments

*We wish to thank the following for their services:*
*Typesetting, Dix Type Inc.; Color Separations, Gamma One, Inc.;*
*Text Stock printed on S. D. Warren's 60# Somerset Matte;*
*Cover Material provided by Holliston Mills, Inc.;*
*Printing and Binding, R. R. Donnelley & Sons, Co.*